ॐ Sri Devi Lila ॐ

ॐ

Sri Ganeshaya Namaha!

Sarva vigna haram devam,
Sarva vigna vivarjitam,
Sarva siddhi pradhadaram,
Vandeham Gananayakam

"I bow to Lord *Ganesha*,
Who removes all obstacles,
And gives all knowledge."

Ambikahridayanandam
Mathrubi paripalitam,
Bhaktapriyam madonmatham,
Vandeham Gananayakam

"I bow to Lord *Ganesha* of supreme intellect,
Who is the delight of his mother *Ambika*,
And beloved by his devotees."

ॐ **Sri Devi Lila** ॐ

The Play of the Divine Mother

As found in the

Srimad Devi Bhagavatam

and

Sri Devi Mahatmyam

and

various other scriptural sources

Narrated by

Vanamali

Aryan Books International
New Delhi

Sri Devi Lila

ISBN: 978-81-7305-304-7

First Published: 2006

Reprinted in **2017** by:

Aryan Books International

Pooja Apartments, 4B, Ansari Road, New Delhi-110 002 (India)
Tel.: 23287589, 23255799; Fax: 91-11-23270385
E-mail: aryanbooks@gmail.com
www.aryanbooks.com

Computer Typeset and Printed in India at
ABI Prints & Publishing Co., New Delhi

ॐ

Sri Adbhutacharitrayai Namaha!

Amale Kamalasana sahide,
Adbuda charithe,
Palayamam.

O Amala! Who sits on a lotus,
Whose stories fill us with wonder,
Pray, protect me.

Dedicated To

My Beloved Daughter
Amala

ॐ

Brahmanyai Namaha!

I meditate on the beginingless *Brahmavidya*, who is of the nature of All Consciousness (*Satchidanandarupini*). May She stimulate our intelligence to the realization of THAT.

ॐ

Ambayai Namaha!

PREFACE

by

Swami Kriyananda, Donald Walters

Founder of *The Ananda Community*

Author of "The Hindu Way of Awakening"

Mata Devi Vanamali – Mataji, as I shall refer to her hereinafter, is a fit person to write about the Divine Mother of the Universe. Mataji is a deep devotee who is also filled with India's ancient concept of wisdom or *jnana.* Because my own devotion to God finds particular expression to the Divine Mother, I was deeply touched when Mataji asked me if I would write a few words of introduction to this beautiful book.

There are two aspects of the important subject of the cosmic Mother: the scriptural and the experiential. Mataji has rightly given us the scriptural slant on the subject. In this age, when most of us think of God as 'He', it is necessary to point out, as Mataji has done, that God is neither male nor female, and at the same time God is both! In the words of a great Kaali bhakta of Bengal, Ram Prasad, "A thousand Vedas declare that my Tara (a name for the divine mother) is *nirakara* (without form)."

Yet religion in these times has become too rationally formal and therefore too rational altogether. Years ago in America, the inspiration came to me to spread the concept of God as Mother and not only as Father. I wasn't thinking of the virgin mother only, as is more common in the West but of the formless Infinite in its motherly aspect. I went to many Western shrines dedicated to the Divine Mother and worshipped there. I received in each of them great inspiration and love. And I say now, is it not time for dogmatic religion to be replaced by devotion and love? There has been too much *thinking* about God. Mankind must learn to love Him, to talk with Him and to experience Him. And that 'Him' needs to be understood, first in its higher impersonal aspect, then brought down to earth in its more truly personal aspect as the Divine Mother.

For god in 'His' different aspects, though one in essence, is different in every aspect. It matters not only how we ourselves look upon God and define Him in our minds, it is a question also of how God views us. If we invoke God as the Divine Mother, She comes closer to us. The Infinite – beyond all sexual differences, is the maternal as well as paternal principle – opens its heart to us when we appeal to it as Mother.

There is a story from the life of that same poet, singer and saint, Ram Prasad. He was mending the fence before his house. At one point, someone, he thought was his own daughter, came up to him and offered to help with his job. He had been singing. She said to him, "Whom have you been singing to Papa?"

"I've been singing to my Divine Mother," he replied. "But She's very naughty. I keep calling and calling Her but She won't answer!"

"If She doesn't answer, Papa, why do you waste your time calling to Her?" The little girl then ran off with a childish laugh.

When Ram Prasad came indoors later on, he told his wife how their daughter had come and helped him with the fence and talked to him playfully.

"But that's not possible," answered his wife. "Today she's gone to visit the other side of our village."

"But I know it was she," he exclaimed. Later on, when their daughter returned home, he pressed her, "Wasn't it you helping me with our fence today?"

"Why, no Papa. You can ask anybody, I was with friends on the other side of our village."

Thus did Ram Prasad come to know that the Divine Mother Herself had come to him and teased him.

"O my Mother!" He cried, "what a naughty dear you are! Though you pretend to be inaccessible, you are ever near me and Mother, ever dearest to me."

All aspects of God hear us when we pray, but the Divine Mother listens to us – I don't say more so but more particularly. For we are her children.

She cares for each one of us in a special way. When we err, she will spank us through the law of *karma.* But when we love her, she also forgives. For she is ever anxious for us to understand that we may return with outstretched arms to her lap of infinity!

ॐ *Aim, hreem, kleem* ॐ

"What is love? Is it only ours?
Or does love whisper in the flowers?
Surely we, Children of this world,
Could not love by our own powers.
What is joy? Is it a dream?
Or does joy laugh in every stream?
Are the clouds mindless after all?
Or is joy all Nature's theme?"

— Swami Kriyananda

ॐ

Sri Matre Namaha!

CONTENTS

Preface vii
List of Illustrations xiii
Introduction xv

1. Prakriti 1
2. Parameshwari 11
3. Maha Devi 22
4. Rajarajeshwari 32
5. Maheswari 40
6. Parashakti 46
7. Lalitha 51
8. Tripurasundari 59
9. Kameswari 65
10. Durga 69
11. Chandika 78
12. Mahishasura Mardini 87
13. Chamunda 98
14. Sati 110
15. Dakshaayini 119
16. Parvati 124
17. Aparna 131

18. Gauri 139
19. Ganga 146
20. Maha Kaali 158
21. Maha Lakshmi 170
22. Maha Saraswati 180
23. Radha 188
24. Tulasi 198
25. Sita 204
26. Savitri 212
27. Shivaduti 219
28. Adi Shakti 228
29. Smashan Tara 239
30. Narayani 252
31. Devi Kundalini 262
32. Shivani 280

Glossary of Sanskrit Terms 287
Scriptures 307
Names of Gods 309
Names of Demons (Asuras) 312
Names of Goddesses 314
Mantras 320
Bibliography 323

ॐ *Aim, hreem, kleem* ॐ

ॐ

Devyayai Namaha!

LIST OF ILLUSTRATIONS

All illustrations except the *Chakras* are by Sri Sahadevan

	Facing page
1. *Durga*	69
2. *Lakshmi*	170
3. *Saraswati*	180
4. *Sri Chakra*	258

Illustrations of *Chakras* are taken from various sources.

Blessings and thanks to Ted Cutler for his help in colouring the *Chakras*.

ॐ *Aim, hreem, kleem* ॐ

Note : Names of gods, goddesses, demons, rivers and some mountains have been put in italics to remind the readers that these are all personified in the Hindu scriptures. In fact they have all been deified.

ॐ

Paramatmikayai Namaha!

INTRODUCTION

Ya Devi sarvabhuteshu, Vishnumayethi shabdita,
Namasthasyai, Namasthasyai, Namasthasyai Namo Namaha!

"O goddess, who is known as *Vishnu Maya* in all creatures,
Hail to Thee, Hail to Thee, All Hail to Thee!"

The ancient sages of India looked at this amazing world, filled with beauty; filled with fascinating and horrifying forms and wondered what it was all about. Was this the only face of the creator or was there something beyond this? Somehow they were sure that this extraordinary universe with its myriad structures was only the mask that hid the visage behind.

The *Rig Vedic* hymn says,
"By a golden lid
Is hidden the face of Truth,
Uncover it O Sustainer!
Let the seeker behold it!"

There are many paths laid in the scriptures for discovering the truth underlying the phenomenal world as well as the truth of one's own self and these are known as *yogas*. But what we should remember is that all the paths of *yoga* are only different methods by which this golden lid can be removed.

Hindu philosophy asserts that the *Brahman* is the Supreme Reality underlying both the manifest and unmanifest states of Being. It is an integrated state, which is changeless, indivisible, without distinctions and utterly beyond human comprehension. It can only be known by direct experience by penetrating through and transcending the levels of the mind on the material plane. By this, consciousness becomes aware of its own real, undying nature, which is also the nature of the Supreme unmanifest.

The individual spirit or *atman* is a centralised or contracted expression of the *Brahman.* It contains the whole in a potential form. Even though it is nothing but an expression of the Supreme Consciousness, it has been obscured by the limited, mental world of the individual. When Pure Consciousness descends to the individual frame, it begins to relate to its limited body and displays itself in different ways according to its inherent nature and thus plays its own distinct role in the drama of manifestation. Although these centres of consciousness in the individual frames appear to be many, they are actually not separate. In the manifested realm they function separately through the agency of their separate minds. In the realm of the unmanifest, however, they cannot be considered as separate since they have emanated from the One Supreme Consciousness. This is a divine mystery, which can only be solved by the direct realisation of the source from which they have sprung. Thus, a reverse process is possible and the *jivatman* (embodied soul) is capable of withdrawing inwards to its central source through *yoga* and contemplation and developing to its full divine status. Cosmic evolution proceeds from the Absolute, super conscious, unmoving, unknowable, and unmanifest to the conscious, moving, knowable and manifest microcosm. Human evolution is a return journey from the gross physical plane of the microcosm back to the Absolute. In one case the force is centrifugal and in the other centripetal. Thus, all embodied souls represent different expressions of the Ultimate Reality of the *Brahman*, which is whole, indivisible and integrated through different centres of consciousness.

Brahman is the uncaused cause of everything, the one source of all qualities and forms, though in itself it has no qualities or forms. From this basic standpoint, Hinduism gives us freedom to worship God in whatever shape that appeals to us. Each individual is given the liberty to accept any form of the divine that appeals to her or him as her personal aspect of Reality, dearest to her heart. The logic being, that which is formless, can take any form. This is the basis of the great tolerance found in the Hindu religion. Since the *Brahman* is formless and qualityless, any form can be worshipped as 'Its' form.

The *Vayu Purana* asserts, "He who fanatically affirms the superiority of one deity or incarnation over another is a sinner."

The purpose of life according to Hinduism is to return to the source from which we have come. The embodied soul *(jivatman)* comes from the *Brahman* and goes through the dramas of its many lives and then at last desires to return to its origin. All Hindu scriptures and epics, all Hindu ceremonies and festivals are charged with this spiritual connotation. They have an esoteric significance which is far-reaching and which is not apparent in the outer rituals and show. Every ritual – even those, which we perform automatically – is a spiritual dedication of the soul for that single aspiration which it has been enshrining within itself from eternity. This significance is brought out in all our scriptures. Unfortunately, the casual reader does not understand this.

In India, therefore, there was no contradiction between science and religion. The ancient *rishis* or philosophers were both scientists as well as spiritualists. This was so because from ancient times these *rishis* understood that the basis of all matter was spiritual. Their investigation into the material world took them to the spiritual without any difficulty since they did not have any preconceived notions in their minds about a world that existed apart from its spiritual foundations. Modern western science however started from the unfortunate hypothesis that nature, man and God were totally unconnected, so it took a very long time for them to understand this truth. Even now they have not fully grasped it. It was only in the twentieth century that glimpses of this have been perceived.

Not long ago it was thought by advanced thinkers that science would ultimately overthrow all age-old spiritual concepts and reconstruct human society on a purely materialistic basis. But now we see that a totally different picture is emerging.

Einstein himself said, "The most beautiful and the most profound emotion we can experience is the sensation of the mystical. It is the source of all true art and science. He to whom this emotion is a stranger, who can no longer pause to wonder and stand rapt in awe, is as good as dead; his mind and eyes are closed. The insight into the mystery of life, coupled though it may be with fear, has given rise to religion. To know that, what is impenetrable to us, really exists, manifesting itself as the highest wisdom and most radiant beauty which our dull faculties can comprehend only in their most primitive forms – this knowledge, this feeling is at the centre of true religiousness."

This is the knowledge that the *rishis* of ancient India experienced through deep personal understanding brought about by intense austerity and meditation.

Indian thought is famous for its symbolism and from ancient times the pictorial representation of God took the form of both male and female. The universal form of the motionless Absolute came to be associated with the manly structure and the manifested energy of nature with the female form. The Absolute and Nature are therefore not two, but two-in-one. They are necessary to each other as complementary manifestations of the One.

In the *Skanda Purana, Indra*, the king of the gods, asks *Vishnu* how the *Brahman* projects itself as male and female.

Vishnu replies, "Listen O *Indra*, the male and female are eternal principles involved in the projection of the universe. They are never separate. Fundamentally they are one, as gold and ornaments made of it are one."

This two-in-one existence came to be known as *Purusha* and *Prakriti* or *Shiva* and *Shakti.* It is something like the dynamo and the force that charges it. One is powerless without the other. *Shiva* and *Shakti* are polar opposites, inseparable but having a varying relative predominance under different directions. But in the unmanifest, the *Shakti* aspect of the One Reality is only a potential. It is merged in the Pure Consciousness of *Shiva* and is indistinguishable from it. It is only when manifestation takes place after a period of *pralaya* or dissolution that *Shakti* separates from *Shiva*, pierces the *bindu* or point from which everything expands and descends in the form of the sound of *hreem* and creates this entire paraphernalia of existence. In the *tantric* view, sound is a vibration of undifferentiated intelligence, which acts as the catalyst that sets into motion the unfolding of the manifest cosmos. A primal shudder disturbs the slumbering equilibrium of *Shakti* and arouses *rajas,* the principle of activity to carry out the creation of the manifold universes. This vibration or *sabdabrahman* is undifferentiated, soundless sound. It is that wavelength that is experienced only by the Divine.

This vibration splits *Shakti* into two opposite fields of magnetic force – *nada* and *bindu*. As the centrifugal, positive male force, *bindu* is the centre from which *nada* operates. As the centripetal, negative, female force, *nada* unfolds the manifest universe. *Bindu* is the ground from which *nada* operates. These are regarded as the Father and Mother aspects of the supreme power. The bifurcation of *Shakti* is not a separation but a duality in unity. This duality of poles in the substratum of manifested *Shakti* provides the magnetic force that holds together in a state of vibration the molecules of the physical world.

So we find that in Hindu mythology *Prakriti* and *Purusha* or *Shiva* and *Shakti* are always found together, though in each organism one or the other predominates according to its own stage of evolution. If the *jivatman* wants to realise its own divine nature, it has to extricate itself from the illusory haze created by *Maya Shakti* and penetrate through its own centre and emerge on the other side of the point as it were. It is then in the realm of Pure Consciousness and is able to have a direct experience of that consciousness which is both *Shiva* and *Shakti*. This is explained in detail in the chapter on *Kundalini Yoga*.

Devi or *Shakti* presupposes all forms of existing knowledge – past, present and future. She is the creative aspect of the *Brahman*. It is through her that the One becomes the many. She is *Adi Shakti*, the primeval force, and the first emanation of power from the Absolute – *Brahman*. She is the womb of the universe.

Creation and dissolution follow each other. It is a cyclical process and not linear as found in western philosophy. During the period of dissolution, *Shakti* lies quiescent. Just as the tree lies latent in the seed, so this universe of names and forms lies enfolded in *Shakti*. Within it rests the three *gunas* or qualities known as *sattva* (purity), *rajas* (activity), and *tamas* (inertia). This *Shakti* is a mass of latent, undifferentiated energy, which contains the seed power of many universes. It rests in the *Brahman*. During the period of creation it flowers into the manifest, evolved cosmos and during dissolution it withdraws everything into itself and remains in the latent state till the next period of evolution and creation. This expansion and contraction continues throughout eternity. Like day and night the universe alternately expands into matter and recedes into primal energy or *Mula Prakriti*. From her comes this entire manifestation of myriad forms – from the stars to the earthworms, from the oceans to the dewdrops! She is cosmic energy. Energy is the physical ultimate of all forms of matter. Matter is nothing but energy in motion as modern physics has come to acknowledge. Spirit and Energy are inseparable. They are essentially one. They are like fire and heat.

Lord *Krishna* tells *Arjuna* in the *Bhagavad Gita*, "Earth, water, fire, air, ether, mind, intellect and ego – these constitute the eightfold division of my nature. Know this to be my lower nature. My higher nature O *Arjuna,* is that spiritual Being, which sustains the entire universe. That is quite different from this. These two natures form the womb of all beings. I am thus the origin and the dissolution of the entire universe."

This spiritual being of which *Krishna* talks about is what the *Devi Purana* describes as the *Devi* or *Adi Shakti* or *Mula Prakriti.*

In poetic language it is said that *Prakriti* or the embodied energy of the Supreme leaps into creative activity at just one glance from the *Purusha.* This manifestation is her dance of ecstasy at the joy of being able to perform for her Lord. The sun is her glory and the moon her glow. The stars are the jewels in her hair and the moonlight her radiance!

The Mother power or divine energy has many forms and symbols. All beauty and all ugliness flow from her. She is *Lakshmi*, the auspicious, bestower of boons and beauty. She is *Saraswati,* the giver of all wisdom and art. She is *Tripurasundari,* the most beauteous in the three worlds. But she is also *Kaali,* the destroyer, whose wrath ignites the storm, the thunder and the lightning. She is *Mahishasuramardini*, destroyer of evil. She is *Chandika,* the terrible, who lets loose the typhoon, the flood and the tidal wave.

The *Shakti* cult is one in which the divine is worshipped in the form of the *Devi* or the Divine Mother. This has fascinated all minds at all times since the mother is one with whom everyone can have an intimate relationship. In fact this is the primary relationship. The devotee has greater freedom when he conceives of God as Mother. The great sage of Bengal, Sri Ramakrishna said, "Just as a child can force its demands on the mother, so a devotee can force his demands on God as mother."

The system of worshipping *Shakti* or the Goddess is said to have begun in ages long past among the uncivilized and uncultured tribes of prehistoric India. In fact it can be traced back to neo-Palaeolithic times. Archaeologists have unearthed figures of the Goddess in the earliest strata of Indian settlements. It kept on growing and growing until today it is a full-fledged sect with adherents amongst all the other cults that exist in India. It might have begun with a simple divinity of one universal Goddess representing the earth deity, but it has slowly assumed different forms and names until at last we have a whole pantheon of female goddesses with different functions. But we must understand that all of them are merely powers of the one universal *Shakti* – *Adi Shakti* or *Parashakti.* Some savants assert that *Shaktism* is an intrusion of non-*Aryan* thought into the mainstream of *Aryanism.* They affirm that the Mother cult is pre-*Aryan* and originally belonged to the Sumerian and other cultures. Whatever the truth may be we can only assert that the worship of the Mother aspect of God is as deep-rooted in human nature as the worship of the Father aspect. Today it is an integral part of the Hindu culture. It has been practised and elaborated by millions of seekers through the ages. Poor and rich alike can approach the Divine Mother, some with wisdom and some out of despair but all have love in their hearts. *Shaktism* has inspired saints and *yogis,* artists and poets.

The worship of god as Mother is found in all civilizations. In Egypt she was known as *Isis.* In Babylon and Assyria as *Ishtar,* in Greece as *Demeter* and in Phrygia as *Cybele.* Judaism, and later on Islam, put an end to Mother worship in the Middle East. Christianity repressed it in the beginning but later started to venerate Virgin Mary as the Mother of God.

The first word uttered by the infant is '*maa*'. Our first relationship with the world is through the mother. The earliest memory of any person is that of lying on the mother's lap and gazing into her love-filled eyes. In the mother is centred a whole world of tenderness, love, nourishment and care. She is the embodiment of security. She personifies the ideal of love, from which the child draws sustenance, comfort, protection, and nourishment. To transfer this concept to a cosmic being was a natural step, which the ancients took. Therefore we can understand that the concept of the Divine as Mother is as old as life itself. It is only natural to think of the Divine as the Cosmic Mother, who loves all, nourishes all, cares and protects all. *Devi* is the Divine Mother, the eternal womb of all creatures, human, animal and sub-human. She cradles her children in her loving arms, suckles them and nurtures them with her infinite love in all forms. Wherever you see maternal love, in a bird or an animal or a human being, know that to be but an aspect of her love for the universe, for she is the universal mother.

"Man is a child of the universe, an infant tied by the umbilical cord of space and time to that great nurturing mystery out of which he has been born and to which he will inevitably return. Our dependence on that mysterious Mother is absolute, our intimacy is also absolute. No human relationship can compare with it. Is it any wonder that humanity has worshipped and tried to propitiate this maternal mystery at the very heart of our lives. Is it any wonder that we have personified her, prayed to her, confessed our deepest secrets to her, cried out in pain to her, danced for her, sung for her and wept before her?"

It is astonishing how this modern age seems to have forgotten her very existence. This is the Dark Age, *Kali Yuga*, in which our increasing engrossment with the physical or worldly aspect of life has torn us away from our metaphysical roots and alienated us from our Mother. The ancients were nurtured by the milk of kindness which is always oozing from the breasts of our Divine Mother and that is why they had a sense of the high purpose of human life.

According to scholars in India, the worship of the Divine Mother is a cultural gift from pre-*Aryan* times. It has an unbroken tradition right from ancient times. In the *Vedas* there are a number of hymns addressed to the *Devi.* Much later a whole body of literature known as the *Tantras* were written, dedicated solely to the worship and philosophy of the Divine Mother. In the aspect of all power the Mother has a dual aspect – one as *avidya* or cosmic delusion and also that of *vidya* or cosmic deliverance. She binds us with her bewildering *maya* of cosmic illusion in this world-play of birth, death and enjoyment. On the other hand, it is she who releases us from this wheel of existence. Artists have depicted her as holding a noose in one hand, with which she binds us, and a sword in the other with which she cuts the knot.

Another beautiful imagery is that of the Indian kite, which is a game that children play. The Mother also plays this game. The thread which holds her kite, has sharp bits of glass in it and as the kites soar up into the sky, she cuts the thread of some of them and releases them from their bondage! The kites stand for souls in bondage. In both these aspects as the deluder and the releaser she has set up this cosmic drama. She is the one who has brought about this amazing play of duality on the stage of the universe. *Sri Ramakrishna* gives another beautiful allegory. As long as the child is playing with his toys, the mother busies herself with household chores, but when the child throws away the toys and cries for its mother, she puts down the cooking pot and runs to the child. This analogy illustrates the strong bond that exists between the Divine, conceived as the Mother and the devotee.

One who has become fed up with this vain and futile running about in the game of the world has only to turn to her and beg her to release him from it. She will do it if our desire is strong enough. Her grace is infinite. Her compassion and love for all human beings and especially for true seekers is indescribable. The Mother is ever ready to take back the straying child into her arms. It is true that she is the one who has set about this momentary play, this divine drama upon the stage of this physical universe. But she is ever ready to take back into her loving bosom those children who have lost interest in the play and have had enough. The child which has wandered far away from the Mother one day realises that she is the only source of security and runs back to her and begs her to take her back into her arms. The Mother opens her arms wide and the errant child jumps into them and regains her original bliss.

The *Purusha* is that which we cannot know or conceive. It is the Supreme Being – the transcendental *Para Brahman.* That which we know through our mind and senses is nothing but the manifestation of the Mother. Everything that we can think of or know is the form of the Goddess. But she has a transcendental aspect as well. She is not contained in this little universe of which the earth is a part, with its countless stars, a sun and a moon and all the terrestrial and stellar, lunar and solar systems. All this is but an infinitesimal speck in the vastness and infinity of the Mother. Innumerable such universes have their rise and fall within her ample bosom. She is all-power and all-manifestation through eternity and infinity.

The *Devi Bhagavatam* describes her as the Mother of the Trinity. The three dynamic manifestations of the Absolute as *Brahma, Vishnu* and *Maheswara (Shiva),* are all manifestations of *Adi Shakti*, or the first force. As *Brahma Shakti*, she manifests herself in the form of *Saraswati.* This is her *rajasic* aspect. As *Vishnu Shakti* she manifests in the form of *Lakshmi*, which is her *sattvic* aspect, and as *Shiva Shakti*, she manifests in the form of *Durga*, which is her *tamasic* aspect. These are not three distinct *Devis* but the one energy of the *Brahman* worshipped in three different manifestations. She is the creator of many worlds and universes; numerous *Brahmas, Vishnus* and *Shivas* have emanated from her.

In her transcendental aspect she is *Parabrahma Swarupini*, the form of the Absolute *Brahman*. Therefore when we worship the Divine Mother, we are not only offering adorations to the Supreme in its aspect of motherhood but we are also adoring the Supreme Absolute. She is that aspect of the Supreme power by whose grace alone we shall be ultimately released from the darkness of ignorance and the bondage of *maya* and taken to the abode of immortal knowledge, immortality and bliss.

The problem in writing about the Divine Mother is that there is no complete story about her. She has taken many manifestations in order to help her devotees and especially the gods. All these are described in various *Puranas,* so her stories will not have a consecutive order but will be chosen at random from various sources. May she bless this poor scribe with the power to write about her mysterious *lilas.*

"For one was there Supreme behind the God,
A Mother Might brooded upon the world.
A consciousness revealed its marvellous front.
Transcending all that is, denying none,
Imperishable above our fallen heads,
The undying truth appeared, the enduring power,
Of all that here is made and then destroyed,
The Mother of all godheads, and all strength
Who, mediatrix, binds earth to the Supreme."

— "Savitri" by Sri Aurobindo

ॐ *Aim, hreem, kleem* ॐ

ॐ

Prakrityai Namaha!

CHAPTER ONE

PRAKRITI

Sarvamangala maangalye, Shive sarvartha sadhike,
Sharanye Tryambake Gauri, Narayani namosthuthe!

"Salutations to the *Devi Narayani*, who is blessed with every felicity,
Filled with auspiciousness, able to accomplish everything,
Who is the protrectress, the three-eyed *Gauri*!"

The word *'pra'* in Sanskrit means exalted, superior and excellent and the word *'kriti'* means creation. So the Divine Mother is known as *Mula Prakriti* since she is the Supreme Creator of the world. *Prakriti* or primordial matter is not to be confused with physical matter. *Prakriti* is the eternal matrix from which all the components of reality have sprung. She is the dot in the centre of the ocean of energy which is the ultimate source of all the fields which western science knows – the field of gravity, the electromagnetic field and so on. *Tantric* philosophy calls this the Divine Mother, *Devi Prakriti* or *Parashakti.* She is the very source of the subtle dimensions of reality that our physical senses can never perceive. Her energy is described in the *Puranas* as the ocean of primeval waters on which *Vishnu* lies, in which the Island of Jewels or the *Mani Dwipa* floats. Her throne, which is described in the chapter on the Island of Jewels, is the *bindu* or dot from which all energy eddies in circles to create the expanding universe.

Prakriti contains the core of the three *gunas.* These three *gunas* contain the very essence of the Divine Mother's *avidya maya* by which she binds the immortal soul to the mortal frame of the body. They are known as *sattva, rajas* and *tamas. Tamas* has the ability to distort reality, *rajas* to veil reality and *sattva* to allow it to be seen, though dimly. Scientifically speaking we can describe these three as the qualities of inertia, activity and equilibrium which are found in various combinations in all matter, including people, animals and plants. *Tamas, rajas* and *sattva* have different colours according to Indian thought and these are black, red and white respectively, which are the colours of the Goddess herself. *Kaali* is black, *Lakshmi*, red and *Saraswati,* white.

'Pra' signifies *sattva*, *'kri'* denotes *rajas* and *'ti'*, *tamas.* These qualities are found in their pristine nature in *Prakriti.* She is known as *Maha Maya* or the great deluder. But her *maya* has two aspects. One is *vidya maya* and the other, *avidya maya. Vidya maya* is omnipotent and omniscient and is capable of revealing the *Brahman,* which is her receptacle. Remember, she is known as *Parabrahma Swarupini*, or the very form of the *Brahman.* When the Supreme Self is reflected in *avidya maya* it is known as the *jivatman* or the embodied soul. This *avidya maya* conceals the Supreme and thus the *jivatman* experiences all kinds of sorrows. In actuality the Self or *atman* is self-luminous. It is the eternal and blissful fountain of love. *Jnana* or knowledge is the very nature of the *atman.* It is the basis of the knowledge of 'I am' which every *jiva* possesses. It is also the source of all love.

The *jivatman* is said to have three bodies – the gross body, the subtle and the causal. *Prakriti* resides in the subtle body in two different forms – *vidya* and *avidya maya.* The *jivas,* who are in essence nothing but the Supreme Self, appear different due to the different composition of the three *gunas* in them.

When *Himavan,* King of the Mountains, did *tapasya* to the *Maha Devi* in order to procure her as his daughter, she appeared to him in her most spectacular form and promised to incarnate herself as his daughter. After this she proceeded to enlighten him as to her true nature since he was eager to know her secret essence. This discourse by the *Devi* to *Himavan* is known as the *Devi Gita.*

"Hear this O *Himavan,* by knowing which all *jivas* will become liberated. Before creation I alone exist – eternal, immutable. My real Self is no different from the *Para Brahman.* In that state I am pure *sat* (existence), *chid* (consciousness), *samvit* (intelligence) and *ananda* (bliss). At that time I am beyond all attributes or transformations. *Maya* is my power of illusion and it is inherent in me. It is co-eternal with me. It arises out of me like heat from fire and rays from the sun. Though it has no beginning it is possible to end it with the attainment of supreme knowledge. *Maya* can neither be called existent nor non-existent. If it existed eternally there would be no liberation for the *jiva*. But if it were not present at all, the practical world would not exist, so it cannot be non-existent. It can be destroyed with the knowledge of *Brahman* so it cannot be called existent either. It is thus my mysterious power of delusion and it can be overcome only through my grace.

"In essence I am *nirguna*, without qualities but when I relate myself to *avidya maya*, I become *saguna* or endowed with qualities. Then do I become the cause of the universe of names and forms. Thus, *avidya maya* is the cause of this whole creation. From the point of view of the *Brahman*, there is no *maya* and no creation. Therefore I am ever pure even though involved in creation just as the sun's rays are not defiled by illumining dirty objects."

"When *maya* unites with *chid* or consciousness, it becomes the efficient cause of the universe and when it unites with the five original elements it becomes the material cause. *Avidya maya* is what creates the delusion of time, space and causality and its characteristic is to hide my true nature but *vidya maya* has the ability to liberate the *jiva* from this illusion.

Actually, infinite and endless creations are threaded on me as pearls on a string. I myself am the Lord that resides in the causal and subtle bodies of the *jivas*. I am *Brahma*, *Vishnu* and *Shiva*. I am the sun, moon and stars. I am the beasts and the birds, the *Brahmin* and the untouchable. I am the noble soul as well as the hunter and the thief. I am male, female and hermaphrodite. Wherever there is anything to be seen or heard, I am to be found there, within and without. There is nothing moving or unmoving that can exist without me. This world cannot appear without a substratum and that substratum is I."

"The world is composed of twenty-five *tattvas* or elements. The first five – *akasa* (ether), *vayu* (air), *agni* (fire), *apas* (water) and *prithvi* (earth) – are known as the *Maha Tattvas*. When the *Para Brahman* (Supreme *Brahman*) relates to my *avidya maya* the sound '*hreem*', which is my seed sound, is produced. Within this sound are contained my three *shaktis* known as *iccha shakti*, the power of desire, *jnana shakti* or power of intelligence and *kriya shakti* or power of action. These three are absolutely essential for creation. This sound – *hreem*, which denotes me – the *Adi*

Shakti or the first force, who is of the nature of the *Brahman* and is known as *Parabrahma Swarupini*, is the twenty-fifth *tattva* or element. The rest of the twenty-four *tattvas* come out of this.

The five qualities of sound, touch, form, taste and smell are known as *tanmatras* or subtle elements. The subtle quality of sound is the first *tanmatra* to manifest from *'hreem'*. Then come the subtle elements of touch, form, taste and smell. Out of the subtle *tanmatra* of 'sound' is manifested the gross element or *tattva* of *akasa* or ethereal space. The zero-point field, which has only recently been discovered by modern science, roughly corresponds to this element. Strangely enough, western science has begun to call this the mother of all fields. The vibrations in the element of space cause the moveament of air. Thus, from *akasa* appears *vayu* or air which has its own subtle feature of 'touch' and also the added quality of 'sound' which it incorporates from the previous *tattva* of *akasa.* Friction caused by the continuous movement of the air principle creates heat which we call fire. Thus from *vayu* comes *agni* or fire which has its own subtle feature of 'form', plus 'touch' and 'sound'. Condensation of the density of these forces results in the formation of liquid or water. So the next to manifest is *apas* or water, which has its original subtle quality of 'taste', plus those of 'form', 'touch' and 'sound'. The solidified form of all this is the earth. So the last to appear is *prithvi* or the earth element that has its basic subtle feature of 'odour', as also the qualities of the other four elements of taste, form, touch and sound.

What we have to understand is that creation proceeds from the subtle to the gross and not the other way round as we might suppose. The subtle elements or *tanmatras* are sound, touch, form, taste and odour. The gross elements or *tattvas* corresponding to these are space, air, fire, water and earth, which are all derivatives of the subtle elements. These five elements represent the entire gamut of our advanced modern physics. From the *Shakta* point of view, physical matter and its fields represent only a tiny fraction of reality. These five elements all have *sattvic, rajasic* and *tamasic* qualities.

The five *jnanendriyas* or the sense organs of knowledge are created out of the *sattvic* portion of the first five subtle elements. These are the ears, skin, eyes, tongue and nose, which are the necessary instruments through which these elements can operate in the material world. These sense organs function as a whole. When they are engaged in the process of forming resolves and having doubts they get a collective name – *manas* or mind. When this mind reasons and makes judgements it goes by the name of *buddhi* or intellect. When it simply rests in itself with the feeling of 'I' and 'mine', it is called *ahamkara* or ego.

The *karmendriyas* or the organs of action come from the *rajasic* portion of the *tanmatras.* These are the organs of speech, hands, feet, organ of generation and the anus or organ of excretion. The subtle element of sound gives rise to space and ends in speech. The subtle element of touch projects as air, which is felt by the skin especially the skin of the hands. The subtle element of form gives rise to fire, which eventually takes the form of the feet. The subtle element of taste gives rise to water, which in turn produces the organ of procreation. The subtle element of odour produces the earth, which results in the production of the anus.

The five *pranas* or subtle breaths, which control all these functions, arise from the *tamasic* portion of the *tanmatras.* They are known as *prana vayu* which resides in the heart and takes care of blood circulation; *apana vayu* residing in the lower portion of the body which expels waste matter; *samana vayu* which resides in the navel and takes care of digestion; *udana vayu* which resides in the throat and controls speech; and *vyana vayu* which pervades the whole body. These five winds or *pranas* take care of the involuntary functions of the body.

The gross sensations of sound, touch, form, taste and smell are important components of our experience of life. Indian philosophy claims that these exist in other worlds in their intangible and subtle forms. These are visible to our inner eye and are the very essence of our dreams. However, they are not to be experienced by the gross body.

The *linga sarira* or subtle body of the *jiva* is made up of these seventeen *tattvas* in their subtle forms. *Yogis,* who have perfected the ability to leave their physical bodies at will, realised that their subtle or astral bodies were able to travel unhampered through space. Gross matter could not stop them from passing through. However, since they could still hear, touch, smell and feel in this state, they concluded that the actual experience of these five sensations lay in the subtle body and not in its physical counterpart. Thus creation proceeds from the subtle to the gross and not vice versa, as modern science would have us believe.

The mind is a psychic organ that operates through a physical nervous system in this life, allowing it to interact easily with physical matter. While in the physical body it has three functions with separate names. The part that receives, processes and stores information is called *manas* or mind. That part which relates to a particular individual, giving him a strong sense of individuality, the feeling of 'my' and 'mine' is called *ahamkara* or ego. That part which weighs alternatives and makes decisions is called *buddhi* or intellect. However it has another aspect that is most subtle, which is capable of obtaining data from our inner dimensions of reality and which is actually a storehouse of all information. It is in direct contact with what the modern scientists call the zero-point field and this is known as *chitta.* It has no equivalent english term unless you want to call it the super consciousness, which is actually not an accurate translation.

After death or for *yogis* during their astral travels, the mind separates from the physical organism and operates in the realm of the *tanmatras* or subtle elements. Then it is pure *chitta* alone. *Yogis* have demonstrated the difference between this higher mind and the brain. In some EEG experiments conducted on *yogis* it was found that even when the machine registered total lack of brain response, the *yogi* when coming out of his self-induced sleep state was able to accurately report the events that occurred in the laboratory. The brain was asleep but the *chitta* was fully awake. Only *yogis* are able to achieve this type of complete mastery over their physical nervous system.

This brings us to another important point that Indian philosophy has always claimed. The first three aspects of the mind (*manas, buddhi,* and *ahamkara*), which is the basis of our personality, are all material constituents and not spiritual entities. These have their roots in *Prakriti* or primordial matter and not in the Spirit or *atman.* The mind changes every moment and eventually perishes with the perishable body but the *atman* or Spirit remains. This is the eternal Self that never perishes with the perishing of the body and is always the undying witness and never the doer.

The Newtonian world was a law-abiding, but desolate place with which we were totally unconnected. Next came Darwin who stripped life of all its spiritual potential and left us bereft. Our only purpose was survival. The pinnacle of humanity appeared to be the terrorist who could efficiently dispose off all weak links. Life is not about sharing and interdependence but about winning and warring if need be. It is theories like these that have produced the modern psyche and led to our great technological advancement. Unfortunately it has been at the cost of our humanity and of our divinity. No wonder suicides appear to claim more lives than homicides and wars! Science has torn the human being from his roots and left him with a sense of brutal isolation.

With the advent of quantum physics, in the early part of the twentieth century, there was a dramatic reversal by many scientists of these old views of man and the universe. Modern science is slowly coming to realise some amazing facts of material life. It is slowly coming to understand that all living beings are a coalescence of power in a field of energy that is connected to every other thing in the world. This pulsating energy field is the central engine of our being and our consciousness – the alpha and omega of our existence. There is no duality between the universe and us. We are connected to every single thing in the cosmos by one underlying energy field. The tiniest bit of matter isn't matter at all but energy in motion. What is more interesting was the discovery that these sub-atomic particles had no meaning by themselves but only in relation to everything else! This is the astonishing finding of modern physics that is slowly replacing the old Newtonian physics where everything had a set pattern and was totally predictable by the human mind!

"There is a field of energy which is responsible for our mind's highest function, the information source guiding the growth of our bodies. It is our brain, our heart, and our memory – indeed a blueprint of the world for all time. This field is the force, rather than germs or genes that finally determines whether we are healthy or ill, the force which must be tapped in order to heal". The field as Einstein put it, "is the only reality".

This is what the *Puranas* call the ocean of undifferentiated energy in which *Vishnu* resides or the Goddess lives in her Island of Jewels. It is the ethereal space or *akasa* that is the twenty-third *tattva.* The closest scientific terminology that can be given to it is the zero-point field. It is a timeless, spaceless quantum that provides the ultimate blueprint of the world for all time – past, present and future. Any person who desires or professes to see the past and future has to tap this source. Quantum physics has also come to realise that pure energy as it exists on the quantum level is not bound by the ordinary laws of time and space. It exists in a vast continuum of fluctuating change. When we bring this energy to our conscious awareness through the act of perception, we create the separate objects of our world that exist in time and space. In fact we create our own worlds in time and space and thereby create our separate individualities. This brain-boggling theory which western science has only recently become aware of and is still wary of accepting, is something which has been recognised by Indian philosophy from ancient times. In fact this is what the *Devi* told *Himavan* in the *Devi Gita.* Of course, the words used were different but the meaning is the same.

All the *Puranic* stories like the churning of the ocean and the Island of Jewels, point out this amazing truth. For instance, in this particular story of the churning of the milky ocean, the *devas* and *asuras* represent the positive and negative sides of each person's personality. This personality churns the ocean of all possibilities (the zero-point field), using the churn of space (*Mandara*), and the rope of time (*Ananta)* and thus draws out for himself many wondrous things including the nectar of immortality if he so wishes it. Thus each one creates his own separate world.

Time has generally been considered to be a primary, independent and universally applicable order both in physics and in common experience. It is one of the fundamental orders known to us. Now modern scientific research is slowly coming to accept the fact that it is a secondary order and, like space, it is derived from a higher dimensional ground. Both depend on another multidimensional reality that cannot be comprehended fully in terms of any time order. If human consciousness operates on this quantum level, it would have to reside outside space and time. In theory this means that we would be able to access information of both the past and the future. This means that every moment of our lives could be made to influence every other moment both forward and backward! These are breath-taking ideas which science is loath to accept. But Indian *yogis* have known them from time immemorial.

There is a particular step called *sankalpa* or intention in every *puja* or ritual in which the gods are invoked. This is the intention, for the accomplishment of which the priest is doing the ritual. It may be for some physical purpose like the curing of a disease or passing an exam or anything else. This intention is supposed to be so important that it can actually change the chain of events and cause something to happen as desired by the one who performs the ritual. The Quantum Age has shown modern science that the intention of the experimenter has a lot to do with the final result to be achieved from the experiment. The human factor influences the end result of any experiment!

The individual is not an isolated phenomenon, a piece of flotsam floating aimlessly in the sea of the world, totally unconnected with everything else, with freedom to pursue his own selfish ends. He is part of an interconnected whole in which all of us are deeply involved. The human consciousness is absolutely essential to the making of some objective sense out of the constant flux of sub-atomic particles! This is the amazing discovery of quantum physics that many scientists are still unable to accept.

In the *Devi Gita*, the *Devi* says,

"I am the intelligence from which the universe emanates and in which it abides. The ignorant believe me to be nothing more than nature or *prakriti* but the wise experience me as the true Self within. They glimpse me in their own hearts when their minds become as still and clear as an ocean without waves. The supreme wisdom is that which ends the delusion that anything exists apart from me. The fruit of this realisation is a total lack of fear and the end of sorrow. When one understands that all the limitless universes are but a fraction of an atom in the unity of my being, that all the numberless lives in the universes are the wisps of vapour in one of my breaths, that all triumphs and tragedies, the good and the evil in all the worlds are merely games I play for my own amusement, then life and death stand still and the drama of individual life evaporates like a shallow pond on a warm day."

"This world that you are experiencing now is nothing but my power. The only remedy for your ignorance is to worship me as your innermost Self. Surrender yourself to me with one-pointed devotion and I will help you discover your true being. Abide in me as I abide in you. Know that even now at this very moment there is absolutely no difference between us. Realise and be fulfilled this instant."

"Its mind of error was stripped off from things,
And the dull moods of its perverted will.
Illumined by Her all-seeing identity,
Knowledge and Ignorance could strive no more.
No longer could the titan opposites,
Antagonist poles of the world's artifice,
Impose the illusion of their twofold screen,
Throwing their figures between us and Her!"

— "Savitri" by Sri Aurobindo

Thus ends the first chapter of the *Sri Devi Lila* known as 'Prakriti', describing the process and nature of creation and the relationship between *Brahman* and *Prakriti.*

ॐ *Aim, hreem, kleem* ॐ

"Love that was once an animal's desire,
Then a sweet madness in the rapturous heart,
An ardent comradeship in the happy mind,
Becomes a wider spiritual yearning's space."

— "Savitri" by Sri Aurobindo

ॐ

Ambikayai Namaha!

CHAPTER TWO

PARAMESHWARI

Ya Devi sarvabhuteshu chetanethyabhidiyathe,
Namasthasyai, Namasthasyai, Namasthasyai Namo Namaha!

"O goddess, who is designated as consciousness in all creatures,
Hail to Thee! Hail to Thee! All Hail to Thee!"

The central concept of Hindu philosophy is the belief that wisdom is something to be recovered rather than discovered. Absolute truth is not something to be discussed as an intellectual conception but it is something to be lived. It is a way of life – the *Sanatana Dharma.* In fact this is the original name of the Hindu religion. This way of life gets lost or gets diluted in the process of time but great incarnations appear from time to time, in order to uplift this eternal *dharma,* as Lord *Krishna* tells *Arjuna* in the *Bhagavad Gita.*

The *Vedas* are the most ancient source books of Indian wisdom. They are the heritage of the world. They were revealed to, or recovered by, the *rishis* when they were in a state of super consciousness. The *Puranas* or the epics, on the other hand are of human origin and the sage *Vyasa* is said to be the compiler of the eighteen *Puranas* which deal with the Supreme, under eighteen different names. The literal meaning of '*purana*' is 'narratives from ancient times'. Indians as a whole did not believe in writing history but the *Puranas* give us a good view of the different phases and aspects of the life of the diverse ages of this land. These books allow us a glimpse into ancient religion, philosophy, history, sociology, politics and other subjects. These *Puranas* were normally recited by a class of people called '*Sutas*', during periods of rest between the various rituals of a *Vedic* sacrifice. They are divided into two classes – the *Maha Puranas* and the

Upa Puranas. Each class contains eighteen books. Thus, the total number of *Puranas* is thirty-six. The *Maha Puranas* are classified into different categories – *Vaishnava, Brahma, Shaiva* and so on, depending on the preferential treatment which is given to each of the three deities, *Vishnu, Brahma* and *Shiva.*

The *Puranas* are intimately related to the *Vedas.* They interpret and adapt the metaphysical truths of the *Vedas* so that they can be understood and appreciated by the common man. The *Puranas* do not proclaim any new truths but only make the *Vedic* truths available in a contemporary and relevant manner. The *Veda* is the revealed truth and is known as *sruti.* The *Puranas* reveal the same truth in a modern setting and are known as *smriti.* The *Vedas* are reserved for the *Brahmin* class and the initiates alone and may not be taught to all. Whereas, all others may hear the *Puranas.* Recitations are done in public to audiences of all classes. The *Puranas* are thus of great importance to us, especially in this Iron Age of *Kali* when the *Vedic Dharma* is almost on the verge of decline. The *Puranas* contain an easier form of truth adapted to the conditions of the age. They are in complete harmony with the truth contained in the *sruti* or the *Veda.* Their job is to reveal the eternal, immutable reality, in a comprehensible form, to all humanity. The process of revealing truth is a never-ending process. The truth, which was revealed in the *sruti,* has to be newly interpreted in the '*smriti*', which is the collective name for the *Puranas.* With its usual flexibility of approach to spirituality, the Hindu tradition believes that each generation and each individual must make the *Vedic* truth his very own in his own way. Thus, though the *Vedic* truths remained fixed and unalterable, the *Puranas* could and did change with the changing times and incorporated the devotional teachings of numerous cults and saintly teachers that arose from time to time in this holy land. They also gave a lot of information on a variety of subjects – scientific, occult, social and historical.

The original *Purana* is said to have emanated from the fifth mouth of the creator *Brahma* and comprises a billion *slokas.* This original *Purana* is said to exist only in the world of the gods. In every *Dwāpara Yuga Veda Vyasa* abridges this original into the thirty-six *Puranas*, which exist in the mortal world.

All Hindus can be classified under four or five broad-based divisions. The worshippers of the Supreme in its aspect as *Shiva* are known as *Shaivites.* The worshippers of *Vishnu* are known as *Vaishnavite*s and those who worship the Supreme, as *Devi* are known as *Shaktas.* There are two lesser-known sects called *Ganapatyas* or those who worship the Supreme as *Ganesha* and the *Souryas* who worship the sun as the Supreme. Of course there are also the *Advaitins* who worship the Supreme as the formless non-dual *Brahman.* The *Upanishads,* which come at the end of the *Vedas,* deal with the non-dual *Brahman* but the *Puranas* deal with all other deities.

Time, according to the *Puranas,* is without any modification and without any beginning and end. Basically it is insubstantial but it gets a form when it causes the stirring of the three *gunas* of *Prakriti* at the beginning of each creative cycle. It is the basis for the sport of the Supreme Being in his creative manifestation. The sun is the visible form of the Lord as Time. The smallest particle of matter is known as a *paramanu.* The shortest period of time is called a *paramanukala* and this is the period of time taken for the light of the sun to pass one *paramanu,* which is the tiniest particle of matter. The time taken for the light of the sun to pass through the twelve *rasis* or constellations round the earth, which is a huge amount of matter, is known as a year. One human year is only one day for the gods. Six months from January fourteenth to June fourteenth is a divine day and from June to January is one night of the gods. Twelve thousand divine years is divided into four *yugas* called *Krita Yuga, Treta Yuga, Dwapara Yuga* and *Kali Yuga.* These four together are known as one *Chaturyuga.* This applies only to the human world. Even this period of time is mind-boggling and the modern world has only recently called a certain period of astronomical time as 'light years'. The *rishis* of ancient India had already named the tiniest speck of time up to the longest period of time, many centuries ago. This is amazing when you consider the fact that they had no modern instrumentation to do this. All they had was their mighty intellects.

A thousand *Chaturyuga*s is only one day in the world of *Brahma,* the creator. His night is another thousand *Chaturyugas.* The lifespan of each *Brahma* is a hundred such years and is known as a *kalpa,* which is an astronomical period of time as can be seen! We are now living in the dawn of the first day of the present *Brahma* who is in his fifty-first year!

Each day of *Brahma* is divided into fourteen *Manvantaras.* The lawgiver, *Manu* who rules for his span of seventy-one *Chaturyugas,* is in charge of each *Manvantara.* All the lesser gods including *Indra*, the seven sages and various other celestial beings, are found in each *Manvantara.* In each *Manvantara* the Supreme Lord *Vishnu* and the *Maha Devi*, incarnate themselves in order to keep up the balance of righteousness.

In the *Puranas*, creation is cyclic in nature. A vast period of creation is followed by a vast period of *pralaya* or dissolution. There is no absolute beginning for creation at any point of time and therefore no absolute end. Time is not linear as in western philosophy but cyclic. A period of evolution is followed by a period of involution called *Maha Pralaya* in which all things remain in a latent state. At the time of *Maha Pralaya* or the great deluge everything in the cosmos is taken back into the primeval essence. After the passage of eons, when the time is ripe for another creation, the One eternal *Brahman* takes on the form of duality just as one face becomes two when reflected in the mirror. *Maha Maya* is the Lord's power of illusion or differentiation that creates the illusion of time, space and causality. At the commencement of a new period of evolution, *Maha Maya* sets into being the process of evolution by which all things come into existence once again. During *pralaya,* the universe is in a state of latency and after *pralaya* it comes into a state of manifestation. It never gets completely destroyed. This is all the play or *lila* of the Supreme.

There are three different types of *pralayas* based on time, substance and the attributes of *Prakriti.* The first is called *Nitya Pralaya*, which is based on Time alone which all of us experience when we go to sleep. Each night is a *pralaya* for the *jiva* or individual soul. When we sleep there is no world or individuality. It has not totally disappeared but is merely in a state of latency, submerged in the total consciousness. The moment the person awakes, the world springs into being and individuality asserts itself.

The next type of dissolution is called *Naimittika Pralaya* or *Maha Pralaya,* which is the night of *Brahma*, the Creator. This happens after one day of *Brahma* that lasts for a thousand *Chaturyugas.* During *Maha Pralaya* or the night of *Brahma* the whole universe, up to *Satyaloka* or the world of *Brahma*, goes into a state of involution. At the end of this vast period of Time, *Maha Maya* employs her power as Time and causality and another period of creation and evolution follows.

The third type of dissolution is called *Prakritika Pralaya* when all the categories and attributes of *Prakriti* go into total dissolution into their ultimate cause, which is *Maha Prakriti* or *Mula Prakriti*. This in turn reverts into its ultimate cause – the *Brahman*. This *pralaya* will last for eons. But it is to be noted that even during this dissolution, nothing is destroyed. Everything merely remains in its latent state.

Creation is necessary in order to exhaust the *karmas* which have been acquired by the *jivas* during their sojourn on the earth. The causal body or *antah karana* of every embodied soul or *jiva* consists of the mind, intellect and ego and this bundle of thoughts continue to exist in the astral plane, waiting for an opportunity to take birth in a physical body in order to exhaust its desires. Hence creation takes place due to the *karmas* of the *jivas* who are lying latent in the causal waters.

All creation is made up of a combination and permutation of the three *gunas*, which are the three qualities of *Prakriti*. They are called *sattva*, *rajas* and *tamas*. These *gunas* are to be found in all aspects of creation. They are the qualitative building blocks of creation. Without them there would be no qualities. If we employ the terms used in physics, we can say that *rajas* has the feature of kinesis, *tamas* of inertia and *sattva*, the balancing principle of harmony. *Sattva* is white in colour and is the source of pleasure and happiness. It induces a person to all types of good thoughts and activities. *Rajas* is red in colour and is the source of hyper-activity leading to pain and unhappiness. *Tamas* is black in colour and leads to laziness, sloth and sleep. However, these qualities are never found in their pristine state. They are always intermingled and dependent on each other. One should always try to encourage *sattvic* qualities, control *rajasic* qualities and destroy *tamasic* qualities. This is the way to liberation. The *jiva* has been caught in the illusion of duality by its identification with the *gunas*, so the way out is by taking the return path that leads beyond the *gunas*. It is only by controlling *rajas* and *tamas* that *sattva* can become pure.

The *gunas* are the agents of *Prakriti* by which the immortal and imperishable *atman*, which is nothing but the Pure Consciousness, imagines itself to be the mortal and perishable body. Out of these three strands (*guna* means a thread), *Maha Maya* weaves a net in which the *atman* is caught and identifies itself as the temporary and perishable body. This imperishable *atman* not only identifies itself with the perishable body but also takes delight in its own pitiful and limited personality. This is the wonder of the work of *Maya.* The mind has a predilection to enjoy the limitations of its body. It is happy to shrink into the cocoon of its small, prejudiced individuality and refuses to believe in its universality. Once caught in the net of *Maya*, the immortal Self delights in its mortality and frailty. *Moksha* or enlightenment is liberation from the shackles of this puny individuality; from the limitations of particularised existence. The only way out of this web of delusion as *Krishna* tells *Arjuna* in the *Bhagavad Gita*, is to go beyond the three *gunas.* It is not enough to become purely *sattvic* since we have just seen that none of the *gunas,* including *sattva,* can exist by itself. There is always an admixture. At different times and in different people one or the other might become prominent. So long as we are in their power we will always live in dread of a fall. So Lord *Krishna* advises *Arjuna* to become a *gunatita* or one who has gone beyond the *gunas.* Only such a person can have no fear of a fall. Such a person comes to realize his own divine nature as Pure Consciousness and is thus freed from the bondage of *Maya.* This can come only with the grace of *Maha Maya* herself since she is the one who has caught us in this net of delusion. Therefore those who desire liberation have to pray to her to remove the veil of illusion from their eyes.

The whole of creation is at first only an idea in the mind of the Supreme *Brahman.* This idea is given a concrete reality and expressed to the world by his *Shakti* or *Prakriti*, which is the *Maha Devi* or the great Goddess. Without her, he would remain aloof, inert, passive and inactive. *Prakriti* is absolutely necessary for creation. It is only through her that the *Purusha* can manifest his full potential in creation. Without her there would be no creation. Therefore one can say that *Prakriti* not only complements the *Purusha* but also completes him.

We are now living in the *Kali Yuga* or the Iron Age. In every *Dwapara Yuga* of each *Manvantara*, Lord *Vishnu* himself incarnates as *Veda Vyasa.* His duty is to divide the *Vedas* into four parts so that they become easier to memorise. In every succeeding *Yuga,* people's memory become poorer and poorer and they are unable to memorise the vast *mantras* of the *Vedas.*

Not only are their memories poor but also their intellects, so in order to reach out to the common person, *Veda Vyasa* compiles the *Puranas*. The *Puranas* are an outpouring of his compassion for the masses. The *Vedas,* as mentioned before, are reserved for the *Brahmins* and other selected persons. But the *Puranas* can be heard and read by all classes and both sexes and even by children. The present *Manvantara* is known as *Vaivasvata* and the *Veda Vyasa* of this epoch was known as *Krishna Dwaipayana.* It is to be noted that though *Vyasa* is the author of all the *Puranas,* in each one of them he extols the uniqueness of that particular deity. There are two reasons for this. The first is to show people that all deities are only aspects of that Supreme Truth and that sincere devotion to any of them will give us liberation from our mortal coils. The second reason is to convince the votaries of each particular deity of the greatness of his or her own personal god.

In the *Bhagavad Purana,* all the stories revolve round *Vishnu* and his *avataras.* But in the *Devi Bhagavatam* we find that all the gods and great kings have recourse to the *Maha Devi* in order to get her blessings. In this book all her different incarnations are dealt with as well as the different forms that she takes like the river *Ganga*, the plant called *Tulasi* and so on. All these will be dealt with in the following chapters.

The *Devi Bhagavatam* has eighteen thousand *slokas* and is divided into twelve books. It is the earliest literary work in which the character of the Goddess stands fully revealed. Even today she is conceived as she is pictured in this scripture. Obviously this *Purana* depicts the ultimate reality as feminine. It is classified as a *Maha Purana.* Every *Purana* has to deal with at least five topics. They have to discuss creation or *Sarga*, secondary creation or *Visarga,* the age of the *Manus* or *Manvantaras*, genealogies of various kings and a description of their heroic deeds. It is said that *Veda Vyasa* narrated this *Purana* to his son, *Shuka* who then taught it to others.

The *Devi Bhagavatam* describes creation thus: The *Devi* is beyond attributes, eternal and omnipresent. She is formless and immutable. But for the sake of the world she assumes the form of many *shaktis.* In these forms she takes on the attributes of the three *gunas.* Her *sattvic shakti* takes the name of *Maha Lakshmi*, her *rajasic shakti* is known as *Maha Saraswati* and her *tamasic shakti* is called *Durga* or *Maha Kaali.* In the *Sarga* portion of the *Devi Bhagavatam*, these three *Shaktis* of the *Devi* assume different forms for the creation of this universe of diverse forms. These *Shaktis* take on male counterparts known as *Vishnu, Brahma* and *Shiva* for the preservation, creation and dissolution of the universe. This is known as secondary creation. Thus all male gods have their *shaktis* or inherent powers which enable them to create.

The origin of the world according to the *Devi Bhagavatam* differs from other *Puranas* since the *Devi* is the supreme power and creator of the cosmos. She herself describes the process of creation to the creator, *Brahma.* She is *Maha Devi, Maha Maya, Maha Prakriti* and *Maha Shakti.* She is also *Lakshmi, Saraswati, Parvati, Durga, Kaali, Chandi* and a host of other powers, which are depicted in the *Purana* as goddesses.

The book begins with the sages questioning the narrator, *Suta,* to describe the qualities and glories of the *Devi.*

The *Suta* responds, "I bow at the lotus feet of the *Devi* – *Bhagavati,* who is worshipped by *Brahma, Vishnu* and *Shiva* and who is the sole source of liberation to all. This is the best of all *Purana*s and contains all the sentiments that a human being can conceive. It is known as the *Srimad Devi Bhagavatam.* May that highest primal *Shakti,* who is known as *Vidya* in the *Vedas,* who is omniscient, who controls all and who is skilled in cutting the knot of the world, give me the intelligence to describe her glories. I meditate on that Divine Mother who creates this universe, whose nature is both real and unreal, who creates, preserves and destroys everything in her *rajasic, sattvic* and *tamasic* aspects, and who eventually dissolves everything back into herself and remains alone during the period of universal dissolution."

There is no difference between the *Devi* and the *Purusha* or the *Para Brahman* who is the Supreme, from which everything emanates. Before creation, she lies latent in the Supreme, undifferentiated consciousness of the *Brahman.* All creation has to be done through the *Shakti* of the *Purusha,* which is always depicted as feminine. *Shakti* is the force that underlies and impels creation. To make a difference between 'force' and the 'receptacle of force' is an error. *Prakriti* is the inherent tendency of the *Purusha* to express itself in concrete forms and individual beings. However, she has to be set in motion by the will of the *Purusha* and acts according to his force and design. It is only through this *Shakti* or *Prakriti* that he is able to express himself in creation. *Brahman* is the cause of everything. Without

Brahman, *Maya* cannot exist. Therefore, *Maya* or *Prakriti* rests in the root cause, which is *Brahman.* Though they are one in essence, differences are conceived during creation. When everything melts and goes back to its original causal state of *pralaya*, then there is no distinction between *Purusha* and *Prakriti*, *Maya* and *Brahman.* There is neither male nor female. There is only *Brahman* with *Maya* latent in it.

Many beautiful allegories are given in the *Puranas* to give us an idea of this interdependence of *Purusha* and *Prakriti.* He is the Supreme Subject and she is the essence of all objects; he is the ocean and she the waves; he is the sun and she the light; he is the sky and she the earth; she is all qualities and he the enjoyer of all qualities; she is all activity and he, the sole witness of all activity; she is the form of everything in the cosmos and he, the thinker of the forms; she is speech and he, the meaning. In other words, she is creation and he the creator.

Prakriti and *Purusha* have no beginning and no end. *Purusha* is the universal consciousness that exists in everything. He is the Highest Self. He is *nirguna* or without qualities. *Shakti* is the energy of the Highest Self and is inseparable from him. No human being can know the essence of this union even by the study of the scriptures or the *Vedas.* All *jivas* are the products of the three *gunas* – *sattva, rajas* and *tamas.* They can never know that which is *nirguna* or beyond all *gunas.* The *gunas* spring from the cosmic *ahamkara* or ego and unless one is totally free of ego one cannot understand the relationship between *Purusha* and *Prakriti.*

The cosmic *ahamkara* is made up of the three *shaktis* or powers of *Prakriti* – *jnana shakti* or power of knowledge, *kriya shakti* or power of action, and *iccha shakti* or power of will. These three have to combine to produce all material objects. *Jnana shakti* is a product of the *sattvic ahamkara, kriya shakti* of the *rajasic ahamkara* and *iccha shakti* of the *tamasic ahamkara.* All creation proceeds from these three *ahamkaras* or egos.

Out of the *tamasic ahamkara* are produced the five *tanmatras* or subtle essences of the five elements. These are sound, touch, form, taste and smell. Out of these are produced the five gross elements of ether or *akasa*, air or *vayu*, fire or *agni*, water or *ap*, and earth or *prithvi.* Sound is the quality of ether or *akasa*, touch is the quality of *vayu* or air, form is the quality of fire or *agni*, taste is the quality of water or *ap* and smell is the quality of earth or *prithvi*. As has been mentioned in the previous chapter, each of these elements combines in them their own quality as well as the quality of the element previous to them. So the first substance – ether – has only the quality of sound but air has the quality of both sound and touch. Fire has sound, touch and form and water has sound, touch, form and taste and the earth element has all five – sound, touch, form, taste and smell.

These ten subtle and gross materials are the building blocks of the whole universe of matter. All creation takes place as a consequence of the *tamasa ahamkara* or the *iccha shakti* of the *Maha Devi* which is endowed with the desire to create material substance.

The *rajasic ahamkara* produces the five types of perception – sound, touch, taste, sight and smell. The organs corresponding to these are the ears, skin, tongue, eyes and nose. These are called the *jnanendriyas* or the organs of knowledge. Then there are the five *karmendriyas* or organs of action. These are the mouth, hands, feet, anus and the organ of generation. Then there are the five *vayus* or winds or forces that control all the involuntary actions of the body. These are called *prana, apana, vyana, samana* and *udana.*

Out of the *sattvic ahamkara* come the presiding rulers of the five sense organs. Their names are *Dik, Vayu, Surya, Varuna* and the *Aswins. Dik* refers to space or all the quarters, *Vayu* is air, *Surya* is the sun, *Varuna*, the Lord of waters and *Aswins*, the twin gods of the earth. The causal body or astral body consists of mind (*manas*), intellect (*buddhi)*, ego (*ahamkara*) and super consciousness (*chitta).* Their presiding deities are *Chandra* (moon), *Brahma* (the creator), *Rudra (Shiva*) and *Kshetrajna* (the all-knower). These presiding deities are filled with consciousness and enter into the five gross elements. As soon as these deities enter into their respective organs, *ahamkara* or egoism comes into play and this is the beginning of the false identification of the Supreme Consciousness with the bodies thus created.

Brahman, or the Highest Self has two forms, one subtle and the other gross. The formless Self is Pure Consciousness and can never be known.

The second form projects itself as the Supreme Goddess or *Maha Maya,* and is conditioned by space, time and causality.

Brahman is the undecaying principle of fullness – the ultimate substratum of everything. It is totally without desire or qualities. Therefore it is not able to create or accomplish any action without the help of its inherent force or *Shakti* – *Maha Maya,* which is the feminine principle, the great goddess. All the gods like *Brahma, Vishnu, Shiva, Ganesha, Indra* and so on can only do their respective work if they are united with this *Shakti.* So *Maha Maya* can be considered as the sole cause of this entire universe of movable and immovable objects. She is the cause of all causes and manifests as *Maha Lakshmi, Maha Saraswati* and *Maha Kaali.* One should worship her with all adoration. Even the gods worshipped her in order to perform their allotted tasks.

This is the philosophical teaching of the *Devi Bhagavatam.*

"Infinity turned its gaze on finite shapes.
Observer of the silent steps of the hours,
And the passing scenes of the Everlasting's play,
In the mystery of its selecting will,
In the divine comedy a participant.
The Spirit's conscious representative.
God's delegate in our humanity,
Comrade of the universe. Transcendent's ray.
She had come into the mortal body's room,
To play at ball with time and circumstance."

— "Savitri" by Sri Aurobindo

Thus ends the second chapter of the *Sri Devi Lila* known as '*Parameshwari*', describing the *Devi Bhagavatam* and its view of creation.

ॐ *Aim, hreem, kleem* ॐ

ॐ

Sarvabhuteshwaryai Namaha!

CHAPTER THREE

MAHA DEVI

Ya Devi sarvabhuteshu, buddhi rupena samsthita,
Namasthasyai, Namasthasyai, Namasthasyai Namo Namaha!

"O Goddess, who resides in all creatures in the form of intelligence, Hail to Thee! Hail to Thee! All Hail to Thee!"

It was the dawn of the first day of the present *Brahma* – the very first dawn of this present cycle of creation. There was nothing but water everywhere. *Brahma,* the creator in the Hindu trinity, opened his eyes to find himself seated in the centre of a lotus in the middle of a vast expanse of water. The stalk of the lotus was forlornly moving to and fro in the waves of a mighty ocean. The whole scene was bleak and lonely. There was no sun or moon or stars or earth. *Brahma* looked around him for something that would give him a clue as to how he got there and what was the purpose of his existence, but could find nothing. After some thought he decided to try and find the source of the lotus. For a thousand years he searched in the water but could find nothing. The stalk of the lotus seemed to be endlessly thrusting down into the water. Exhausted with his futile search he came up again and sat on the lotus, wondering what he should do. Then came a celestial voice asking him to practice *tapasya* (meditation). Content with this, he took his seat on the lotus and meditated for another thousand years. At the end of this period of time he heard the voice again, commanding him to create. Brahma was perplexed as to how to proceed with this command. While wondering what to do, two gigantic demons appeared out of the waters and challenged him to fight.

Brahma was dreadfully frightened and hurriedly climbed down the stalk of the lotus seeking help. When he reached the end of the stalk, he saw a blissful vision. A most beautiful being appeared to be sleeping on the coiled up body of a serpent. He was the colour of a dark blue rain cloud. He was wearing a luminous yellow garment and had four arms, holding the conch, discus, mace and lotus. Round his neck was a garland of wild flowers. He was the most fascinating figure that *Brahma* had ever seen and he had the instinctive knowledge that he was looking at *Narayana* (Lord *Vishnu*), the Lord of the Universe. The lotus flower on which he was sitting was coming out of the navel of this wonderful Being. But unfortunately he appeared to be in deep sleep and *Brahma* did not dare to awaken him. The demons were thrashing about the ocean and intimidating him with their baleful looks so *Brahma* decided to take recourse to the goddess – *Bhuvaneswari.*

He praised her thus,

"O *Maha Maya! Bhuvaneswari!* You are the imperishable one. You are the nectar of the gods. By you alone is the universe created, by you supported and by you consumed at the end of Time. At its emanation, you take the form of the creator; for its protection, you take the form of steadfastness and at the end of this epoch, you take on the form of destruction. You are *Maha Vidya* (the great knowledge), *Maha Maya* (the great illusion) and *Maha Medha* (the great memory). You are the primordial material (*Mula Prakriti*) of everything, manifesting as the three *gunas.* You are *Kalaratri,* the great night of destruction as well as *Moharatri,* the terrible night of delusion. You are all auspiciousness, modesty, intelligence, tranquillity and forbearance. You are terrible with your sword and spear, cudgel and discus, conch and bow, sling and mace. Yet you are gentle, gentler than other gentle ones, exceedingly beautiful, the supreme queen! Whatever and wherever anything exists, whether it be real or unreal, you alone are the power. How then can I adequately praise you?

By you, *Vishnu,* the sustainer of the world, the protector of the world has been brought under the influence of sleep. Kindly condescend to awaken him, the Lord of Lords so that he may slay these two great *asuras.*

Pray! Remove yourself from the form of Lord *Vishnu* so that he can kill the two demons who are threatening me.

All Hail to Thee! Hail to Thee! All Hail to Thee!"

Pleased with *Brahma's* hymn, the goddess in the form of sleep left the body of *Vishnu* from all quarters. It is said that in this episode it was *Maha Lakshmi* who had taken on the form of *yoga nidra,* the mystic sleep and it was she who now condescended to leave the body of Lord *Vishnu.* One by one she left his eyes, his mind, his hands and every limb.

As soon as she left his body, the great Lord of the world woke up and revealed himself in all his inexpressible grandeur. He fought with the two mighty titans and killed them by placing them on his thighs.

The goddess was still in the sky and it was her *shakti* which enabled *Vishnu* to kill these mighty demons. As *Brahma* and *Vishnu* gazed at her, they were joined by *Shiva* and all three of them sang hymns in praise of her. Pleased with their hymn, she cast her benign glance over them and told them to go ahead with their respective duties of creation, preservation and destruction.

Brahma looked at her in distress and said, "O Mother! There is nothing here except this wide expanse of water. With what am I to create?"

Hearing this, the goddess smiled and told them, "Beyond the ken of the material world there lies an island made of priceless gems, resting on a sea of bliss. In the centre of that island is a temple of light, where I sit on my throne of limitless dimensions, made of numberless universes – both material and non-material. If you draw your awareness up your spine into my antechamber, I will take you to that island and admit you into my throne room".

So saying she beckoned them to get into an aerial chariot, which had just appeared. The chariot was decorated with jewels and pearls and tinkling bells. The three gods got into the vehicle and were transported to the Island of Jewels or the *Mani Dwipa.* On the way they passed the worlds of the other gods and even saw themselves sporting in their own worlds. There was *Brahma* in his world known as *Satyaloka* and there was *Vishnu* lying on the celestial serpent in *Vaikunta* and there was *Shiva* in deep meditation on the icy peak of *Kailasa.* The three gods were totally bewildered when they saw this and asked each other, "Who is this *Brahma* and who this *Vishnu* and *Shiva*?" None of them could think of a satisfactory explanation.

Before they could make further conjectures, the chariot reached the Island of Jewels. They saw all the glorious features of this island and were taken to the *chintamani griha,* which is the sanctum sanctorum of the *Maha Devi.* They were struck with wonder to see the form of the *Tripurasundari* (most beautiful in all the three worlds). She was the colour of the rising sun and her beauty was indescribable. Even the birds there were chanting her *mantras.* While they gazed at her in wonder they saw that her four arms had become a thousand. She was thousand-eyed and thousand-footed. Her form filled the entire universe. As they gazed in astonishment, she regained her original form and smiled at them.

Vishnu was the first to recognize her and spoke to the others.

"She is *Maha Maya, Maha Vidya* and *Mula Prakriti.* She is the cause of all causes. She is the eternal *Brahman* as well as that which is non-eternal. She is the power of will of the Supreme. It is she who creates the cosmos and displays it to the *Paramatman* (the Supreme Soul). O *Brahma!* O *Shiva!* Today we are indeed fortunate that we have got this blessed vision of the Divine Mother. I recall how I was once in the form of an infant, lying in the cosmic waters on a *peepul* leaf. At that time it was she who rocked me lovingly in her tender arms. Let us bow down to her and receive her blessings."

As the three gods came closer to her they were amazed to find that the entire universe of movable and immovable things, was reflected in her toenails. They themselves were there as well as the two demons, which *Vishnu* had just killed.

Each of them in turn extolled the *Devi* with beautiful hymns.

"O Mother, we realize that this whole universe rests in you. It rises from you and folds back into you. It is you who creates the elements at the time of creation and through them, this manifest universe, in order to beguile the *Purusha* who is the sole enjoyer. His nature is Pure Consciousness and he is untainted by any desire to create. You alone have the power to create. Without you there would be no objects and no universe. You alone have the knowledge to create *(jnana shakti),* the will to create *(iccha shakti)* and the ability to create (*kriya shakti*). Even we cannot fathom your inconceivable glory, let alone those who are steeped in ignorance. You have created countless universes by your power. On our way here we saw many such, with other *Vishnus, Shivas* and *Brahmas.* Such is your divine power and majesty. We – *Brahma, Vishnu* and *Shiva* – create, preserve and destroy only through your command and grace.

It is your endless might that is supporting this entire universe. You are in essence one with the *Purusha*, the attributeless Self, but by the power of your *maya,* you appear in the form of this universe of attributes. You alone are the ancient, eternal *Prakriti* and the Mother of the universe. The three of us are products of your creation and thus we also come under the power of the *gunas. Rajas* is predominant in *Brahma*, *sattva* in *Vishnu* and *tamas* in *Shiva.* It is because of this that we are able to carry on our work of creation, preservation and destruction.

O *Devi!* You are the intelligence of the intelligent; you are the fame of the famous, the beauty of the lustrous, and the wealth of the wealthy. You are the source of both desire and dispassion leading to bondage and liberation. You have expanded and manifested this whole phenomenon of the visible cosmos for the liberation of the *jivas.* When the *jiva* comes to realize fully that all this is your work and your *lila* (play), then it understands that it is only a participant in this divine drama. With the dawn of this understanding it comes to an end of its role in the cosmic comedy.

"O Divine Mother! Help us to overcome your *maya* and continue our work according to your commands."

Thus saying, the gods bowed before her and begged her to explain everything to them. The goddess then described her divine nature to them.

"This entire universe which appears so real to the finite intelligence is no more real than a reflection in a mirror. All the entities in all the worlds from the gods to the barely conscious creatures are but fragments of my glory. I am worshipped by all beings in many such universes. Though many worship me, few know me in truth. Creatures imagine that they exist apart from me but this is not true. The realization that they are integral parts of my being comes only through deep, sustained devotion to me. When the mind is directed solely towards me, the *jiva* discovers its unity with me. When obstructions limiting the *jiva* fall away, it recognizes that it is not limited by the body, has never been and will never be anything but my very Self. The devotee who cleanses the mind with tranquillity, concentration and loving devotion, will discover me at the root of all things – self-luminous, transparent and perfect. With this realisation, all doubts will vanish. Such a person will go beyond suffering and will overcome all fear."

"There is no difference between the *Brahman* and me. We are the same. Without *Brahman* there would be no *maya* and without *maya* there would be no creation. At the beginning of creation *Brahman* and *maya* have to appear different or else there would be no creation. Out of this apparent duality, all the differences – visible and invisible – have come forth. There is nothing in the universe which is not a part of me. When you perform the act of creation, O *Brahma,* it is my *shakti* that will enable you to create. It is my *shakti* that will enable *Vishnu* to take care of the universe and *Shiva* to destroy.

Sattva guna is prominent in *Vishnu* so he is superior to *Brahma.* If any difficulty arises in the world of *Brahma's* creation, *Vishnu* will take an incarnation and go down to the earth in order to uplift the *Sanatana Dharma.* He will take birth in the wombs of women and sometimes in the wombs of birds and animals in order to destroy the demons and uphold *dharma.* There is no difference between *Hara* and *Hari* – *Shiva* and *Vishnu.* He who worships one, worships the other and he who makes a difference between them is ignorant of the truth.

Everything springs from the supreme reality of *Brahman.* He is neither cause nor effect. I am his *maya* or power of illusion that creates this world of duality. From me come the three illusory powers of time, space and causality. The first to come out of me is *avyakta* or *ahamkara,* which is the essence of the three *gunas.* These *gunas* are known as *sattva*, *rajas* and *tamas. Rajas* is the power of kinesis and *tamas* is the opposite – inertia. In between them is the harmonizing principle of *sattva.* There is nothing in this world that is devoid of these three *gunas* including the three of you. Everything that is visible is endowed with the three *gunas.* Whatever was or will be, cannot exist without them. Only the Supreme Self or *Purusha* is without these *gunas* and he is not visible. I myself am *Adi Shakti* or *Mula Prakriti.* At times I am with *gunas* and at times without. I am always the cause and never the effect. When I take on my causal nature I am with *gunas.* When I am enfolded into the Supreme Essence, I am without *gunas.* From this Supreme Essence comes *ahamkara.* From it comes *mahat tattva* or the cosmic intellect. From this comes the five *tanmatras* or subtle elements. From these come the gross elements and then the organs of perception, action and the mind, intellect, ego and super consciousness *(manas, buddhi, ahamkara* and *chitta*). Out of these the whole universe of forms is created. At the end of one cycle of creation this universe, including the three of you, will be dissolved and will fold back into me, the *Maha Maya*, the primeval energy and I myself into that Supreme Essence.

It is not possible for the embodied self or *jiva* to know me in my *nirguna* state that is devoid of attributes nor is it possible for the mind that is born out of *ahamkara* to know the *Nirguna Brahman* or the Quality-less Supreme. But we can be realized through deep meditation when the mind has transcended the three *gunas. Purusha* and *Prakriti* pervade everything and exist in everything. Nothing in this universe can subsist without both of them. Both are *nirguna,* devoid of qualities, undecaying and without impurities. The Universal Consciousness that is felt in all beings is the *Purusha*, the highest Self. The energy that is felt in all beings is *Prakriti*, the universal *Shakti.* The *jivas* are all *saguna* or endowed with qualities. How can they ever see that which is *nirguna* or beyond all qualities?

This universe is both eternal and non-eternal. It is non-eternal in as much as it is always changing. But I am in all things and I am eternal so in that respect the universe, even though ever changing can still be considered as eternal. The unreal can never come into existence. The real can never cease to be. The forms change but I am that Supreme Reality, which upholds these various forms and I am eternal. So do not confuse yourselves with questions about the reality and the unreality of this world. Plunge yourselves into your respective functions and have recourse to my name by which alone you will be able to discharge your duties.

Now I will give you my nine-syllabled *mantra* by which you will be able to realize me and carry on with your work."

So saying the *Devi* gave them the nine-syllabled *mantra* that has to be preceded by the *pranava* or *Aum* and followed by '*namaha*'.

"Aum Aim, hreem, kleem, chamundayai vicchai namaha!"

This is the supreme and most esoteric *mantra* of the *Maha Devi* that should be chanted constantly in order to get liberation.

The *Devi* blessed the three of them and told them to go to their own worlds and commence their work in this present cycle of creation. She also presented them with her *shaktis.* She gave the *Shakti* known as *Maha Saraswati* to *Brahma* whose predominant trait was *rajas* since he was the one to undertake the task of creation as detailed by the *Maha Devi.* He was to take her and go to his abode of *Satyaloka.* To *Vishnu,* she gave the beauteous *Maha Lakshmi* and told him to go and live in the world known as *Vaikunta. Sattva guna* would be preponderate in him and *rajas* and *tamas* would be secondary. To *Shiva* whose basic *guna* was *tamas,* she gave *Gauri,* and told him to go and live in *Kailasa.* He was told to take recourse to *rajas* and *tamas* in order to undertake the act of destruction but also to resort to *sattva* and perform austerities.

"All three of you are my *devas,* born of my *gunas.* You will undoubtedly be worshipped and respected by the whole world."

What we have to understand by this is that the whole of creation is but a revelation and a manifestation of the One and the sole divine essence. *Advaita* proclaims the truth that Brahman alone is real and the world unreal – '*Brahma satyam, jagat mitya*'. But here we see that the *Maha Devi* asserts something quite different. She seems to make a wholesale, indiscriminate sanctification of everything on the earthly plane so that there is no need to think that liberation can be gained only through an ascetic renunciation of the world. We are all in immediate contact with the Divine here and now if we can only look on everything as part and parcel of Its ever-changing, everlasting self-revelation. Here the popular picture of *maya* as the dreaded delusory power of the Supreme, which is so difficult for even the sternest ascetic to overcome, takes on a surprising aspect. She, the *Maha Maya,* is herself the revelation, the incarnation of the divine energy of the Absolute. Life with all its dualities, its extremes of peace and strife, of dread and bliss, is holy and divine and is only a screen for the Divine within it. Just beneath the veil of *maya,* the magic mirage of the universe, dwells the Supreme Spirit. The energy of *maya* is nothing but the energy emanating from that Spirit. The *Maha Devi* emerges in the forefront, masking the Absolute but also displaying his inner potentialities.

As she herself tells the three gods, the process of creation is a conversion of the static repose of the Absolute into a procreative power. In every cycle of creation there are two steps. First, there is the Absolute *Purusha,* which is complete inactivity, inertia and voidness. From that we come to the infinite activity and dynamic differentiation of a universe with its abundance of creations and variety of forms. All this happens in this world bound by time, space and causation, which is the very essence of *maya.*

These three are categories of our limited, individual consciousness, the most elementary frames and limitations of our human perceptions and conceptions. They do not apply to the transcendent Absolute. We view the world with this three-framed glass. What appears to our human consciousness as a gradation from the Absolute is not a gradation at all when seen from the standpoint of the Absolute. The three are only aspects of a single, unique and eternal essence. The truth is voidness and plenitude, everything and nothing.

The Absolute rests in its transcendental quietitude, all comprehensive and enigmatic. It is serenely unaffected by the tensions produced by the three *gunas* which is the work of *maya.* It never feels the joys and agonies of their mutual interactions. The restless effects of the three-fold play of creation, manifestation and destruction, is subsumed in its eternal repose. This glorious presence is, as if indifferent, to the processes of the universe and the dualities experienced by the individual. So also the *atman*, the Self of man, rests unconcerned with the sufferings and delights of the personality, which is enshrouded within the various sheaths of the physical body, the astral body, and the mental and intellectual bodies.

When viewed against the background of eternity, the drama that is enacted on the stage of space and time is as insubstantial as the play of light and shade. They are all creations in the mist of the mind, which pass, flow and vanish into thin air. The true work of *maya* is the production of a phenomenal world, which has its basis in nescience or *avidya. Maya* is what produces this extraordinary universe – both personal and collective as experienced by us within our limited, individualised consciousness. It is experienced both when we are awake and asleep, remembering and forgetting, enjoying and suffering, always grasping for that which is ephemeral and unable to grasp the reality of its own existence. This is the paradox of *maya.* The universe as well as our own personalities is as real or as unreal as the dualities, which seem to emerge from the Supreme Centre and which are ignored by it. *Brahman* and *Maya* co-exist. *Maya* is the continuous self-manifestation and self-disguise of *Brahman* – its self-revelation as well as its concealing mask. Hence everything in the universe is divine. Nothing can be scorned or cast aside as below par and worthy of contempt. *Maha Maya* herself is the sum total of all and is worshipped as the Mother and life energy of even the gods as well as of all creatures.

The *yogi* should concentrate on this truth and realize that the individual personality is one with the universal Self who is none other than the *Maha Maya*. That which is mortal in us is also that which is imperishable. What is change and what is above change is one and the same. Thus, the *yogi* should learn to accept the *maya* of his frail, transient existence as the dynamic radiation of the eternal, absolute Self.

The three gods then took leave of the *Maha Devi* and ascended the aerial chariot that took off into ethereal space. When they turned round to look at the island they found that there was no *Mani Dwipa*, no *Devi* nor the ocean of nectar!

"Her look, Her smile awoke celestial sense,
Even in earth stuff and their intense delight,
Poured a supernal beauty on men's lives.
A wide self-giving was her native act.
A magnanimity as of sea or sky,
Enveloped with its greatness all that came
And gave a sense as of a greatened world,
Her kindly care was sweet temperate sun,
Her high passion a blue heaven's equipoise."

— "Savitri" by Sri Aurobindo

Thus ends the third chapter of the *Sri Devi Lila* known as 'Maha Devi', describing the nature of the *Devi* and creation.

ॐ *Aim, hreem, kleem* ॐ

ॐ

Rajnyai Namaha!

CHAPTER FOUR

RAJARAJESHWARI

Ya Devi sarvabhuteshu, kshuda rupena samsthita,
Namasthasyai, Namasthasyai, Namasthasyai Namo Namaha!

"O Goddess, who resides in all creatures in the form of hunger,
Hail to Thee! Hail to Thee! All Hail to Thee!"

The Island of Jewels or *Mani Dwipa* to which the three gods were transported is the esoteric island in which the *Maha Devi* resides with her attendant *shaktis,* which are numerous in number. It is situated somewhere in etheric space far above the worlds of the gods, so it is known as *Sarvaloka* because it is superior to all other worlds.

The *Devi Bhagavatam* gives a graphic description of the island. It is set in the middle of an ocean known as *Sudha Samudra* or the sea of nectar. Many types of fish with brilliant hues play and leap about in this ocean. The shores of the island are made of the dust of millions of gems and that is how the island got its name – *Mani Dwipa.* The Sanskrit word *'mani'* means gem. The trees that line the beach have clusters of jewels hanging from them and the sand is made of jewel dust. An aerial view of this island shows that it is designed in the shape of a mystic *Yantra.* There are many enclosures, some circular and some square in shape. The squares cut into the circles and thus make the *Yantra.*

A few yards away from the beach is an iron enclosure with four gates. Many guards are stationed here. All the gods who come to this mystic island have to alight from their vehicles at this place to be taken forward by the *Devi's* attendants. After this they are made to pass through a second enclosure, the walls of which are made of white copper. In this there are many trees laden with fruit and fragrant flowers. Forests, gardens and lakes abound here with cuckoos cooing sweetly and stately swans and other aquatic birds swimming in the lakes.

The third enclosure is square in shape and is made of copper. The forests are filled with *kalpavrikshas* or wish-fulfilling trees, bearing golden leaves and flowers and fruits of gems. The Lord of the spring season is the king of this place. His throne is made of flowers. A canopy of flowers is held above him. His ornaments are also made of flowers. His food is the nectar of a thousand newly opened buds. The sweet perfume of full-blown blossoms drenches the air. One can see the beauty of the vernal season everywhere.

The next enclosure is made of lead. Within this is the *Santanaka* tree with flowers that look like gold. But they have an intoxicating perfume that spreads to several miles around. This tree is always in full bloom. Its fruits are luscious and sweet. The king of the summer season lives here. It is very hot and the inhabitants have to seek the shade of the trees and anoint themselves with sandal paste in order to remain cool. All of them carry flower fans in their hands. Many *yogis* are seen practising severe austerities at this place.

The wall of the fifth enclosure is made of brass. The prominent tree here is the sandalwood and the ruler is the king of the rainy season. Lightning flashes from his amber eyes and rain clouds are his armour. Thunder is his voice and the rainbow his weapon. There is a constant drizzle here. The trees have new leaves all through the year and are entwined by tender buds and creepers. The rivers are ever full and flow swiftly and forcefully. The tanks are filled with muddy water like the minds of materialistic people!

The sixth enclosure is made of five types of iron. The gardens are filled with beautiful trees, flowers and creepers. The ruler is the king of the autumn season. Many *siddhas* or perfected souls live here.

The seventh enclosure is made of silver. The gardens are filled with *parijata* trees, the flowers of which drench the air with their sweet perfume. The ruler of this is the *Hemanta* season, which comes immediately after autumn and is characterized by pearly mists and clouds.

The eighth enclosure is made of molten gold. In the centre is a garden of *kadamba* trees. They are covered with fruits and flowers from which honey drips constantly. The ruler of this is the winter season.

Next comes the ninth enclosure with walls of topaz. Even the drains and roads here are made of topaz. Various enclosures made of many types of gems lead out from this one. The regents of the quarters reside in the different directions. *Indra* and his retinue live on the eastern side. The south-eastern enclosure belongs to *Agni*, the god of fire. To the south is the abode of *Yama*, the god of death. On the south-western corner dwell the demons and on the west, *Varuna*, god of waters and drink. His vehicle is the king of fishes and his subjects are all aquatic animals. On the north-western corner dwells *Vayu*, the wind god. The *yogis* who have practiced *pranayama* or control of breath live with him. On the northern side resides, *Kubera*, the corpulent king of the *Yakshas* who are the guardians of wealth.

On the north-eastern corner is the abode of *Rudra.* His eyes are always red with anger and his attendants have distorted faces. Around his neck is a garland of skulls and tiny snakes are twined round his fingers. He wears a tiger skin and his body is anointed with the ashes of the dead. *Bhadrakali* is his mate. The sound of his *damaru* (drum) reverberates through the universe in the form of thunder, crashing waves and furious storms. Spirits, ghouls and phantoms surround him.

The tenth enclosure wall is made of deep red coral, the colour of the rising sun. All the gates, temples and arbours are made of the same stone. This is the place where the sixty-four *kalas* or subsidiary powers of the *Devi* reside, each with her separate vehicle and weapons. Fire is always coming out of their lolling tongues. Their eyes are red with anger. Wherever there is war, death and destruction, they will be present. They are ever ready to swallow the entire universe at the command of the *Maha Devi.*

After this comes the eleventh enclosure made of hessonite. The whole ground is covered with the dust of these gems. Here live the thirty-two *maha-shaktis* or super forces of the *Devi,* adorned with many ornaments and holding weapons of destruction. They are ever ready to fight and any one of them can destroy a million universes if the *Devi* so commands. They can never be defeated at any time. They will always be present at the time of universal destruction.

Next to the hessonite enclosure comes the one made of diamonds, which is the twelfth. The entrance gates are also made of diamonds and even the trees are resplendent with diamond drops. This is the residence of the maids of the *Bhuvaneswari* (goddess of all the worlds). Her eight main ladies-in-waiting dwell on the eight sides of this enclosure.

The thirteenth enclosure is made of cats-eye. The courtyards and houses are all made of the same gem. This is the residence of the *sapta matrikas* or seven mothers known as *Brahmi, Maheswari, Kaumari, Vaishnavi, Varahi, Indrani, and Nrisimhi.* Their forms are similar to those of *Brahma, Vishnu* and his *avataras.* They are fierce goddesses, always present at the time of wars. At the four gates of this enclosure the various vehicles of the *Maha Devi* are stationed, always ready to start at her slightest command. These vehicles are not merely chariots but also include swans, lions, peacocks and bulls.

The fourteenth enclosure is made of blue sapphire. In the centre of this enclosure is a huge lotus with sixteen petals. On each petal resides one of the sixteen main *shaktis* of the great goddess. All are dark blue in colour like sapphire. They are in charge of all the other *shaktis.*

Next to the sapphire enclosure comes the one made of pearls, which is the fifteenth. Courtyards, roads and houses are all made of pearls. Here again is a huge lotus with eight petals on which reside another eight *shaktis.* They are the ministers of the *Maha Devi* and her *jnana shaktis* or powers of knowledge. They know everything that takes place in the entire universe and it is their duty to keep her informed at all times.

The sixteenth enclosure is made of emeralds. It is a hexagonal *yantra* and *Gayatri Devi, Savitri Devi,* the *Vedas, Puranas* and *Smritis* live in every corner of the hexagon. *Ganesha* also resides in a special corner.

The seventeenth enclosure is made of opals. The goddesses of the five elements reside here. Their bodies resemble the colour of the elements over which they preside.

The eighteenth enclosure is made of *navaratnas* or the nine precious gems. Here dwell the different *avataras* of the *Maha Devi* – the incarnations she had taken in order to kill various demons.

The twentieth enclosure is the final one. This is the crowning place of the *Rajarajeshwari,* and is called the *ratnagriha* or house of gems. It is situated in the mathematical centre of all the other enclosures. In the middle of this is the *chintamani griha, which* is made of the precious gem known as *chintamani* that is capable of fulfilling the wishes of all devotees. All the artefacts within this enclosure are made of the same gem. Rivers of gems and other precious metals stream from all sides of this palace and flow into the ocean of nectar. At the time of creation and dissolution this *griha* or enclosure expands and contracts like a piece of cloth. On all sides flow rivers of ghee, milk, curd, honey, nectar, pomegranate juice, etc. Different parts are lit up with the lustre of the various jewels to be found there, like emeralds, sapphires and diamonds. Even the sky reflects the glory of these jewels. The mountains looming in the distance are made of gems and jewels. All the tanks are filled with beautiful red lotuses. The enclosure has four halls with pillars which shine like the sun, moon, stars and lightning. Over these are canopies that look like rainbows.

These halls are known as the Hall of Beauty, the Hall of Liberation, the Hall of Wisdom and the Hall of Solitude. They are surrounded with perfumed gardens overflowing with flowers. The *Maha Devi* sits in the Hall of Beauty when she wants to listen to the songs of all the creatures of the universe, sung to her through the mouths of her maids. When she wants to give liberation to her devotees, she sits in the Hall of Liberation and when she expounds on the wisdom of the ages, she sits in the Hall of Wisdom. Seated in the Hall of Solitude, she gives commands to her ministers.

In the centre of these halls is a dais in the shape of a *satkona yantra* or mystic six-angled figure of two triangles intersecting each other. The throne of the *Maha Devi* is placed in the centre of this. The throne is also made of the gem known as *chintamani.* The ten steps leading to this throne are made of the *tattvas* or primary qualities, which make up the universe. *Brahma, Vishnu, Rudra* and *Shiva* support the four legs of the throne.

The *Maha Devi* sits here in all her glory. She is also known as *Lalithambika* or *Maha Tripurasundari*, the supreme beauty who is beyond the triple bonds of the physical, subtle and causal dimensions. Though she is the ancient one, she appears to be in the full bloom of youth. Her face has the brilliance of a thousand suns. She has three lotus-petalled eyes. The third is the eye of wisdom and is placed in the centre of her pearly forehead. It opens only when she wants to destroy anything. The other two eyes are filled with compassion and overflowing with love. Below the third eye is the red mark known as a *tilaka,* made of musk and saffron. Her nose ornaments are tiny replicas of the planet Venus and are made of minute crystals, which cast their rainbow lights over her rose tinted cheeks. Her lips are red as the *bimba* berry. Her lustrous locks are twined with jasmine flowers and crowned with a tiara, which has jewels in the shape of the sun and moon. Her earrings are shaped like the *Sri Chakra* and enhance the beauty of her small, delicate ears. Her slender neck is adorned with necklaces of various shapes and wonderful hues. A jewel-studded bodice covers her full and enticing breasts. Her waist is adorned with a delicately wrought jewelled girdle with golden bells that tinkle as she moves. Her armlets are made of burnished gold, studded with rubies. Her wrists are heavy with bangles with tinkling bells. Her long, delicate fingers with pink-tipped nails have curiously carved rings set with precious gems. She has four hands holding the noose, goad, bow and arrow and the *abhaya mudra* or the sign of grace and fearlessness. Her voice is sweeter than a lute. This is the most exalted and mysterious residence of the *Maha Devi* as described in the *Srimad Devi Bhagavatam.*

We should now try to understand the esoteric significance of this island. The deep blue tranquil waters are the substance of life. This is the ocean of eternal life, the *Sudha Samudra* or the ocean of immortality in its primal state. In the mythology of Lord *Vishnu* we find him recumbent on the cosmic serpent, which is floating on the ocean of nectar. In both these allegories, the ocean is the vast water of endless life energy. It is the ocean of nectar, and the elixir of immortality and in its centre is the mystical island. The ocean, though apparently dormant, is full of infinite potential. It is the field of all possibilities which modern physics has just come to recognise. The field is never static. It is capable of unlimited combinations and permutations. Modern physics has only now understood that there is nothing called a static universe. This field or ocean as described in the *Devi Bhagavatam* contains the germs of all conflicting opposites, all the pairs of co-operating antagonisms. All these energies evolve and concentrate at the centre, which is the Island of Jewels, the abode of the *Maha Devi.* The ocean, which stands for universal consciousness, is comparable to the subtle element of *akasa* or ether that constitutes all space and is the stage for all subsequent evolution and development.

The island is the metaphysical point of power. It is the *bindu* or dot, which spreads, unfolds, expands and becomes transmuted into the tangible realm of our limited consciousness and this universe of myriad forms. This *bindu* is the first concentrated drop of the dynamic force of the universal divine substance. From it the creative process starts as a primeval sound or *nada* and spreads out in waves of beauty and bliss. Therefore, the universe is nothing but the projection of her majesty and glory. The island, which is made in the form of a *Yantra,* has to be visualized and meditated upon with great devotion before it yields its esoteric secrets. The *Maha Devi* is *Mula Prakriti*, the power behind the *Purusha*, the original force that projects this phenomenal world. The weapons she carries have an esoteric meaning apart from the obvious one of being used to kill demons. The bow and arrow denote the power of her supreme will known as *iccha shakti.* Without this will, creation would not be possible. The noose is usually the lasso, which catches and fetters the enemy. This denotes *jnana shakti,* or the master force of the intellect which seizes and fixes with a firm hold on its objects. Again this is essential for creation. The goad which is used for urging a beast to move, denotes action and is known as *kriya shakti.* These are the three *shaktis* that she uses for creating the objective world of duality. She is the feminine, active principle, the efficient and material cause of the universe, the *Maha Maya* that evolves the different elements and beings.

The modern mind might dismiss these descriptions as the wild imaginations of the ancient *rishis* bound as they were to the infancy of the world. But when we see the consistency and uniformity of the descriptions in the various *Puranas,* we will be able to accept the truth that these are the recorded impressions of the memory of a race created by a powerful impact of vivid and similar spiritual experiences. The portrayal is symbolic and in our inner worship the *sadhaka* will be able to unravel the truth represented by the symbols.

Every aspect of the Island of Jewels is meant for meditation and is to be visualized in the innermost recesses of the heart. At first it appears that it is a vindication of our hidden desire for the splendid and the beautiful alone. But in time we will come to realize that in its total acceptance of the beautiful life which appears almost trans moral, it is also quite as stern as the total negation of life which is the way of the ascetic. In India this pendulum of thought has always existed – the sway between these extremes that point to inhuman attitudes and extra human goals. On one hand we find the pessimistic criticism of life, which leads to practices of the severest ascetic character, which will enable the devotee to shatter the nightmare of life by a great awakening into the reality. Human existence is but a springboard to help us in the bound into the supra human, supra divine sphere of Being which is beyond the spell of *maya.* The literal meaning of *maya* is that which measures the immeasurable. *Maya* sees limitation where none actually exists. But in this symbolism of the goddess in the Island of Jewels, we find the same *maya* in her most benign aspect. She is the very essence of the Absolute, pure bliss and pure spirit.

She also displays the true feminine nature – the life-bearing, life-nourishing maternal principle. She is benign, beneficent and bright. She exhibits only the positive aspect of *Maya Shakti* or power of illusion. We have also to see how the opposite side of the coin is depicted in the fearless world of Indian myth and folklore. Her negative aspect of an ever-destructive function, which takes back and swallows time and time again all that she has created, gives us a shock of horror if it is to be duly expressed. To this end we will have to see her pictured as *Kaali*, the black one. *Kaali* is the feminine form of the word *kaala,* which means Time, which is the all-producing and all-consuming principle. Time alone is the vanquisher and the killer. Everything that comes into existence vanishes again after the passing of its brief spell of allotted time.

The vision of the *Mani Dwipa* was shown to the three gods, *Brahma, Vishnu* and *Shiva* at the beginning of this *Kalpa* or cycle of creation after *Vishnu* had destroyed the gargantuan demons known as *Madhu* and *Kaitabha.*

"A joy in the world her master movement here.
The passion of the game lighted her eyes.
A smile on her lips welcomed earth's bliss and grief,
A laugh was her return to pleasure and pain.
All things she saw as masquerades of Truth,
Disguised in the costumes of ignorance.
Crossing the years to Immortality."

— "Savitri" by Sri Aurobindo.

Thus ends the fourth chapter of the *Sri Devi Lila* known as 'Rajarajeshwari', describing the Island of Jewels or the *Mani Dwipa.*

ॐ *Aim, hreem, kleem* ॐ

ॐ

Maheswaryai Namaha!

CHAPTER FIVE

MAHESWARI

Ya Devi sarvabhuteshu, nidra rupena samsthita,
Namasthasyai, Namasthasyai, Namasthasyai Namo Namaha!

"O Goddess, who resides in all creatures in the form of sleep,
Hail to Thee! Hail to Thee! All Hail to Thee!"

The birth of the two terrible demons, *Madhu* and *Kaitabha* is a curious phenomenon. At the end of the *Maha Pralaya* when the whole universe was dissolved in the cosmic waters, Lord *Vishnu* was sleeping on the cosmic serpent called *Ananta.* At that time it is said that a drop of honey (*madhu)* came out of his right ear, which changed into the enormous demon known as *Madhu.* Out of his left ear came a small pellet of wax, which turned into the mighty demon called *Kaitabha.* What is the esoteric meaning of this strange episode? Lord *Vishnu* is the preserver in the Hindu trinity and he is the one who is always aware of what goes on in the universe. The *Upanishads* describe him as having many limbs, many eyes and many ears. This means that he hears all that happens in the world, both good and evil. All the slanderous and ugly tales that have been told by so many countless people, all the lies and falsehoods that have been related, all these were collected as wax in his ears. The driving passion for comfort, luxury, power, fortune and wealth was transformed into a drop of honey. The *karmic* effect of the uncontrollable desire for wealth and comfort and the accumulated amount of negative, self-destructive thoughts and talk were transformed into two terrible demons who threatened to destroy the creator – *Brahma,* himself. This happens at the beginning of every *Kalpa* or cycle of evolution. This is the power of collective negativity. It is this that erupts into world wars. The terror that we are facing now is nothing but the work of these two demons that have been brought to life out of our own negativity.

These two titans who had thus been born out of Lord *Vishnu's* ears found themselves splashing about in the cosmic waters pondering on the where and why of their existence. At last the idea came into their minds that the mighty goddess, *Maha Devi,* was their cause. They determined to discover her whereabouts. As they cogitated over the matter, they heard the celestial voice of *Devi Saraswati*, who told them to meditate on her seed *mantra.* They decided to try this out and proceeded to repeat the *mantra* and meditate on her for a thousand years. At the end of this period of time they heard the celestial voice once again.

"I am very pleased with your *tapasya* and you can ask for any boon you like."

The *asuras* immediately asked for immortality. The divine voice said that no one could be granted that. So they opted for death at their own volition. This was granted and the demons became bloated with pride and thrashed about the mighty ocean searching for a suitable opponent on whom to try their valour. Their arms were itching for a fight and they did not think *Brahma* to be a suitable candidate on whom to display their prowess. They ordered him to give up his lotus seat and accept their suzerainty or fight! *Brahma* was frightened out of his wits and desperately searched in the waters for some aid. At last he was given the vision of Lord *Narayana.* But as has been narrated before, *Vishnu* was in the thrall of *Yoga Nidra*, the goddess of sleep. It was only after she left him that he rose up from his couch and saw *Brahma.*

Brahma bowed low before *Vishnu* – the Lord of all Lords and begged him to deliver him from the threat of these two mighty demons. *Vishnu* pacified him and told him to retire to his own abode and leave him to deal with the demons. At this point the bloodthirsty demons arrived on the scene, glad to have found a more worthy opponent!

They saw Lord *Hari* (*Vishnu*) of unspeakable beauty lying on his divine bed, the coil of a snake that was many leagues wide and many leagues long. He was clad in a yellow robe and had a diamond diadem on his head. On his chest flashed the enormous ruby known as the *Kaustubham.* He glowed with an ethereal splendour and beauty. From his navel sprouted a lotus with the lustre of the sun and within the lotus was seated *Brahma*, the four-faced one, the *guru* of the world with four arms, holding the four *Vedas.*

The eyes of the *asuras* were totally blinded by the brilliance emanating from the Lord. They were astonished to see this sight but nothing daunted they roared and tried to intimidate the trembling *Brahma.*

"There is nothing greater than us in this world, O Great Sage! We are the ones who cover this whole universe with darkness (*tamas)* and passion (*rajas).* We, whose nature consist of *tamas* and *rajas,* are the main cause of *dukkha* (sorrow) to the world. We are deceitful among those of virtuous conduct and invincible among all embodied ones. We are born age after age and delude the world. We are made up of those objects which are desired by everyone – wealth, possessions, happiness, joy and fortune."

"We will kill you first and then kill this one who seems to be sleeping on a serpent", they cried.

Brahma immediately disappeared from the lotus and took up a safe position behind the Lord.

Lord *Vishnu* laughed and leisurely got up from his bed and told the demons that he was ready to fight with them if they so desired. The brothers were delighted to put their might to use.

Madhu came first and challenged the Lord. After some time when he saw his brother getting tired, *Kaitabha* joined the fray. *Vishnu* used only his fists since the demons had no weapons. A tremendous battle ensued between the war-lusty demons and Lord *Vishnu. Brahma* and *Adi Shakti* witnessed this spectacle from above. After fighting for a thousand years the titans were still not tired. Lord *Vishnu* started wondering why this was so.

The *asuras* were elated at their success and taunted him. "If you are too tired to fight you can give up and become our slave!"

Vishnu replied, "O *danavas* (demons)! You are two in number and mighty in size whereas I am single and puny when compared with you. Therefore, let us rest a while and then we will recommence our battle".

The *asuras* agreed with alacrity since they were sure of the outcome and did not mind a small rest themselves. While they rested the Lord began to think of the reason for the apparent invincibility of the two brothers. He soon came to know of the boon of the goddess. "If this is the reason, they can never be slain since no one ever wishes for their own death. So my only hope is to appeal to the *Devi* herself who has granted them this boon."

So thinking he looked up at *Yoga Nidra Devi* who was shining in the sky and extolled her.

"O *Maha Kaali! Bhuvaneswari! Chandika*! You have given them these boons and puffed up their pride. Kindly help me to destroy them since they are threatening to kill *Brahma.*"

Pleased with his hymn, the *Devi* told him sweetly, "O *Narayana!* Do not fear. I will delude these two heroes by my *maya* and then you will be able to kill them easily. Let it be a battle of wits between you and not just of fists."

It is to be noted that from the very commencement of this *yuga* or cycle of time, the gods had to depend on the *Devi's* power to help them in their tasks.

In all his encounters with foes Lord *Vishnu* is noted for using his intelligence, thus showing the superiority of brains over brute strength. Once again he proceeded to challenge the *asuras* who were still thirsty for battle. Fist for fist, arm for arm, thrust for thrust, the fight went on and on, interminably. At last *Vishnu* shot a desperate look at *Maha Maya* who was shining with all her beauty in the sky. Seeing his look, the *Devi* came down to the ocean and cast her sidelong glances enticingly at the two demons who became quite bemused by her.

To those *asuras* who were thus swollen and drunk with pride, Lord *Hari* spoke, "O *Danavas!* I am pleased with your prowess in the art of wrestling and wish to give you a boon. Go ahead and ask for what you want".

The haughty demons were quite insulted by this and told him, "We are not beggars to accept boons from you. On the other hand, we are the ones who should be giving you boons. We are donors, not receivers! We are your benefactors so you can go ahead and ask us for whatever you want!"

The Lord smiled at the enormity of their egos and sweetly replied, "I accept your boon, O heroes! Indeed there is something I desire. I know you have great prowess. There is none equal to you. But for the good of the world I have to ask you for something. I wish that the two of you will allow yourselves to be killed by my hands."

The *asuras* realized that they had been neatly tricked by *Vishnu's Maya,* which is a power of the divine mother. They thought for a minute and saw that there was nothing but water everywhere so they swiftly hit upon a ruse to save their skins.

"O Mighty Being! No one is equal to us in strength, beauty, bravery, generosity, might and self-control. We will always keep our word. Yet we want to change our minds and ask you for the boon which we refused previously. You have our permission to kill us, provided you do it on some space which is not covered by water."

"So be it," said the blessed Lord and allowed them to put conditions on their commitment even though he could not see any space that was not covered with water. He then happened to glance at his own uncovered thighs, which had not a trace of water on them and expanded them so that they appeared like solid earth.

"O Mighty *Danavas*! He said. Place your heads on this solid foundation and keep your word as I will keep mine!"

When they saw this, the demons were terrified and expanded their forms to double their size. *Bhagavan Hari* also expanded his thighs interminably. This game went on till the demons realized that they were beaten. They laid their gargantuan heads on *Hari's* thighs and the Lord took his discus – the *Sudarshana Chakra* – and sawed off their mighty heads. The marrow *(medhas)* from their bones filled the ocean and was sucked into the earth and that is how the earth got the name *Medini.* It was after slaying *Madhu* and *Kaitabha* that *Vishnu* came to be called *Madhusudana.*

It will be noticed that in this episode of the killing of *Madhu* and *Kaitabha,* the goddess did not take an active part. The episode establishes her cosmic, transcendental status. She is *Maha Maya*, the great illusion who deludes the *asuras* into thinking that they could outwit the divine. How great was their opinion of themselves when they talked to *Brahma*! This is typical of the *asuric* ego that thinks itself to be superior to God. As they themselves proclaimed to *Brahma,* these *asuras* are born at the beginning of every cycle of Time and the earth is nourished by the fat of their enormous egos. Naturally they are the ones who are at the root of all our desires for earthly pleasures. But behind it all is the power of the *Maha Maya* who leads human beings to impute absolute reality to life in this world and thus make their own futile attempts to outwit the divine. These attempts will end in failure for only the Divine truly abides.

"He who would save the world, must be one with the world,
All suffering things contain in his heart's space.
And bear the grief and joy of all that lives.
His soul must be wider than the universe,
And feel eternity as its very stuff.
Rejecting the moment's personality,
Know itself older than the birth of time."

— "Savitri" by Sri Aurobindo

Thus ends the fifth chapter of the *Sri Devi Lila* known as 'Maheswari', describing the defeat of the *asuras – Madhu and Kaitabha* – by Lord *Vishnu.*

ॐ *Aim, hreem, kleem* ॐ

"Thence I extend pervading all the worlds;
And yonder heaven I closely touch and penetrate,
With the showering and flowing body of mine."

— *Rig Veda*

ॐ

Bhavanyai Namaha!

CHAPTER SIX

PARASHAKTI

Ya Devi sarvabhuteshu, chaaya rupena samsthita,
Namasthasyai, Namasthasyai, Namasthasyai Namo Namaha!

"O Goddess, who resides in all creatures in the form of shadow,
Hail to Thee! Hail to Thee! All Hail to Thee!"

Once the creator *Brahma* went to *Vaikunta,* the abode of Lord *Vishnu* and found him in deep meditation. When the lord came out of meditation, *Brahma* asked him a pertinent question.

"O *Janardana!* You are the Lord of Lords! The Lord of the present, past and future! Kindly tell me who or what is the object of your meditation? I myself have sprung from the lotus, which grew from your navel and have been ordered to create. It is due to your will that I have been able to do this. By your command the sun shines and the winds roam, fire heats and clouds shower rain. Then what is the need for you to meditate and on whom are you meditating?"

Hearing his words *Bhagavan Narayana* (*Vishnu*) spoke, "O *Brahma*! Listen to me carefully. Though it is well known by everyone that you and I and *Shiva* are the cosmic triad for creation, preservation and destruction, a little consideration will tell you that these three acts are actually performed by the *shaktis* or forces of creation, preservation and destruction. Therefore, this force that resides in you, *Rudra* and me is all-powerful. When these *shaktis* are absent, then you are powerless to create, *Rudra* to destroy and I to preserve. Directly or indirectly we are always under that *Shakti.* At the time of *Maha Pralaya,* I lie down on my bed – *Ananta.* At the time of creation I wake up, swayed by her power of Time.

It is on her that I meditate, O Lord of Creation! All of us are subservient to her!"

"O *Brahma!* Don't you remember that in one *Kalpa*, the four *Vedas* were stolen from your mouth and you were searching for them in vain? At last you came to know that they had been stolen by the *asura*, *Hayagriva* and begged me to restore them to you. At that time I had to take the form of a person with the head of a horse in order to kill the demon."

Brahma confessed that he had forgotten that episode and begged to be told the whole story, and *Vishnu* proceeded to do so. In ancient days there was a demon called *Hayagriva* who practiced severe austerities on the banks of River *Saraswati.* He repeated the *bija mantra* of the goddess in her *tamasic* aspect until she appeared to him, seated on her vehicle – the lion. On seeing her, the *asura* was greatly pleased and began to hymn her.

"Obeisance to Thee, O *Devi Maha Maya*! You are the creator, preserver and destroyer of the universe. You are skilled in giving boons to your devotees. All things moving and unmoving are fashioned by you."

The *Devi* was pleased with his devotion and asked him to choose a boon. He immediately asked for immortality.

She spoke, "Birth brings death in its wake and death brings birth. This is the inevitable law of life. Therefore O *Daitya*! Ask for some other boon".

"O Mother! If you do not want to grant me the boon of immortality, then grant me this, that I may be killed only by one who is horse-faced."

The *Devi* granted this and vanished. After getting this boon the demon roamed over the whole universe destroying everything and troubling both gods and humans. It was he who stole the four *Vedas* from the mouth of *Brahma* so that all wisdom disappeared from the world. In despair the gods went to *Brahma* to ask him to intercede on their behalf and request Lord *Vishnu* to take an *avatara* in order to kill this demon who was harassing the world.

Lord *Vishnu* had to undertake a severe sacrifice in order to fulfil this prayer of the gods. But he is the *Uttama Purusha* – the Supreme Person. He is compassion incarnate. He has infinite love for creation and is ever ready to sacrifice himself if need be, for the sake of the world. For this particular bit of work he would have to acquire a horse's head! He was prepared to do anything for the sake of his devotees.

A cause has to be found for everything and therefore he created a cause. He seated himself in *padmasana* (lotus posture), in a beautiful spot and rested his head on the front of his bow, which had been tautly strung. It appeared as if he was fast asleep. It was at this time that the gods along with *Brahma* came to request his help. When they saw that he was resting, they feared to disturb him. They thought of a clever plan to wake him.

Brahma created white ants and told them to eat the string of the bow so that it would break and disturb *Vishnu's* sleep. The white ants were not too happy at this order. To disturb someone who is sleeping is supposed to be a heinous crime so they wanted to know what benefit they would get out of this. *Brahma* promised them that at the end of every fire sacrifice they could eat the *ghee* that had fallen from the sacrificial pit.

Satisfied with this, the insects ate the end of the string that rested on the ground. Immediately the string gave way and the bow flew up with a tremendous sound. The earth trembled, the ocean rose up in huge tidal waves, violent winds began to blow, the mountains shook, and ominous portents like comets and falling meteors, were seen in the sky. All the quarters assumed a terrifying aspect. The sun sank down and the entire world was enveloped in total darkness. The gods were petrified and did not know what to do. While they huddled together, the darkness slowly disappeared and they were horrified to see the decapitated body of Lord *Vishnu* lying on the ground. There was no sign of his head anywhere.

They started crying and wailing, "O Lord of Lords! O Eternal One! You are incapable of being cut or pierced or wounded or burnt! How is it that now your head has been cut off? O Lord of Gods! Where are we to go now? Whom shall we approach for help? You have always been our only help and succour. What are we to do now?"

Seeing their plight, *Brihaspati*, the *guru* of the gods said to them, "O *Devas*! Instead of bewailing your bad luck, start thinking of how you can recoup yourselves and regain what you have lost. Remember that destiny is not all-powerful. It can be overcome by using your intelligence. So start thinking how this can be managed".

Brahma now said, "However auspicious or inauspicious it may be, that which is ordained by destiny, has to be borne by everyone. When one takes up a body, one must experience both pain and pleasure. However, fate can be offset by the grace of the *Maha Devi*. She is the Mother of all, the supporter of all and ever ready to bless anyone who approaches her. So let us begin to chant her hymns".

"*Maheswari* is seated above the mind and will and sublimates them into wisdom. She is the wise one who opens to us the cosmic truths of infinity and eternity. She is ever calm and immutable for she knows everything. She comprehends everything about creation. Nothing is hidden from her. Her strength is the power of knowledge coupled with the power of action and thus none can go against her. She is equal, patient and unalterable in her will. To the wise she gives luminosity, to the wicked she imposes the consequences of their own wickedness, to the ignorant and stupid she deals according to the levels of their understanding. She handles everyone and everything at its own level. She is bound by nothing and attached to nothing. But she has the heart of the universal mother, over-flowing with a compassion that is limitless and unending. Every creature including the *asura* is her child. Her so-called punishments are part of her grace. Her sole mission is to build and mould our nature so that it merges into the divine." Thus, *Brahma* told the gods to approach her for she alone was capable of helping them.

So all the gods started to hymn the *Maheswari*– the great mother of the universe.

"O *Devi!* Thou art the merciful mother of the whole universe. No one is able to know your true form. You are the one who has created all of us, including *Brahma, Vishnu* and *Shiva,* so how can we ever know you, who are the cause of all? You are the knower of everything so you should know the reason why *Vishnu's* head has fallen off. We don't know where his head has flown off. O Thou who gives life to all creatures, kindly bring life to the headless body of Lord *Vishnu*."

At this, the gods heard an ethereal voice. "O gods, do not fear. You are all immortal. None of you can be killed, least of all *Vishnu*, the God of all Gods! There is a cause for everything. The *asura*, *Hayagriva* who has been troubling all of you, has been given a boon by me, that only one who has the head of a horse can kill him. So, go to the divine architect, *Vishvakarma* and ask him to fit the head of a horse on the headless body of *Vishnu*. Then shall your desires be fulfilled".

Hearing these words, *Vishvakarma* cut off the head of a horse and fixed it on Lord *Vishnu's* trunk. The Lord, who had been prepared to sacrifice himself for the sake of the world, now proceeded to destroy the invincible demon, *Hayagriva,* who had been creating havoc in all the three worlds. In this *avatara,* Lord *Vishnu* takes on the name of the *asura* and hence it is known as the *Hayagriva avatara.*

The Lord as *Hayagriva* advised the sage *Agastya* to worship the *Maha Devi* in her form as *Lalitha* or *Kameswari* – the Queen of Desire. The thousand and one names of *Lalitha*, known as the *Lalitha Sahasranama*, was given to the sage by the Lord and comes in the *Brahmanda Purana.* It is one of the most famous poems to the *Maha Devi* and is recited by all *Shakti* worshippers to this day.

"She knew herself the beloved of the Supreme,
These gods and goddesses were He and She,
The Mother was she of beauty and delight,
The word in *Brahma's* vast creating clasp,
The world puissance in almighty *Shiva's* lap,
The Master and the Mother of all lives.
Watching the world their twin regard had made."

— "Savitri" By Sri Aurobindo

Thus ends the sixth chapter of the *Sri Devi Lila* known as 'Parashakti', describing the defeat of the *asura, Hayagriva,* by Lord *Vishnu.*

ॐ *Aim, hreem, kleem* ॐ

"The goddess Lalitha, whose body is the universe
Is verily one's own Self."

— Tantra Raja

ॐ

Ishwaryai Namaha!

CHAPTER SEVEN

LALITHA

Ya Devi sarvabhuteshu, shakti rupena samsthita,
Namasthasyai, Namasthasyai, Namasthasyai Namo Namaha!

"O Goddess, who resides in all creatures in the form of power,
Hail to Thee! Hail to Thee! All Hail to Thee!"

The *Brahmanda Purana* is one of the eighteen *Puranas.* In it we find the incarnation known as *Lalithambika* or *Tripurasundari*, which is the most pleasing and beautiful form of the goddess. In fact the very word *Lalitha* means lovely, elegant and charming. This incarnation was taken to destroy the demon known as *Bhanda.* The *Brahmanda Purana* devotes practically the whole of Book 1V to the story of *Lalitha.* Out of the forty-four chapters that make up this book, forty are devoted to *Lalitha* and are known as the *Lalithopakhyana* (the story of *Lalitha*). Her worship is more common amongst the orthodox Hindus since she represents the best of all feminine qualities. Her form evokes lofty spiritualism and philosophic calm. The *Brahmanda Purana* lays down the origin of the goddess, the construction of her city known as *Sripura* which was modelled on the *yantra* known as the *Sri Chakra*, the preparation of the war with *Bhandasura* as well as the actual war and the final triumph of the *Devi* over the demonic forces. *Adi Shankaracharya* wrote a commentary on the *Lalitha Trisati* and thus attached special significance to her worship. He addresses her with three hundred names in the *Trisati.* The *Tripura Rahasya* says, "That which shines within as pure being is her Majesty, the Supreme Empress, Absolute Consciousness. The universe and all the creatures that range within it are that One Reality. Yes, all this is she alone".

The *Saundaryalahari* (intoxication of beauty), again by *Adi Shankaracharya,* emphasises her extraordinary beauty. It describes every detail of her physical self. The *Lalitha Sahasranama* (thousand-and-one names of *Lalitha*) describes her every feature in the first few names from thirteen to fifty-one. This is given as an aid for concentration so that the devotee can visualise the goddess in all her beauty. The *Saundaryalahari* says that *Kama's* (god of love) great power of attraction was bestowed on him by just one glance of the *Devi.*

The *Lalitha Sahasranama* gives her many epithets that identify her with sexual desire and points out that she is the one who manifests in all creatures as sexual attraction. She is called *Ramya* – the beautiful one, *Kanta* – the lovely one, *Vamanayana* – the one with beautiful eyes, *Vamakesi* – the one with beautiful hair, *Kamya* – the desirable one, *Sringararasapurna* – the one who is filled with amorous sentiments, *Lolakshikamarupini* – the one whose tremulous eyes are the desire of the world, *Mohini* – the enchantress, *Kamakelitarangita* – the one who overflows with desire and pleasure.

She has all the three *shaktis* – *iccha shakti, jnana shakti* and *kriya shakti. Iccha shakti* or the power of desire constitutes her head, *jnana shakti* or the power of wisdom, her body and *kriya shakti* or the power of action, her feet.

The necessity for her incarnation is told in the *Brahmanda Purana.* There was once a powerful *asura* called *Taraka.* He had got a boon from *Brahma* that only the son of *Shiva* could kill him. He knew *Shiva* to be a confirmed celibate who might never have a son and he thought he could outwit *Brahma* by asking for such a boon. He then proceeded to destroy *dharma* on earth and ousted the gods from the heavens. The defeated gods went to *Brahma* to beg for his help. Of course *Brahma* was helpless and accompanied them to *Vaikunta* (abode of *Vishnu*), to get his advice. The Lord answered that since the *asura* could only be killed by the son of *Shiva,* the obvious thing would be to divert the mind of *Shiva* from his *tapasya* and make him fall in love and marry. In the meantime, *Parvati,* the daughter of *Himavan,* King of the *Himalayas* was doing severe penance in order to get *Shiva* as her husband. The gods decided to help her by sending *Kama* or *Manmatha,* the god of love and his wife *Rati* to disturb *Shiva's* penance.

Accompanied by his wife *Rati, Kama* proceeded to the icy abode of Lord *Shiva* and carefully prepared themselves for the task. As soon as *Kama's* feet touched the barren land clothed in ice, the snows melted and turned into gurgling rivulets. Spring spread her exquisite carpet of flowers and fruits and new shoots on the trees. The celestial damsels who had accompanied them danced in abandon, churning the minds of the severest ascetic. The full moon rose to shed its dazzling brilliance on a perfect setting for a lover's tryst.

When *Shiva* opened his eyes, he noticed this untimely intrusion of spring into his wintry hermitage and wondered at it. However, he closed his eyes again and continued with his meditation. Then *Kama* took on his most beguiling form and together with *Rati,* they started a wonderful dalliance filled with amorous gestures, calculated to rouse passion in the hearts of even the sternest *yogi.* The celestial damsels were playing enticing music all the while. But *Shiva* seemed undisturbed and *Kama* began to doubt his own prowess to rouse the *Maha Yogi.* Just at that moment *Parvati* appeared and started her morning *puja* of the Lord. She was used to doing it even if he was in the deepest *samadhi* state. At the end of the worship, she stood shyly beside him hoping that he would open his eyes. As luck would have it, Lord *Shiva* opened his eyes for a split second and turned his gaze on *Parvati. Kama* took the opportunity and shot his enchantment-filled flower arrow straight at the Lord. Usually the Lord, even though he happened to open his eyes, would close it again even though *Parvati* stood before him. This time, all due to *Kama's* intervention, he found that he could not tear his gaze away from *Parvati's* loveliness. But master *yogi* that he was, he realised immediately that something had happened to churn his mind. He looked round to find out the cause for this and his gaze fell on *Kama* who stood with *Rati* beside him, proud of his prowess in having brought the great *yogi* to heel. *Kama* was holding his bow taut, ready to discharge a second arrow if necessary. As the arrow sped from his bow he felt the full blast of *Shiva's* wrath sweep over him and he cried out to the gods to help him. Before any of them could come to his aid, Lord *Shiva* opened his third eye and a great flame of fire shot up from his forehead like a fiery meteor. It dropped on *Kama's* hapless head and reduced him to a heap of ashes.

Seeing this piteous spectacle and hearing the wails of *Rati*, an inspired artist called *Chitrakarma* gathered up the ashes and shaped it into the figure of a human being. When *Shiva's* glance fell on this figure, it started to breathe and was filled with life and effulgence. *Chitrakarma* was enamoured by his own creation and asked the creature to pray to *Shiva* by repeating the hymn to *Rudra.* Pleased with this, *Shiva* blessed him with unequalled over-lordship of the world for six thousand years. He also got the boon that he would be able to drain half the energy of his enemy, in any encounter with an opponent. The creator *Brahma* was quite disgusted with this show of leniency on the part of *Shiva* and proceeded to express his opinion in no mean way by the expletive, '*bhand! bhand!*' Thus, the person came to be known as *Bhanda.* Since he was born of the wrath of *Shiva,* he had all the most fearful aspects of the Lord's nature and behaved like a veritable demon. Unlike *Kama* who represents pure love and is the sacred movement of nature to nurture and propagate, *Bhanda* was a caricature of this and symbolises distorted, aggressive and selfish lust. He subdued the gods with his ferocity and forced *Mayan,* the architect of the gods to build a magnificent city called *Sonitapura* for his residence. *Shukra*, the preceptor of the demons had him anointed as overlord of the whole world. Thus, the *asura's* position was firmly established and he started to wield his iron hand over the gods.

The gods as usual were desperate and asked the sage, *Narada* to help them. *Narada* asked *Indra*, the king of the gods, to perform a great sacrifice to the goddess, *Parashakti*, who alone would be able to conquer *Bhanda.* Thus, the gods performed a wonderful fire sacrifice and propitiated the *Devi* by offering animal sacrifices. A circular mass of blazing light rose up over the fire. In the centre was the shining wheel of Time on which sat the lovely form of the goddess, resplendent as the rising sun. She was the colour of the pomegranate flower and the quintessence of beauty and desire. In her four hands she held the noose, a goad, a sugarcane bow and five arrows tipped with flower petals. She was the manifestation of *Lalitha,* the embodiment of self-awareness. The gods were enchanted by this vision and praised her as the universal Mother and Father and begged her to save them from the scourge of the demon, *Bhanda.*

They extolled her thus:

"Victory to the Mother of the Universe. You are greater than the greatest. You are the source of all prosperity and well-being. You are the holiness of the act of love!

Hail to the inexpressible beauty of consciousness, unparalleled in all the three worlds.

Pervading unlimited space, yet fully manifest in every atom, it is you who in an act of overflowing love, gave birth to all creatures.

The dawn is your robe. Past, present and future are your body, and the scriptures, your words."

Hearing of the bewitching appearance of the goddess, the *Trimurtis* (*Brahma, Vishnu* and *Shiva*) came to offer their homage to her. *Brahma* in his role of the universal grandsire declared that a suitable spouse should be found for her. But who in the world would be worthy of this enchantress except Lord *Shiva* himself. But *Shiva* was standing beside him, clad in tiger skin, with matted locks and ash-covered body. Would she deign to look at him? Sensing the creator's thoughts, *Shiva* assumed the incredibly handsome aspect of *Kameswara*, or the Lord of Desire and turned to look at *Lalitha*. It is said that even *Shiva*, who had incinerated the God of Love, found himself unable to withstand the extraordinary beauty of the Mother of the Universe. *Lalitha* returned his gaze and appeared to be totally captivated by his strikingly handsome form. He was indeed the Lord of Desire. *Lalitha* agreed to marry him but on certain conditions.

"Remember that whatever I say or do is according to my own will alone. Whoever accepts me as his wife must also accept my complete independence."

Shiva agreed to this since he knew her to be *Parashakti* without whom he was powerless to act. She took the wedding garland, which Lord *Vishnu* gave her in his role as her brother and tossed it, high into the sky. The garland circled the heads of all the gods in turn and gently landed on the neck of *Kameswara*. Thus the couple were married and *Lalitha* came to be known as *Kameswari* – Queen of Desire.

This was the union of *Kameswara* – the Lord of Love, with *Kameswari* – the Supreme Desire. Actually *Kameswari* grants all desires – from the hunger for sexual fulfilment to the yearning for union with the Supreme. *Lalitha* is worshipped on full moon days because its waxing phases represent the increasing light of the soul as it expands to its greatest stature, which is the desire for liberation.

Though married to *Shiva*, we find that *Lalitha* was self-willed and independent. At the same time she was also the devoted consort of *Kameswara.* She existed in a state of harmony most of the time, but since the form she had taken was for the fulfilment of a certain purpose, she had to take up arms immediately in order to restore the balance of good and evil in the world. The sage *Narada* who was at the wedding ceremony took the opportunity to remind the goddess of the reason for her incarnation, before he departed.

In order to keep her promise to the gods, *Lalitha* proceeded to make preparations for the great battle. The *Brahmanda Purana* enumerates the names of all her *Shaktis* and the names of their separate chariots. All these names come in the *Lalitha Sahasranama*, or the thousand-and-one names of *Lalitha*, which was given to the sage *Agastya*, by the Lord in his incarnation as *Hayagriva.* This hymn is one of the most important part of the *Brahmanda Purana* and is chanted even today by countless Hindus all over India. This is because every name mentioned in the hymn, is a special *mantra.* The names were not randomly chosen but each has an esoteric significance.

The powerful commanders who accompanied her were all her *Shaktis* or demi-goddesses, eager to free the world from evil, riding on extraordinary chariots. These *Shaktis* are the innate energies of the subtle body and their chariots are *yantras* or mystic *mandalas* in which these energies embody themselves, so that they are available for worship.

Her two commanders-in-chief were *Mantranayika* or *Mantrini* and *Dandanatha* or *Dandanayika.* Her chief attendants were *Yantrini* and *Tantrini. Mantrini* was mounted on the great chariot known as *Geyachakra. Lalitha Devi* herself was on another chariot called *Chakraraja* – King of Chariots. This had nine joints on each of which were stationed various *Shaktis*, all armed to the teeth. On the ninth joint were the *ashta shaktis* or eight powers. On the eighth point were the *gupta shaktis* or secret forces, armed with bows and arrows. In the seventh joint were the two *shaktis* known as the embodied and the swift! In the sixth were the *ajna shaktis.* In the fifth were the *shaktis* whose weapons were the ploughshare, noose, mace and bells. In the fourth came the ten goddesses whose arms were the thunderbolt, spear and wheel. Goddesses known as *Vagadeeswarees* took their stand in the third joint. In the second was the secret police known as *Atiguptarahasya* – extremely confidential. These had the full confidence of the goddess.

The *Geyachakra* of *Mantrini* had seven joints. She sat in the first joint. In the second were seated *Rati, Preeti* and *Manoja.* These describe the different types of love. The fourth joint had the five *shaktis* whose function was to create delusion in the minds of the enemies. Another joint had *Bhairavis* with terrific aspects. All these chariots were in the shape of *yantras* as will be described in the chapter on the *Sri Chakra.*

The chariot occupied by *Dandanatha* was known as *Kirichakra.* Her weapons were the ploughshare and the pestle. The joints of this chariot also had many *shaktis,* all well armed. In the sixth joint of this chariot were the *Ashtadevis,* representing the eight directions.

These three amazing chariots were drawn up in front of the army. Many musical instruments were playing; drums were booming and bugles blowing to announce the approach of the army. The *Devi's* chariot known as *Chakraraja* had six charioteers including *Lalitha* herself while the other two had only one each. Over every chariot were held satin umbrellas in dazzling colours. Loud cries of "Hail to *Lalitha*! Victory to the *Maha Devi*!" rent the air as the expedition set out.

The terrific war cries from *Lalitha's* camp were heard far away in *Bhanda's* city of *Sonitapura* or *Shunyaka* near the ocean. The citizens noted a number of bad omens and informed *Bhanda* about them. He decided to have a council of war and went to the council chamber accompanied by his brothers.

One of them addressed the council and said that the gods were sending an army of women to fight with them. *Bhanda* laughed in scorn when he heard this but his brothers advised him not to dismiss this as being unworthy of him but to send a counter-force immediately before they reached the city.

Bhanda said, "Even if all the gods came to her aid, they would still be unable to withstand our forces". However he called his commander-in-chief and told him to guard all the entrances to the city. He also sent his general, *Durmada,* to forestall the advancing host.

"Spiritual beauty illumining human sight,
Lines with its passion and mystery Nature's mask.
And squanders eternity on the beat of Time,
As when a soul drawn near the sill of birth,
Adjoining mortal time to Timelessness,
A spark of deity lost in Nature's crypt."

— "Savitri" by Sri Aurobindo

Thus ends the seventh chapter of the *Sri Devi Lila* known as 'Lalitha', describing the birth of *Bhandasura* and the advent of the *Devi* as *Lalitha.*

ॐ *Aim, hreem, kleem* ॐ

"That one lived without breath by his self-law.
There was nothing else nor aught beyond it.
In the beginning, darkness was hidden by darkness,
All this was an ocean of inconscience.
When universal Being was concealed by fragmentation,
Then by the greatness of its energy, that One was born.
That moved at first as desire within,
Which was the primal seed of mind."

— *Rig Veda*

ॐ

Mahashaktyai Namaha!

CHAPTER EIGHT

TRIPURASUNDARI

Ya Devi sarvabhuteshu, Trishana rupena samsthita,
Namasthasyai, Namasthasyai, Namasthasyai Namo Namaha!

"O Goddess, who resides in all creatures in the form of thirst,
Hail to Thee! Hail to Thee! All Hail to Thee!"

Seeing the *asura* hosts marching towards them, *Sampatkari* along with her *shaktis* offered to meet them. When *Durmada*, the general of *Bhanda's* army found that he was being beaten by her general, he decided to confront the *Devi* herself. He was riding on an enormous camel while she was on an elephant. A bitter battle was fought and *Durmada* jumped on to the elephant and wrested her crown jewel from her tiara, much to the delight of his followers. But their mirth was short-lived since she smote him on his head and killed him in one stroke.

Bhanda was astonished to hear of this and commanded one of his best generals, *Kuranda* to wreak vengeance on *Sampatkari. Kuranda* was an expert in creating illusions but another *shakti* called *Aparajita* killed him in no time.

Bhanda now sent five commanders with a huge army who created an illusion in which thousands of reptiles swarmed over the *Devi's* militia and harassed them sorely. At last they hymned Lord *Vishnu's* vehicle called *Garuda*, which was an enormous eagle who was the enemy of snakes and thus overcame the illusion created by the reptiles and killed all the five commanders.

Bhanda was dumbfounded and sent the seven great warriors known as the *Balahaka* brothers to meet the opposing army. They enveloped the

Shakti army in total darkness but the *Shakti* known as *Tirasankaranika* caused all seven brothers to become blind and thus killed them easily.

This news totally paralysed *Bhanda* and he soon realised that the opposing host was not to be trifled with. He called a secret war council and ordered his general *Visunga* to attack the army from the rear for he had the knowledge that *Lalitha* was stationed at the back and he felt that if she could be captured, the others would automatically become demoralised. The army left without music or any outward show and stealthily crept behind the camp where the *Chakraraja* chariot was stationed. This was *Lalitha's* own chariot. In the meantime, another general approached from the front and fought a battle with the *shaktis* who were positioned there. *Lalitha* came to know of the attack from the rear and went forth as *Kameswari* and put *Visunga* to the sword. This battle was fought in the night and by dawn the whole *asura* host had been routed.

Lalitha's army now decided that they had to protect themselves from all sides since the *asuras* were resorting to all types of unrighteous acts like creeping up from the back and fighting in the night. So they put their whole army inside a camp encircled by a garland of fire made by the *Shakti* known as *Jwalamalini*. *Lalitha's* chariot was kept in the centre flanked on both sides by the *Geyachakra* and the *Kirichakra*.

Hearing about these preparations *Bhanda* asked his own sons – thirty in number – to proceed to the front and to take *Lalitha* alive by any means. The expedition set out with great enthusiasm. When this news reached the *Shakti* camp, *Kumari* or *Bala*, *Lalitha's* nine-year-old daughter, begged to be allowed to fight the sons of the demon chief. *Lalitha* demurred but gave in reluctantly when she saw that the child was adamant to fight. She gave the child her own armour and weapons. *Bala* set forth in the *Chakraraja* with *Mantrini* and *Dandanatha* on either side. She fought with great skill and dexterity and was untired even though the battle went on for two days. Everyone was surprised at the ease with which *Kumari* vanquished the enemy. Finally she defeated and killed all of them by sending the powerful *astra* (missile) known as the *Narayanastra* – the weapon of Lord *Narayana*.

Bhanda was heartbroken when he heard of the death of his sons but rallied round and ordered another general to go forth immediately. When he saw the ring of fire which was protecting *Lalitha's* camp, he threw a *yantra* into the camp, creating laziness and sloth in the minds of the *shaktis*. *Mantrini* and *Dandanatha* alone were not overcome with lassitude and they reported the matter to *Lalitha*. She immediately deputed *Ganesha*, her elephant-headed son to go forth and counter-act the effects of this *yantra*. On his completing the task successfully, *Lalitha* granted him the boon than any ritual done to any deity should begin with the worship of *Ganapati* or *Ganesha*.

Next, *Bhanda* sent his two brothers to war. *Dandanatha* and *Mantrini* fought with the two of them and slew them. *Bhanda* was wild with rage when he heard this and this time decided to go himself. All the remaining males in the city were mustered and *Bhanda* marched forth to meet the Mother of the World. A mighty battle ensued in which she countered every missile that *Bhanda* sent with its counter correlative. Thus you find that in the *Sahasranama*, that she is invoked as '*Bhanda-surendra nirmukta, sastrapratyastra varshini*'. Despite this, many of her *Shaktis* fell to *Bhanda's* missiles and *Lalitha* was pained to see this.

She created a *Shakti* called *Yashaswini* who was given weapons by all the gods. She rode on a lion and plunged into battle with terrific war cries. *Bhanda* did not lose heart. He called forth all the great *asuras* of yore starting with *Hiranyaksha* and *Hiranyakashipu*, *Ravana* and *Kamsa*. *Lalitha* retaliated by calling all the *avataras* of *Vishnu*, starting from the boar to *Rama*, *Krishna* and *Kalki*. Then she asked *Kameswara* (Shiva), for his weapon, the *Paasupata*, and with this the whole army of the *asuras* was decimated. This gave rise to another appellation of the *Devi* in the *Lalitha Sahasranama* – '*mahapaasupatastragni, nirdaghtasura sainaka*'. *Bhanda* was undaunted and fought on by himself. At last *Lalitha* slew him with the *Mahakameswarastra*, the missile of her husband, *Kameswara*. This again is mentioned in the *Saharanama* – '*Kameswarastra nirdagdha sa Bhandasura sainika*'.

Thus the object of the *avatara* of the Divine Mother as *Lalitha* was fulfilled and the gods rejoiced and praised her.

Let us try to find out the esoteric significance of this battle. It is not just a bloodthirsty war as one might imagine. *Bhanda* represents the reproductive energy of Nature gone wild. He is a caricature of *Kama*, the God of Love. In him the sacred magnetism of love is used to manipulate and destroy. It is no longer love but lust – lust for power and for self-aggrandisement. You will find that even the greatest of sages have been overcome by this *Bhandasura* – this demon in the form of lust for power and sex. Every stage of the battle represents a stage in spiritual purification. The battle is an allegorical representation of the march of the human soul from bestiality to humanity and thence to divinity. The *Shaktis* are the various divine forces within us, which the Mother gives us in order to overcome negativity, which tries to bring us down again and again. Even with the most sincere will in the world many spiritual aspirants find that they fall a prey to all types of difficulties. Most of these originate in our own mind. The external enemies are easier to overcome. For instance, one of *Bhanda's* tricks was to induce lassitude and laziness amongst the *Shaktis*. This is very common with all *sadhakas*. *Bhanda's* forces of *tamas* try to tell the aspiring *sadhaka* that it is not necessary to strive so hard. Why not go back to sleep for a few more minutes. Why should we be so disciplined? Here we find that only the two supreme *Shaktis* – *Dandanatha* or breath control and *Mantrini* or the power of the *mantra* – were strong enough to overcome this. So, obviously the advice for all aspirants is to resort to *pranayama* or breath control or sit down and start vigorous chanting of the *mantra* to help us to overcome laziness.

Next we find that *Lalitha* calls *Ganesha* to come to her aid. So also when we feel we are failing in our spiritual determination, call upon Lord *Ganesha* to remove the obstacles in our way. He represents firm determination and good humour. If our mind is resolute and we can keep up a sense of humour we will be able to proceed on our path.

Bhanda's attack by producing darkness over the camp is an allegory for the darkness of ignorance and despair that might assail the mind of the *sadhaka* now and again. The sincere seeker is asked to practice *pranayama* or breath control to ward off this evil. *Mantrini* and *Dandanatha* are *Lalitha's* most trusted generals. They are constantly alert and trying to repair and reinforce the weak points of the army. So we find that the chanting of the *mantra* and *pranayama* should be practiced diligently every day and this will help us to control our minds and overcome our weaknesses.

The two of them protect the whole campus with a ring of fire. The command of the *mantra* and the power provided by breath control can indeed make a ring of fire around us which will protect us at all times.

Meditating *yogis* and evolved souls at the time of death often experience this ring of fire or a shining globe, which seems to be surrounding the highest truth. Only *yogis* are supposed to be able to pass through this inner sun and proceed on their onward journeys. The *Bhagavad Gita* also mentions that the departing *yogi* has to pierce the orb of the sun.

Lalitha's daughter, *Bala* or *Kumari* is an allegory for all who consider the Divine to be their own mother. We will be allowed to fight for the cause of right and justice if we so wish. She will provide us with her own armour and accoutrements in order to protect us, for we are very dear to her. We are all daughters of the Divine Mother and every aid will be given to us to help us pass all spiritual tests enumerated in this battle. She loves us more than we are capable of realising. In the chariot of our body, we ride into the battle of life protected by the two *shaktis* of our Mother who will never leave our side.

In the final description of the battle when *Lalitha* herself comes to confront *Bhanda*, we find that she destroys each of his *astras* with its opposite or counter-correlative. He despatches missiles of fear, illness, materialism, apathy and neglect of sacred teachings. She counters them with the missiles of courage, health, spiritual insight, compassion and the countless *avataras* like *Krishna* and *Rama* who put us on the right path. Finally, *Bhanda* despatches the missile known as *Mahamoha* or the supreme delusion. This is the delusion that makes us believe that sacred and secular are different – that everything exists by itself without any necessity for the divine, unsupported by God.

Lalitha blasts this view as well as *Bhanda* himself by the *Mahakameswarastra,* the missile of pure divine love which none can gainsay. Thus, the most powerful force in the universe – the power of divine love, kills *Bhanda* who is selfish lust, born from the ashes of love. *Bhanda's* capital city of *Shunyaka* was also destroyed. '*Shunya*' means zero or nothingness. This citadel, which the power-hungry, lusty ego builds for itself is nothing but emptiness for it does not recognise the divine truth of an all-embracing love. *Bhanda's* boon that he would be able to drain half the energy of his opponent worked in all cases except this one. *Lalitha* is the fullness of the Infinite and the truth is that you can never deplete the Infinite even if you keep taking out of it. The *Veda* says, '*Poornamada poornamidam, poornath poornamudachyathe, poornasya, poornamadaya, poornamevaavashishyathe.*'

The lines have been translated as:

"That is full and this is also full. If you take away the full from the full, fullness alone will remain."

All the gods appeared to eulogise *Lalitha* as the *Tripurasundari*, the most beautiful in all the three worlds. They begged her to restore to life, *Kama,* the god of love and make *Rati* happy and bless him with success in his second endeavour with Lord *Shiva.* They wanted *Shiva* to marry *Parvati* and thus get a son – *Kumara*, who alone would be able to vanquish the great demon – *Taraka. Lalitha* brought *Kama* to her mind and immediately *Rati* felt her husband materialise beside her. She blessed him with power to roam about the world creating love in the hearts of all. She also commanded him to go to *Shiva* and promised him that this time his arrow would not fail and so it came to pass that *Shiva* opened his eyes just as *Kama's* flower-tipped arrow pierced his heart. Just at that moment he saw *Parvati* and fell in love with her.

"A nature throbbing with a heart divine
Was felt in the unconscious universe;
It made the breath a happy mystery,
And brought a love sustaining pain with joy;
A love that bore the cross of pain with joy
Eudaemonised the sorrow of the world."

— "Savitri" by Sri Aurobindo

Thus ends the eighth chapter of the *Sri Devi Lila* known as 'Tripurasundari', describing the battle with *Bhandasura* and his final demise.

ॐ *Aim, hreem, kleem* ॐ

ॐ

Kamakshyai Namaha!

CHAPTER NINE

KAMESWARI

Ya Devi sarvabhuteshu, Kshanti rupena samsthita,
Namasthasyai, Namasthasyai, Namasthasyai Namo Namaha!

"O Goddess, who resides in all creatures in the form of patience, Hail to Thee! Hail to Thee! All Hail to Thee!"

During the time of the *Brahmanda Purana*, the goddess was worshipped by most people in the form of *Lalitha.* The principal centres of her worship were *Srinagar* in *Kashmir* and *Kanchipuram* in *Tamil Nadu*, even though *Tripurasundari* is also enshrined in the city of *Ayodhya.*

The work of building her city of *Srinagar*, which exists even today in the *Himalayas*, was entrusted to *Vishvakarma*, the architect of the gods and *Mayan,* his principal engineer. Another name of the city was *Kameswaripuri* or the city of *Kameswari.* The fine points of the city are almost like the details of the *Mani Dwipa* except that *Srinagar* is placed in the midst of nine mountains while the island was in the middle of the ocean. *Srinagar* was also made of *yantras* and *mandalas* intersecting at various points, thus producing many types of mathematical figures filled with the ability to concentrate the mind. Here also there was the *Chintamani griha* or the palace made of the sacred, wish-fulfilling gem. Another name for this was *Mahapadmatavi* which is a name found in the *Sahasranama.* Within this enclosure was kept her sacred chariots called the *Chakraraja*, *Geyachakra* and *Kirichakra.* In the south-east, which was the direction of the Fire God, there was the big pit known as the *chidagnikunda* in which a fire blazed for all eternity, for this was the cremation pyre of all creatures. This whole town was lit by bejewelled lamps and in the centre was the splendid throne of *Kameswari*, which had miraculous powers.

The ninth enclosure was known as the *Bindu peetha. Bindu* means dot and this is the place from which all creation emanates. Here is the sacred cot, the four legs of which are *Brahma, Vishnu, Maheswara* and *Iswara.* On this cot lies *Kameswara*, the Lord of Desire, the ever-youthful consort of *Kameswari. Lalitha* as *Tripurasundari* reclines on his lap. The thirty-six *tattvas* form the steps to the cot. The *tattvas* are both on the gross and on the subtle levels. The subtle ones can only be experienced by the mind when it sinks to deeper levels of awareness during meditation.

Esoterically speaking, the city of *Srinagar* is the human body. The human body is a huge *yantra* and the many palaces and abodes are the mysterious places through which the mind of the meditating *yogi* has to pass before reaching the *Bindu peetha* where the union of the *jivatman* and the *Paramatman* takes place. The different chambers are the different *chakras*.

The many enclosures are the petals of the *Sahasrara Chakra,* which is the vortex of psychic energy established in the roof of the brain. These enclosures contain the countless treasures of the Spirit and the passageways take us into dimensions of being which are utterly unfamiliar to the modern mind but which, no doubt, psychology will eventually come to discover. Great *yogis* have actually experienced the truth of all these things while in a state of *samadhi. Kameswari* herself is the *Kundalini Shakti,* which has to be uncoiled from the base of the spine and taken up to the thousand-petalled lotus on the crown of the head before this blissful union can take place. The *Purana* gives the esoteric method of doing *puja* to the *Devi* that will bring about this union and eventual liberation from mortal coils.

The *sadhaka* should bathe early in the morning, put on clean clothes and worship the sun. Then she should enter the *puja* room and remain in silence for the duration of the rite. She should meditate on this city of *Srinagar* within her heart *chakra* and perform the *puja* rituals as prescribed in the *Agama shastras.* After this she should do *japa* or repetition of the sacred *mantra* of *Lalitha*, thirty-six lakhs of times. One who does this daily can gain many extraordinary *siddhis* or super normal powers.

Another city that is closely related to the *Lalitha* cult is *Kanchipuram* in the state of *Tamil Nadu* in South India. The author's *Guru* is the

Shankaracharya of this place. Here, *Kameswari* is known as *Kamakshi* or the one with eyes filled with love. This is the spot where *Sati's* navel is supposed to have fallen and hence it is a *Shakti Peetha* of great importance, since the navel is the place of the *Manipura Chakra* – a seat of enormous spiritual potential. *Kanchi (Kanchipuram)* and *Kasi (Varanasi)* are supposed to be the two eyes of Lord *Shiva.* It is in *Kanchipuram* that *Brahma* performed *tapasya* in order to propitiate *Sri Devi.* At last there appeared before him, *Adi-Lakshmi* accompanied by Lord *Vishnu.* Seeing her eyes brimming with love for humanity, *Brahma* addressed her as *Kamakshi.* He begged her to permeate that holy spot with her presence in order to bless all people for eternity. She agreed, provided her brother, *Vishnu* would also establish himself there. The *Sri Chakra* or the mystic *yantra* of *Rajarajeshwari* is established in this spot and all the three gods – *Brahma, Vishnu* and *Shiva* – are supposed to have worshipped this and gained glory. The priests of the *Kamakshi* temple perform daily worship of the *Sri Chakra.* The mode of making these *chakras* is also mentioned in this *Purana* and people buy these *chakras* and install them in their own homes. The *chakra* should only be worshipped according to the advice of the *guru.* The *Devi Suktam* and the *Lalitha Sahasranama* are normally chanted at the end of the *puja.* Everybody, irrespective of caste or sex, can adore the *Devi* in this way. The worship of *Lalitha* is the sweetest and most effective form of the adoration of the Divine Mother. Those who cannot do daily *puja* can also do it on full moon days.

"He heard the far and touched the intangible,
He gazed into the future and the unseen.
He used the powers earth instruments cannot use,
A pastime made of the impossible.
He caught fragments of the Omniscient's thoughts,
He scattered formulas of omnipotence,
Thus man in his little house made of earth's dust,
Grew towards an unseen heaven of thought and dream,
Looking into the vast vistas of the mind,
On a small globe, dotting infinity,
At last climbing a long and narrow stair,

He stood alone on a high roof of things,
And saw the light of a spiritual sun."

— "Savitri" by Sri Aurobindo

Thus ends the ninth chapter of the *Sri Devi Lila* known as 'Kameswari', describing *Srinagar*, the abode of the goddess and her method of worship.

ॐ *Aim, hreem, kleem* ॐ

"The gods saw there a concentrated mass of light like a blazing mountain,
Pervading all the quarters with its flames.
That unique light emanated from the bodies of all the gods,
And pervaded the three worlds with its lustre.
It combined into the one flaming form of a wondrous female."

— *Devi Mahatmyam*

ॐ

Durgayai Namaha!

CHAPTER TEN

DURGA

Ya Devi sarvabhuteshu, jati rupena samsthita,
Namasthasyai, Namasthasyai, Namasthasyai Namo Namaha!

"O Goddess, who resides in all creatures in the form of birth,
Hail to Thee! Hail to Thee! All Hail to Thee!"

Durga is one of the most impressive and formidable goddesses in Hindu mythology. She is a warrior queen with eighteen arms each wielding a particular weapon. Her primary function is to combat with the demons that threaten the stability of the cosmos. Despite this, when we gaze at her we see that she has a benign look on her face. This is because she does not attack in order to kill but only when we invite her to come and deliver us from the devilish ego, which threatens our spiritual life.

There are many accounts of *Durga's* origin but the most well known is told in the *Devi Mahatmyam* and is connected with her defeat of the demons *Mahisha* and of *Shumbha* and *Nishumbha*. The *Devi Mahatmyam,* or "The Text of the wondrous essence of the Goddess", describes her as an unconquerable, sublime warrior-maid, who came into being out of the combined wrath of all the gods gathered in council. She was created because the situation called for a female warrior since the buffalo demon, *Mahishasura* could only be killed by such a combination of power, which she alone possessed.

Another story about how she got her name is found in the *Devi Bhagavatam*.

Once there was a great *asura* known as *Durgama.* He realised that the *Vedas* were the main source of strength of the *devas* and decided that the best way to weaken the gods would be to steal the *Vedas.* With this in view, he started to do rigorous *tapasya* to the creator *Brahma.* When *Brahma* appeared, the demon asked for the gift of the *Vedas*, which was promptly given over by *Brahma.*

With the disappearance of the *Vedas* from the world, the *Brahmins* forgot their chanting and *mantras.* No longer did the gods receive the fire sacrifices by which they had been nourished and they became weaker and weaker. Unrighteousness reared its ugly head in the world. There was a severe drought and the earth refused to yield any grain, and famine swept the land. Countless numbers of people, cattle and plants died for want of food.

The *Brahmins* went to the *Himalayas* and did great penance to invoke *Adi Shakti*, the Supreme Power. They begged her to restore the *Vedic mantras* to them so that they could start performing their daily rituals.

At the end of their penance, *Maheswari,* the Great Goddess, appeared before them in all her glory. Her colour was dark blue, the colour of eternal space. She had hundred eyes, large and lustrous like blue lotuses, and her breasts were round and elevated. She had four hands. In her right hand she was holding arrows, and in the other a lotus. The left hand held a great bow and the other carried vegetables, fruits, flowers and roots. She was the essence of beauty, luminous like a thousand suns, the ocean of mercy. When she heard the sad tale of the *Brahmins* and saw the pitiful condition of the earth she began to shed water from her lovely eyes. For nine days and nights tears poured down from her eyes until all the rivers and ponds and lakes began to fill up. This incarnation of the *Devi* was known as *Satakshi* (hundred-eyed), since she took a form with many eyes from which water poured to save the world from drought. The gods who had been hiding in caves and mountains now started to come out and began to sing her praises. The *Devi* now showered the earth with plenty. Grains, vegetables, fruits and roots were made available for all. Grass started to sprout so that the cattle could feed. From that day she came to be famous by the name *Shakambari* – the giver of food.

When the demon, *Durgama* heard this he was furious and set out to fight with the *Devi.* Seeing this *Shakambari* produced countless *Shaktis* out of her body who started annihilating the army of the *asura.* But *Durgama* vanquished the *Shaktis* and eventually confronted the *Devi.* She shot fifteen arrows at the demon. The arrows killed his horses and charioteer and pierced his two eyes, cut off his arms and flag and, finally the fifteenth arrow pierced his heart and killed him.

The world became a peaceful place once again and the *devas* extolled her. She blessed them and said, "The *Vedas* are parts of my own body, so cherish them well. If you lose them great calamities will fall on you as you have seen. Henceforth I will be known as *Durga* since I have killed the demon, *Durgama*".

About the fourth century, images of *Durga* slaying a buffalo began to be common throughout the sub-continent. By the sixth century *Durga* had become a household name and was worshipped everywhere. *Lalitha* is always depicted as a *shanta murti* or one with all peaceful qualities despite the fact that she killed the demon *Bhanda* but *Durga* is ever the warrior goddess astride her fierce vehicle, the lion. She has more mass appeal than *Lalitha.* She appeared at a time of cosmic crisis, which was precipitated by a demon that the male gods could not subdue. She is in fact a classic example of the modern-day feminist and it is to the credit of the ancient *rishis* that they conceived of such a personality many thousand of years before the present century.

Durga's enormous appeal seems rather strange when we consider the fact that she violates the norms of the model Hindu woman. She is not submissive nor is she subordinate to any male deity. She does not fulfil household duties and excels mainly in battle. She reverses the normal role of females. She is the original anti-feminine! She does not lend her power or *shakti* to any male deity but takes from them in order to perform her own heroic exploits. On the other hand, they are said to willingly surrender their potency to her! She is *Shakti* personified. She is not the *Shakti* of one or other of the male gods but she is pure *Shakti* or power unattached to anything else. She is not the consort of any one of them. She herself is shown to contain various *Shaktis* within her, which she can call forth any time she wills. She creates many female helpers out of her own power and never asks the help of any male allies. Some of the demons become enamoured by her beauty but she will have nothing to do with them and refuses to marry any of them.

In her role as a reversal of the usual picture of an Indian woman, *Durga* exists outside the normal, social structures and provides an invigorating view of the feminine power, which lies repressed in most societies. The law books of *Manu* declare that women should always be protected by some man – in childhood by her father, in youth by her husband and in old age by her sons. A woman was considered to be incapable of looking after herself and was always to be kept under the protection of some male! Women are significant primarily as sisters, daughters, wives and mothers! It is to the credit of the *rishis* that in *Durga* they portrayed a goddess who totally violates all the traditional portraits of women that they themselves have projected in all the other *Puranas.* She suggests the extraordinary feminine power, which lies suppressed and depressed and forced into submissive and dependent roles, by a male-oriented society. Her favourite haunts are also totally different from places where one would expect beautiful young ladies to frequent. All her myths associate her with mountains, especially the *Himalayas* and the *Vindhyas,* where fierce tribes still exist.

Thus, *Durga* portrays the divinity who stands outside the so-called civilised order of established *dharma* and who can be found only by one who has the courage to step out of the orderly male-protected world, as we know it. The gods themselves refer to her by many dubious names. She is known as *Mahamoha* or *Mahamaya* – the great delusion, as *Mahasuri* – the great demoness, as *Kalaratri* – the black night, *Maharatri* – the great darkness, *Moharatri* – the night of delusion, and *Tamasi* or delusion. She is full of numbing, deluding and dark qualities, as her names imply. She is continuously referred to as *Mahamaya,* the power that throws people into the bondage of delusion and attachment. All the negative qualities found in the world are found in her. Her greatness lies in the fact that she alone is qualified to destroy these qualities in us, because she possesses all these qualities within herself. It is the homoeopathic principle of like destroying like. This is the reason that her worship has such a hold on this society.

This juxtaposition of auspicious and terrible qualities in the picture of *Durga* is meant to show that she is really a portrait of the macrocosm. The universe is conceived as a living organism in the form of the *Devi.* In her auspicious forms she depicts the world as unceasingly fruitful, beautiful and filled with the energy of the divine, which supports and nourishes. As the mother she dotes on her children and spoils them with all her bounties. As food, she offers herself to be eaten by her children, and as sexual desire she prompts all creatures to take part in the universal dance of creation and procreation. She gives unstintingly. She is life itself.

But she is also death, which is always necessary to sustain life. If she gives life she must also be nourished by life in the form of death. Any gain in any part has to be compensated by a loss somewhere else. Just as there is no life without death, so also there is no gain without loss. Hence she is shown to have many terrible manifestations. The universe is an economical system of continual exchanges. No hoarding or over-spending is allowed if it has to run perfectly for eternity. *Durga's* dual personality is absolutely necessary and inter-related. She reveals the inescapable truth of this world that if life and nourishment have to continue, there has to be continuous slaughter and death. Food that sustains life can be procured only through death and carnage. Life and death constitute a continuous process of giving and getting, a process in which the energy of the goddess is continuously re-cycled.

There are nine types of *Durgas* described in the *Puranas.* First and foremost, she is the goddess of inspiration who gives us the impetus to start on the spiritual path. Secondly, she is the goddess who tells us to undertake studies from spiritual books, which will encourage us to continue on the path. Thirdly, she is the goddess of spiritual practice who instigates us to take up some sort of *sadhana* or spiritual discipline. Then comes the goddess of inner refinement by which our mind is progressively cultured. Fifth is the goddess who takes us closer to the divine within us. Sixth is she who makes us completely pure. Seventh is the one who enables us to give up this delusion of duality. The eighth is the one who urges us to unite with the inner light and the ninth grants us liberation. These are the *Navadurgas* who are worshipped by all Hindus even though only the *yogis* know their esoteric significance. These are actually the nine psychic forces which will lead us to our spiritual goal. At every moment on the spiritual path, one or the other is guiding us.

Durga's association with food is another of her distinctive characteristics. She is that mysterious power which transforms the apparently lifeless seeds into life-giving food when they are sowed. All types of fertility are apparent in her. She possesses the power to invigorate all beings and give them a new lease of life. All plants and creatures on this planet are identified with her, for she is the manifestation of the fertile power that resides in the earth and brings into life all creatures. She manifests as infinite organisms, which in turn feed more complex organisms. This impulse is triggered and sustained by her in the form of food. She is also the sexual impulse that characterises all created beings. She is manifest wherever sexual desire appears. Even *Kama,* the god of love is her agent. This is part of her benign aspect. Her terrifying forms demand blood, for nourishment and finally the very lives of all creatures. This is one of the main points of difference in *Shakta* texts and other *Puranas.* The *Shaktas* emphasise the paradoxical nature of the Goddess who is the ultimate reality. She is both beautiful and grotesque, both maternal and martial. Most of the texts that show her benign form insist that she possesses a terrible aspect.

The *Mahanirvana Tantra* describes her as drenched in blood, grinding up the world at the time of dissolution.

The *Kurma Purana* also shows *Parvati* in her cosmic form. She blazes fiercely, wears a tiger skin and is armed with many weapons.

In the *Devi Bhagavatam,* the gods asked her to show them her *vishwarupa* or universal form, just as *Arjuna* asked *Krishna* to show his universal form in the *Bhagavad Gita.* She agreed and the gods were stunned to see her. She had thousands of heads, eyes and feet; her entire body blazed with fierce, destructive flames and her teeth made horrible, grinding noises. Her eyes burned with flames brighter than a million suns, and the gods trembled as they saw her consume the universe. They pleaded with her to resume her gentle aspect.

In the *Devi Mahatmyam*, she is said to be quaffing wine at intervals and roaring and behaving in a most atrocious manner. At the end of the episode her devotees are requested to worship her with their own flesh and blood.

During the process of *yoga,* the human consciousness is lifted up from *chakra* to *chakra*, starting from the *Muladhara* at the bottom of the spine to the *Sahasrara Chakra* on top of the skull. At this time it encounters inner demons ranging from immature emotions like jealousy, fear, greed and lust up to more serious forms of derangement including paranoia and megalomania. Each weapon in *Durga's* hands is meant to eradicate these emotions ranging from the violent and brutal, to the sly and cunning. The devotee can meditate on any of them in order to clear himself of these negative emotions. Her weapons in fact serve two purposes. They can combat negativity as well as instil positive traits of thought, like self-discipline, introspection, selfless service, prayer, devotion, clarity of vision and a cheerful outlook. *Durga* is the Divine Mother seated between the eyebrows in a radiant light.

The biggest festival connected with her is known as *Durga Puja* and is celebrated during the first nine days of the bright half of the lunar month of *Asvin,* which coincides with the autumn harvest in North India. It falls in October. On the very first day a clay pot containing *Ganga* water, in which are placed sheaves from the harvest and some banana leaves, is decorated and kept on the altar. This pot is identified with the pot of the nectar of immortality, which the gods churned from the ocean of nectar. On one side of the altar some earth is kept on which are sowed the '*navadhanyas*' or the nine types of grain.

As each type of grain is sowed, the priest chants, "*Aum*, you are rice, you are life, you are the life of the gods, you are our life, you are our internal life, you are long life, you give life. The sun with his rays gives you the milk of life and *Varuna* nourishes you with water". This ritual denotes *Durga's* power to induce plant fertility. By the tenth day these grains sprout and are distributed as *prasada.*

In some parts of India, especially Bengal, animal sacrifices are offered during this festival. The buffalo especially, is killed to indicate her killing of the buffalo demon – *Mahisha. Durga's* thirst for blood is established in various texts. As mentioned in the previous paragraph, this custom arose from the fact that after having reaped the life-giving benefits of her potency during the harvest, we are bound to return strength and power to her in the form of the blood of sacrificial animals.

These fierce aspects are also meant to portray those dark qualities in the human being that thirst for violence and warfare. She is the personified wrath of the whole of humanity. Human beings cannot stay peacefully and happily with themselves for a long time. They long for blood and warfare. When she apparently loses control over herself, she personifies the mob mentality, the thirst for violence, ever lurking in the human heart, which totally loses control over its humane side and forgets all benign qualities when aggravated by the mob. The rabble can be instigated to kill, ravage, rampage, pillage and destroy. Soldiers are known to become berserk when they start fighting and the thirst for blood will instigate even the mildest of men to slaughter and kill and undertake bloodcurdling deeds. It is not the art of war but the thirst for blood which instigates these people and this is that part of the dark nature of the human being that she depicts when she dances on corpses and drinks human blood. In these aspects she portrays the distilled, furious, savage power and lust of the frenzied warrior. Thus, she shows how such a power when it is left to itself can prove to be a terrible threat to the world.

Usually *Durga* is petitioned in one of her gentle aspects to combat the demons or for victory in war, but when confronted with these fearful beings, which are a threat to world peace, she takes on her dark and menacing aspect in order to enter into the battle. This is shown in the *Devi Mahatmyam* in the episode of the killing of the *asuras*, *Mahisha, Shumbha* and *Nishumbha.*

She is indeed the victorious force of the Divine and it is by her grace and passion and speed that great achievements can be made immediately rather than put off to a later date. She is the warrior maiden who never retreats from battle. In ancient India all kings invoked *Durga* for victory in battle. *Shivaji,* the great *Maratha* hero, is supposed to have got his sword from her. A sacred sword belonging to her was also kept in the princely state of *Mewar.* In the royal state of *Mysore*, the king with all his citizens concluded the *Durga Puja* on the tenth day, which was called *Dussehra*, by worshipping the Goddess.

The *Mahabharata* states that when King *Yudhistira* set out to battle with the *Kauravas*, he remembered the promise made by the Mother in the *Devi Mahatmyam* and praised her with the famous *Durga Stotram* before proceeding for the battle. Needless to say, *Durga* granted him victory. All the kings of India have chanted hymns to *Durga* before setting out for battle.

"Twilight, night, light, sleep, moonlight, loveliness, patience, compassion.
When honoured, you cause to perish the bondage of men,
Their delusion, death of sons, loss of wealth, sickness, death and fear.
Fallen from my kingdom, I submissively take refuge in you,
Just as I have bowed my head to you, O Goddess! Queen of the Gods!
Protect me, one of lotus-petal eyes! Truth! Be true to us,

Be a refuge for me, O *Durga*!
O refuge! O One, who is fond of her devotees!"

To this, *Durga* answers,

"Victory in battle will soon be yours,
Having by my grace conquered and slain the *Kaurava* army,
Having made your kingdom free from troubles,
You will again enjoy the earth,
Together with your brothers O King, you will obtain abundant favour,
And by my grace happiness and health will be yours."

— The *Mahabharata*

Thus ends the tenth chapter of the *Sri Devi Lila* known as 'Durga', describing the form and function of the warrior goddess.

ॐ *Aim, hreem, kleem* ॐ

"The auspicious let us hear with our ears,
The auspicious let us see with our eyes,
O objects of our worship!
With firm limbes and bodies let us laud you,
And enjoy the term of life allotted by the gods."

— *Rig Veda*

ॐ

Chandikayai Namaha!

CHAPTER ELEVEN

CHANDIKA

Ya Devi sarvabhuteshu, lajja rupena samsthita,
Namasthasyai, Namasthasyai, Namasthasyai Namo Namaha!

"O Goddess, who resides in all creatures in the form of modesty, Hail to Thee! Hail to Thee! All Hail to Thee!"

The *Devi Mahatmyam* is a part of one of the early *Puranas* known as the *Markandeya Purana.* It is more commonly known in North India as the *Durga Saptashati* since it contains seven hundred verses to *Durga.* It is also frequently called 'The *Chandi*' since the *Devi* is often referred to in the text as *Chandika.* The *Devi Mahatmyam* is one of the most famous of the *Shakta* and *tantric* literatures. Though it comes in the *Markandeya Purana* it has always had a separate life of its own. This is because of the pristine quality and exquisite beauty of its hymns. It is called a *mantra shastra.* Every verse is a *mantra* in itself. The very first line of the book which gives the outward meaning, 'Listen to the story of King *Suratha* who was the eighth *Manu*', actually holds the esoteric meaning – Now I shall describe to you the glory of the *mantra 'hreem'.* This is the *bija* or seed *mantra* of the Divine Mother. Similarly, every line contains some esoteric meaning, which only *tantric* initiates can decipher. It is truly a majestic poem that describes to us the epic march of the human soul to its destination, which is liberation from the cycle of births and deaths. Countless devotees through the ages have chanted the verses sung by the *rishis* in this book.

The manuscript describes the different battles fought by the Goddess with the demons who were terrorising the world. This is in-keeping with the purpose of her advent. She herself says in verse fifty-five of the eleventh chapter, "Whenever troubles arise from the fall of religion, I shall incarnate myself and destroy the enemy." First she destroyed *Madhu* and *Kaitabha*, then *Mahishasura* and finally *Shumbha* and *Nishumbha*. The sage *Medhas* describes these battles to a king called *Suratha* and a merchant called *Samadhi* in order to help them overcome the illusion of this earthly life and gain the life immortal.

Some people complain that the *Chandi* is full of fights and battles and cannot generate a feeling of devotion. This is only a superficial understanding of the book. Actually all these battles have esoteric meanings. It is an allegorical representation of the life of the human being, which is beset with battles of opposing interests. Life itself is a struggle against opposing forces. The fight between good and evil is an eternal one. This is seen both in cosmic life as well as on the individual level. The story of the *Devi Mahatmyam* is that of the combat which goes on in the evolved human mind between the higher and the lower self.

Mahishasura is the conditioned ego, which projects its own distorted view of the universe. Everything is defined within the narrow limits of its own selfish interests. Everything has meaning only if it is connected with these interests in some way or other. The higher Self has no other recourse but to embody all its spiritual qualities in the form of the Supreme Mother of the world, who alone has the power to kill this bloated ego. She will come to our aid only if we importune her to do so. We have to admit that we are lost in the forest of *samsara* (worldly life), beguiled by our narrow vision of the world, abandoned by those whom we consider dear, just because they happen to have been born from our loins, like the king and the merchant. If we have the courage to give up everything and beg her to save us, she will most definitely do so. This is the esoteric story of the *Durga Saptashati*.

The book is grouped into three sections devoted to three goddesses, describing the three aspects of the march of the soul to freedom. During our ascent up the ladder of evolution we come to three major halting places where there is a complete transformation of outlook and attitude. These three transformations are presided over by the three deities known as *Maha Kaali*, *Maha Lakshmi* and *Maha Saraswati*. We invoke *Maha Kaali* to destroy our negativity, then we pray to *Maha Lakshmi* to plant the seeds of positivism in our minds and finally we beg *Maha Saraswati* to give us liberation. In the first section *Adi Shakti* awakens *Maha Vishnu* so that he may destroy the original demoniacal forces. In the second stage the same *Shakti* manifests as *Maha Lakshmi* and overcomes *Mahishasura* and *Raktabija.* In the third, *Maha Saraswati* destroys *Shumbha and Nishumbha.* These three forces are representations of the powers of the spirit manifesting within us and urging us onward to freedom. When we walk along the spiritual path we do not walk alone. The forces of the Divine Mother walk beside us.

Now let us take a quick look at the different chapters before going into a detailed study. The goddess is designated in a number of ways in this text. The most common is '*Devi*' or goddess. The next commonly used name is '*Chandika*'. *Bhagavati* is another important name of the goddess. It means the illustrious and beneficent one. There are many other names of the goddess to be found in this book, each one of which is a *mantra* on its own. It is a book that is charged with the power of the divine *Shakti* and is capable of imparting *bhakti* and *mukti* – devotion as well as liberation. It is also supposed to fulfil the desires of anyone who reads it with complete faith and devotion. The normal way to read it is to complete the text in seven days. It is also to be recited daily during the nine-days festival in October known as *Navaratri* or *Durga Puja.* In fact many *Devi* devotees recite the *Chandi mantras* every day. Every verse in this text is pregnant with the *Shakti* of the Divine Mother. As has been mentioned earlier, the first verse of the text implies that the whole book is an explanation of the seed *mantra* of the goddess – *hreem.* The book has had many commentaries, some giving mystical explanations and some giving a straight forward account of the battles, but whatever be the manner in which we read it, we cannot fail to be amazed by the power of the hymns which are charged with great spiritual potential. This book is capable of averting both individual and universal calamities. A regular daily recital of this amazing scripture can avert wars and epidemics and help us to destroy our inner psychological enemies.

The word *Chandika* means the violent and impetuous one. This epithet is applied to the goddess twenty-nine times in the *Chandi,* hence its name. In the poem known as the *Chandikashtaka*, which is the composition of the seventeenth century poet *Bana*, she is described thus:

"Spoil not thy coquetry, O brow;
O lower lip, why this distress?
O face, banish thy flushing;
O hand, this *Mahisha* is not living;
Why dost thou brandish a trident, with desire for combat?
Caused by these words as it were, the *Devi Chandi*,
Caused the parts of her body that displayed signs of rising anger,
To resume their normal state.
Her foe, which took away the life of *Mahisha*
Foe of the gods was set down upon his head.
May the foot of *Devi Chandi*, destroy your sins!"

Since The *Devi Mahatmyam* is a *Shakta* text, its main aim is to postulate the Ultimate Reality as feminine. Next, it goes on to prove that the reality of the goddess is both transcendent and immanent. Her transcendent character is established at the very outset of the text. But she is also immanent, operative both as the material world and *in* the material world. As *Prakriti*, she is Nature, or the whole of the material world, in its multifarious forms. She is also the one who protects and the one who responds instantly to the cries of her devotees.

By characterising her as *Maha Maya* and *Maha Nidra*, under whose influence Lord *Vishnu* lies in *yoga nidra* or the mystic sleep, it is shown that it only by her withdrawal that he can act at all. The transcendental state, which is normally ascribed to Lord *Vishnu*, seems to apply equally to the goddess. She is also shown as being an interior and inward phenomenon. She is *nitya*, the eternal and *sraddha*, the movement of the heart with faith. Over and above all she is *Shakti*, the universal expression of power, regardless of how she is projected in the external form of its manifestation. The devotee of *Shakti* sees both sides of the Mother. She is both gentle and terrible. She is soft and mellow with devotees but when dealing with evil forces, she is forceful and even violent. In the gentle forms she is surpassingly beautiful and in the fearful forms, she is exceedingly terrible. The devotee has to see her in both forms. She has to steel herself against all weaknesses. She must give up all fears and hesitation and selfishness and be prepared to overcome all obstacles. She has to have the courage of the lion on which the Mother is seated. She has to brandish the sword of faith and fearlessness and fight against all types of negativity.

The *Markandeya Purana* is set in the eighth *Manvantara* known as *Savarnika*, which is the epoch of the *Manu* known as *Savarni.* The first chapter starts with the story as told by the sage *Markandeya* as to how the *Devi* had promised King *Suratha* that he would be born as *Savarni*, the son of *Surya* and would become the *Manu* of the eighth *Manvantara.* The frame story of the text is very simple. It deals with the deep sorrow of the *kshatriya Suratha* and the *vaisya Samadhi*, with their families and with life in general and how they turn to the sage *Medhas* for comfort.

A king of the illustrious line of the *Surya vamsa,* called *Suratha* was defeated by his enemies and had to flee the country. Deprived of his wealth and retinue, he took shelter in the forest. He wandered about dejected and forlorn but all the time his mind kept returning to the very people who had deprived him of everything – his family, his countrymen and his ministers. Lost and helpless, he stumbled upon the hermitage of the sage called *Medhas.* It was a beautiful *ashrama* filled with trees and flowers – full of peace and tranquillity. He decided to stay there. While at this place he met a *vaisya* (one belonging to the merchant community) called *Samadhi.* His story was very similar to the king's. He had lost all his wealth and had been thrown out of his house by his own relations and family. He too was forced to wander in the forest and had at last taken shelter at the feet of the sage, *Medhas.*

The king and the merchant found that they had a lot in common. Both had lost their wealth and been cheated by their own people. Both were puzzled by the nature of the mind, which despite the cruelty they had received from their kinsmen, kept returning to the very people who had spurned them. They discussed the character of the mind, which keeps lingering on the very things that have caused it sorrow. Unable to find out the reason for this, they approached the *rishi* and begged him to instruct them. The question that had been voiced by the king and the merchant is one that poses a burning problem for the whole of mankind. The entire *Devi Mahatmyam* is the reply of the *rishi* to this question. The seer expatiates on the relativity of knowledge and the folly of sensual attachment.

The word '*suratha*' means 'attention' and '*samadhi*' is 'a state of super consciousness' where the mind is not aware of the external world. '*Medhas*' is that intelligence which has been infused with divine love. The esoteric meaning of the simple story is that of the *jivatman* which has lost its focus with the higher self (both king and merchant have lost their wealth). It is the sage *Medhas* or the intelligence infused with love that redirects them to their essential wealth.

The sage said, "O best of men! Human beings crave for offspring in the belief that they will reciprocate their feelings and help them when they are old. This is how they fall into the pit of delusion made by their own egos. This mysterious delusion forces them to cling to those very objects and persons from whom they have been subjected to so much pain and suffering. All creatures have been given a certain amount of intelligence yet they keep falling into the pits created by their own weaknesses. Their intelligence seems to be mainly used for filling their bellies and satisfying their animal wants. Moths are drawn to a blazing fire and keep hurling themselves into it, regardless of the fact that they will be consumed in the flames of their own attraction. Men fall into the fire of sensual objects. What difference is there between the two"?

"The blessed goddess *Maha Maya*, who is the cause of this cosmic delusion, forcibly seizes the minds of even the man of knowledge. All are deluded and controlled by that Great Power – the *Maha Maya*. It is due to her power that this whole world is functioning. Because of her all are suffering. She drags down even great men of knowledge. She creates this whole universe of movables and immovables. It is due to her mysterious veiling power that the one seems to have become the many and the formless appears to have taken many forms. She is nothing but the power of the *Brahman*, emanating from him and setting into motion the mighty cosmic drama of creation, preservation and ultimate withdrawal into the transcendental state of Pure Being. It is her *lila* that binds, in order to release. She is the cause of both bondage and liberation. She is the Supreme Knowledge (*Maha Vidya*) which grants final liberation."

Naturally, both the king and the merchant wanted to know more about this mysterious power. The sage expounds on the nature of the Divine Mother of the universe in the seven hundred verses of the *Devi Mahatmyam*. In the first chapter before the *rishi* goes into the actual account of the *Devi's* glories, he recounts the story of *Yoga Nidra* as found in the *Madhu Kaitabha* episode that has already been narrated in the fourth chapter. From this we can see that it is due to *Maha Maya's* mysterious powers of delusion that the *asuras* thought they could defeat the divine. The implication is clear. She is the great deluder who entices human beings into believing that they are the greatest, thus perpetuating this wheel of existence (*samsara chakra*). But she is also *Maha Vidya*, Knowledge Supreme that makes us finally realize that this ego with its conflicting and constant demands and its total belief in the reality of this existence is nothing but a myth.

The word *maya* comes from the *Rig Veda* where it means 'wile' or 'magic power'. This meaning of the word connects it in some way with the *asuras*, who are noted for their wiliness and magic powers. From this it follows that *Maha Maya* is herself the Supreme *Asura*. In fact, *Brahma* in his hymn to the goddess before the killing of *Madhu* and *Kaitabha* by *Vishnu*, calls her *Mahasuri*, the great *asura*. One of the reasons why she has such power over the *asuras* is because she is one of them, just as she is also one with the *devas*.

The *rishi*, *Medhas* now goes on to explain the workings of *Maha Maya* to the questioners. "She is *nitya* (eternal), having the universe as her form. She spreads all this out. Even though eternal, she is said to be born when she becomes manifest for the sake of accomplishing the purpose of the gods. It is through the power of this *Maha Maya* that people impose solidity on this ephemeral universe".

From this we can understand that she is both eternal and co-existing with the manifest universe at the same time. The text also tells us that at certain times, she takes on a tangible form. At the very beginning of the *Madhu-Kaitabha* incident, we find the famous hymn of *Brahma*, the creator, known as the *Tantrika Ratri Sukta*. *Maha Kaali* with the predominant quality of *tamas* or inertia is *Yoga Nidra* who is the goddess of the first part of the *Chandi*.

"Thou art *svaaha*, thou art *swadha*, and thou art *vasatkara*. Speech is thy very soul. Thou art the nectar of the gods. Thou art imperishable and eternal and thou art the one who abides in the three-fold syllable. Thou art she, the goddess, the Supreme Mother – *Savitri*." From this we can understand that wherever the spoken word is operative, she is present. She is 'the highest of all things, high and low – the highest queen.' She is the essence of the three deities, *Brahma*, *Vishnu* and *Shiva*.

The first chapter gives the *Devi's* orientation as transcendent to the cosmos. The function of the second chapter is to show how she is identified with the universe and is actually a crystallisation of the glories of all the deities. The third describes her exuberant plunge into the mundane. It not only points out that she has an earthly career but also that she is the Supreme Ruler of the changing world. She is shown to be the ultimate agent of power in the universe. This is very necessary for she is called upon to grapple with the forces of the mind as typified by *Mahisha, Shumbha* and *Nishumbha.* Only one who wields ultimate power in the world's own terms can cope with all these disturbing elements in the mind.

The third chapter describes the killing of *Mahisha* and the fourth chapter the eulogy of the gods and the promise of the goddess to help them whenever they call on her. The fifth chapter tells the story of the origin of the demons, *Shumbha* and *Nishumbha.* Once again the *devas* request *Durga* to help them. The famous hymns starting with '*Ya Devi*', which are sung by the gods, come in this chapter. The sixth, seventh and eighth chapters describe the fight between the *Devi* and the various agents of *Shumbha,* like *Chanda, Munda* and *Raktabija.* The ninth and tenth chapters describe the battle between the *Devi* and the two brothers, *Shumbha* and *Nishumbha* and their final annihilation. The eleventh contains the beautiful '*Narayani Stotram*' in which the gods hymn her as the goddess '*Narayani*' and the *Devi* foretells all the different incarnations she will take in future to protect the universe. In the twelfth chapter, the *Devi* promises to look after and bless all those who read this book and all those who worship her with faith and devotion.

The sage *Medhas* then concluded the account of the *Devi's* extraordinary manifestations thus, "O King! The *Devi* comes to manifest herself in the world from time to time for establishing righteousness and for protecting her devotees. She deludes the whole world as *Maha Maya,* yet protects it as the Mother. All this is pervaded by her alone. That great power creates this whole universe of pleasure and pain. Thus, she herself is the cause of both sorrow and joy"!

The thirteenth chapter brings the tale of the king and the merchant to its happy conclusion. They were both deeply impressed by the tales of the goddess and decided to do severe austerities immediately. Both of them penetrated into the thick forest and started doing rigorous penance on the banks of the river. After three years of intense *tapasya,* in which they denied themselves even the bare necessities for life, the *Devi* appeared to them separately and asked them what they wanted. King *Suratha* asked that he might be given back his kingdom.

The *Devi* declared, "O King! In a few days you will regain your kingdom and possessions and become a mighty monarch and rule the land happily for many years. After death you will be born in the *Surya Vamsa* (lineage of the Sun) as the eighth *Manu* called *Savarni"*.

When the goddess appeared before *Samadhi*, his request was totally different. He asked for spiritual knowledge that removes sorrow and delusion forever. The Mother was charmed with his request and granted it immediately. The *Devi* said, "O wise One! Your desire shall be fulfilled. You will get both wisdom and liberation!"

The *rishi, Markandeya*, who is the author of the *Markandeya Purana* in which the *Devi Mahatmyam* occurs, now concluded the tale that he had begun, with this same account of how the *Devi* had promised King *Suratha* that he would become the eighth *Manu* called *Savarni*. This *Purana* was written in the *Savarnika Manvantara* or the epoch of the *Manu* known as *Savarni* who was none other than the King *Suratha* mentioned in the *Devi Mahatmyam,* round whom the whole story revolves.

"O death thou lookest on an unfinished world,
Assailed by thee and of its road unsure.
Peopled by imperfect minds and ignorant lives,
And says God's not and all is vain.
How shall the child be the man?
Because he is ignorant shall he never learn?
In a small fragile seed a giant tree lurks,
In a tiny gene a thinking being is shut.
A little element in a tiny sperm,
It grows and is a conqueror and a sage."

— "Savitri" by Sri Aurobindo

Thus ends the eleventh chapter of the *Sri Devi Lila* known as 'Chandika', which gives an outline of the story of the *Devi Mahatmyam.*

ॐ *Aim, hreem, kleem* ॐ

ॐ

Raudrayai Namaha!

CHAPTER TWELVE

MAHISHASURA MARDINI

Ya Devi sarvabhuteshu, Shanti rupena samsthita,
Namasthasyai, Namasthasyai, Namasthasyai Namo Namaha!

"O Goddess, who resides in all creatures in the form of peace,
Hail to Thee! Hail to Thee! All Hail to Thee!"

There are three myths describing the glorious deeds of *Durga* in the *Devi Mahatmyam.* The second, third and fourth chapters exalt her as *Mahishasura Mardini* or the killer of the *asura, Mahisha.* Her encounter with the buffalo demon known as *Mahisha* is one of the most famous episodes connected with the goddess. While the *Madhu-Kaitabha* episode stresses her cosmic and transcendental stature, this incident describes the reason for her incarnation on earth and her universal purpose, which is the saving of all creatures.

Once, there were two *asuras* known as *Rambha* and *Karambha* who did great austerities in order to beget sons. *Asuras* are noted for undertaking impossibly severe austerities in order to force the gods to grant them boons meant for their own selfish purposes. *Karambha* did *tapasya* under the waters of a river. This infuriated *Indra,* the king of the gods who knew well the purpose behind this. *Indra* killed him before he could conclude his vow. *Rambha* heard about this and decided to make the supreme sacrifice of immolating himself in the fire so as to force one of the gods to grant him his boon. *Agni,* the god of fire appeared before him and advised him to desist from this silly act since it would serve no purpose. Instead he told *Rambha* to ask for a boon and it would be granted.

Rambha concluded that this was a sensible suggestion and asked for a son who would be able to assume different personalities at will and conquer the three worlds and destroy all his enemies. He was granted this boon and *Rambha* roamed around the forest to find a suitable mate. His eyes fell on a beautiful she-buffalo who was in full heat. He fell for her charms and had intercourse with her. When she conceived, he took her off to the nether world to keep her under his protection but unfortunately another buffalo became enamoured of her and in the battle that ensued, *Rambha* was killed. His carcass was cremated and the disconsolate she-buffalo decided to immolate herself in the fire. When she jumped in, an astonishing thing happened. The foetus, which was in her womb, rose out of the fire and achieved enormous proportions and became the *asura, Mahisha. Rambha* also got another form and rose up from the fire and became known as *Raktabija*, close friend and ally of *Mahisha.*

Mahisha now proceeded to the mountain known as *Sumeru* and performed severe *tapasya* for many years. Pleased with his austerities, *Brahma* appeared and asked him to choose a boon. The *asura* immediately asked for immortality.

Brahma replied, "O *Mahisha!* Birth has to be followed by death and death by birth. This is the inevitable law of nature. The highest mountains and the deepest oceans and all created things will come to an end when the time comes. So I cannot grant immortality but you can choose some other boon".

Mahisha immediately said, "O Grandfather! Grant me the boon that I can never be killed by any god, demon, human being or animal of the male sex".

Brahma acceded to this request and *Mahisha* exulted, for he could not imagine any woman to stand up to his might.

Puffed up with pride after his success, *Mahisha* first proceeded to conquer the earth. Then he looked towards the heavens and routed the gods and forced them to take to their heels. The dejected gods now went to *Brahma* and asked for his help. *Brahma* was, however, unable to help them as it was he who had granted the boon. So they went to *Kailasa.*

Shiva cast a meaningful look at *Brahma* and said, "O worshipful one! You are the one who has given this demon these boons that have made him invincible. None of us will be able to defeat him. How can we ask our wives to go and fight with this fiend? That is not possible, so let us go and ask *Vishnu* to find a solution".

The gods then went to *Vaikunta*, the abode of *Vishnu.*

With a smile on his face, Lord *Vishnu* said, "O *devas*! Since this demon cannot be killed by a male, the only remedy is to create a female out of our combined energies who will surely be able to defeat him".

Hardly had he finished speaking when a fiery energy, red in colour, rose out of the face of *Brahma*, which was soon joined by a silvery white fire from *Shiva*. A dazzling blue light emanated from *Vishnu* and joined the other two lights. The glow that came out of *Indra* was multi-coloured. Masses of fiery sparks soon came out of the other gods and united to form a humongous mass of energy, blazing like a thousand suns. These eventually took on the form of a ravishingly beautiful young woman adorned with divine clothes and ornaments, having eighteen arms, each wielding a different weapon.

Her enchanting face was created out of the fiery energy of *Shiva*; her glossy black hair came from *Yama*, the god of death; her three eyes emitting sparks of anger came from *Agni*, the god of fire; her arched eyebrows came from *Sandhya*, the spirit of twilight. Her ears were fashioned by the light from *Vayu*, the god of wind; and her nose, from *Kubera*, the god of wealth; her pearly teeth came from *Daksha*. Her deep red lips came out of the energy of *Aruna*, the charioteer of the sun and her eighteen arms from the glory of *Vishnu*. Her breasts came from *Soma*, the moon god and her navel from *Indra*. Her thighs and legs were from *Varuna*, the god of waters and her loins from the earth deity. Her form was exquisitely beautiful and the *devas* were in raptures when they saw her. Now *Vishnu* asked them to present her with their separate weapons.

The milky ocean on which *Vishnu* reclined brought forth an exquisite crystal necklace and some heavenly clothes, bright red in colour. *Vishvakarma*, the architect of the gods, bedecked her with intricately designed jewels intended to adorn each and every part of her body. *Varuna* the lord of waters presented her with a crown of never-fading lotuses and a *vanamala* or garland of mixed wild flowers. The mountain, *Himalaya*, offered a tawny lion as her vehicle.

Then the gods presented her with many weapons. *Vishnu* created another discus with thousand spokes and offered it to her. *Shiva* gave his trident and *Varuna*, a conch. *Agni* offered her a splendid, blazing weapon known as *Shatagni* and the wind god, a bow and unlimited arrows. *Indra* gave his thunderbolt and *Yama*, the god of death gave his staff, with which he used to take away the life of all beings at the time of death. *Kubera*, the god of wealth, gave her a golden goblet filled with intoxicating wine. *Brahma* gave his own *kamandalu* or water pot, filled with *Ganga* water, *Vishvakarma* made a mace for her and the Sun god gave his sparkling rays that surrounded her head like an aureole.

We have to understand that the gods did not create the goddess out of their own imaginations. Instead, they consciously constructed a body through which the unborn and deathless Mother of the universe could manifest in this plane of reality. They willingly abdicated their various masculine attitudes – royal, valiant and heroic – so that the demon might be destroyed. Into the hands of the Supreme Mother they delivered their various weapons, utensils, ornaments and emblems containing their particular energies and traits. Into the all-comprehending source out of which they themselves had originally evolved, they now merged their separate natures and powers of action.

On beholding this most auspicious personification of the Supreme Energy of the universe, this miraculous amalgamation of all their powers, the gods rejoiced and paid homage to her. They called her '*Tripurasundari*', 'the fairest maid of all the three worlds'. She was the perennial, primeval female in which all the particular and limited forces of their various personalities had powerfully amalgamated. Such an overwhelming totalisation signified omnipotence. By a gesture of perfect surrender they had returned their energies to the primeval *Shakti*, the fountain-head of power from which they had stemmed. The result was a great renewal of the original state of universal potency. When the cosmos first unfolded into a system of different spheres and forces, life energy was parcelled out into a multitude of individual manifestations. But these had now lost their force. The Divine Mother, the life energy as the primeval maternal principle had reabsorbed them into her universal womb. She was now ready to go forth in the fullness of her being.

Seeing her thus resplendent and adorned, filled with startling beauty, the gods extolled her,

"O *Devi!* Thou art ever constant and ever existent. Thou art *nirguna* (without qualities), yet for the sake of thy divine play, thou dost assume different forms, *sattvic, rajasic* and *tamasic*, like an actor who takes on various roles for the entertainment of the people. Pray, help us to rout this wicked *asura* who has driven us out of our abode and is bent on destroying the entire universe."

The *Devi* now spoke in a melodious voice and assured the gods that she would accomplish their purpose and slay the demon.

Sitting astride the huge lion she gave a mighty roar which reverberated through heaven and earth and made the earth and sky rock with its impact. The oceans churned and volcanoes belched lava. Heaven and hell trembled with fear. Her head grazed the sky while the ground sank beneath her feet. The *devas* were delighted to see this most astonishing form of the *Devi,* which was guaranteed to make the mightiest *asura* quake with fear. Along with the *rishis,* they extolled her with many hymns.

When *Mahisha* heard this hideous, fiendish laughter it is said that for a minute even his adamantine heart trembled with the unknown sentiment of fear. He ordered his ministers to go and find out the source of this dreadful sound. They returned with the message that the sound had emanated from the enormous figure of a woman, undoubtedly beautiful, but all the same, fearful to behold. She appeared to be quaffing wine from a golden goblet and was seated on a vicious lion. She twanged her gigantic bow with her eighteen arms and made the very air shiver with its vibration.

When he heard that his enemy was a woman, *Mahisha* decided to use conciliatory methods and told his ministers to go and try to win her over with sweet words and bring her to him and he would make her, his consort. The ministers scurried to do his bidding and tried their best to beguile *Devi Durga* with many sweet words in the hope of tempting her.

Durga smiled sweetly and said, "I am pleased with your words but know me to be the Mother of the universe. Understand that I have come here at the request of the gods with the sole purpose of killing *Mahisha* and giving heaven back to them. I have come here alone, without an army. Tell him to restore heaven to the gods and return to the nether regions or else fight and be killed by me".

The minister replied, "My master is invincible. All the gods have fought with him and failed to kill him. How can you, a delicate female, alone and helpless, ever hope to subdue him? It would be far better for you to surrender to him and become queen of all the three worlds".

Durga laughed at his words and said, "Your master received a boon from *Brahma* that he could be killed by no man and that is why I have taken on a woman's form. Inherently I am neither male nor female. I am the Supreme *Purusha* itself. Tell your master that when death beckons, even a grass can turn into a thunderbolt so why not a woman! Your master's end is approaching and not all his warriors or his own valour can save him".

When *Mahishasura* heard this, he decided on battle and sent his commanders one after the other to kill *Durga*, but to his amazement, one by one each of his best generals were killed even though they were supported by huge numbers of infantry, cavalry and elephants. Seated on her lion and wielding her weapons to deadly effect, she made short work of the *asuras*. The lion also did his bit, by gobbling up those who came near him. Those who remained ran back to their master and gave a report about this unnatural turn of events.

At last *Mahishasura* decided to face her himself. But first he changed his buffalo form to an elegant human shape so as to entice her. Primed and puffed up with pride and armed with all his accoutrements, he advanced towards her, confident that she would succumb to his charms. When she saw him, she blew the conch that had been given by *Varuna*. The sound made all the worlds quail with fear. *Mahisha* advanced towards her and spoke flattering words, designed to beguile her.

He said, "O lotus-eyed one"! "I will make you queen of all the three worlds if you will give in to my request and become my wife. I have already defeated the gods and there is no one in the universe who is capable of withstanding my prowess".

Durga laughed and said, "O *Daitya!* I do not desire anyone other than the Supreme Lord. I am his power of will – his *Prakriti.* Because of his proximity, I appear as the Eternal Consciousness, manifesting itself as this cosmos. As iron can be moved due to the power of the magnet, so I am inert. I work consciously due to his proximity. Formless, birthless and deathless am I, yet at times I take on forms to uphold *dharma.* If you are desirous of saving your life, make friends with the gods and go your way. I will not harm you but if you desire to die, then fight, for I will undoubtedly kill you"!

Rather reluctantly, *Mahishasura* decided to fight, for he was quite enamoured by her charms. He started to shoot arrows filled with virulent poison. In the meantime his warriors surrounded her and kept raining arrows from all sides, while he kept hurling one missile after another at her. She laughed as if in sport and reduced his weapons and his army to ashes in a second. *Mahisha* could not believe his eyes and fell upon the lion with his club. The lion rent his leg with his claws. The *asura* immediately took on a lion's form and clawed the lion. *Chandika* became very angry at his assault on her pet lion and rained inexhaustible arrows at him. He now turned into a maddened elephant and hurled huge boulders at the *Devi* with his trunk. But she shattered them to pieces with her arrows. The *Devi's* lion sprang at the head of the elephant and rent it with its claws. The *asura* immediately assumed the form of a *sarabha*, an animal more powerful than any creature known to man. *Chandika* instantly tore the *sarabha* to shreds.

The supernormal energies of this lusty tyrant, gathered through years of self-torture and inhuman austerity, was powerful enough to unseat the gods and bring the universe to heel and this is the power that now broke into different forms.

This bewildering series of transformations is an example of the mythological trait of externalisation or projection found in the *Puranas*. The buffalo demon, employing his illusory power, which again is a power of the goddess, projected his vital energy into new forms. His aggressiveness, his ambition, his will to win, are all projected into one form after another and relinquished one after the other in order to survive.

The human vital energy of body and soul, when aroused, flows forth in either beneficent or destructive forms, demonic or divine, depending on the nature of the desire that prompts it to externalise. The battlefield of the world is filled with such godly and demonic characters – the Hitlers, the Mussolinis, the Gandhis, and the Christs. In fact, the universe itself is such a transformation of the Absolute. Our individual worlds are also made up of such projections. Each one of us projects our individual *shakti* (vital energy) into our little universe – our immediate environment. We colour the neutral screen of the Supreme Consciousness with the dramas and dreams of our inner personalities and get caught in the web of our own make-believe world. The world as we perceive and react upon, is the product of our own *maya* or delusion. Thus, we are captives of our own *maya-shakti* and get caught up in its dramatic events, delights and calamities. Whenever we are entangled and enmeshed in any vital or passionate issues, we are dealing with the projection of our own imaginations. This is the spell of *maya.* It is the spell of creative, life-engendering, life-maintaining energy. It is also the spell of nescience or ignorance. Since the mind is the chief producer of our personal dramas, ancient Indian wisdom is based on mind-transcending experiences in *yoga* and meditation and aims at a total transmutation of human nature, a new awareness of both the world and of itself. It seeks to release human beings from the spell-binding projections of their own *maya shakti* and thus expose their hidden divinity.

Indian philosophy gives many types of *yoga* in order to do this. One of these is to worship the *Maha Maya* who spins this web of illusion and thus become the Lord of *maya* rather than her slave.

Once more the *asura* resumed his original form of a mountainous buffalo and started to harass the *Devi*, piercing her with his horns, kicking her with his hooves and lashing her with his gigantic tail. Then he fell on the lion with a mighty sword but the lion tore his legs into pieces. Nothing daunted *Mahisha* lashed his huge tail and scattered the clouds, which scuttled across the sky. The oceans rose up as if they had been thrashed. His horns rent the sky and his hooves ploughed the entire earth.

Then *Devi Chandika* opened her third eye in fury and roared, "O wicked one! Your end is nigh! Go on ranting a moment more while I sip my fill of this delicious brew". Thus saying, she took a deep draught of wine from the golden goblet. Tossing it aside, she leapt into the air and came down on the back of the buffalo. Pinning *Mahisha's* throat with her foot she drove her trident into his heart. The demon tried to escape through the buffalo's gaping mouth in the shape of a heroic warrior but before he could drag himself out, she caught his hair and cut off his head with her discus. The severed head rolled to the ground like a colossal mountain. The headless buffalo body remained upright for a few minutes and appeared to be vibrating to the beat of the drums. Then it fell to the ground with a tremendous thud that shook the earth with its impact. Blood flowed like a river from the headless body. The lion was delighted with all the blood and lapped it up. He also chased and devoured those warriors who were fleeing for their lives. The gods and sages rejoiced. The earth and its denizens were free once again to worship the Supreme and the *Yakshas* and *Gandharvas* danced with joy.

It is an interesting fact that in all the statues depicting her slaying of the demon, the *Devi's* face shows no signs of wrath. She is steeped in the serenity of eternal calm. Though the deed in time and space has to be accomplished, the expression on the countenance of the goddess reduces its importance to the minimum. For her, the whole course of this cosmic performance, including her own appearance, is only a part of the celestial dream. It is only another scene in the universal drama. She has assumed a form in order to play her part in the universal dream and enacts the leading role, fully aware that it is only a dream. The *Maha Maya* remains totally unconcerned with her own triumphant manifestation. On the other hand, *Mahisha's* ego is constantly striving to elude this cleansing power of the divine within us. We have to have recourse to the sage *Medhas,* who is the loving intellect, which is full of inspiration and joy in order to show us the way to *Durga.*

The gods now extolled her with many hymns.

"O *Devi!* You are the prime cause of the preservation and destruction of this whole universe. You are the supreme origin of the whole world. The gods are helpless to do anything without your energy. You are *Gauri, Lakshmi* and *Saraswati.* How beautiful you are, yet how dreadful! Salutations to you, O Mother! Having vanquished this *asura*, you have brought peace to the whole world. Pray, protect us from all evil."

Having blessed them, the Divine Mother repaired to her own abode known as the *Mani Dwipa* or the Island of Jewels. She was born again through the body of *Parvati* in order to kill the demons *Shumbha* and *Nishumbha.*

The killing of *Mahisha,* as with all the other blood curdling stories told in the *Devi Mahatmyam* describing the greatness of *Chandika,* has to be seen from an esoteric angle before we can understand the great impact it has had on the mind of the Indian continent.

The first section deals with the slaying of the demons *Madhu* and *Kaitabha.* They originated out of the dirt or wax of *Vishnu's* ear. The lowest category of opposition on our spiritual march comes from dirt.

Psychologically, this dirt has the form of *kama, krodha* and *lobha* – desire, anger and greed. According to the *Bhagavad Gita,* these three are our greatest enemies. They are the triple gates to hell. So the first step is to remove this dirt with the help of the *Shakti* within us.

In the second section we are faced with a more dangerous enemy. This is the ego-filled mind that, like *Mahishasura,* changes its shape constantly and just when we think we have conquered it, it turns into another million desires like *Raktabija.* We think we have killed one desire but a million others crop up in their stead. The root has to be dug out and here the *Devi* asks *Kaali* to spread out her tongue so that not a drop of blood falls on the ground. Even a person who looks peaceful may be tormented with a hundred desires going on inside him. The *mala* or dirt-like desire, anger and greed can be routed through constant practice of *karma yoga* or disinterested service but the churning of the mind, known as *vikshepa,* can only be ended by devotion to the goddess.

Chandika represents the ever-victorious higher principle within us and *Mahisha*, the demonic ego continually seeking to elude the transformative powers of the divine force within. The battle depicts the conquest of this ego. The ego is necessary for us to function in this world but it also has the ability to separate us from the higher reality within. *Mahisha* is the personification of the selfish ego at its basest form, filled with pride and sensuality. His legions are spite, pettiness, greed, falsehood and all the other negative emotions. His chief commanders are desire, anger, arrogance, attachment, greed and self-centeredness. Fortified with these powers he usurps the gods who represent the divine powers of the mind. Once this mighty *asuric* ego is killed, the gods or the helpful forces within us resume their rightful roles in our lives. *Chandika's* weapons include self-discipline, chanting of the *mantra,* selfless service, introspection, prayer, devotion, meditation and cheerfulness.

"O slayer of the demon *Mahisha,*
The gods themselves worship you for the protection of the universe.
You are victory itself and therefore give victory in battle,
Goddess, blazing with light, be kind to me!

Show mercy in my hour of darkness,
Grant me conquering power."

— "Durga Stotram", The *Mahabharata*

Thus ends the twelfth chapter of the *Sri Devi Lila* known as 'Mahishasura Mardini', which describes the killing of the demon *Mahisha.*

ॐ *Aim, hreem, kleem* ॐ

"Mahishasura saw the Devi pervading the three worlds with her lustre,
Making the earth curve with her footstep,
Scraping the sky with her diadem.
Shaking the nether worlds with the twang of her bow.
Standing there with her thousand arms,
Pervading all thc quarters."

— *Devi Mahatmyam*

ॐ

Chamundayai Namaha!

CHAPTER THIRTEEN

CHAMUNDA

Ya Devi sarvabhuteshu, sraddha rupena samsthita,
Namasthasyai, Namasthasyai, Namasthasyai Namo Namaha!

"O Goddess, who resides in all creatures in the form of faith,
Hail to Thee! Hail to Thee! All Hail to Thee!"

The chapters from five to ten of the *Devi Mahatmyam* are devoted to the killing of the *asuras, Shumbha* and *Nishumbha* and their allies. This is the third section of the epic and is devoted to *Maha Saraswati.* It deals with the overthrow of another most powerful enemy – ignorance or *avidya.* All our troubles arise from the fact that we are in total ignorance of who we are, what is happening to us and what may happen to us. Thus, *ajnana* or ignorance is the subtle power that really binds us. The churning of the mind is only due to unawareness of the truth. We desire so many things because we do not know the nature of Supreme Truth. When the sun of wisdom is covered with clouds, there is nothing but darkness in our minds. In this darkness the cyclone of desire starts to blow that can sweep us off our feet and project us into a maelstrom of hate and anger. As long as the *jivatman* is unaware of its own effulgent nature, the tornado of desire will keep blowing. This nescience has its root in cosmic *tamas, rajas* and *sattva.*

What is depicted in the epic is the overcoming and transformation of cosmic nature in the form of these three *gunas. Sattva* is a subtle medium of obstruction. It is like a clear glass pane that does not obstruct our view but obstructs our approach to the reality within. The psychological traits characterising *sattva* are the complacency and satisfaction that we feel with what we have achieved. These two are typified by *Shumbha* and *Nishumbha.*

Only *Maha Saraswati*, the power of higher wisdom, can dispel these. Liberation is not an individual effort. It is a cosmic endeavour in which we are helped by the great celestial powers. When stepping into the spiritual path, we must leave our petty individual concepts behind and cross into the way of cosmic relationships. A spiritual seeker is not just another individual but a special person, for he has connected himself with the universal reality. The *Devi Mahatmyam* involves us in this cosmic dance that overcomes the powers of *tamas, rajas* and *sattva* and helps us to attain Supreme Realisation. In this we are helped by the great forces of the *Adi Shakti.*

After killing *Mahisha*, *Durga* had promised the gods to come to their aid any time they needed her. Now the time had come when once again they were sorely troubled by the demons and had to run to her for help. The fifth chapter contains the beautiful hymns beginning with '*Ya Devi*', which extol her as the one who is immanent in all creatures, in all forms. Every chapter of this book begins with a couplet from this famous hymn.

In days of yore there were two mighty *asuras* called *Shumbha* and *Nishumbha* who decided to practice *tapasya* in order to wrest some boons from the creator. They practiced severe austerities in the lake known as *Pushkara,* till eventually *Brahma* revealed himself and prompted them to ask for a boon. Of course in the nature of all demons they immediately asked for immortality, which was denied to them. *Brahma* told them to ask for any other boon and, after due consideration, they requested, as *Mahisha* had done, that they should be granted invulnerability from the hands of any male creature whether demon, god, animal or bird. This was promptly approved. No doubt *Brahma* knew in his heart that he could always depend on the goddess to rescue him. The constant repetition of this pattern makes us think that *Brahma* must be re-enacting the whole drama only in order to give a chance for us to enjoy the divine *lilas* of the *Devi.*

The brothers returned and installed *Shumbha*, who was the elder, on a golden throne specially made for him by the sage *Brighu* whom he had propitiated. They then started to amass a large army of *asuras* headed by their powerful commanders, *Chanda, Munda, Dhumralochana* and *Raktabija.* The last demon, *Raktabija* was invincible because he had a boon that every drop of his blood that fell on the ground would give rise to another *asura*, equal to him in valour and carrying the same weapons. Many heroes arrived and pledged their allegiance to *Shumbha* and *Nishumbha* until their armies swelled and rolled like a mighty ocean. *Shumbha's* army marched to the heavens and conquered the host of gods, lead by *Indra*, in no time. He then proceeded to overthrow the rulers of the quarters and established his suzerainty over the three worlds.

The dejected gods went to their *guru* and begged him to chant some *mantras* that would free them of their troubles. *Brihaspati*, *guru* of the gods, told them that good by itself could not resist evil since 'good' is only the counter correlate of evil. Only that which is neither good nor evil (*nirguna*, without qualities) can defeat evil.

He Said, "Don't you remember the time when she killed the mighty *asura, Mahisha,* the Divine Mother promised to help you whenever you were afflicted by evil. Go to her therefore and praise her with hymns and she will surely come to your aid".

The *devas* hopefully departed to the *Himalayas*, the abode of the goddess and started to extol her with many beautiful hymns. The hymn starting with '*Ya Devi*' in the *Devi Mahatmyam* is part of the paean of praise sung by the *devas.*

The *devas* said, "Salutations to the blessed *Devi.* Salutations again and again to *Prakriti,* the auspicious. Prostrations to the dreadful, to the eternal, the pure and the effulgent. Prostrations to *Durga*, the essence, the doer of everything. All hail to her who manifests in all creatures as *Vishnu Maya,* as consciousness, as intellect, as sleep, as hunger, as shadow, as power, as thirst, as forbearance, as birth, as modesty, as memory, as mercy, as contentment, as mother, as delusion and who is known as the sustainer of all. May that *Devi* bestow her blessings on us, who are forlorn and helpless".

Hardly had they finished eulogizing her, when they saw goddess *Parvati* coming out of her cave in order to take bath in the river, *Ganga.* She was incredibly beautiful, adorned with divine clothes and jewels. In sweet accents she asked the *devas* what they wanted. They made their request and begged her to help them.

As they spoke she smiled and out of her bodily sheath or '*kosha*' another supremely beautiful form emerged, known as *Kaushiki.* When *Kaushiki* came out of her body, *Parvati's* body changed its colour and turned black and terrible to behold. Thus, she came to be known as *Kalika* or *Kaali*. *Kaushiki* told the gods to return to their own abode and promised to settle the matter with their enemies.

The beautiful *Kaushiki* or *Durga* then seated herself on the branch of a tree while *Kalika* sat below her and started to sing in a melodious voice. Just then *Chanda* and *Munda*, the bodyguards of *Shumbha* and *Nishumbha*, happened to pass by. They saw the enchanting form of the goddess seated playfully on the tree. They were enthralled by her appearance and ran to inform their masters of this beautiful vision.

Asuras are noted for their vanity and lust and immediately *Shumbha* asked his minister *Sugriva* to go and woo the beauty and ask her to become his bride.

The minister pleaded his master's case with great dexterity.

He said, "O *Devi! Shumbha*, the king of the *asuras* is Lord of the three worlds. He has sent me here to request you to become his bride. He is capable of giving you anything you desire".

The *Devi* smiled sweetly when she heard these words and told the minister, "I have no doubt that you are speaking the truth and that your master is the greatest in all the three worlds. I will gladly marry him. But there is one condition. I have taken a vow to marry only one who can defeat me in battle. So let either *Shumbha* or *Nishumbha* come here and defeat me and I assure you that I will marry the one who vanquishes me".

The messenger was shocked when he heard this and begged her to reconsider her foolish vow but the *Devi* merely smiled her secret smile and told him to return to his master and repeat her words!

When *Shumbha* heard this strange vow of the *Devi* he decided to send his general *Dhumralochana* to capture and bring her to him.

Dhumralochana tried his best to persuade *Kaushiki* to accompany him back to his master but she refused to talk and merely sent *Kalika* to confront him. After a fierce fight *Dhumralochana* charged at her, shouting imprecations. *Kalika* merely gave a mighty '*hum*' and he was immediately burnt to ashes. His frightened soldiers ran back to *Shumbha* to give a report of these extraordinary happenings. *Shumbha* was astounded to hear this and did not know what to do. His brother *Nishumbha* now offered to go and conquer *Kaali* but *Shumbha* said,

"It is not necessary to send an elephant to kill a rabbit, so let us send our generals, *Chanda* and *Munda.* They will be able to kill *Kalika* easily and bring *Durga* to me."

Now it was the turn of *Chanda* and *Munda* to march towards *Durga* and try their hand at defeating her. When they tried to lay their hands on her, the *Devi* became furious. Her face became black with rage and from her furrowed brow there emerged another hideous form of *Kaali.* The demons were horrified when they saw her. She was gaunt and terrifying with thin, pendulous breasts, sunken eyes and a lolling tongue hanging from her bloodstained, cavernous mouth. She belched fire and gave the most hideous, blood-curdling roars. She wore a necklace of human skulls and wielded a colourful staff topped with a skull. She was clad in tiger skin and had sunken blood-shot eyes, which rolled revoltingly as she roared. The *asuras* fell unconscious at the very sound. The earth trembled with every step she took. She pulverised the *asuras* with her teeth and swallowed them whole. Taking up handfuls of *asuras,* she stuffed them into her cavernous mouth and munched them with apparent relish. Chariots and elephants and horses also went the same way without too much of difficulty. She swallowed even the weapons they flung at her, crunching them into bits. Soon the entire army was destroyed. Undaunted, *Chanda* and *Munda* ran at her with upraised weapons. She caught hold of them as if they were puppets and brought them to *Durga,* who was sitting on the lion, and presented them to her as human sacrifices. Taking up her axe, *Kaali* cut off their heads and offered them to *Durga* and drank the blood that was gushing out of their severed necks.

Ambika said, "Since you have brought me the heads of *Chanda* and *Munda,* you will be renowned in the world by the name of *Chamunda*".

The eighteenth century poem by *Bhavabhuti* glorifies her thus:

"Hail! Hail! *Chamunda*! Mighty goddess hail!
I glorify thy sport, when in the dance,
That fills the court of *Shiva* with delight,
Thy foot descending spurs the earthly globe.
The elephant hide that robes thee, to thy steps,
Swings to and fro; the whirling talons rend,
The crescent on thy brow;
And from the torn orb the trickling nectar falls,

And every skull that gems thy necklace,
Laughs with horrid life!"

The remaining soldiers were terrified by this gruesome spectacle and ran back to their masters and reported all that had taken place on the battlefield. *Shumbha* now ordered his best general *Raktabija* to go with another huge army to capture *Durga*. The *asura* hordes encircled her along with her lion and *Kaali*, and prepared to rush at her. At this time the watching gods sent their powerful *shaktis* to help her. The energy of *Brahma* appeared as *Brahmaani*, riding on a swan, carrying a *kamandalu*. The energy of *Shiva* came as *Maheswari*, riding on a bull, holding aloft a trident, wearing the crescent moon in her hair. As the force of *Skanda*, came *Kaumari*, riding on a peacock, holding a spear. As the energy of *Vishnu*, appeared *Vaishnavi*, flying on the eagle *Garuda*, holding the discus, conch, mace and bow. As the energy of *Indra*, came *Indraani*, riding the white elephant and brandishing the thunderbolt. The *shaktis* of the *avataras* of *Vishnu* came as *Varahi* – the boar, and as *Nrisimhi* – the man-lion. Another fierce *shakti* came out of the *Devi* herself, howling like a jackal. She told Lord *Shiva* himself to go as her ambassador to *Shumbha* and *Nishumbha* and therefore she came to be known as *Shivaduti* – one who sent *Shiva* as an emissary.

First to arrive on the scene of battle was *Brahmaani*, who sprinkled the waters of her *kamandalu* over the *asura* army, and drained all their strength. Then came *Maheswari*, who flung her trident, discus, spear and thunderbolt at them and arrested the onslaught. The boar, *Varahi*, came next and tossed the *asuras* hither and thither with her tusk and then came *Nrisimhi*, who began to devour them.

Seeing this destruction, *Raktabija* came forward. From every drop of blood that was spilt from him there arose another demon, as fearsome as he. All of them started to fight *Durga* with renewed vigour. With one throw of her thunderbolt his head was severed but again every drop of blood that fell on the ground turned into a clone of himself. Thousands of warriors rose out of his flowing blood, enough to fill the earth. The gods were filled with horror when they saw this. Then all the *shaktis* and the seven mothers, like *Vaishnavi*, fell on *Raktabija* but thousands of *Raktabijas* rose up and filled the battlefield, to the dismay of the watching gods. The whole world seemed to be filled with *asuras* and only the seven mothers or *matrikas*, *Durga* and *Kaali* were left on the battlefield to fight with these hordes.

Then *Chandika* told *Kaali,* "Widen your face and spread your tongue as far as the eye can see. When I kill these *asuras* with my weapons, don't let even a drop of blood fall on the ground. Drink up every drop with your wide and long tongue and eat up as many *asuras* as possible at the same time. Only then will we be able to stop this demon's onslaught."

With these words, *Durga Devi* pierced *Raktabija* with her trident and *Kaali* spread her tongue and drank up his blood before a drop could fall on the ground. *Raktabija* roared with pain and fell upon *Chandika* with great force. She put an end to his life with her discus and there was another great flood of blood. *Kaali* drank all the blood and ate all the *rakshasas* who had been created by the few drops that had escaped her tongue.

Raktabija is an allegory of our unhealthy thoughts, which multiply if left to feed on the negativity that is surrounding us. They have to be caught before they take root in our sub-conscious and multiply beyond our control. *Kaali* has to be invoked to do this. If left alone, these thoughts will harden into our personality and then we will never be able to eradicate them. 'Constant vigilance is the price of spiritual liberty.'

The remaining *asuras* fled in terror and reported the matter to *Shumbha.*

"O King! *Devi Ambika* has killed all the *asuras* and *Chamunda* has drunk all their blood and ate the rest. We advise you not to keep on with this battle if you fear for your life. She is not an ordinary woman. She is *Maha Maya.* There is no doubt about this. She has manifested herself only to help the gods and is bent on destroying our whole race."

Shumbha was furious when he heard this and told them scornfully, "You are all cowards to be chased by a woman. You may go down to the nether world if you wish but I will go and destroy her, myself".

Then *Nishumbha* said, "Brother! Fear not! I will go first and kill this woman. There is no need for you to bestir yourself".

Seeing the approaching army, *Durga* laughed and spoke in her soft, sweet voice to *Kaali,* "O *Kaali!* See how foolish they are. Hope springs ever in the human breast. Even after witnessing the death of so many of their generals they still think they can defeat me".

Nishumbha fell upon *Maha Maya* and fought with her various manifestations like *Kaali, Vaishnavi, Shaankari, Brahmaani, Kaumari, Indraani, Varahi* and *Nrisimhi.* The last seven are known as the *sapta matrikas* or the seven mothers. *Shumbha* had followed close on the heels of his brother and was supporting him from the rear. When *Nishumbha* wounded her lion, *Chandika* became angry and immediately stuck him down. He rose up and flew at her in his chariot holding aloft many weapons. Seeing him approach, she blew her conch and the sound made the blood freeze in his bones. However, he rallied himself and fell upon the lion with his club and then made as if to lunge at *Chandika.* She immediately struck off his head with her axe but to the horror of the *devas*, the headless demon danced around, lashing at everyone with his club. *Chandika* now cut off his hands and feet and at last the lifeless trunk fell to the ground with a mighty thud.

The soldiers ran back and told *Shumbha* about the death of his brother and advised him not to proceed.

Shumbha said, "Fools! Do you expect me to run away and save my skin when I have been the cause of the death of my brother and my ministers? This woman is a woman only in name. She has the strength of a hundred heroic warriors. Since death is certain for every creature, let me die on the battlefield rather than rot in the nether world"!

So saying, *Shumbha* got into his chariot and advanced towards *Durga.* When he set eyes on her, he was smitten by her charms and tried to woo her with conciliatory words,

"O thou of delicate limbs, why do you want to fight with me? A woman's eyebrows are her bow and her looks are her arrows. Her gestures and postures are her weapons. Give up these fierce ministers of yours, this ugly *Kalika* and *Chamunda* and come with me. I shall serve you as you deserve to be served."

Durga laughed at his words and said, "O stupid one! If you think I'm too beautiful to fight with you then fight with this ugly *Kalika* or fierce *Chamunda.* I will stand and watch".

Then turning to *Chamunda* she said, "O *Chamunda*, your nature is violent and this person likes to fight with ferocious people; so please go and humour him".

Hearing this command, *Chamunda* pounced on him with her axe and cut off his left hand adorned with jewels and weapons. Then *Shumbha* said "O wicked *Durga*, you are fighting with the help of so many others while I am all alone."

Then *Devi Chandika* said, "Look at me. I am alone. There is none other than I. I alone exist in this whole universe. You are imagining that you see people other than me".

As soon as she said these words all her other appearances like *Kaali* and the seven mothers re-entered her body and *Durga* remained alone, holding aloft her trident, but *Shumbha* was too immersed in his own ego to understand the message. He continued to think that he could conquer the divine. He still believed that he could manipulate the divine and control her. He failed to understand the inner meaning of the show she had just put forth, which was to point out to him that he was also a part of her and could merge himself in her if he so wished.

Shumbha now waged a terrific battle with the goddess. He hurled his most powerful weapons at her and the gods watched with bated breath as she smashed his chariot and made him fall to the ground. He fell on her with his most powerful *astra* (missile), but she sliced it with her arrows. Now he hit her on the breast with his club. She retaliated and beat his chest with her mace and he fell down senseless. She waited till he regained consciousness. Then he soared into the sky and rained arrows on her. She immediately flew after him and brought him down to the ground. The infuriated *Shumbha* charged at her as if to throttle her with his bare hands. Thus the fight went on and on. The *Devi Mahatmyam* says that *Durga* allowed *Shumbha* to wrestle with her for a long time.

At last *Durga* decided to put an end to *Shumbha's* life and tore his chest into two with her trident. As he fell, the whole earth trembled and the oceans were churned. The celestials rejoiced and danced. The trees began to bloom and the rivers to flow swiftly. Fires in all hearths burned vibrantly and the wind blew softly while the sun shone brightly. It seemed as if the earth had got rid of her burden.

Shumbha typifies that part of our nature which keeps resisting the truth that we are all fundamentally the same and all emanate from the Supreme. We are confirmed individualists and will not give up our separate egos even if we are promised the kingdom of God. We find it difficult to accept the fact that we cannot force the Divine to obey our will! When she doesn't bend to our will, we feel the same frustration and anger as *Shumbha* did. We are allowed full freedom to entertain this idea and combat with her for a long time until the moment comes when she decides that we should be made aware of our true nature.

The *Devi Mahatmyam* is the story of an inner battle. Victory comes to us only when we find the strength to surrender our negative emotions to *Durga's* purifying influence. The different types of conflicts that are described here actually happen daily within our hearts and in the external world. We are constantly waging a war between our negative and positive emotions. It is a battle which has to be fought by every generation. The answers have to be given by the Divine Mother herself. Unless we surrender to her, we can never end the conflict. If, like *Chanda* and *Munda,* we try to defy the goddess and usurp her special powers for our own benefit, we will only invite her wrath and out of her beautiful form will emanate the terrible figure of *Kaali,* the power of Time, which will devour us with her fierce fangs.

In the eleventh chapter, the gods rejoiced and came to hymn *Chandika* with the famous *Narayani sthuti.*

O *Narayani!* Destroyer of woes! Be pleased O Mother of the universe. Supreme controller! Protect us all! You are the support of the universe.

You are *Vishnu Maya,* cause of both bondage and liberation. All knowledge is thy form. All women are thyself, O Mother!

O *Narayani!* Thou art Time, Space and Causation. All this is filled by thee alone.

Thou art intelligence. O *Narayani!*

O blessed refuge of the distressed, O *Narayani!* Salutations to thee!

O destroyer of all troubles of the devoted, who take refuge in thee!

O *Narayani!* Salutations to thee!

O *Devi,* whenever evil prevails, you manifest yourself.

You are that power of the Eternal which manifests as the power of creation, sustenance and destruction. O queen of all, you protect all. Having all for your very soul, you support all.

O Mother of all the worlds! Destroyer of woes! Support of the universe! Please continue to protect the world. O *Brahmaani* carrying the *kamandalu,* riding on the swan, O *Maheswari* with the trident sitting on a bull, O

Kaumari with the spear sitting on the peacock, O *Vaishnavi* carrying the conch, discus, mace and bow seated on *Garuda,* salutations to you!

O *Devi* of the dreadful form of *Varahi* and *Nrisimhi*, O *Narayani,* salutations to you!

O *Lakshmi!* O *Kaali!* O *Saraswati*! Pray protect us.

O *Narayani!* Salutations to you again and again!

Wherever there is unrighteousness, there will you manifest. Those who take refuge in you have no cause for fear.

O adorable one! Pray protect us who rest under your feet!

O Mother be gracious! Just as you rescued us from the demons today, please promise to save us whenever we call out to you in all the times to come".

The twelfth chapter contains the promises of the *Devi* to the devotees of the future. She was pleased with the hymn of the gods and told them of her future incarnations.

"In the *Vaivasvata Manvantara*, in the twenty-eighth *Dwapara yuga*, I will be born in the house of *Nandagopa* in *Yasoda's* womb and will destroy *Shumbha* and *Nishumbha* once again in the *Vindhya* mountains, where I will take up my abode and be known as *Vindhya Vaasini*."

"Again I will be invoked by *rishis* at the time of a universal famine and I will be born in order to relieve the distress of the people. At that time I will be known as *Satakshi* and *Shakambari.*

"Whenever there is oppression by evil forces, I shall descend into the three worlds and save you, if you call to me with hearts full of faith. Whoever contemplates my saving grace with full concentration and loving devotion, will be relieved of disease and misfortune. They need fear neither weapons, fire nor floods. I will never abandon that abode where prayers are offered to me continually. Listening to the tales of my deeds one becomes fearless and is unaffected by evil dreams and the influence of malefic planets."

"Whenever there is trouble anywhere I shall manifest myself and bring peace on earth. The mere reading of my stories will destroy the troubles of my devotees."

Thus saying, she blessed the gods and disappeared from their sight.

This brings us to the end of the *Devi Mahatmyam.* The thirteenth chapter as has been said concludes the tale of the king and the merchant.

"When worshipped by your devotees,
You remove their ignorance and bondage.
Their fear, disease and threat of death.
You protect their children and their goods.
I, who have lost everything, appeal to you for help
Protect me O lotus-eyed saviour.
I am fighting for truth,
Protect me with all the power of truth.
O Durga, shelter me in your wide lap.
You who are ever loving and merciful to devotees,
Help me!"

— "Durga Stotram", The *Mahabharata*

Thus ends the thirteenth chapter of the *Sri Devi Lila* known as 'Chamunda', which describes the killing of the demons – *Shumbha* and *Nishumbha.*

ॐ *Aim, hreem, kleem* ॐ

"Queen of the gods, she leapt to land,
A lotus in her perfect hand,
And fondly of the lotus sprung,
To lotus bearing Vishnu clung,
Gods above and men below,
As beauty's queen and fortune know."

— Account of Sri in the *Ramayana*

ॐ

Sathyyai Namaha!

CHAPTER FOURTEEN

SATI

Ya Devi sarvabhuteshu, kanti rupena samsthita,
Namasthasyai, Namasthasyai, Namasthasyai Namo Namaha!

"O Goddess, who resides in all creatures in the form of beauty, Hail to Thee! Hail to Thee! All Hail to Thee!"

As we have seen earlier, the *Maha Devi* takes on various births in order to fulfil the demands of her devotees and for the protection of the world. One of the most famous of these was her incarnation as *Sati,* daughter of the *Prajapati*, *Daksha.*

Daksha was one of the mind born sons of *Brahma.* He was a *Prajapati* or patriarch. *Daksha* was an arrogant man with a long face and deep furrows on either side of a hooked nose. His lips curled with disdain at anything that did not meet with his ideas of propriety. He was the champion of orthodoxy and conservatism. He was addicted to rites and ritualism and was the greatest supporter of the *Vedic* tenets. He had been requested by his father *Brahma* to marry and create people through the normal way of union between male and female. So far creation had been through the mind of *Brahma* and had not proved to be too successful.

Daksha had two wives called *Asikni* and *Virini.* From his first wife he got two thousand sons whom he commanded to marry and thus multiply the human species. Unfortunately, the sage *Narada* advised them to become ascetics and contemplate on the Supreme Truth and thus deflected the boys from their marital plans. *Daksha* was furious and cursed *Narada.* Then he decided that daughters might prove to be more pliable and so he begot sixty daughters from his second wife. When they came of age, he got them married to suitable husbands amongst the *rishis* and demi-gods. Much to his relief their progeny slowly started to fill the world.

But for the one daughter on whom his mind always dwelt with great fondness, he had been unable to think of a suitable groom. He remembered her birth. His father had asked him to do *tapasya* to the goddess – the *Maha Devi* – and beg her to be born as his child. He had done intense austerities and eventually had the vision of the goddess. She came in a haze of darkness in which appeared two pinpoints of light. One point turned out to be a brilliant blue lotus and the other a flashing sword. And then as he peered into the gloaming, he saw her – *Durga* seated on a lion and looking at him with great tenderness. He got up and threw himself down before the growling lion and begged her to become his daughter. She graciously agreed.

Daksha returned home and along with his wife *Virini*, worshipped the goddess and begged her to keep her promise. The Supreme Mother of the universe now took birth in the house of *Daksha*. As she was the embodiment of Supreme Truth, she was named *Sati*.

At a tender age, *Brahma* had instructed *Sati* that the only fitting mate for her was *Mahadeva* – *Shiva*, the Lord of Lords. Even as a child her mother noticed that she was quite unlike her other sisters. The rest of them would laugh and gossip and invent stories of the ones they would marry but *Sati* kept to herself. She was often found wandering alone in the forest singing to herself and painting pictures of the Lord of *Kailasa*. It was a frightening face which she drew, quite incomprehensible to her mother and sisters. When she reached adolescence, she approached her mother and informed her that she was going to undertake a year-long vow in order to propitiate *Shiva*. She underwent rigorous tortures of her body until one full year had passed. At the end of the year she concluded her worship of the three-eyed Lord and sat and concentrated on him. This news was reported to *Daksha* who was quite dismayed. He was the patriarch of organised religion, following strict rules and conducting continuous fire sacrifices (*yajna*) to the gods, who in turn were supposed to support and upkeep the sanctity of the social order. *Shiva* stood for the very opposite of all this.

Daksha ranted and raved, "I will never agree to my beloved daughter marrying this crazy man, this woman stealer! He is the enemy of all rules and rites, he smears himself with the ashes of the dead, and he consorts with the lowest of the low, grows his hair long and bedecks himself with bones. He stands for the opposite of everything that I stand for. Why did I compose so many rites and rituals and why did I beget the Mother of the universe if she is to be snatched away from me by that mad man! I will never agree to this marriage! You may tell her that"!

But though her mother and sisters tried their best to dissuade her and warned her of the dire consequences of her father's wrath, *Sati* was adamant and refused to be deterred from her firm resolve. She determined not to stir from the place she had chosen for her austerities, till the Lord of her heart appeared in person to take her. As the months passed, she grew thin and emaciated yet her body shone with an extraordinary lustre. Even the sages came to see her, for she had reached an exalted state. They determined to make her wish come true and along with the gods they went to Lord *Vishnu* and begged him to intercede with *Shiva* on her behalf. All of them now proceeded to *Kailasa* and praised *Shiva* and begged him to accept *Sati* as his wife.

Shiva said, "O sages! Only a person of imperfect knowledge will desire marriage. It is a great bondage; I am a *yogi*, ever delighting in the bliss of the Self. I am always engaged in *tapasya* and totally detached from the world. What interest would I have in marriage? Moreover I am the friend of ghosts and goblins. I visit the burning *ghats* and crematoriums. My body is covered with the ashes from the cremation ground. Serpents and reptiles are my ornaments. Which woman would want to marry me"?

The gods begged him to reconsider his decision, so *Shiva* smiled and said,

"If you can find me a woman who will come up to my requirements I shall certainly marry her. When I am *yogi,* she will have to be a *yogini,* when I desire her she will have to be a wife, when I go into *samadhi*, she should not approach me for she will be burnt to ashes in the fire of my austerity. If she refuses to do what I say, I shall abandon her. Now see if you can find such a woman."

Brahma was delighted at these words and said, "Indeed O Lord, such a woman has already been born in the household of *Prajapati Daksha.* She is known as *Sati* and is a fitting mate for you. At present she is performing rigorous penance in order to secure you as her husband. She is an incarnation of the *Maha Devi* who takes on many forms in order to bless the world".

Shiva was intrigued by this description and agreed to meet *Sati*, On the eighth day of the bright half of the month of *Aswin* (September/ October), *Sati* observed her final fast, which concluded her one-year worship of Lord *Shiva*. She sat in the dense forest engrossed in meditation on his form. Suddenly she felt her whole body tremble. Her mind became agitated and refused to concentrate. Wondering what had happened to distract her, she opened her eyes and saw her beloved standing before her, just as she had imagined him. He appeared before her in his incomparable form with five faces, three eyes and crescent moon adorning his locks. He was holding the trident and drum and his neck was entwined with serpents. He was covered with ashes and clad in a tiger skin. Such was his brilliance that *Sati* could hardly look at him.

Although hc knew her desire, he asked her to choose a boon, for he wanted to hear her wish from her own mouth. But she was very shy and would not speak. Again he urged her to openly express her desire. At last she whispered, "O Lord! Why do you play with me? You know my desire. Let me have the bridegroom of my choice".

Hardly had she finished when he replied, "You shall indeed be my wife, O *Dakshayini!* (daughter of *Daksha*). I shall take you away immediately to my mountain fastness before anyone sees us. Your father will surely obstruct us if he could".

Sati begged him to approach her father and marry her with all proper rites. *Shiva* shook his head in foreboding but since she insisted he gave in to her wishes. He grasped her tender hand in his strong one and hastened to *Daksha*.

Daksha, the impeccable priest of orthodoxy, looked at *Shiva* in utter contempt. He was a wild beggar clothed in the stench of pyres. He broke out in a fierce expletive when he saw that *Shiva* held *Sati* tightly in one strong arm while he stroked his garland of bones with the other. *Sati* herself looked different. She was no longer his beautiful daughter. The long year of penance had turned her skin dark. She was clad in dirty and torn clothes but her eyes were bright and radiated happiness. She was looking adoringly at her divine lover and seemed oblivious of her father's wrath.

"You scoundrel! What have you done? Are you trying to snatch my beloved daughter from me"? Looking at *Sati* he said, "I will never let you marry this wretch".

Sati Said, "O father"! "I have made my choice. This is the man I wish to marry, and none other."

Daksha exploded, "In that case you can marry him without my consent and without my blessings. You will be shunned forever, condemned to wander like an outcaste with this madman"!

Sati's eyes pleaded with her father for understanding but he refused to meet her eyes. This child who had been so dear to him was now cast out of his heart and house. *Sati* clung harder to *Shiva's* arm. Without a word he lifted her into his arms and placed her on his vehicle – the bull *Nandi* who had been waiting for his master's command. The couple set off without any pomp or show. There was no music or trumpets; no priests and no rituals. They had no home or shelter. From the palace of *Daksha Prajapati* in which she had enjoyed every comfort, *Sati* was taken to a bleak and barren mountain where there were only beasts and reptiles to welcome her. She cared not for the lack of comforts. All she wanted was to roam about wildly in the wake of her unpredictable husband across the desolate Himalayan ranges and peaks inhabited by wild animals, followed by a hoard of goblins. At first he tested her resolve and hardly glanced at her but she ignored this callous treatment and continued to follow him. At last one day he chased his followers away and gathered her into an embrace that lasted for twenty-five years without his ever emptying his seed into her.

This was the union of *Purusha* and *Prakriti.* So long as they embraced and became One there would be no advance in creation. *Sati's* role was to make *Shiva* function in the mundane world. He was *Bhava* or Pure Being and she, *Bhavani* or Becoming. Unless she bestirred herself and broke out of his embrace all creativity would be at a standstill. The portrait of *Shiva* is always one that alternates between the extremes of asceticism and eroticism. *Shiva's* stored up potency which accumulates during asceticism has to be coaxed into being released into the world to invigorate creation. *Sati's,* and later *Parvati's,* role was to lure *Shiva* from this ascetic isolation to creative participation in the world.

At last she uncurled herself from that endless embrace and started to question him on the meaning of the Self.

"Ever since I was a little girl I have practised *tapasya,* not for liberation but to get you as my husband. Now that I have my desire, I long for liberation too. I have been told that you are 'liberation' itself. All my devotion has been to you but now I want knowledge."

Shiva said, "O *Sati,* in the age that is to come, the Iron Age of *Kali,* devotion is the easiest method of getting release. So you should continue with your devotion to me and I shall set you free".

"My Lord, I know what devotion is but I would like to learn about *jnana* also from you."

"You don't need it, O *Sati,* for you and I are one. That is knowledge."

"But who are you?" Asked *Sati.*

"I am That," said *Shiva.*

"What is That?" She insisted.

At last *Shiva,* the Supreme Soul gave in to the wishes of the Divine Mother and gave her, who is omniscient, all wisdom in order to benefit the world.

"O *Sati,* I shall give you that knowledge which shall free all souls in bondage. O Beautiful One! Know that Supreme Knowledge consists in experiencing the great truth, 'I am *Brahman*'. In the enlightened intellect, nothing else is remembered. This sort of consciousness is very rare in this world. But O beloved! Remember, that I myself am the supreme *Brahman* as is *Vishnu.* As for you, my love, you are nothing but the Supreme *Shakti (Parashakti).* You are not separate from the *Brahman.* Devotion to you or to me or to *Vishnu* will give liberation from these mortal coils and is easier to practise. One who is steeped in devotion enjoys perpetual bliss. Devotion has the power to attract me as nothing else can. Why do you think I was attracted to you? I go even to the houses of outcastes if they are devotees. In the decadent age of *Kali,* wisdom and detachment have been misused and neglected. People who can grasp them are rare. Devotion or *bhakti* can give the same benefits and is more appealing."

Listening to this discourse, *Sati* was satisfied. She questioned him on a thousand other things also. These wonderful dialogues between *Sati* and *Mahadeva* form the basis of much of the sacred lore found in Hindu philosophy. Thus, *Shiva* and *Sati* who are both intrinsically nothing but the Supreme *Brahman,* who are all knowing and eternal, carried on their dialogue in the Himalayan region in order to help human beings to rise out of the ocean of *samsara* or the wheel of human existence.

At times *Sati* used to wander off by herself when *Shiva* was immersed in *samadhi.* At these times she would feel a weight of grief pressing on her breast for she knew that her father *Daksha* hated *Shiva.* She remembered the great *yajna,* which the *rishis* had once conducted at *Prayaga* – the confluence of the three rivers, *Ganga, Yamuna* and *Saraswati.* She had gone there with her Lord and all those assembled there had got up from their seats to pay homage to *Mahadeva.* When *Daksha* arrived with his entourage, everyone except *Shiva* rose from their seats to honour him. *Daksha's* face became dark with rage when he noticed this lack of humility on the part of his son-in-law. He broke out into a host of invectives against *Shiva.*

"How is it that when the rest of the world honours me, this fellow alone refuses to pay me homage. His monkey-eyes are not fit to meet the doe-like eyes of my lovely daughter. By giving her to him, I have given the fragrant flowers of the *Veda* into the hands of an unclean outcaste! In future he shall not be given a place in any of the *yajnas* conducted by anyone!"

Sati would have jumped up immediately to vindicate her husband, but *Shiva* restrained her with a touch.

He said, "My dearest! This is not the time and place for you to denounce your father. Don't you know that I myself am the sacrifice, the sacrificial rite and the very Self of the sacrifice. Who is this *Daksha*? Who are you? Who are all these people? In reality I am all. Knowing this, you should not grieve. *Daksha* has done this out of pride, for which he will be forced to pay a heavy price. But you are my wife and should be free from anger"!

At that time *Sati* had held her tongue but often as she wandered alone on the mountain slopes, a great load of sadness pressed on her chest. She felt sure that some dire incident was approaching. She knew that her husband did not reciprocate *Daksha's* hatred for he had no aversion to anything in the world, but still the nameless sorrow gnawed at her vitals.

One day as she was wandering on the mountainside, she noticed many of her sisters travelling in their aerial vehicles up in the sky accompanied by their husbands. Many other celestial beings were also going the same way. She called to them to find out where they were proceeding.

They said, "Don't you know that our father is conducting a grand *yajna* to which everyone has been invited. It is going to be the greatest show the world has ever known. we are sure you will be invited and we will meet you there".

Sati ran to *Shiva* and asked him whether they had received an invitation.

Shiva replied, "I thought you know that your father hates me. He is conducting this *yajna* with the express purpose of humiliating me and will certainly not invite us".

Sati looked crestfallen and said, "Of course you cannot go to a place where you have not been invited but I am his daughter. Children can go to their father's house without invitation. Moreover I long to meet my mother and sisters and talk to people other than *Nandi* and the goblins, so will you permit me to go"?

At this, *Shiva* said, "I cannot stop you from going where you please, but remember that no good will come of it. In fact you may have to face dire consequences if you go. You will be dishonoured and forced to listen to your father's insults"!

But *Sati* was adamant. She had made up her mind and nothing could deter her. With great sadness *Shiva* watched her depart. He sent *Nandi* as her vehicle and all his *ganas* accompanied her to protect her if necessary. She was wearing pomegranate flowers in her hair. Her pet parrot sat on the bull beside her. The white umbrella of royalty was held above her head and pennants and banners waved merrily beside her. Trumpets and conchs blared forth as she set out. *Shiva* watched her sadly for he knew that he would never see her in this form again.

Sati came from the realms of established religion, the order of *dharma.* She married into the order of asceticism, thus combining the two conflicting worlds. Her role was to act as the mediator between these two opposing poles, both of which are basic to the Hindu tradition. Her final sacrifice of herself forced *Shiva* to look favourably on the sacrificial cult that is meant to maintain and nourish creation, and from which he had so far kept aloof.

"How has He through the thickets of the world,
Pursued me like a lion in the night,
And come upon me suddenly in the way,
And seized me with His glorious golden leap.
Unsatisfied He yearned for me through time,
Sometimes with wrath and sometimes with sweet peace,
Desiring me since first the world began.
He rose like a wild wave out of the floods,
And dragged me helpless into seas of bliss."

— "Savitri" by Sri Aurobindo

Thus ends the fourteenth chapter of the *Sri Devi Lila* known as 'Sati', which describes the advent of the goddess as *Sati*, daughter of the patriarch, *Daksha.*

ॐ *Aim, hreem, kleem* ॐ

ॐ

Sarvaswarupe, sarveshe,
Sarvashakti samanvite,
Bhayebhyastraahi no Devi,
Durge Devi namostute.

"I prostrate to the goddess Durga,
Who can take on any form,
Who is the Source of all power,
And resides in every object.
Protect us from all fear."

ॐ

Shivaayai Namaha!

CHAPTER FIFTEEN

DAKSHAAYINI

Ya Devi sarvabhuteshu, smriti rupena samsthita,
Namasthasyai, Namasthasyai, Namasthasyai Namo Namaha!

"O Goddess, who resides in all creatures in the form of memory,
Hail to Thee! Hail to Thee! All Hail to Thee!"

Sati could hardly recognise her ancestral home when she reached there, for it was spectacularly decorated and abounded with wondrous sights. She descended from the bull, *Nandi* and went inside alone. The *ganas* waited outside in trepidation. They knew that something momentous was about to happen. As *Sati* entered the sacrificial hall, everyone became immobilised and none dared to look at her face, for fear of *Daksha.* Only her mother and sisters flocked to welcome her but she waved them aside. Her father alone was totally unaware of her entrance, for he was immersed in his rituals. Her trained eyes instantly noted that offerings had been kept for all the gods except *Shiva.* His place was deliberately kept empty and bare. With measured steps she walked towards the centre of the *yajnashala* where her father was seated beside the blazing fire, offering ghee and various other herbs into the pit, muttering incantations all the while. Everyone watched with bated breath as *Sati* approached.

Her complexion, which was normally quite dark, became even darker. Her long, black tresses, which had been knotted up were shaken loose and swung like a black cloak around her. Her lotus eyes were red with anger and blazed like hot coals and as she looked at her father; sparks of red light flew out. *Daksha* turned and saw her and visibly paled beneath her scorching gaze. It was the first time that *Daksha* had broken off his mutterings in the middle of a ritual.

Sati looked at him with scorn and said, "O father! Your end is near. You are trying to perform a sacrifice without inviting the One who is the very soul of all sacrifices. *Shiva* is the essence of fullness and you have excluded him from your *yajna*. You think the world revolves round your rites. The flowers of your ritual are but rain which falls from the feet of *Shiva*. You have insulted him – the great Lord *Mahadeva* – without whose blessings no sacrifice can be complete. My Lord warned me of what I would find here and I disregarded him. How can I return to him? I can no longer bear to have my beloved call me '*Dakshaayini*' (daughter of *Daksha*). This body that was born from your seed, is hateful to me. I can no longer inhabit it. Your daughter shall be the supreme human sacrifice for your great *yajna*. Here and now I shall abandon this body which has sprung from your loins".

So saying, *Sati* turned towards the north and fixed her mind on her Lord. She covered herself with her upper garment and went into a *yogic* trance. She raised her *Kundalini Shakti* from the *Muladhara Chakra* at the bottom of the spine up to the seventh *chakra* – the *Sahasrara* on the crown of the head. Her spirit disappeared through the orifice at the crown of her head, leaving the empty calcified shell of her body standing like a translucent statue. Everyone gazed in terror at what remained of *Sati's* body.

The *ganas* flew back to *Shiva* and reported the whole wretched story of the disastrous turn of events. *Shiva* jumped up from the rock on which he had been sitting and plucked off one of his braids and dashed it on the rock. Out of this sprang the gigantic figure known as *Virabhadra*. He had the same features, embellishments and dress as *Rudra*, the destroyer. He had hundreds of feet and arms, brandishing a multitude of weapons. He was decked with snakes, tiger skins and flower garlands. *Shiva* commanded him to proceed to *Daksha's* palace and destroy the entire hall of sacrifice. He set out, followed by *Kaali* and a host of goblins and spirits.

Far away in the *yajnashala* there was total silence and gloom. Into this silence crept a noise, which grew and grew like the awesome approach of a tornado. It was inexorably approaching from the north. *Virabhadra's* approach was heralded by a dust storm that filled every nook and crevice of the hall. Then out of the shadows came his mountainous figure with flailing arms and weapons, indiscriminately destroying every single thing in the hall. Those who could flee, ran for their lives, others had their limbs torn from them and still others were brutally trampled upon. The once beautiful *yajnashala* had become a battlefield soaked with blood and scattered with limbs. The *ganas* desecrated the whole place that had been sanctified by the Brahmins. They urinated in the hollows in which fires glowed and splattered blood on the offerings. *Virabhadra* was looking around for the Master of the sacrifice and at last spied him huddled in terror near the altar. One of *Virabhadra's* hands gripped him by the neck and hauled him off to the sacrificial pit where the animal sacrifice was normally carried out. *Virabhadra* cut off *Daksha's* head and threw it contemptuously into the fire; the final offering into the fire – the head of the Master of the sacrifice!

Having done their worst they returned to their Lord. In the meantime *Brahma* and *Vishnu* also went to *Kailasa* and begged *Shiva* to withdraw his form as *Rudra* and allow *Daksha* to complete the sacrifice. *Shiva* agreed but since *Daksha's* body had no head, he told them to fix the head of a goat on the headless figure and allow him to complete the sacrifice, which was for the well being of the world.

Though he had forgiven *Daksha, Shiva* was filled with agony at the death of his beloved *Sati.* Picking up her lifeless corpse, he wandered over the whole world, holding her aloft. His *ganas* followed him silently, tears rolling down their cheeks, not knowing how to console their grief-stricken Lord. He wandered on, repeating the steps of the *tandava*, the dance that always preceded creation and destruction. The whole of creation was filled with grief and the gods begged *Vishnu* to do something before the whole world drowned in *Shiva's* sorrow. *Vishnu* took his discus and cut off pieces of *Sati's* body, limb by limb. At last when the whole body had been cut off, *Shiva* realised that there was nothing more in his arms. He retired to his mountain fastness and went into deep *samadhi* and refused to meet anyone.

Those places where *Sati's* limbs had fallen came to be known as *Shakti Peethas*, where the power of the *Maha Devi* was most keenly felt. Even today they are filled with divine potency and attract thousands of devotees from all over the country. The *Peethas* are hundred-and-eight in number and are found all over the sub-continent of India. *Shiva* is always present in these *Peethas* where the remains of his beloved *Sati* had fallen, so these places are considered even more holy. Her vulva fell in the place called *Kamarupa* or *Kamakhya* in the state of modern Assam. It is said that *Shiva* assumed the form of the *linga* and plunged himself into her and there the two remain conjoined eternally. There is a saying in Sanskrit that the penis will always ejaculate automatically when placed in a vagina. But this is not true of *Shiva.* He has completely obliterated lust from his consciousness. His *linga* always resides in *Sati's yoni* and yet he never loses his semen. The same story is repeated with *Parvati* when she and *Shiva* embrace each other for eons with no apparent display of lust. This is why he is known as the perfect *yogi.*

The *yoni* actually stands for all womenkind and the *linga* for all mankind and this story is meant to show that men and women will continue to attract each other eternally. *Sati's* eyes are supposed to have fallen in the holy spot of *Varanasi* and here she is known as *Vishalakshi* – the wide-eyed one. Her navel fell in *Kanchi.* This is a most famous *Peetha* and here she is known as *Kamakshi* – the one with love-filled eyes. She is known as *Kumari* in *Haridwar*, as *Rukmani* in *Dwaraka* and *Radha* in *Vrindavan.* She is *Sita* in *Chitrakuta* and *Vindhya Vaasini* in the *Vindhya* mountains. These places are said to be her favourite abodes. In the form of Truth she is present in the hearts of all creatures all the time.

Even in death, *Sati* succeeded in her attempt to bring *Shiva* from ascetic isolation to creative participation. He dwells forever in the form of the *linga* embedded in her *yoni.* She performed the same feat when her body was cut to pieces and fell to the earth. By following her, *Shiva* was literally forced to return to the kind of life that he had hitherto shunned. Previously he had dwelt in the mountains and was totally immersed in *tapasya,* indifferent to creation. But *Sati* succeeded in involving the great ascetic god in the world of creation, by capturing him in her *yoni* and forcing him to accept a creative role. Thus, even though *Shiva* keeps performing his asceticism in his mountain retreat, he continues to be accessible to the world in the form of the *linga.* This theme is fully developed in the story of *Parvati.*

"A spirit within looks into the Eternal's eyes.
It hears the words to which our hearts were deaf,
It sees through the blaze in which our eyes grew blind.
It drinks from the naked breasts of Truth,
It learns the secrets of eternity."

— "Savitri" by Sri Aurobindo

Thus ends the fifteenth chapter of the *Sri Devi Lila* known as 'Dakshaayini', which describes the *Daksha Yaga* or the Sacrifice of *Daksha.*

ॐ *Aim, hreem, kleem* ॐ

"O Devi! We bow to you.
You are the good fortune of the virtuous,
The bad fortune of the vicious,
Intelligence of the learned,
Faith in the hearts of the good,
Modesty in the hearts of the noble
Pray protect the universe."

— *Devi Mahatmyam*

ॐ

Yoginyai Namaha!

CHAPTER SIXTEEN

PARVATI

Ya Devi sarvabhuteshu, vritthi rupena samsthita,
Namasthasyai, Namasthasyai, Namasthasyai Namo Namaha!

"O Goddess, who resides in all creatures in the form of activity,
Hail to Thee! Hail to Thee! All Hail to Thee!"

One of *Sati's* sisters, *Swadha,* had been given in marriage to the *pitris* or the manes. She had three daughters called *Mena, Dhanya* and *Kalavati.* Once in their youth, the sisters had gone to *Vaikunta* to receive the blessings of Lord *Vishnu.* At that time they failed to show respect to the four boy-sages known as *Sanat Kumaras.* They had been cursed that they would be born on earth as mortals. They felt very sad and begged the sages to retract their words. The *Kumaras* told them that the curse of a sage was always for the good of the world. It always fulfilled the inscrutable purpose of the Lord. They comforted *Mena* by telling her that she would become the wife of *Himavan,* the king of the mountains known as the *Himalayas* and that the *Maha Devi* herself would be born as her daughter and would be known as *Parvati. Dhanya* would become the wife of the great sage-king of *Videha* known as *Janaka* and *Lakshmi Devi* would be born as her daughter and would be called *Sita.* This *Sita* would become the wife of *Vishnu* in his incarnation as *Rama,* prince of *Ayodhya.* The third sister *Kalavati* would be born in a cowherd family and would be married to their chieftain called *Vrishabhanu.* The goddess *Parashakti* would be born as her daughter – *Radha,* who would become the beloved of *Krishna.*

The sisters were very happy when they heard this and thanked the sages for their curse that would prove a blessing not only to them but also to the whole of humanity.

After the death of *Sati*, *Shiva* had become a permanent recluse. He wandered to those holy sites where the different parts of *Sati's* body had fallen, immersed in meditation on that Supreme *Parashakti* who had embodied herself in human form as *Sati* and spent some years with him. How could he forget? Because of his intense *tapasya* the rivers dried and the earth lost its prosperity. The hearts of all beings became dried up and lost the power to love. All creatures became immersed in an ocean of sorrow from which there seemed to be no reprieve. Disease and famine stalked the world.

The only one who prospered was a demon called *Taraka*. He had got a boon from *Brahma* that he could not be killed by anyone but the son of *Shiva*. Since he knew *Shiva* to be a confirmed ascetic, he felt secure to continue with his atrocities on gods and humans alike. He had all the three worlds under his control and declared himself to be *Indra*, king of gods. *Indra* ran in despair to *Brahma* even though he knew that the grandsire was the cause of all their troubles since he insisted on giving boons indiscriminately to fiends like *Taraka*. Where could they find a woman who was capable of luring a *yogi* like *Shiva* into marriage? They trouped off to *Vishnu* and begged him to help them in their impossible task. *Vishnu* told them that their only hope lay in enticing Lord *Shiva* to marry and get a son since only such a person could kill *Taraka*.

Parashakti, the divine Mother alone was the fitting bride for *Shiva*; so they prayed to her and begged her to incarnate herself as the daughter of *Himavan*. Like *Vishnu*, the *Mahadevi* also deigns to incarnate herself from time to time in order to maintain the balance of *dharma* and *adharma*.

At the end of their great *tapasya* the goddess appeared.

She said, "O *devas*! I know your desire and my *Shakti* will incarnate as *Parvati*, in the house of *Himavan*. She will become the wife of *Shiva* and will beget a son who will destroy the demon known as *Taraka*".

The gods were very happy to hear this and departed. *Himavan* however stayed back and begged the goddess to give him true knowledge. The advice given by her to *Himavan* is known as the *Devi Gita*, and has been given in the first chapter of this book.

Along the northern boundaries of India stand the magnificent mountains known as the *Himalayas* or the abode of snow. It is the king of all mountains. It has some of the highest peaks in the world. This was the place Lord *Shiva* loved the most. It is known as the land of the gods, for sages from time immemorial have performed austerities there and the place is saturated with spirituality. The intense *tapasya* practiced in these regions have soaked into the very rocks so that the heat of austerity shimmers in the air. *Himavan* was the king of these mountains. His wife was called *Mena* and she was the daughter of the manes. This was the fortunate couple who were to become the parents of *Parvati,* the Divine Mother.

Thus the goddess incarnated herself in the house of *Himavan,* much to the joy of her parents. The word *Parvati* means, 'she who dwells in the mountains'. Though her parents had many heroic sons, their fond gaze always followed the antics of their beloved daughter. Once the sage *Narada* visited the palace of *Himavan* and foretold the future prospects of the child.

"The palms of your daughter, O *Himavan*, are filled with auspicious signs. She will heighten the glory of her parents and delight her husband, but her husband will be a naked *yogi.* He will have neither mother nor father and will be indifferent to honour and dishonour. His manners and mode of dressing will appear inauspicious."

Mena and *Himavan* were greatly distressed to hear this but *Parvati* smiled secretly for she knew that the description given by *Narada* matched with the portrait of *Shiva,* which she had imprinted in her heart from birth.

Seeing the distress of the parents, *Narada* comforted them, "O Lord of the mountains! Don't be unhappy. Lord *Shiva* will be her bridegroom. In him there is neither good nor bad, neither auspiciousness nor inauspiciousness. He is *nirguna* – beyond qualities. Let her propitiate him with austerities and he will definitely agree to wed her. Love such as is found between them will not be found anywhere in the world. She will become part of him and he will get the name '*Ardhanareeswara*' – half male and half female".

However, *Himavan* had another doubt, "O celestial sage, I have heard that after the death of the daughter of *Daksha, Shiva* has sworn never to marry again and is always in *Samadhi.* How will he agree to marry *Parvati*"?

Narada, the omniscient sage, replied smilingly, "Have no fear, O

Himavan! This daughter of yours was formerly the daughter of *Daksha* and was called *Sati*. There is no doubt that she will become the wife of *Shiva*. Now she resides on your lap but her permanent place will be the lap of *Shiva*"!

The main theme in the story of *Parvati* is similar to that of *Sati*. *Shiva* represents the ideal of asceticism and *Parvati* the ideal of the householder. These two typify the eternal tension in Hindu philosophy. One path insists that the world is *maya* and should be shunned, and the other asserts that the world is real and leading an ideal householder's life can also lead to the goal of liberation from mortal coils. *Parvati's* mission was to lure *Shiva* into a world of marriage, sex and children – to lead him away from asceticism, *yoga* and solitude. *Shiva* had no family, no lineage and no interest in progeny. He lived beyond the realm of established society, outside the recognised law of *dharma*. *Parvati* came from a noble family and longed for marriage, children and a home. *Shiva* is the destructive fire that burns up the juices of life, and *Parvati* the flowing sap that promotes life.

The famous fourteenth century saint of *Tamil Nadu*, *Manikkavachakar*, calls *Shiva* the madman and *Parvati*, the goddess who tames this unpredictable *yogi* and makes him behave in a civilised manner.

Parvati's mother *Mena* was not too happy at *Narada's* predictions and did not want her lovely daughter to marry a madman but she was persuaded by her husband to allow *Parvati* to go to the mountains to perform austerities in order to attract the ascetic.

Just at this time it is said that *Shiva* himself came to the territory of *Himavan* in order to do penance. *Himavan* hastened to welcome him and asked him how he could serve him. *Shiva* replied that the only service he could do for him was to leave him alone!

Himavan took some fruits and offerings and went to wait upon *Shiva*, accompanied by *Parvati*. He begged *Shiva* to accept the services of his daughter who was anxious to provide him with all his needs.

Shiva took one look at *Parvati*, who was in the first flush of youth, beautiful beyond words, and quickly averted his eyes. Very sternly he told *Himavan*, "A woman is a phase of illusion. What use would I have for a young woman as beautiful as your daughter? Please don't send her here in future".

Himavan was struck dumb and did not know what to say, but *Parvati* was undeterred in her determination to woo him and spoke boldly,

"O Lord! Have you considered that all activity comes under the sway of *Prakriti*? Even *tapasya* is an activity and can be done only with the consent of *Prakriti*."

Shiva replied, "I am destroying the *gunas* of *Prakriti* with my penance. In reality I am *nirguna,* and without any attributes".

Parvati spoke up again, emboldened to make a bid for her love.

"Don't you know that I myself am *Prakriti* as you O Lord are the *Purusha?* Without me, you will be attributeless no doubt, but you will also be actionless and incomprehensible!"

Shiva laughed and said, "O *Parvati!* I see that you are a champion of the *Samkhya* system of philosophy but seem to know little of *Vedanta.* Know me to be the Supreme *Brahman*, beyond *maya* and beyond *Prakriti,* comprehensible only through spiritual insight".

Quick as a thought *Parvati* countered, "If as you say, you cannot be affected by *Prakriti*, why should you fear me? Why can't I serve you? Surely I cannot pose a threat to one like you"?

Shiva was delighted with her quick wit and determination and agreed to let her serve him.

Parvati was elated by her success. Every day she would go with all the prescribed materials for *puja* and wash his feet with holy water and make all offerings to him. She would sing and dance for him and clean the precincts with her own hands. Many years passed, with the Lord in deep *samadhi,* totally oblivious of what was going on around him. *Parvati* continued to serve him day after day unperturbed by his indifference.

But the gods were getting worried. *Taraka's* harassment went on unabated and *Shiva* showed no signs of responding to *Parvati's* overtures. *Indra* decided to employ *Kama,* the God of Love, to help them in their mission.

Kama boasted, "I can overthrow both gods and demons with one single arrow from my bow, so why not Lord *Shiva*?"

Kama's five arrows were like flowers and his bow looked as if it was made out of a row of bees, for Spring followed him wherever he went and the inebriated bees were drunk with the nectar of the flowers. He proceeded to the territory of *Himavan,* accompanied by his soulmate *Rati*

to the place where *Shiva* was doing *tapasya. Kama* and *Rati* – desire and pleasure – always went together. They were followed by Spring with her full retinue of perfumed breezes and running brooks. She danced like a breath of fresh air into the wintry surroundings where Lord *Shiva* was seated in motionless contemplation. Everything she touched or glanced at, turned into beauty. Ice flowed into gurgling brooks and bare boughs became loaded with fragrant flowers and buds. Spring even crept into the hermitages of the *rishis.* At her approach they felt an indescribable longing for all that they had forsaken.

Kama crouched behind a thicket and watched fascinated as *Parvati* came forward to perform her daily worship of the Lord. As she placed the flowers at his feet, Spring sent a little breeze that lifted her shawl and exposed her enticing breasts covered with a scanty bit of cloth. Just then *Shiva* opened his eyes and saw *Parvati* in the full beauty of her budding youth. Her complexion was that of a blue lotus, her maturing breasts ended in a slender waist that could be spanned by his two palms. Her black, curly locks tumbled about her shoulders as she bent forward. *Kama,* who was waiting for just such an opportune moment, shot his flower arrow straight at *Shiva's* chest with unerring accuracy. Usually even if *Shiva* happened to open his eyes, he would close them again without any change in his demeanour. But at that moment, due to *Kama's* intervention, he could not tear his gaze away from *Parvati's* delectable form. He gazed deep into her eyes and thought to himself,

"She is indeed a storehouse of perfection. If I get so much pleasure just from looking at her, how much would I get by embracing her?"

Thinking thus, he was just stretching his hands to touch her when *Kama* shot his second arrow. At the twang, *Shiva* turned his head and saw *Kama* standing proudly with *Rati* beside him. The full blast of *Shiva's* wrath swept over *Kama* like a fiery flame. Mentally he invoked the help of *Indra* and the other gods who were lurking in the bushes to see the show. Before they could come to his aid, *Shiva* opened his third eye. A great flame of fire shot up into the sky like a fiery meteor. It dropped to the earth and covered the ground, engulfing the trembling *Kama* and reducing him into a heap of ashes which eddied around with the dust. *Rati* scrambled on the ground trying desperately to save what she could of her lover's remains. Her loud sobs shook *Parvati* out of her petrified state. She ran home sobbing to the arms of her mother, followed by her terrified maids who described the whole ghastly scene to the parents.

The gods were frightened out of their wits and did not know how to comfort the sorrow-stricken *Rati.* They begged *Shiva* to restore him to life.

"What have you done"? Cried *Rati* in agony. "By killing *Kama*, you have condemned all creatures to live a life devoid of desire. Life will come to a standstill and collapse if desire is destroyed. The bull will forsake the cow and the horse, the mare, the bees, the flowers and man, his wife. Desire is not just the cause of suffering but it's the basis of all joy. What is life without love? It is mere existence, like a flower without perfume. Life has its price which is suffering but it also has its reward, which is joy and it cannot exist without *Kama*".

Shiva's anger was always short-lived and he could not bear the sight of *Rati's* suffering.

He said, "I destroyed *Kama's* body but not his spirit. He will live on as *Ananga* – the bodiless one and will be reborn as *Pradyumna*, the son of *Krishna* and you, O *Rati,* will be joined with him once again as his wife".

So saying, *Shiva* lapsed into silence, closed his eyes and went into deep *samadhi.*

(We have already heard the story of how *Kama's* ashes were made into a fiend called *Bhanda,* and of the incarnation of the goddess as *Lalitha.*)

"And now his burning breath assailed the soil,
The tiger heats prowled through the fainting earth.
All was licked up as if by a lolling tongue,
The Spring winds failed; the sky was set like bronze."

— "Savitri" by Sri Aurobindo

Thus ends the sixteenth chapter of the *Sri Devi Lila* known as 'Parvati', which describes the birth of *Parvati* and the death of *Kama.*

ॐ *Aim, hreem, kleem* ॐ

ॐ

Mahamayyai Namaha!

CHAPTER SEVENTEEN

APARNA

Ya Devi sarvabhuteshu, daya rupena samsthita,
Namasthasyai, Namasthasyai, Namasthasyai Namo Namaha!

"O Goddess, who resides in all creatures in the form of compassion, Hail to Thee! Hail to Thee! All Hail to Thee!"

Parvati returned home in a highly agitated frame of mind. "What is the use of physical beauty if it can't get me the one thing I most desire? *Shiva* is a true *yogi*. Physical charms have no fascination for him. What he admires most is asceticism, so that is what I should practise if I want to marry him".

She decided to go to the forest and practise intense austerities. At that time the sage *Narada* came to the palace and spoke privately to *Parvati*. He gave her the famous five-syllabled *mantra* of *Shiva* and told her to concentrate totally on that, and she would surely win him over.

Parvati went to her parents to get their consent. *Himavan* was agreeable but her mother could not bear to see her go. "Why don't you meditate in the house? All facilities are here and I'll see to it that you are left alone; *u-ma*". This means 'don't go'. Thus, *Uma* came to be another of *Parvati's* names.

But *Parvati* was adamant. Discarding her fineries and ornaments, she clad herself in the bark of a tree tied at the waist with a girdle of grass. She told her maids not to accompany her and went straight to the place where she had last seen *Shiva* after *Kama* had been burnt down. It was bare and empty, the leaves had withered and the season was no longer spring. *Parvati* could have wept for her Lord, but she controlled herself and took her seat in the same place where *Shiva* had sat. She made a *linga* out of mud in front of her and started her penance. Still and steady as a rock, she kept her mind fixed on the beloved form of her Lord and kept repeating the *mantra* given by *Narada.*

In summer she sat in the midst of five fires, in the monsoons she sat in the rain and did not seek shelter and in winter she sat in the snow, inured to the icy winds that howled around her. For the first year she subsisted on fruits alone, and in the next year on leaves, thus getting the name *Aparna* or the one who subsisted on leaves. Her mind was a canvas on which was painted the picture of *Shiva* alone. She had neither father nor mother, no other life except this one. She felt as if she had been meditating all her life. Her parents came to try and persuade her to return but she did not even notice them. The heat created by her *tapasya* was so great that the ground under *Indra's* feet began to burn. He ran to *Brahma* to find out the reason for this phenomenon. *Brahma* was equally perplexed and they went together to Lord *Vishnu* who told them the reason for the sudden rise of heat in the world. It was the power of *Parvati's tapasya* and she had sworn not to stop her austerities till *Shiva* became her husband. So they went to *Shiva* and eulogised him and begged him to save them from the threat of *Taraka.* They told him of the heat which was being produced by *Parvati's* penance and how only he could save them from both the dangers!

The great *yogi* looked at them with a glimmer of smile in his eyes?

"I thought you'd be happy that *Kama* is out of the way and you can do your meditations without being troubled by his arrows. If I marry *Parvati*, *Kama* will have to be revived and you will be unable to perform penance!"

Vishnu now spoke, "Your beloved wife *Sati* has been re-born as *Parvati,* the daughter of the mountains, and she is performing intense *tapasya* to procure you as her husband. Only a son born of your loins is capable of killing the demon *Taraka.* So for the good of the world, please accept her as your wife".

Shiva mused to himself, "A wife is ruinous to the life of a *yogi.* Even the *Vedas* say that, but then I have always been a rule to myself. Nothing can fetter me, not even a wife. Moreover, I am always anxious to please my devotees. How can I resist her plea when she's undergoing such tortures for my sake? She has proved that she can be a *tapasvini* (anchorite), fit to be the wife of a *tapasvin* like me".

He told the seven sages to go to the place where she was performing austerities and test her resolve.

Seeing her emaciated form, shining with brilliance, they bowed to her and begged her to give up her *tapasya. Shiva* was a confirmed *yogi,* they said and had declared that he would never marry.

"In that case I shall die unwed," said *Parvati* with no change in her composure. "As you know I am the daughter of the mountain and therefore immovable. Do not waste your time on me. It is better for you to go back to your contemplations. The sun may rise in the west, fire may refuse to heat but my words will never be false. I shall continue my penance until he comes to me or I shall give up my body in this very place".

The sages were delighted with her determination and reported the matter to *Shiva.* Now *Shiva* himself decided to test her. He appeared before her in the guise of a very old sage in ascetic's garb, and told her to desist from her *tapasya* since *Shiva* would never marry her. *Parvati* merely smiled and said, "In which case I shall immolate myself in the fire that I have kept ready."

Without speaking another word she lit the pyre and jumped into it but the fire became cool and could not burn her. The old man stopped her from making another fire and listed *Shiva's* bad qualities to her.

Parvati was furious and cried out, "Why have you come here to poison my mind with your vile accusations against my Lord. Whatever *Shiva* is or is not, I love him and will have none other as my husband".

She turned away in disgust and was on the point of running away when *Shiva* assumed his real form and caught her by the hand.

"Why are you running away from me"? He teased. "You have won me by your extreme austerities and I am your ardent slave. Come with me to my abode in the *Himalayas.*"

But *Parvati* could not be persuaded so easily.

She said, "My Lord", "I eloped with you once in my incarnation as *Daksha's* daughter and you know what happened. This time I want a proper marriage with all due rites, and with the full consent of my parents. So you will have to go to them and ask for my hand if you want to marry me".

To this, *Shiva* said, "My sweet *Parvati*, this entire world in one of illusion. I stand above all prophecies and planets. But if it's your wish to perform the marriage rites by propitiating all the planets, so be it. I can refuse you nothing. I shall approach your father and ask for your hand in the proper manner".

Parvati returned home jubilantly and was welcomed back with great love. But as expected *Shiva* could not conform to rules. He went to *Himavan's* court in the guise of a mendicant dancer and delighted the court with his skill. *Mena* offered him money and jewels, which he refused.

"What is it you want then?" She asked.

"I want your daughter," he replied.

Mena was furious and ordered that he should be chased out of the court. *Parvati* alone had been shown his true form and begged him mentally to take on a more conventional appearance. So the next time he came, he took the guise of a noble Brahmin, a devotee of *Vishnu* with crystal beads in his hand and a *saligrama* round his neck. The Brahmin strongly advised *Himavan* against giving his daughter to *Shiva*. He then left the way he came, muttering on his beads. *Parvati* was desperate and mentally prayed to him to stop playing these tricks.

So *Shiva* commanded the seven sages once again to go to *Himavan* and request him to give his daughter to him. They were overjoyed to do his bidding and went to *Himavan* and said, "*Shiva* is the father of the universe and *Parvati*, the mother. It behoves you to give your daughter to him alone. By this gift your life will be fulfilled".

Himavan was very happy to hear this but *Mena* was stubborn in her refusal to give her tender daughter to a mad man, as *Shiva* appeared to be. The gods then sent *Arundati*, the wife of sage *Vasishta*, who was noted for her wisdom and chastity, to persuade *Mena* to agree to the union of her daughter with *Shiva*.

"*Parvati* is the great cosmic intellect, the mother of the universe. You will gain honour and glory only if you give her in marriage to *Shiva*."

Hearing this, *Mena* was pacified and agreed to the betrothal. Preparations were immediately started for the consummation of the joyful event.

Himavan was determined that this should be the grandest occasion ever held in the world. Everyone was invited – the gods, the sages, the rivers, the mountains, *gandharvas*, *apsaras*, and all other celestial beings. Different mansions were made for the gods, with the best one reserved for the bridegroom. On the auspicious day, all the gods went to *Kailasa* to accompany *Shiva*. They begged him to dress as befitting a bridegroom. He smiled his secret smile and complied with their request. The crescent moon took the place of a crown, his third eye became a beautiful jewel adorning his forehead, the serpents twined round his ears turned into earrings and the ones round his neck into necklaces and garlands. The ashes that were smeared on his body turned into sandal paste and the elephant hide into a silk garment. The *ganas* from all over the world flew in to accompany the bridegroom party. Nothing could dissuade them from coming.

Thus the wedding party set out amidst the blare of trumpets, beating of drums and blowing of conchs. When they reached the outskirts of the mountain city, *Himavan* came out with a large retinue to meet them. He was enchanted to see the divine form of *Shiva*, totally contrary to what he had been expecting. The Lord had taken on the form of *Sundaramurti* – the handsome one! He was seated on the white bull of crystal purity and beauty, the very symbol of *dharma*.

As can be imagined, *Mena* was in a fever of impatience to see the man for whom her daughter had been prepared to forsake everything she held dear and spend so much time doing intense austerities. She went to the balcony and looked down on the bridegroom party, which was just arriving. *Shiva* knew of her qualms and decided to play one of his usual pranks. *Mena* was delighted to see the splendid procession. First came the *gandharvas*, who were the celestial musicians noted for their sartorial elegance. Heavenly nymphs waving banners of brilliant hues accompanied them. *Mena* thought that one of them might be *Shiva* but was told that they were merely his attendants. How striking he must be, she thought, if his attendants were so handsome. Then came *Agni*, *Yama* and *Indra*, all looking equally fantastic. When *Vishnu* arrived on the scene, *Mena* nearly fainted. She had never seen such a handsome personality before and was sure that this was *Shiva*, but again she was disappointed. Next came *Shiva* accompanied by the *ganas*.

"Here is your daughter's bridegroom," someone whispered in her ears. *Mena* stared aghast at the motley crew that now appeared. The spirits, ghosts and goblins came first. Some of them were in the form of violent gusts of wind, making hissing sounds, some had crooked faces and deformed bodies, some were lame and some blind, some hobbled on one leg and others carried staffs and tridents and had distorted faces.

Were these creatures *Shiva's* escorts? She could hardly believe it.

"There is *Shiva*! There is the bridegroom," they shouted.

On seeing him, *Mena* trembled and nearly fainted. He had five faces and three eyes. His hair was matted and had the crescent moon on it. His body was smeared in the ashes of annihilated desire and he had ten hands, all brandishing gory weapons. His upper cloth was an elephant's hide and lower, a tiger's. He had a wild look in his eyes and appeared to have been drinking. In fact the whole party seemed to be intoxicated and were rolling about in a drunken orgy and singing obscene songs. They flung skulls and bones up into the air instead of flowers.

Mena gazed at this horrifying scene for a few seconds and then mercifully fainted. As soon as she recovered, she wept and cried and swore that she would certainly not give her charming daughter to such an unkempt and uncivilised creature whose sole attendants seemed to be a motley crew of fiends.

"What shall I do," she moaned. "My life is utterly doomed and so is my daughter's. Where are those sages who have cheated us? I shall pluck out their beards with my own hands". Turning to her daughter she cried, "Is this the fruit of your penance. Surely your intellect must be deranged. Setting aside cooked rice are you bent on eating the husk? Oh! What have I done to deserve such a fate?" So saying, the poor lady beat her breasts and wept uncontrollably, bewailing her lot.

Narada and the other sages came to reason with her but she would not listen. Her husband came and told her that this was all a sport of *Shiva* who wanted to test her. She shut her ears. *Brahma* came and told her that *Shiva* had many forms and this was all his divine *lila*. Still she was unconvinced.

Parvati asked her, "O mother! Why has this delusion overtaken you? Please give me to Lord *Shiva*. I have wooed him mentally, verbally and physically for many years. I shall wed none other". *Mena* cried bitterly when she heard this.

At last Lord *Vishnu* approached her and spoke to her in a sweet accent.

He Said, "O *Mena*!" "You are the beloved daughter of the manes and you should be able to appreciate the greatness of *Maheswara.* He is devoid of all attributes, yet possesses all attributes. He is hideous as well as handsome. It is only because of your daughter's great penance that he has agreed to marry her. Consider yourself to be fortunate that he has blessed you. O wife of *Himavan*! Stop your tears and accept him as your son-in-law and all will be well".

Hearing these soothing words *Mena* relented and said, "I will agree to this wedding only if he assumes a pleasing aspect. Otherwise whatever any of you might say, I will not consent to this marriage".

Vishnu reported the matter to *Shiva* and mentally *Parvati* begged her Lord to stop playing tricks. *Shiva* laughingly agreed and when the appropriate time came for the bridegroom to enter the marriage hall, *Shiva* strode in. Much to *Mena's* surprise his form was wondrous to behold.

He was fair and handsome and his face shone with a divine radiance. He was the personification of masculine splendour. His dark silky hair flowed to his broad shoulders. His long, lithe limbs were clad in silk and he was wearing a garland of fragrant, jasmine flowers. His lustrous dark eyes turned towards *Mena* and penetrated to the very depths of her soul. There was a glimmer of a smile on his face as he noticed *Mena's* discomfiture. *Mena* went forward with her husband and worshipped him with sandal paste and whole rice grains mixed with turmeric. The wives of the sages came and waved ghee lamps and camphor flames in front of him and escorted him to the ceremonial stage reserved for the bridal pair.

Now the wives of the sages brought *Parvati* forward. Her beauty entranced all those present there. Her complexion was as dark and radiant as a blue lotus. Her thick black hair was plaited and covered with flowers and jewels. Necklaces covered her breast, and bangles and bracelets her arms. Her lips which had been coloured with red lac, opened slightly to reveal her pearly teeth. Her pink feet tinkled with the sound of anklets as she walked. She carried an exquisite mirror, set with gems in one hand, and a play lotus in the other. The intoxicating perfume of sandal paste, musk and saffron emanated from her body. On seeing the fascinating form of the Mother of the Universe, all the gods stood up and bowed to her. She looked up for a second and met *Shiva's* appreciative eyes and gave a small secret smile.

Himavan took his daughter's hand and repeated the age-old *mantras* of the *Rig Veda* and gave her hand to Lord *Shiva.*

Shiva grasped the lotus-like palms of *Parvati* and repeated the appropriate *mantras.* He then placed the auspicious red mark on *Parvati's* forehead. Grasping her trembling hand in his strong one, he led her thrice round the sacred fire and thus plighted their troth. Thus was the wild one tamed and made to conform to the rules of normal society.

Thinking this to be an appropriate time, *Rati,* the wife of *Kama,* came forward and begged to have her husband restored to his bodily form. *Shiva* smilingly agreed and much to *Rati's* delight, *Kama* appeared before them looking as handsome as ever.

As was the custom, *Shiva* stayed for four days in the mighty mansion made for the bridal couple. He, who was used to sleeping on rocks and stones and in cremation grounds, was cajoled by *Parvati* to lie on silken coverlets covered with flowers. At last the festivities came to an end and *Shiva* returned to *Kailasa* accompanied by *Parvati* and followed by the host of *ganas.*

ॐ

"But now the destined spot and hour were close,
Unknowing she had neared her nameless goal.
For though a dress of blind and devious chance,
Is laid upon the work of all-wise fate,
Our acts interpret an omniscient force,
That dwells in the compelling stuff of things,
And nothing happens in the cosmic play,
But at its time and in its foreseen place."

— "Savitri" by Sri Aurobindo

Thus ends the seventeenth chapter of the *Sri Devi Lila* known as 'Aparna', which describes the wedding of *Shiva* and *Parvati.*

ॐ *Aim, hreem, kleem* ॐ

ॐ

Bhuvaneswaryai Namaha!

CHAPTER EIGHTEEN

GAURI

Ya Devi sarvabhuteshu, matre rupena samsthita,
Namasthasyai, Namasthasyai, Namasthasyai Namo Namaha!

"O Goddess, who resides in all creatures in the form of the mother, Hail to Thee! Hail to Thee! All Hail to Thee!"

Though she was transported from the comfortable palace of her parents to the chilly caves of the *Himalayas*, *Parvati* was in a state of bliss. She had chosen her path, and was fully conscious of the kind of person she had married and had absolutely no regrets. Henceforth, these caves would be her boudoirs and these snowy slopes, her gardens. She had goblins in lieu of maids and her only friend was *Nandi*, the bull. The brilliant peak of *Kailasa* was the place chosen by *Shiva* for his wife's delectation. Close by was the scintillating lake called *Manasarovar* (lake of the mind) where celestial damsels sported with their lovers. In these icy waters *Parvati* had to bathe. The austere beauty of her new residence enthralled her. She was fully aware that she had conquered the heart of this great *yogi* only due to her asceticism and she had come prepared to pay the price.

However there were times when *Parvati* did long for a normal household as she had enjoyed in her father's house. The *Vamana Purana* gives an interesting anecdote. Oppressed by the intense heat of summer, she approached her husband and requested him thus.

"O Lord! The heat increases in violence. Can we not go to a house which is protected from heat, wind and cold?"

Shiva replied, "I am O lovely one, a constant wanderer in the forests, without any shelter. You knew that when you married me"?

So *Parvati* was content to remain with her beloved under the shade of the trees till the hot summer season passed. Then came the rainy season with its consequent storms and winds.

Parvati was agitated and told *Shiva*, "These storms terrify me O *Maheswara.* I entreat you to build a house on *Kailasa* where we can abide in comfort".

Shiva replied, "My Beloved! I have no riches to spend on houses. I possess nothing but an elephant's hide for a garment and serpents as ornaments".

Parvati spoke again, "O Beloved Lord! How can we pass the rainy season under the trees as we passed the summer"?

Shiva replied, "With our bodies covered with a cloud, O Lovely One, the rainy season shall pass without a drop of water falling on your tender body".

Having said this *Shiva* stopped a passing cloud and they made their abode within the cloud for the duration of the rainy season and remained snug and warm, much to *Parvati's* delight.

At other times, she sported with him on the frosty mountain peaks and verdant slopes of the *Himalayas* and bathed in the icy waters of the lake *Manasarovar* amidst lotuses and royal swans. She was as gentle and graceful as he was wild and forceful. When he performed the *tandava* dance, filled with vigour and violence, she would do the steps of the *laasya,* with full of grace and soft, slow movements. This was the perfect combination. If *Shiva's* principal function was destruction, her's was preservation and reconstruction, thus offsetting his violence. She had a calming, civilising influence on *Shiva.* Under the soothing effect of her charming presence, he changed his wild, rude and often mad behaviour. Many *Shiva* devotees are said to approach *Parvati* first in order to have access to *Shiva.* She was known to be kind and considerate to all devotees and she herself was his greatest follower. The great *Shiva bhakta*, *Manikkavachakar* emulated *Parvati* and prayed to her to give him steadfast devotion to *Shiva.*

The recurring theme in Hindu philosophy is that the way of the ascetic is superior to the way of the householder. These opposing principles were brought to a successful reconciliation by *Parvati. Shiva* was the god of excesses – both ascetic and sexual – and *Parvati*, the modifier. She represents the householder's ideal of married sex that is opposed to both asceticism and eroticism. *Shiva* yielded to her persuasions and reconciled himself to a mutual interdependence of husband and wife, which is the basis of a harmonious, married life. This is shown in many images which combine the two deities into an integrated whole – as *Shiva-Shakti*, and again *Shiva* as *Ardhanareeswara* or half-male and half-female, and that of the *lingam* and the *yoni*.

Many comparisons are given in the *Puranas* to show this inter-dependence. *Shiva* is the sky, *Parvati*, the earth; *Shiva* is the ocean, *Parvati*, the shore; *Shiva* is the sun and *Parvati* the light. *Parvati* is all qualities and *Shiva*, the enjoyer of all qualities. *Parvati* is the embodiment of all souls and *Shiva*, the Supreme Soul itself. *Parvati* is all forms and *Shiva*, the thinker of the forms. *Parvati* is speech and *Shiva*, meaning. The *Ardhanareeswara* figure emphasises that the two deities are absolutely necessary to each other and only in union can they satisfy each other and fulfil the cosmic purpose. This image actually transcends all sexual particularities and demonstrates the fact that God is both male and female, both father and mother, aloof and active, fearful and gentle.

The representation of the *linga* and the *yoni* also points to another aspect of this inter-dependence. As a great *yogi*, *Shiva* accumulates great sexual potency that has to be released in creation or else it has to be utilised for destruction. Both *Sati* and *Parvati* enabled the great *yogi* to use his accumulated potency for the good of the world. The *linga* and the *yoni* symbolise the creative interaction between the world of the ascetic in which sexual abstinence is compulsory and the life of the householder in which sex is absolutely necessary. *Shiva* and *Parvati* portray the ideal of wedded bliss. They have a deep understanding and harmony between them. In this aspect *Parvati* is the perfect wife who makes herself subservient to her Lord and master, unlike *Durga* and *Lalitha*. They actually depict that opposites can unite in perfect harmony. They represent the two poles – *Shiva* is the figure for *moksha* or liberation and *Parvati* for *dharma* or righteous living in the world. Neither of them give up asceticism entirely, thus teaching the lesson that asceticism actually enhances the intensity of sexual life and keeps the householder from being obsessed with eroticism alone. Thus, *dharma* and *moksha* complement and complete each other in the divine pair.

Many years passed while the great *yogi* appeared to have been tamed by *Parvati's* exquisite beauty and charm. She stimulated him to share with her all the accumulated wisdom he had gained from his great *tapasya*.

Because of her, the whole world gained this wisdom that is contained in the *shastras* and *tantras* of Hindu philosophy. There was no end to her thirst for knowledge and no end to his wisdom. She was the perfect student and he was *Dakshina Murti*, the perfect teacher.

One day he is supposed to have teased her about the dark colour of her skin. In a fit of temper she went to the forest and started *tapasya* in order to change her colour. Seeing her intense austerities, *Brahma* came to her and requested her to take another form and rid the world of the two demons, *Shumbha* and *Nishumbha* who had been re-incarnated and were terrorising the world.

Acceding to this request, the goddess *Parvati* shed her dark skin and became fair in colour and came to be known as *Gauri*, the radiant one. The word *Gauri* comes from the root 'ruc' which means 'to shine'. She is the shining one; the fair one and this is another of *Parvati's* many names. The dark outer skin took the form of *Kaali*, the virgin goddess, with the lustre of a black rain cloud. She held the conch and discus of *Vishnu* as well as the trident of *Shiva*, for she had the strength of both. *Parvati* told her to go with *Brahma* to slay the demons. She went to the *Vindhya* mountains where the demons were residing and vanquished them and stayed on there as the goddess known as *Vindhya Vaasini*. The *Maha Devi* had already foretold this event in her incarnation as *Durga*.

Gauri returned to *Kailasa* and delighted her Lord in her new role as the goddess with the colour of molten gold. She longed to have a child and prayed to *Shiva* to grant her this boon. *Shiva* drew her into himself and the couple were locked together in an embrace that lasted for eons. Excess was always *Shiva's* norm. He never followed the via media and did nothing according to the accepted modes of conduct. With him life was an everlasting turbulence or a total renunciation. Neither of these states was suitable for a peaceful life on the earth. If *Shiva* practised *tapasya* and ignored the world, then life lost its fragrance and drooped and died. If he indulged in a game of pleasure with *Parvati*, it went on for centuries till the constant friction threatened to burn the whole world. The world was capable of absorbing only a tiny fraction of his energy. Thus, the gods had decided long ago that whatever he was doing, he would have to be interrupted so that the equilibrium of the world would be restored. They were still sorely troubled by the menace of *Taraka* and though they had arranged the marriage of *Shiva* and *Parvati* for the express purpose of producing a child there was no sign of such a happy event. They decided to visit *Kailasa* and remind him of the reason for his marriage. They went to *Vishnu* and requested him to accompany them.

"*Shiva* might well wait another eon before producing a child," *Vishnu* said musingly.

They went to *Kailasa* and found the entrance to the cave guarded by the *ganas* who had been warned to keep everyone out. After waiting for a long time they became impatient and started eulogising *Shiva* and begged him to come out and grant their plea for a child who would save the world. *Shiva* had been on the point of giving in to *Parvati's* request to have a child, when the gods came with their persistant demands. He loosened his hold on *Parvati* and went out.

The seed that he had been withholding for ages was now discharged into the air and flew like a fiery meteor and fell to the earth. The earth could not contain it and begged *Agni,* the god of fire, to help her. *Agni* took up the seed but even he could not bear the heat and spat it out into the *Ganga.* As the fiery seed was taken down the river it got stuck in some reeds. The constellation known as the Pleiades or the *Krittikas,* which are a group of six stars, were drawn to the flame. The seed divided itself into six mouths and the six *Krittikas* nourished one seed each in their wombs. It was impossible for one womb to contain the heat of *Shiva's* seed, made extraordinarily potent by ages of *tapasya.* At last out of their collective wombs the child who was to be the saviour of the world was born. The reeds rustled and six pairs of hands lifted the child above the surface of the water and caressed it. Six women gave suck to him. The divine infant's six mouths sucked the milk of the *Krittikas.* Hence he got the name *Shanmukha,* the six-faced one. Since he was born among the reeds, he was also known as *Sharavanabhava.* Since the *Krittikas* nurtured him, he was called *Kartikeya.* His actual name was *Skanda,* the war god, born to destroy the evil created by the demon *Taraka.*

The gods had been keenly watching the progress of the seed. They now came down and took the child from his six mothers much to their dismay, and wafted him off to *Kailasa.* When *Parvati* saw the child, milk oozed out of her breasts for she knew it to be her own. You are the product of my *tapasya* and my bliss. Even though you were not born from my womb yet you exist because *Shiva* touched me. She took him on her lap and caressed him. *Skanda* then went to *Shiva's* lap and played with the snakes round his neck.

The selfish gods hardly gave a chance to the fond parents to cuddle their child. They clamoured that he should be crowned immediately and sent forth to accomplish the deed for which he had been born. Water from all the holy rivers of the land were consecrated and poured over his head to the chanting of *Vedic* hymns. *Brahma* gave him the knowledge of the *Vedas* and the sacred *mantras.* All the gods blessed him and gave him all types of weapons and insignia. The spear was his weapon, the peacock, his vehicle and the rooster, the emblem on his flag. *Shiva* told the gods to take *Kartikeya* or *Skanda* as their general and fight with *Taraka.* A terrific duel was fought between *Taraka* and *Kartikeya* in which the latter defeated the demon by driving the spear into his chest.

Parvati longed to have another son who would be her very own and listen only to her, who wouldn't be appropriated by the gods for their own selfish purposes. When she asked *Shiva*, he was evasive.

"I am not a creator, how can I create a child?" He asked teasingly. "You know what happened the last time I tried!" *Parvati* didn't say a word. They were lying side by side and her body as well as *Shiva's* was drenched with perspiration.

"I am the mother of the world. I can create a child for myself," she said. She anointed her body with sandal wood oil and turmeric powder and mixed it with her sweat and that of *Shiva's.* She rubbed her palms hard all over her body and made a soft dough out of it. She shaped the dough into the figure of a beautiful little boy and breathed life into it. The child was big and handsome, filled with strength and valour. She named him *Vinayaka* since he was born without a husband – '*vi-naayaka*'. She gave him clothes and ornaments and told him that he should be her bodyguard alone. She gave him a staff with which to ward off intruders.

The very next day when she went for a bath, she stationed *Vinayaka* outside and told him to keep off anyone who tried to enter. It so happened that the first person to come was *Shiva* himself. He ordered the boy to make way for him. At first he refused politely but when *Shiva* tried to enter forcibly, the child dared to hit *Shiva* with his staff. *Shiva* was amazed by the boy's audacity and sent his *ganas* to capture him. The *ganas* were defeated and returned dejected. At this *Shiva* became quite angry and severed the head of the boy with his trident.

Parvati was furious when she heard this and was all set on creating many *Shaktis* to defeat the *ganas*. *Shiva* placated her with great difficulty and promised to restore her son to her. He told the *ganas* to cut off the head of the first creature they saw who was sleeping with his head turned to the north. As it happened, they saw an elephant first and cut off its head and brought it to *Shiva* who affixed it to the boy's neck. *Parvati* was delighted to see her boy come back to life even though it was with the head of an elephant. She insisted that he should become the leader of the *ganas* and that is how he got the name of *Ganesha* and *Ganapati* – lord of the *ganas* and master of the *ganas*. She also insisted that he should be worshipped first before commencing any *puja* or ritual.

Parvati adored him and always kept him by her side. He would lie beside her with his trunk curled up and scribble on leaves with his stylus. Thanks to his mother's blessings, he is one of the most adored gods in the Hindu pantheon.

Parvati points out the fact that the way to liberation is to be had by creating harmony and balance between *Purusha* and *Prakriti*. She was *Prakriti* and *Shiva*, *Purusha*. He could only express himself through her. They are actually one, but project themselves in different aspects of the Supreme reality. He is *Bhava* (Pure Being) and she, *Bhavani* (Constant Becoming). They are always worshipped together as the divine couple – mother and father of the universe.

"He longed to draw her presence and power,
Into his heart and mind and breathing frame,
He yearned to call forever down,
Her healing touch of love and truth and joy,
Into the darkness of the suffering world,
His soul was freed and given to her alone."

— "Savitri" by Sri Aurobindo

Thus ends the eighteenth chapter of the *Sri Devi Lila* known as 'Gauri', which describes the birth of *Skanda* and *Ganesha*.

ॐ *Aim, hreem, kleem* ॐ

ॐ

Gangayai Namaha!

CHAPTER NINETEEN

GANGA

Ganga gangeti yo bruyath,
Yojanaanaam shathatapi,
Muchyate sarvapaapebhyo,
Vishnulokaam sa gachati.

"One who chants the name of *Ganga*
Even from the distance of a hundred miles from her,
Will be redeemed of all sins and attain the adobe of *Vishnu.*"

There are many stories connected with the birth of the *Ganga.* One of them is connected with the great sage *Agastya.* At one time some *Brahmin* ascetics were being constantly harassed by a group of demons. The sages would chase them as far as the ocean but the next day they would return after having their strength renewed by submerging in the sea. At last in desperation they appealed to *Agastya* who was renowned for his proverbial ability to digest anything. He solved their problem by the simple expedient of swallowing the entire ocean. *Vishnu* and the other gods were able to kill the demons that were lurking in the depths of the now-dry ocean and the sages could carry on their fire sacrifices without impediment. When they approached *Agastya* and asked him to disgorge the waters that he had swallowed, he smiled and told them sweetly that he had already digested it all. So, even though he had solved their particular predicament it led to a host of other problems. Rivers ran dry and the land was barren due to lack of water. The celestials were filled with distress. At last *Brahma* comforted them by promising to bring down the waters of the heavenly *Ganga* and thus fill the ocean. This task was fulfilled by the saintly king

Bhagiratha who brought *Ganga* to the earth. Even though he did it to give liberation to his ancestors, he was also able to fill the oceans.

Indian mythology is mixed with fact and what the modern world calls fiction. But to the Indian, the *Puranas* are more real than the so-called realistic fiction of the modern world. The *Puranic* stories were mostly based on observance of the terrestrial bodies and planets and the lives of great saints and kings. Lay people came to know much of geography and science from these stories. Some of the stories have been proved to be based on an acute observation of scientific data, which has been discovered by modern science only with the turn of the twentieth century.

At one time the celestial *Ganga* was what we know as the Milky Way. It was a stream of souls, of subtle essences. It ran from one end of the sky to the other, and then flowed to the earth. Earth and sky were the two banks of this great river of stars. Where was the point at which the river passed from the celestial to the terrestrial bank? The disparity of force between earth and heaven is so great that it would have been dangerous to go directly from one to the other. She had to break her fall on the mountain called the *Himalayas* that lifted the earth to the heavens. Thus the Milky Way became the *Ganga* and *Shiva* caught her as she fell down on the *Himalayas*. If left to herself, her waters would have flooded the earth and washed it away into space. The impact as she charged down, shattered the mass of water that came down to earth in many small streams. Life on earth became possible only because *Ganga* flowed unceasingly over *Shiva's* head like the water that is kept in a pot suspended above the stone *linga*. Theirs was a perennial love, renewed at every instant by a stream that knew no end. In fact *Shiva's* seed which even *Agni*, the god of fire, could not contain was kept and cooled in *Ganga's* womb. Here the seed took on an embryonic form that was later nourished by the *Krittikas* or the constellation known as the Pleiades. Thus, *Ganga* was not only *Shiva's* consort but also the mother of the war-god *Kartikeya*.

The *Puranas* vividly describe these three stages in the evolution of the *Ganga*. First she was a river of stars – *Akasa Ganga* or the Milky Way. This fell as snow on Mount *Meru* on the high plateau of *Pamir* and on the ridges and ranges that surrounded it. Here she was a river of snow. As the snow melted, she divided into the four main rivers of Asia. The river Huang Ho in China is also known as Sita or Sirdaria. Chakshu is the river Oxus or Amu Dario that rises from the Pamir Lake and is also called Sari-kul. Byhadra is the river Obi in Siberia, which is also known as the Yarkhand and Zarafshan. Finally when she reached *Bharata Varsha*, or India, she was called *Alakananda* and flows from the *Narayana Parvata* in *Badrinath* and radiates in different directions. After travelling over mountains, valleys, forests and caves she falls into the Bay of Bengal at the place called *Ganga Sagar*. It is said that she will forsake this planet ten thousand years after *Kali Yuga* has passed. When she leaves, all other *tirthas* or holy rivers will also leave.

There are many other accounts of *Ganga's* origin in other *Puranas*. The *Brahma Vaivarta Purana* says that at one time all three goddesses – *Lakshmi, Saraswati* and *Ganga* – were consorts of Lord *Vishnu*. But due to some misunderstanding, they cursed each other and had to take birth on earth in various forms. *Saraswati* suspected that *Vishnu* loved *Ganga* more than her and spoke harshly to *Ganga*. *Lakshmi* who tried to calm her now got the brunt of her wrath and was cursed by *Saraswati* that she would have to take birth on earth in the form of a river and a plant. *Lakshmi* did not display any anger but *Ganga* was furious with *Saraswati* and cursed her that she would suffer a similar fate and become a river and go to the earth. *Saraswati* promptly retaliated and swore that *Ganga* would get the same fate and she would be forced to come to the earth in the form of a river. Very soon all three of them repented their bad behaviour and begged *Vishnu* to release them from each other's curses. Lord *Vishnu* pacified the three goddesses and told them that all this had happened only to accomplish the divine plan.

"Calamities are a really a cause of happiness to human beings. Without sorrow no one can understand the true nature of joy."

He commanded *Ganga* to go down to the earth in order to help King *Bhagiratha* and eventually help to fill up the ocean that had been drunk by sage *Agastya*. Part of *Ganga* would take refuge in the locks of Lord *Shiva* and thus she would become his consort.

Vishnu further blessed her, "You will be able to release thousands of souls from their sins and give them liberation".

Ganga asked, "O Lord! But what will happen to me? Will I not be tainted with the sins of so many wicked people who are constantly shedding their impurities in me"?

The Lord answered, "Fear not, O Dear One! Even if one pure soul washes his feet in you, all your impurities will be washed away. Such is the glory of my devotees. You shall be the cause for the redemption of thousands of souls".

He commanded *Saraswati* also to accept the curse and go to the land of *Bharata Varsha* (India) in the form of a river. Later she would go to the abode of Lord *Brahma* and become his consort. Only *Lakshmi* was allowed to remain with *Vishnu* in her complete portion, for her nature was peaceful. But the curse of a pure soul could not be gainsaid and in course of time she would also have to go to the earth and become the river *Gantaki.* Furthermore, she would become the sacred *tulasi* plant, which is the beloved of *Vishnu.*

The *Brahma Purana* describes how the *Ganga* came out of *Brahma's kamandalu* or water pot. After the wedding of *Shiva* and *Parvati* in which all the gods took part, Lord *Shiva* is said to have extracted the sacred essences of the earth and created a water pot. He poured all hallowed waters into this pot and consecrated it with *mantras.* Since this pot was made out of the essence of earth and water, it became the cause of creation, preservation and destruction.

Lord *Shiva* handed this pot to *Brahma* and said, "All *dharma* is established here. Sacrifice, enjoyment and salvation are all to be found in this. All the sins of one, who bathes or drinks or performs offerings with this sacred water, will perish. O *Brahma,* take this *kamandalu* which has been consecrated by me with all divine *mantras* and continue with your work of creation".

The next episode of *Ganga's* descent is connected with the *avatara* of Lord *Vishnu* as *Vamana* or the dwarf. *Vishnu* had taken on this particular incarnation in order to subdue the demon king *Mahabali.* The demon had promised to give *Vishnu*, in his role as *Vamana*, three steps of land. But when the time came to offer the gift, *Vamana* took on his universal form and measured the whole earth with his first step. His second stride stretched up to the heavens. His foot pierced a hole in the shell of *Brahma's* world. *Brahma* was amazed to see this phenomenon but he immediately took the opportunity to wash the sacred foot of *Vishnu* with the water from his *kamandalu.* This water was the heavenly *Ganga* that fell on Mount *Meru* as described above. Hence, she is also known as *Vishnupadi* or the one who has come from the feet of *Vishnu.*

The most popular account of *Ganga's* descent to the earth is given in the *Ramayana. Sagara* was a king of the solar dynasty. He had two wives, the elder of whom had a son called *Asamanjas.* The second wife had sixty thousand sons. *Sagara* now held a grand horse sacrifice known as the *Aswamedha yajna.* In this sacrifice the consecrated horse had to be left to wander all over the earth. The king's sons had to follow and defeat anyone who tried to stop the horse. *Indra,* the king of the gods, out of jealousy stole the horse and took him to the nether regions and tethered him next to the great sage, *Kapila* who was immersed in meditation. The heroic sons of *Sagara* followed the horse and suspected the sage to be the thief and spoke harshly to him. When he did not open his eyes, they thought he was pretending and gave him a good kick. The sage opened his eyes and looked at them. Immediately they were burnt to cinders by the concentrated power of his austere gaze.

The king was desperate at the disappearance of his sons. Nobody knew where they had gone and the king sent his grandson, *Amsuman* to find out the fate of his sons. He discovered their whereabouts and was told that the only way they could get reprieve from the heinous sin of having kicked such a great soul and disturbed his *tapasya* was to bring the heavenly *Ganga* down to the spot where the ashes were lying and allow her waters to wash over them. *Amsuman* started his austerities but died before he could complete them. His son *Dileepa* performed more austerities but he also passed away before he could complete them.

At last *Amsuman's* grandson *Bhagiratha,* who was a great devotee of *Shiva,* gave up his kingdom and decided to concentrate entirely on achieving the purpose that had obsessed his race for four generations. He stood with hands upraised and performed terrific austerities in the place known as *Gokarna* in the south. After a thousand years of *tapasya, Brahma* appeared and promised to release the waters of the *Ganga* from his *kamandalu.* He pointed out to *Bhagiratha* that the earth would be unable to sustain her fall and only Lord *Shiva* would be able to do so. *Bhagiratha* was nonplussed. He knew *Shiva* to be the arch ascetic, sitting in splendid isolation on the solitary peak of the *Himalayas,* steeped in meditation, unconcerned with the petty worries of the world. It would be a Herculean task to induce him to co-operate in this endeavour. But *Bhagiratha* was prepared for everything. He performed another thousand years of austerities in the *Himalayas* at the place known as *Gangotri.* At last Lord *Shiva* appeared to him and agreed to accommodate *Ganga* in his matted locks.

This story glorifies the greatness of those who acquire ascetic will power. By enduring self-inflicted suffering, the *yogi* accumulates a vast amount of psychic and physical energy. The universal life-force becomes so concentrated in him that it melts the resistance of the cosmic powers and forces them to give in to his demands. This is true even of the demons. They can also force these powers to bend to their will by the accumulated strength of their ascetic fire. The heat generated by *tapasya* is like a laser beam that can cut through any kind of resistance. *Bhagiratha* by the enormous power of his *tapasya,* coupled with his determination to bring salvation to his ancestors, was able to literally drag the heavenly *Ganga* down to the mundane world. In fact his name has come to be a synonym for any task that needs superhuman effort.

It is said that *Ganga* was rather proud of her celestial status. She looked down upon the snowy peaks of the *Himalayas* from the group of stars known as the Milky Way. She saw the bluish tangled mass of Lord *Shiva's* head where she was told to break her fall before touching down on earth. She was scornful of anyone's ability to hold her.

"I'll sweep him away like a straw," she thought.

Even gods like *Agni, Soma* and *Surya* were nothing to her. Was she now to be frightened of that motionless figure on the peak of *Kailasa* who thought he was powerful enough to break her fall! She laughed scornfully and plunged down with a mighty crash on to his head. She would sweep him off and carry on her way over the beautiful earth. But no sooner had she touched *Shiva's* hair than she was lost. She was enmeshed in a labyrinth of darkness through which there was no exit. *Shiva's* locks were a forest of thick trees through which she turned and twisted in vain to find an outlet through which she could flow out, but she found herself to be totally enfolded in his tresses. Through it all she was aware of a strange mocking laughter that echoed in her ears.

"He held the river on his head,
And kept her wandering where,
Dense as *Himalayan* woods were spread,
The tangles of his hair.
No way to earth she found, ashamed,
Though long and sore she strove,
Condemned until her pride was tamed,
Amid his locks to rove."

Ganga felt desperate. "I'll never see the light of day again if I go on like this," she thought. She had been cut up into tiny streams and made to squirm and wriggle through the maze of his hair. She felt cheated and humiliated. She had been a spoilt princess in the heavens but now she felt her force was nothing compared to the mighty power emanating from this strange ascetic.

In the meantime, poor *Bhagiratha* was frantic. He performed more *tapasya* and begged Lord *Shiva* to allow *Ganga* to come down to the earth and thus purify his ancestors. At last his efforts bore results. Having curbed her pride, Lord *Shiva* relented and released a trickle from his locks, which formed the mighty lake known as *Bindusaras* (lake of drops). It is from here that she flowed down the Himalayan terrain as the mighty river that we see today. Mounted on a splendid chariot, the royal sage *Bhagiratha* went ahead to lead her to the place where his ancestors lay. Unfortunately as *Ganga* meekly followed the chariot, she happened to cross the sacrificial arena of the great sage, *Jahnu* who calmly drank up all her waters since she was disturbing his penance. *Bhagiratha* now had to appease the irate *rishi* who eventually released *Ganga* through his ear. She thus got the name *Jahnavi* or daughter of *Jahnu.*

Ganga then resumed her interrupted course behind *Bhagiratha's* chariot. They were followed by a host of celestials, heavenly nymphs, demons, giants, sages and snakes. It was too good an opportunity to lose and as the *Ganga* hurried onwards in the footsteps of the royal sage, the whole multitude of created beings bathed in her sacred waters and washed away their sins. Soon *Bhagiratha* and the goddess arrived at the dry bed of the ocean. From there they made their descent to the nether worlds where his ancestors had perished. *Bhagiratha's* long penance was now approaching a successful conclusion. Her purifying waters flowed over the ashes of his ancestors and redeemed them. Thus, after superhuman efforts *Bhagiratha* succeeded in delivering his ancestors and taking them up to heaven. Nor was this the only benefit that was achieved. Ever since the sage *Agastya* had swallowed the waters of the ocean, it had remained dry. But now with the coming of the *Ganga* this defect in nature found a remedy and the ocean was replenished to the furthest shore. *Ganga* now got the name *Bhagirathi*.

We have already heard the story of *Parvati, Shiva's* consort. But the story of his wives cannot be summed up without the story of *Ganga. Parvati* and *Kaali* are counter correlates and they stem from the same source but *Ganga* was a different personality altogether. She was a part of *Shiva.* Nothing could separate them. He carried her always with him, nestled in his locks. *Shiva* was never alone, even when he was doing *tapasya,* for *Ganga* was always tucked away in his locks. From his long black hair she dripped constantly. *Parvati* was always a bit jealous of *Ganga.* Though she never actually saw them speak to each other, she knew that *Ganga* was a constant witness to all his doings. Sometimes *Parvati* would be totally lost to all mundane thoughts and immersed in *Shiva's* cosmic embrace. However, her consciousness would revert to normal by the steady drip falling from his locks, flowing over her face and trickling to the ground. She would twist her face away from his chest and look up to meet *Ganga's* steady, unwavering gaze, looking at her with compassion and never with jealousy. Even though all she did was to flow, *Parvati* was always suspicious of her.

"All the time when *Shiva* has me wrapped in his embrace, he is still continuing to be with *Ganga.* How can I ever immerse myself in him if I am constantly meeting her eyes telling me of a pleasure greater than my own?"

Ganga's body was always twisted round her lover's head in a constant caress. *Parvati* could not bear it. When questioned about her, *Shiva* told *Parvati* that he had allowed *Ganga* to break her fall over his head so that the world would not be swept away. She in turn served the world by cooling *Shiva's* head all the time so that his *tapasya* would not scorch the earth. With this *Parvati* had to be content.

Just as the sons of *Sagara* were redeemed from their sins and given an entry to heaven by having her waters flow over their ashes, so all pious Hindus believe that having their ashes or bones thrown into the *Ganga* is a sure guarantee of a safe passage to heaven. Thus, she is known as the ladder to heaven – *swarga-sopana-sharani.* The *Skanda Purana* says that the forefathers are always singing this song:

"May someone take birth in our family who will bathe in the *Ganga* and redeem all of us."

The *Ganga* is a bridge between the worlds of the living and the dead. Any of the rites of *sraddha* and *tarpana* (libations to the manes) which are done with *Ganga* water, are supposed to be more effective. By using *Ganga* water, the ancestors are nourished since she also acts as a means by which the rest of the offerings will reach them. Every devout Hindu house will always keep a pot of *Ganga* water. People come all the way from the south of India to take a dip in the holy waters of the *Ganga* and carry a pot of water back to their homes. This water keeps forever without any decay. At the time of death a few drops are placed on the tongue of the dying person in order to assure him of a safe passage to heaven.

The word '*tirtha*' means a crossing and *Ganga* is known as a *punya tirtha*, for she is the one who aids the human soul in its crossing from the land of the living to the land of the dead.

The *Skanda Purana* says, "*Ganga* herself is all the *tirthas*, *Ganga* is a grove of penance. *Ganga* alone is the holy place of supernatural powers. No one need doubt this".

Ganga water is supposed to be totally pure and it is a fact that this is the only water that can be kept for years without getting putrid. The East India Company discovered this strange fact about the *Ganga*, which the Indians have always known. On their voyages to and fro from London to Calcutta, they found that the Thames water became quite polluted by the time they reached Calcutta but on their return journey the water they took from the mouth of the *Ganga,* though apparently polluted, kept absolutely pure till they reached England and came back to Calcutta.

The *Agni Purana* says, "One becomes purified of all sins just by seeing, touching or drinking *Ganga* water."

"One who touches the *Ganga* attains an eternal spiritual form," says the *Narada Purana.*

From the *Vedic* times all water has been regarded in Hinduism as a tangible manifestation of the divine essence. Just as copper is the best conductor of electricity, so water is known to be the best conductor of divine energy. An important part of every ritual in India is to worship a pot of water representing the power of the divinity and sometimes even serving as a sacred object in lieu of an image. For the duration of the ritual, this pot containing water is considered to be the seat of the deity. Normally, ordinary water is consecrated and made sublime by the chanting of *mantras* and by the addition of sacred herbs. But in the case of *Ganga* water, no such sanctification is required.

Physical contact with the waters of the goddess *Ganga* has the magic effect of automatically purifying the devotee. The base metal of his earthly nature becomes sublimated. The *Ganga* flows from the highest, eternal realm, and has contact with all the three deities – *Brahma, Vishnu* and *Shiva.* He who bathes in these waters becomes an embodiment of that celestial essence. This divine essence is not something remote from our life but the very core of our existence and the source of every moment of our life. The *Ganga,* which flows directly from that mystical realm, takes the devotee back along its blessed course to the place of our beginning and forward to our final goal, which is the ocean of existence!

After leaving the earthly regions, *Ganga* is said to assume a form as a river of punishment, which is for the ultimate purification of all lost souls. She takes on the name of *Patala Ganga* and traverses the seven lower planetary systems. Now she comes to be known as the river *Vaitarini* that encircles the city of *Yama,* the Lord of Death. Here she has a fearsome aspect. She is thick and slimy with blood and grime, and her water crawls with strange and gruesome aquatic creatures. All mortals have to cross this river. Persons who have done good deeds in their lifetime and given gifts and charity can easily cross it. Sinners have to wade through putrid blood and sediment, at the mercy of crocodiles and fish that pierce them with their sword-like snouts. The gift of a cow at the time of death is also known as *vaitarini* and a person who has given such a gift is rowed across by the boatman without difficulty.

The human form of the *Ganga* is visible only to the mystic eye. The *Agni Purana* says that she is white in colour, and is adorned with ornaments. Like the *Maha Devi,* she has three eyes and four arms. She holds a jewelled pot in one hand and a white lotus in the other. The other two hands show the *mudras* of fearlessness and blessing. Her vehicle is a *makara* (crocodile) that is also white like jasmine. The crocodile is associated with both earth and water and it has the power to both redeem and destroy. *Yogis* have perceived the figure of a crocodile in the *Swadhishtana Chakra* at the base of the spine. This *chakra* has water as its element and it is a storehouse of our innate tendencies or *vasanas.* These tendencies are carried by us from life to life and impel us to various actions that bind us more tightly to the materialistic life. The goddess *Ganga*, however, has totally subdued this crocodile of the mind's *vasanas* and stands on top of it, as if it were a domesticated animal.

The *Ganga Mahatmyam* (glorification of *Ganga*), which comes in the *Skanda Purana,* glorifies her thus:

Shiva tells *Vishnu*, "*Ganga* is my own transcendental body in the form of water. Her substance is all auspiciousness. She is the transcendental source of creation and the foundation of countless universes. I carry this mother of the world, who is non-different from the Supreme Truth, in order to protect the universe".

"In *Krita Yuga,* holy places are found everywhere, In *Treta Yuga*, the only holy place is *Pushkara*, In *Dwapara Yuga* the only holy place is *Kurukshetra* and in *Kaali* the only holy place is *Ganga.*"

"In *Krita Yuga*, meditation is the cause of liberation. In *Treta*, austerities, in *Dwapara,* sacrifices and in *Kaali* the only cause of liberation is the *Ganga.*"

"O *Hari!* One can take up residence on the banks of the *Ganga* only through the accumulated merit of many auspicious actions done in previous lives."

"One may be competent, learned, virtuous and charitable but if he has never bathed in the *Ganga*, his life is wasted."

"On the banks of *Srimati Jahnavi* all places are auspicious, all times are auspicious and every person is a fit receiver of charity."

Lord *Krishna* tells *Arjuna* in the *Srimad Bhagavad Gita*,

"Among sacred and flowing things, O *Arjuna*, know me to be the holy *Ganga*!"

Sri Adi Shankaracharya wrote the famous eight *slokas* on the *Ganga*, known as the *Gangashtakam*. The fourth verse gives the entire story of the *Ganga*:

"At first you were the water used for rituals in the *kamandalu* of *Brahma*, the grandfather of the universe. Then you became the all-purifying water that washed the feet of *Vishnu*. Then again you became the jewel adorning the matted locks of Lord *Shiva* and then you became the daughter of the *rishi*, *Jahnu*. My you, O Goddess *Bhagirathi*, who destroys all inauspiciousness, protect me."

Let us conclude the glorious account of the divine Mother *Ganga* with the prayer of *Kunti*, the mother of the *Pandavas*, to Lord *Krishna*, which comes in the *Bhagavad Purana*:

"O slayer of *Madhu*, just as the *Ganga* flows constantly to the sea without hindrance, so let my mind be relentlessly drawn to you without being diverted to anything else."

"I who am the beauty of the green earth,
And the white moon among the stars,
And the mystery of the waters,
Call unto thy soul.
Arise and come unto me,
For I am the soul of Nature,
Who gives life to this universe.
From me all things proceed,
And unto me all things must return.
And before my face, beloved of gods and men,
Let thy innermost divine self be,
Enfolded in the rapture of the infinite."

— "Charge of the Goddess" by Doreen Valiente

Thus ends the nineteenth chapter of the *Sri Devi Lila* known as 'Ganga', which describes the story of the Goddess *Ganga*.

ॐ *Aim, hreem, kleem* ॐ

ॐ

Mahakalyai Namaha!

CHAPTER TWENTY

MAHA KAALI

Ya Devi sarvabhuteshu, branti rupena samsthita,
Namasthasyai, Namasthasyai, Namasthasyai Namo Namaha!

"O Goddess, who resides in all creatures in the form of confusion, Hail to Thee! Hail to Thee! All Hail to Thee!"

Kaala is the Sanskrit word for 'Time' and *Kaali* is the divine consciousness in the form of Time – relentless, all-consuming and indomitable. She is also the beloved of *Shiva. Parvati* is his wife but *Kaali* is his soul-mate. While *Parvati's* role is to subdue and soften his violent nature, *Kaali's* role is the very reverse. She incites him to wild, dangerous and destructive behaviour that threatens the very stability of the universe. She loves carnage, destruction and violence. Friend of ghouls and ghosts, she performs the same functions as *Shiva*, but does it in a more violent fashion. Even *Shiva* cannot tame her spirit. Her wrath is immediate and dire, especially against treachery and falsehood. She is ruthless to the ones who hate the divine. She cannot bear indifference and negligence in the performance of divine works. Force and strength are her characteristics – a divine violence that is quick to shatter every obstacle. Her divinity springs out in the splendour of tempestuous action. There is an overwhelming intensity in *Kaali,* a divine violence hastening to shatter every limit and obstacle. Her sword is swift and straight.

The *Kaali* imagery is a bizarre one. She is portrayed in a number of different fashions but in all of them, her appearance is intimidating and intended to put off all those who are not ready to accept life as it is. She is known as *Bhayankari* or the one who terrifies. Sometimes she is naked and pitch black in colour, with long dishevelled hair that flows like night behind her. She wears a girdle of severed arms and a necklace of freshly cut heads. Her earrings are children's corpses and snakes are her bracelets. She has a cavernous mouth dripping with blood, a lolling, red tongue and long, sharp fangs. She has claw-like hands with hooked nails and her lips are reddened with blood. Her favourite haunts are battlefields, where she gets drunk on the hot blood of her victims, and cremation grounds, where she sits on corpses, surrounded by jackals, goblins and ghosts.

This is the visage she shows to the uninitiated. But this is only one of her façades. Her visible mask is that of *Maya* – Nature bringing forth all beings from her womb, feeding them at her breast, then devouring and assimilating them back into herself. This is her public mask as known to science – a material cosmos that seems to be a superficially purposeless chaos of opposing qualities, creation and destruction, cause and effect, light and dark, good and evil. Here she appears as a randomly wilful despot, elusive and aloof.

But the face she shows to her devotees, who value her for her own sake and not for the evanescent charms of her creation, is altogether different. To those fortunate ones, the untameable *Maya* of Nature becomes a doting Mother whose sole concern is their ultimate well-being. The transformation from one extreme to the other is well brought out by an analogy of the great twentieth century saint, Swami Rama Tirtha. As long as we pursue the things of the world for their own sake, they will remain frustratingly elusive like a shadow that flits ahead, always just out of reach. At this stage the world seems alien and unfriendly. However, the moment we wake up from this elusive creation and turn round to face the Creator, the shadow of creation follows dutifully behind us. Nature supports those who sincerely turn towards God.

So *Kaali*, the embodiment of universal destruction, has two distinct faces. These are the two faces of life. The fact is that all of us long to see only the beauteous facet of life – the face of the all-loving, all-gracious and omnipotent Mother Goddess. We do not wish to see anything bad, evil, obscene or dangerous. But it is a fact of life that all these things do exist. Some forms of *Kaali* show her with a cavernous belly through which one can see her gaunt ribs sticking out. I wonder how many of us have seen malnutritioned children like this, begging on railway platforms and bus stations. Even if we notice them, we prefer to turn our eyes away. At best we might silence our conscience by chucking a few coins to them and muttering some words of sympathy. The next minute these scenes are easily ejected from our minds as we run after some other excitement. The *Kaali* figure forcibly brings to our mind the negative aspects of life. We may shun her, we may scorn her, but one day or other in this life or the next we will be brought face to face with her. To those who insist on swimming against the stream of her laws, who spurn her and seek a false security in the ephemeral things of the world which she herself has created, she manifests as Death. Everything that they cling to so desperately both in the world and in themselves, will inevitably be swallowed up by her and disappear. To those devotees who do not struggle against the flow of the current of Nature, who recognise *Kaali* as life eternal, she shows her benevolent, maternal side.

She is not an easy goddess to love but if you love her without reservations, as a child loves a mother even though she is ugly, then she will come to you in any of the forms that you want her to come. If you are a *Krishna bhakta* she will come as *Radha*, if you are a *Shiva bhakta* she will come as *Parvati* and if you go to her with the love of a child, she will become your Divine Mother and put you on her lap and teach you everything. It is to the everlasting credit of the Hindu mind that many of our greatest saints discovered this esoteric secret and were ardent worshippers of *Kaali*. They realised that the secret of life lay in accepting both sides of the coin of life – the destructive and the constructive. There are two sides to the Divine Mother. One is the feminine side – the maternal, life-nourishing, and life-bearing principle. The counter-balancing side is her destructive function, which takes back and swallows the creatures she gives birth to. This is the aspect that is represented by *Kaali*. She is Time, the all- producing, all-consuming principle, in the flow of which everything that comes into existence has to vanish after the expiry of its brief spell of allotted life.

Adi Shankaracharya, the founder of the *Advaita* philosophy of non-dualism, was also an ardent worshipper of the goddess. His says in one of his poems:

"Who art Thou, O Fairest One? Auspicious One!
You whose hands hold both delight and pain?
Both the shade of death and the elixir of immortality,
Are thy grace, O Mother!"

The world cannot be fragmented into clean and unclean, creative and destructive, male and female, as the human mind attempts to do. The world is a unified totality of the terrible and the sublime, welded together. The so-called unclean female bodily functions like menstruation and pregnancy are natural and universal. Through the *Kaali* imagery we are made to realise that to experience opposites is to be fully human. It is not merely an upholding of these contradictory principles but a realisation of the fact that one is meaningless without the other. Such fearless affirmations from a gruesome divine power like *Kaali* become a comforting directive. It encourages women to feel worthy of themselves as females. In fact the *Kaali* imagery has the potential to become a symbol of completion and release for all women, all over the world.

Both the creative principle and the destructive are one and the same. Both emanate from the same divine cosmic energy that becomes manifest in the process of the unfolding of the history of universe. Most pictorial representations of *Kaali* show her in the wholly negative aspect. She is often depicted as an emaciated, gruesome hag with bony fingers, protruding teeth and prominent canines. She has an unquenchable hunger for flesh and blood. She is cold-blooded, self-centred, ungenerous and selfish. The hunger for life that impels the infant to suck hard at the very lifeblood of its mother through her teats is shown in its most loathsome transformation. The Goddess feeds upon the entrails of her victims. Her victims are all those who are born from her own womb. She haunts the cremation grounds, for she loves to feed on the intestines that are still steaming with the last breath of expiring life. She has a halo of flames like *Shiva Nataraja*. These are the tongues of the universal conflagration that reduces everything to ashes at the termination of an age or a *Kalpa*. But these flames are also to be found all the time – they lick incessantly at the bread of life. Life feeds on death. For every newborn creature that comes into the world, there is another returning to the earth from which it came. Every time we eat something, it is at the cost of the death of something else.

Some *Tantric* texts describe her as standing on a boat that floats on a sea of blood. The sea is made up of the lifeblood of the children belonging to all species that she brings forth, sustains for a brief period and then takes back. She stands and quaffs the warm blood from a cranial bowl. Just as her love is unending, her thirst is unquenchable.

When we conceive of totality we should never forget its ambivalent character. The Hindu mind never balked at the display of stark reality. The Supreme Goddess – the *Maha Devi* – represents both aspects of life. To accept one and ignore the other is a form of childish indulgence that the Hindu philosophy did not cater to. As *Tripurasundari,* she is the embodiment of the feminine principle – the personification of man's desire. But in order to show her full significance, her other side has to be revealed. She has to be shown as *Kaali* – old, black and ugly, the embodiment of man's disgust, holding the symbols of destruction and death. In the figure of *Kaali*, the *Maha Devi's* negative, deadly features are emphasised.

Why is she the colour of the midnight sky? Why for that matter is *Krishna* blue? Space is colourless but when you look at the sky it appears blue. Water is colourless but when you look at the sea, it is dark blue. So also the Infinite when it manifests before human eyes, is dark blue.

Around her neck is a garland of eight gruesome heads. They represent the eight nooses or emotions that cloud the mind and incite it to keep performing endless actions that tighten the knots, which tie us to the wheel of life and death. These eight ropes or *pashas* are lust, anger, greed, delusion, envy, shame, fear and disgust. In the state of ignorance we possess many or all of these grinning heads. *Kaali* chops off these heads one by one to free us from these nooses.

Some of *Kaali's* pictures show her as having huge breasts. This is an appropriate symbol of motherhood. Breasts are the symbol of maternal love. The baby sucks from its mother's breasts all that it needs for life and growth. *Kaali* has a huge belly, for she consumes and digests all the beings in the universe. She takes them in and delivers them out. In order to cover her nakedness she wears a skirt of human arms, freshly severed and dripping with blood. The Sanskrit word for arm is '*kara*' which is closely related to the word '*karma*'. So these arms represent our *karmas* of innumerable births. If you look closely you will find that left and right arms are both there which shows that the *karmas* include both positive and negative ones. She wears them as a covering for her navel and pubis, for most *karmas* are done for the sake of food and sex.

Her anklets are little cobras. Snakes are the symbol of our ancestors. These are to remind us to pray for our ancestors without whom we would never be here.

She has four hands. One holds the cranial bowl that yields an abundance of food and the other the lotus that is the symbol of eternal life. Sometimes she is seen to carry a noose instead of the lotus. This is meant to convey the message that she will free us from the noose of death and confer immortality. The third hand holds a pair of scissors with which she cuts the knots that bind us to embodied existence. In the fourth hand she carries a sword, which symbolises physical extinction and spiritual determination. With this sword she cuts through our error and ignorance – the veil of individual consciousness, our doubts, false ideas and impressions. Her lolling tongue is meant to lick up the hundreds of *asuras* that multiply in us. These are our desires. The moment one is fulfilled, another hundred appear, like in the story of the *Raktabija asura.*

The famous *Kaali* statue at the temple of *Dakshineswara* that the great saint *Sri Ramakrishna* worshipped, has four hands. Each has a precise esoteric meaning and function. The arm on the upper left hand side holds a sword. On the esoteric level this sword stands for the destructive half of the world process. For one who sees no deeper than this, the weapon is naturally frightening. The worldly man senses, quite rightly that the sword is directed at him; in fact it is hanging over his head. He knows not when it might fall. His spiritual evolution is still in the primitive stage and he tries desperately to appease her wrath by offering live animals and money! He does not realise that her sword is directed at decapitating his animal instincts. In fact this is the esoteric truth behind all animal sacrifice. We are supposed to sacrifice our animal instincts at her feet and not goats and buffaloes.

The devotee on the other hand realises this and does not fear the sword, for he knows that it is poised to sever the deadly enemies of spirituality—lust, greed, pride and the rest of the demonic brood. The severed head that *Kaali* holds in her lower left hand is a token of her inevitable success in defeating these demons that are products of our ego. If the left arms show the negative aspects, her right arms portray the positive side. The raised hand, palm facing upward on the upper right side shows the *abhaya mudra*, signifying that divine protection will be given to all sincere aspirants on the path of spirituality. The lower right, with palm turned downwards offers boons, and assures the devotee that anything lacking in him which is necessary for spiritual evolution will be granted unasked, a gift of grace.

Kaali is the embodiment of the very essence of *Shiva*. He loves cremation grounds because death is an eternal reality and Lord *Shiva* is the destroyer, the very quintessence of death. You will always see *Shiva* amongst the dead, amongst corpses and ashes. *Kaali*, as his consort, also roams around cremation grounds.

In the *Mahanirvana Tantra, Kaali* is the most common epithet used for the primordial *Shakti*. In this scripture, *Shiva* who is known as *Mahakaala* or the Lord of Time, praises *Kaali* thus:

"At the dissolution of things, it is *Kaala* (Time) who will devour all and by reason of this I am called *Mahakaala*. Since you are the one who eats *Mahakaala* himself, you are known as the supreme, primordial *Maha Kaali*, or destroyer.

Since you are the devourer of *Kaala*, you are *Kaali*, the original form of all things and therefore you are known as *Adya* (primordial). After dissolving all things, you remain alone, formless, ineffable and inconceivable".

She is destruction incarnate, the destruction that is brought about by constant generation and life bearing. She also destroys the veil that *Maha Maya* has enshrouded us in. She comes like the black night which brings in its wake, the dawn. Without her there would be no death and therefore no life. Terrible is the face she shows to the haters of the divine and ruthless her mood towards them. Intolerant of hypocrisy, she deals roughly with all those who are false, treacherous, indifferent and negligent. Her hands are outstretched both to strike and succour, for she is also the Eternal Mother. Her love is as intense as her wrath and her compassion as deep. Only the great, the strong and the noble worship her. They accept her blows and know that she will melt whatever is negative in their natures, and mould it into strength and perfection. She can achieve for us in one day what might take years for us to achieve by ordinary means. Nothing can satisfy her short of the Supreme, the highest heights and the noblest aims.

One of *Kaali's* great devotees called Ram Prasad writes about her,

"O mother *Kaali*, you dwell in cremation grounds,
So I have made my heart a burning pit where you can dance.
One desire burns in the conflagration of my life,
To watch your blazing dance!
Lord Shiva lies beneath your feet,
Gaping up at your dance,
While I sit waiting on my funeral pyre,
Looking for you with closed eyes!"

The famous pictorial representation of *Kaali* dancing on the prone and corpse-like figure of *Shiva* has a deep, esoteric meaning.

"She, *Kaali*, the black one with blood dripping from her hands and adorned with a garland of heads is seen to be dancing on the prostrate figure of *Shiva*. She is supposed to be his faithful spouse, yet she dances on the body of her beloved and only mate. She is black as death and her tongue is out to lick up the world. Her teeth are hideous fangs. But her body is lithe and beautiful. Her breasts are big with milk. She carries the usual weapons in her hands. The figure of *Shiva* here is nothing but a *shava* or a corpse. His eyes are closed in bliss, sleep, trance or death, we cannot say but he looks like a lifeless and inert figure."

The esoteric meaning of this representation is that *Shiva* without *Shakti* is nothing but *shava*. The Supreme by itself is inert or zero. It is *Shakti* that pulsates with life. She is the infinity of forms. It is only at her touch that he can come alive and become the enjoyer of all forms. The Master of Time (*Mahakaala*) becomes Time itself at the touch of *Maha Maya*. Until then he might as well be considered a corpse. This is what *Parvati* told *Shiva* when he refused to look at her. She claimed that without her, who was his *Prakriti*, he, the *Purusha*, would be unable to move! So also the human body becomes a corpse when the *Shakti* or the power of *Prakriti* leaves it at the time of death.

The mythological story behind this pictorial representation is quite interesting. It is said that at one time *Kaali* began to dance on a battlefield and eventually she lost all control since she had become drunk on the blood of her victims. Nobody could manage her or put a stop to her mad rampage. At last to bring her to her senses, *Shiva* lay down on the battlefield, emulating a corpse. When she started to dance on her beloved husband she came to her senses and stopped the bloody carnage.

As we have seen, *Kaali's* most famous appearance is to be found in the *Devi Mahatmyam* in which she springs from *Durga's* forehead. She is the personification of *Durga's* wrath. When *Chanda* and *Munda* try to catch hold of *Durga*, the goddess turns black with rage and out of her furrowed brows arises the hideous figure of *Kaali*. The *Devi Mahatmyam* describes her thus:

"Carrying a many-coloured staff, topped with a skull, wearing a garland of human skulls;

With a garment of tiger-skin, exceedingly frightening with her dried-out skin,

With widely gaping mouth, terrifying with her lolling tongue;

With sunken, reddened eyes and a mouth that filled the directions with roars!"

Durga exhorts *Kaali* to kill the two demons, *Chanda* and *Munda*. Nothing loath she leapt into the fray and tore the demons apart with her bare hands and pulverised them with her teeth. With one furious blow she decapitated both their heads and presented them as an offering to *Durga*. The goddess playfully told her that from then on she would have another name – *Chamunda*. Later on in the battle, *Durga* summoned her to help defeat the demon *Raktabija*. This demon had the ability to reproduce himself with every drop of his blood that fell on the ground. *Kaali* killed him by spreading her lolling tongue all over the battlefield so as to enable her to catch all the drops of his blood before they could touch the ground. In these two episodes, *Kaali* is the personification of *Durga's* wrath.

In another episode, she is the personification of *Parvati's* wrath. When the gods requested *Parvati* to destroy the two demons, *Shumbha* and *Nishumbha*, *Kaali* came out of *Parvati's* body and went to the *Vindhya* mountains where she defeated the *asuras* and remained there as the goddess of the mountain. The temple of *Vindhya Vaasini* at *Vindhyachala* is dedicated to her.

When *Shiva* went to destroy the demons of the three cities, *Kaali* accompanied him. She was adorned with skulls and her eyes were closed with the intoxication of drinking blood. *Shiva* praised her as being the daughter of the *Himalayas*, which shows her identification with *Parvati*.

When *Shiva* sent *Virabhadra* to destroy *Daksha's* sacrifice, *Kaali* was part of his terrifying entourage.

In the *Mahabharata*, she is mentioned in the context of the killing of the *Pandava* children by *Ashwatthama*. The latter was a devotee of *Shiva* and had invoked him. *Shiva* had apparently sent *Kaali* to help him. The *Mahabharata* gives a vivid description of her:

"*Kaali* of bloody mouth and eyes, smeared with blood and garlands,
With reddened garments, alone, crested noose in hand,
The night of death (*Kalaratri*) laughing derisively and standing firm did the *Pandavas* see.
Binding men, horses and elephants with terrible snares did she sally forth,
Carrying various spirits who were bound with snares, their hair dishevelled."

She appears again in the wonderful work called "*Kumarasambhava*", by the great poet *Kalidasa*, who describes himself as the slave of *Kaali*. He had been a kind of moron until he started to worship the goddess who rescued him and made him the greatest poet of the land.

To become a devotee of *Kaali* is not an easy affair. She makes one suffer and disappoints us in terms of worldly desires and pleasures. *Kaali* does not give what is normally expected. She gives her devotee a vision of himself that is not confined to the normal physical and material limitations. As one of her devotees said, "One who loves *Kaali* can easily forget worldly pleasures." Nothing can satisfy her except the noblest aims. Therefore, the victorious force of the Divine is always with her and it is only by her grace that great achievements can be accomplished here and now.

Her devotee need not bother to ask for worldly joys because she will not give it. It is because of this that *Kaali's* devotees can find a reality that goes beyond worldly comfort and security. Her figure is one that is capable of destroying the comforting, mythical assumptions that one has of the world. One who thinks of the universe as an orderly, beautiful whole in which God as the protecting father sits in his heaven and tenderly looks after the needs of his children, will never be able to understand the significance of *Kaali*.

It is only in this century that scientists have discovered that their notion of the universe as an orderly whole, in which atoms and molecules behave in a set and understandable pattern, is a myth of their own wishful thinking. The energy field from which the whole universe rises is far from being orderly. It is a seething mass of turbulent forces made up of energy particles that seem to have no observable method of behaviour. Even to the scientists this was a shocking revelation. The Indian mind had realised this long ago. The figure of *Kaali* forces us to step out of the every-day world of logics into a world of unpredictability, dramatic reversals, opposites and contrasts.

Ram Prasad writes about her,

"You shine in deepest darkness, O Mother!
So yogis worship you in dark caves.
They find in your unlimited darkness,
Unlimited peace,
Who are you Mother?
Clothed in nothingness,
Glowing in the deepest recesses of my mind?
Your frenzied laughter terrifies,
While your love like lightning from a black cloud,
Shocks the worlds with light."

Kaali is India's gift to the world – the eternal, horrifyingly beautiful, caressing and murdering symbolisation of the totality of the world-creating and destroying process.

"The gods who watch the earth with sleepless eyes,
Have given to man the burden of his mind.
They gave him hungers, which no food can fill
His body the tether with which he's tied.
They cast for fodder, grief, hope and joy,
His pasture ground they fenced with ignorance.
Into his fragile, undefended breast,
They breathed a courage that is met by death,
They have traced a journey that foresees no goal.
Aimless, man toils in an uncertain world,

Lulled by constant pauses of his pain,
Death prowls, baying through the woods of life."

— "Savitri" by Sri Aurobindo

Thus ends the twentieth chapter of the *Sri Devi Lila* known as 'Kaali', which describes the *Maha Devi* in her form as *Kaali.*

ॐ *Aim, hreem, kleem* ॐ

Smashaneshavakrida, smarahara, pishacha, sahachara,
Chidabhasamaalopa strugapi nrikarotiparikara,
Amangalyam sheelam tava bhavatu naamaivam akhilam,
Tadapi smatrinaam varada param mangalamasi.

"You roam around the cremation grounds accompanied by goblins and ghouls,
You smear the ashes of the funeral pyres on your body
And wear a garland of human skulls.
These actions of yours are deemed inauspicious.
However, O Giver of boons!
For those who love you,
You are the embodiment of supreme auspiciousness."

— Shiva Mahima Stotrom

ॐ

Lakshmyai Namaha!

CHAPTER TWENTY-ONE

MAHA LAKSHMI

Ya Devi sarvabhuteshu, Lakshmi rupena samsthita,
Namasthasyai, Namasthasyai, Namasthasyai Namo Namaha!

"O Goddess, who resides in all creatures in the form of auspiciousness, Hail to Thee! Hail to Thee! All Hail to Thee!"

There are four aspects of the Divine Mother by which she guides and deals with the world. Two of these as *Maha Devi* and *Maha Kaali* have already been dealt with. Her third mask as that of *Maha Lakshmi* is one of sweetness, harmony and beauty. She has a compelling attraction and flair for affluence of all types. She opens out to our vision the miracle of eternal beauty, divine harmony and the irresistible charm of God's creation. This is the most attractive aspect of the Divine Mother and that is why she is one of the most popular of the Hindu goddesses. *Maha Devi* can appear too calm and too distant for the earthly nature to approach. *Maha Kaali* is too formidable and swift for our weakness to bear but *Maha Lakshmi* throws over us the intoxicating bliss of the sweetness of the Divine. We feel profoundly happy when she is close to us. Existence becomes rapture. Grace, charm and tenderness flow from her like an inexhaustible fountain and the one on whom she bestows her benevolence is plunged into bliss. Her delicate touch refines the body, life and soul of the human being.

Monastic systems of Hindu philosophy like *Vedanta* and *Yoga* are responsible for giving the general impression that Hindus look down upon wealth and give it a secondary importance in their social structure. But, truth lies in the contrary. *Lakshmi* or *Sri,* as she was initially known, has been revered from *Rig Vedic* times to the present day. Only by appreciating the true nature of *Lakshmi* can one hope to attain *Moksha* or liberation, which is the goal of all Hindu philosophy. Initially the two words *Sri* and *Lakshmi* meant anything that was auspicious and brought good luck or bestowed riches. Just as the word '*Aum*' is associated with the spiritual side of life, the word '*Sri*' is associated with the material side. It is the sacred symbol of cosmic auspiciousness and abundance since *Vedic* times. So it was but natural that the two words eventually became connected and *Lakshmi*, the goddess of beauty and prosperity, came to be known as *Sri Lakshmi.*

The *Sri Suktam* found in the *Rig Veda* is the most ancient invocation to this goddess.

"Invoke for me, O *Agni*,
Lakshmi who shines like gold,
Is brilliant like the sun,
Who is wonderfully fragrant,
Who wields the rod of suzerainty,
Who is the form of supreme rulership,
Who is radiant with ornaments,
And is the goddess of wealth."

In the *Lakshmi Tantra*, the goddess herself says,

"I am inherent in existence,
I am the inciter, the potential that takes shape.
I manifest myself; I occupy myself with activity,
And finally I dissolve myself.
I pervade all creation with vitality, will and consciousness.
Like ghee that keeps a lamp burning,
I lubricate the senses of living beings with the sap of my consciousness."

Wisdom and force are not the only manifestations of the Divine Mother. Above them is the miracle of eternal beauty, the secret of eternal harmony. *Lakshmi* is the one who transforms dreams to reality. To realise her is to appreciate and rejoice in the wonders of life. It is due to her kindness that life on earth is made bearable. Due to the inherent transience and mortality of all things, our journey through life is filled with sorrow. Destruction is always haunting the footsteps of the *jiva* from birth to death. It is due to the radiant and joyful aspect of *Sri Lakshmi* that life becomes endurable. *Maha Kaali* and *Maha Lakshmi* represent the opposite poles of life.

Since she is associated with wealth, *Lakshmi* is often called fickle or *chanchala.* It is not easy to meet the demands of this captivating divinity. She goes only where there is harmony and beauty of mind, thoughts and feelings. She is drawn to harmony and loveliness of surroundings also. She consents to abide only with those who are responsive to the rhythms of the Infinite, who respond to the call of her Lord and who strive to keep everything clean and neat both internally and externally, ever ready to welcome the advent of the Divine. Her delicate steps will not tread where there is meanness and ugliness or amongst those who are coarse and brutal. Where there is no love and beauty, she will not deign to come. This enchanting goddess will not linger in the house and heart of one who is filled with greed, jealousy and hatred. Neither are ascetic bareness and harshness appealing to her, nor the repression of the soul's natural desire for love and beauty. It is through love and beauty that she yokes the human to the Divine. Life is turned into a work of art, and existence into a poem of delight by her touch. Even the simplest things are made fragrant by her breath.

Though we always think of *Lakshmi* as the consort of *Vishnu,* originally she was supposed to belong to the demons. Demons, however, have the reputation of plundering and hoarding wealth, thus hindering its flow. This is why *Lakshmi* deserted them. She is then supposed to have gone to *Indra*, the king of the gods but when he overindulged in wine, wealth and women at the cost of his duty, she was disgusted and left him. *Lakshmi's* name has also been linked with many of the other gods of the *Vedic* pantheon like *Varuna, Soma, Agni and Kubera.* It was only in *Puranic* times that she was truly domesticated and became the consort of Lord *Vishnu.* In *Vishnu* she finally found the perfection she was looking for and having found him, she remained faithful to him ever since. This is because he is the embodiment of *dharma.* Though married to the goddess of affluence, he is totally uninterested in the acquisition or hoarding of wealth. The true nature of wealth was known to the *rishis* who were more powerful than the gods since they knew how to control their minds. Their formula for keeping riches was to allow it to flow, unobstructed, in the desired channels, never to obstruct its flow, never to hoard and never to plunder. This deep understanding of the nature of money is found in all the stories of *Lakshmi*. She appears fickle only because she will not stay with one who hoards and plunders wealth. But what her devotees should realise is that *Lakshmi* has a decided partiality for those who worship her husband – *Vishnu* – and will always go to them un-solicited.

Lakshmi has four hands in which she holds lotuses and vessels of grain and gold. One hand shows the *abhaya mudra* or the sign of fearlessness, and the other has the palm pointing downward to show that she showers her devotees with wealth. She is extremely beautiful since she is the goddess of fertility. Beauty is a life-propagating necessity and a true component of fertility. If flowers were not beautiful, pollination would not take place. Red is the colour of potential energy so she always wears red. Gold never rusts or gets polluted so she is adorned with gold ornaments. She holds a pitcher or the *akshaya patra*, which is the vessel of plenty that never gets exhausted. It is the eternally flowing cornucopia of gold and grain.

The lotus is the most popular flower in Hindu mythology. *Lakshmi* sits on a red lotus and has a strong connection with that flower. Many of her appellations are associated with the lotus. She is called *Kamala* and *Padma*, both of which mean 'lotus' and *Padmavati* which means lotus-born. As has been mentioned before, the lotus takes its birth and strength from muddy waters. It symbolises the growth of existence that is distilled from the life-giving property of water and mud. The lotus coming out of the navel of *Vishnu* marks the beginning of another cycle of cosmic life. The lotus gives a picture of a growing, expanding world, imbued with vigorous, fertile power. This is the power that is revealed in *Lakshmi*. She is the essence of creation and gives it flavour and splendour. Organic life is impelled by her mysterious power to flower into the rich tapestry of the world, as we know it.

Some pictures of *Lakshmi* show her as flanked by two elephants which shower water on her through their upraised trunks. Elephants represent fertilising rains as well as royal authority. They imbue her with those very qualities, which she possesses to the highest degree.

Lakshmi gives us the best of physical life so she has eight forms, known as *Ashta Lakshmis*, which portray the eight things in material life that are most prized by human beings. These are *Bhagya-Lakshmi* or the one who gives good fortune, *Gaja-Lakshmi* or the *Lakshmi* who gives power, *Dhana-*

Lakshmi or the bestower of wealth, *Dhanya-Lakshmi* or the provider of food, *Santana-Lakshmi* or the granter of offspring, *Vidya-Lakshmi* or the bestower of knowledge, *Virya-Lakshmi* or the one who confers strength and *Vara-Lakshmi,* the granter of boons. These figures are very popular in South India.

She also has a supreme form, which portrays her as a totally independent deity or *Maha Shakti.* In the *Pancharatra* and *tantric* schools she is given this independent status. She is known as *Maha-Lakshmi* and *Adi-Lakshmi,* the Supreme Goddess. While *Lakshmi* is the consort of *Vishnu, Maha-Lakshmi* is the embodiment of the divine *Shakti.* Her nature is very much like that of the virgin goddess *Durga.*

Another school considers her to be the root of all creation. *Narayana,* the cosmic soul, was lying on the cosmic waters. The idea of objectifying his divine bliss in the form of creation appeared in his mind, and his *Shakti* lying dormant within him burst forth, manifesting herself as *Maha-Lakshmi.* She placed the seed of his divine desire in the palm of her hand and unleashed the dynamic forces of creation, which emerged in the myriad forms of the universe that we know.

Another story describes *Vishnu* sleeping on the coils of the serpent of time known as *Adi-Shesha* or *Ananta* (endless). Time is endless. *Brahma,* the creator emerged from the lotus sprouting from *Vishnu's* navel and *Shiva* burst forth from *Brahma's* forehead. *Ananta* is conceived as floating on the cosmic waters. But what is the container of these waters? The sages declared that the waters were contained in the womb of the primeval divine Mother, *Adi-Lakshmi* or *Adi-Shakti.* '*Adi*' means first, so she existed before everything else. Gods, demons and human beings can never understand her divine mystery.

The *Puranas* have hundreds of interesting stories, which describe creation. The *Brahmanda Purana* states that this *Adi-Lakshmi* laid three eggs. *Ambika* and *Vishnu* emerged from the first, *Lakshmi* and *Brahma* came from the second, and *Saraswati* and *Shiva* from the third. She paired off *Saraswati* with *Brahma*, *Lakshmi* with *Vishnu* and *Ambika* with *Shiva.* They were sent forth for the purposes of creation, maintenance and dissolution.

Another story states that these three goddesses were the personification of the three *gunas* that emerged from *Adi-Lakshmi. Rajas* or activity was the essence of *Lakshmi*, *tamas* or negativity of *Ambika* and *sattva* or harmony of *Saraswati*.

The beautiful story of *Lakshmi's* meeting with Lord *Vishnu* is found in the myth about the churning of the milky ocean. The narrative has its origin in the dawn of time when *Brahma* created the seven sages to whom he taught the *Vedas*. They were also kept in charge of seeing to the well-being of the world. Six of them used the *mantras* they learnt from *Brahma* to invoke *Saraswati*, the goddess of wisdom through whose grace alone humanity could gain enlightenment. However, they soon realised that wisdom does not appease the hunger of the body and mind.

The seventh sage, *Brighu* learnt from *Varuna*, god of the waters, that ultimately all things are composed of food. There are only two categories of living things – those who eat and that which is eaten. He realised the extreme value of food. He used this knowledge to invoke *Lakshmi*, the goddess of bounty and wealth, through whose grace human beings could get food as well as anything else they wanted. Some of the impoverished sages went to *Brighu* and asked him to help them attain riches. He taught them the science of astrology, palmistry and how to make use of the bounties of the earth in the correct way, by which they could acquire wealth. The collection of his works is known as *Brighu Samhita*. Since he was the one who taught them the science of material prosperity, they concluded that *Lakshmi* was his daughter and thus they added another name to her collection and called her *Bhargavi*.

Later on *Lakshmi* was invoked by the demons and went to stay with them and thus the *asuras* became very powerful. But when they resorted to hoarding and cheating and licentious living, she deserted them and went to *Indra*, king of the gods.

At this time *Durvasa*, the sage known for his irascible nature, took a celestial garland to *Indra's* court. *Indra* was totally inebriated and carousing with the heavenly damsels. He took the garland, which the sage offered and carelessly threw it over his elephant's head. The garland fell off and was trampled by the elephant. *Durvasa* was infuriated by this behaviour and cursed *Indra* that all the gods would lose their health, wealth and youth and become decrepit. No sooner did the sage utter this curse than the gods lost their virility and *Lakshmi* disappeared into the ocean of milk. Instantly, the world lost its appeal. Everything became dull and listless. The earth refused to yield and the cows to give milk. The gods ran to their saviour – *Vishnu,* who advised them to get the help of the demons and churn the milky ocean, and thus get back both *Lakshmi* and the nectar of immortality called '*amrita*', by taking which they would regain their lost youth.

It was a task that needed cosmic preparations. The churn was the huge mountain called *Mandara* and the rope was the serpent called *Ananta. Mandara* represents Space and *Ananta*, Time. The positive and negative forces of life (gods and demons) combined to churn the ocean of causality with the churn of Space and the rope of Time. What they got was the essence of existence and the elixir of life. *Vishnu* had to help them many times, whenever misfortune overshadowed this gargantuan enterprise. When the mountain started to slip down into the ocean, he took on the form of a gigantic tortoise and upheld the mountain. When both parties started to tire, he took a form with thousands of arms and stood in the middle and helped both sides to churn vigorously.

Many wondrous things came out of the cosmic waters. At last, pleased with the determination displayed by both parties, *Lakshmi* emerged from the ocean in all her glory, seated on a glowing red lotus. She was clad in a splendid red-and-gold *sari* and resplendent with jewels from crown to toe. Both parties stopped their exertions just to gaze at her. Along with her came the wish-fulfilling tree called *Kalpataru*, the wish-fulfilling cow called *Kamadhenu* and the desire-fulfilling gem known as the *Chintamani.* Thus, *Lakshmi* brought with her everything that would give pleasure to humanity.

The gods, demons and sages all wanted to please the goddess and begged her to accept them but after inspecting all of them, she found some fault or the other with each of them and refused their advances. Looking around she found one being who was totally disinterested in what was going on. He was sitting alone, dangling his foot in the milky ocean and gazing out over the waters. This was *Vishnu* for whom she had been searching all her life. Taking the *Vanamala* (garland of wild flowers) in her hands she glided slowly towards him and placed the wedding garland round his neck. Hence, it is said that *Lakshmi* blesses those who do not run after her. She goes un-solicited and places her garland of plenty on those who worship her husband. *Vishnu* accepted her and gave her a place on his chest, next to his heart. He also declared that she was his *Shakti* and thus her name should always precede his. So they came to be known as *Lakshmi-Narayana.*

As *Vishnu's* consort, *Lakshmi* lost her reputation for fickleness. She became the model Hindu wife, loyal and submissive to her husband. She is mainly shown as sitting at the feet of her Lord and massaging his feet. The picture of *Lakshmi* at his feet, gives the message that one should not allow worldly power and riches to go to one's head. Wealth has the subtle ability to corrupt, and so one should always be careful in handling it. We have seen that *Lakshmi's* early history connected her with teeming vitality and prolific fertility. In her role as the wife of *Vishnu*, however, she is more involved in helping her husband to upkeep the order of *dharma* or righteousness in the world. Whenever *Vishnu* incarnated himself to uphold *dharma,* she incarnated along with him as his helpmate and consort.

The *Vishnu Purana* says, "As *Hari* descends in the world in various shapes so does his consort *Sri.* When *Hari* was born as a dwarf, the son of *Aditi*, she appeared in the form of a lotus. When he was *Raghava (Rama)*, she became *Sita*, when he was *Krishna,* she became *Rukmini.* In his other descents also she is his associate. When he takes a celestial form, she appears divine, if a mortal, she becomes a mortal too, transforming her own person to suit the character which her husband enacts".

In her role as a model wife she upholds the social order. Thus, it is said that she is always present in a house that is clean and beautifully kept, and to live with those who observe the correct social observances like telling the truth and who are generous and kind.

In the *Mahabharata* she says, "I dwell in truth, gifts, vows, austerities, strength and virtue."

All *Vaishnava* schools of philosophy insist that *Lakshmi* should always accompany *Vishnu* and be invoked along with him. In fact the devotee prays to her to intercede to her Lord on his behalf. She is the embodiment of divine compassion and she ensures easy approach to *Vishnu.*

Lakshmi is worshipped in every house, temple and shop throughout the country but the festival which is most connected with her is *Diwali* or *Dipavali*, the festival of lights, and *Navaratri* or the nine days worship of the divine mother in all her forms.

During the first three nights of the nine-day festival, the goddess is worshipped as *Maha Kaali,* in the next three nights, as *Maha Lakshmi* and the final three nights as *Maha Saraswati.* It is said that the *Maha Devi* stood on a point of a needle and did terrific *tapasya* for nine nights, thus transforming herself from the fierce, *tamasic Kaali* to the ravishing, *rajasic Lakshmi* and finally to the serene, *sattvic Saraswati.* Esoterically speaking, these nine days are to be divided by the spiritual aspirant in the following fashion. During the first three days we concentrate on *Kaali* and beg her to remove all our negative tendencies of hatred, fear, anger and jealousy. Then we start our worship of *Lakshmi* and beg her to replace these with the positive qualities of cheer, joy and love. In such a purified heart, *Saraswati,* the goddess of spiritual success, will deign to come and give us liberation. When we want to plant a garden we have to first root out the weeds and for this we need the help of *Kaali.* When the ground has been prepared we can invite *Lakshmi* to come and plant the flowers. Only then will *Saraswati* appear to give us the fruit.

Diwali or the festival of lights, is another celebration which is closely connected with *Lakshmi.* The actual festival falls on the new moon in late autumn – October/November. But the two days preceding and two days following the festival are also celebrated. On the thirteenth day of the waning moon, all types of shining vessels are brought to the house. Gold, silver, copper or steel vessels are bought according to one's capacity. These are the tangible manifestations of the goddess. The next day is known as *Naraka Chaturdasi,* which is the day on which Lord *Krishna* defeated the demon *Naraka* and rescued the ten thousand damsels who had been incarcerated in *Naraka's* dungeon.

Diwali falls on the new moon day, which is the darkest night of the month. At this time every house is lit with hundreds of little lamps to welcome the goddess. It was on this day that she is supposed to have risen from the milky ocean. On this night the sun enters the constellation of Libra – the scales. Hence, all businessmen balance their accounts on this day and invite *Lakshmi* to come and take up her abode in their shops and houses. On the next day it is usual to distribute new clothes and food to everyone, especially the poor.

The basis of Hindu religious life is to discover our true nature. Before we do this, however, we have to experience life the way it is – to know both its bounties and its pain. For both these we need to worship *Lakshmi*, for she is the divine provider, the source of all nourishment. *Adi Shankara*, the exponent of *Advaita Vedanta*, which asserts the ephemeral nature of life, wrote a famous hymn to *Lakshmi* known as the *Kanakadara Stotram*, which means "the hymn which will make gold flow". This shows that even he, ascetic though he was, realised the necessity of the blessings of *Lakshmi* in temporal life.

"May the eyes that are spellbound by the beauty of *Vishnu*,
Fall on me and bestow upon me prosperity and happiness."
"Salutations to the lotus-faced goddess who emerged from the ocean of milk, along with the moon and the elixir of immortality and became *Narayana's* bride."
"May the breeze of her compassion bring the clouds of prosperity,
And pour rain on the barren life of this poor bird,
And wash away its accumulated demerits."
"With my impoverished heart I surrender myself to your compassion,
That you may watch over me, bless me and forgive me."

— "Kanakadara Stotram" by Adi Shankaracharya

Thus ends the twenty-first chapter of the *Sri Devi Lila* known as 'Lakshmi', which describes *Lakshmi*, the goddess of auspiciousness.

ॐ *Aim, hreem, kleem* ॐ

"O Lord of Fire! Do thou bring Lakshmi,
Who is like a golden deer with glowing body,
Who is playful, adorned with gold and silver,
And who gives pleasure to all, like the moon."

— Sri Suktam, *Rig Veda*

ॐ

Saraswatyai Namaha!

CHAPTER TWENTY-TWO

MAHA SARASWATI

Chithirupena ya krthsnam ethat vyapya sthitha jagat,
Namasthasyai, Namasthasyai, Namasthasyai Namo Namaha!

"She, who abides in this whole world,
Having pervaded it in the form of mind,
Hail to Thee! Hail to Thee! All Hail to Thee!"

Since the universe is the creation of *Maha Prakriti,* the body of the goddess has been identified with different parts of the world as described in the *Devi Bhagavatam.* The earth is her loins, the oceans, her bowels, the mountains, her bones, the rivers, her veins and the trees, the hair on her body. The sun and moon are her eyes and the nether worlds, her hips, legs and feet. She wears the stars as ornaments in her hair.

Unlike other countries, India has a sacred geography. The whole of the Indian sub-continent is a repository of divine power. Every region in India is dotted with sacred and holy places. The sacredness of the land, rather than the unity of its political set-up, has been the force that has made India into a unified nation. The whole of the sub-continent has been rendered sacred by the different parts of the body of *Sati,* which had been scattered by *Shiva* through the length and breadth of the land. The *Puranas* depict the whole of India as a goddess. She is known as *Bharata Mata* – Mother India. Indians consider themselves to be children of Mother India. In many places like *Haridwar* and *Varanasi,* there are temples dedicated to Mother India. The land itself is an inspiring and nourishing presence to all those who are born in it. The Indian national anthem written by Sri Rabindranath Tagore, portrays this feeling in a most beautiful form.

"Thou art the ruler of the minds of all people,
Dispenser of India's destiny,
Thy name arouses the hearts of Punjab, Sind, Gujarat and Maratha.
Of Dravida, Orissa and Bengal.
It echoes in the hills of the *Vindhyas* and the *Himalayas.*
Mingles with the music of *Yamuna* and *Ganga,*
And is chanted by the waves of the Indian Sea.
They pray for thy blessings and sing thy praise,
The safety of all people reposes in thy hands,
Thou dispenser of India's destiny,
Victory, Victory, Victory to Thee!"

Each act of worship to any village goddess is considered to be an act of worship to the divinity of India as a whole. Every river is a *tirtha* or sacred water. Hence, we find that sanctity is conferred on almost every river in the Indian sub-continent. This reverence goes back all the way to the *Rig Veda* where it is said that all the Indian rivers had their origin in the heavens. The earthly river is only a continuation of the waters that flow from heaven to earth.

In the *Vedas, Saraswati* was worshipped as a river. Her name actually means "watery". The early Indians considered this river to be most sacred. At that time the position she held is similar to what the *Ganga* holds today. *Ganga* is actually the prototype of all the rivers of India. All the waters of this land share her magic power of salvation, though to a lesser degree.

The *Rig Veda* proclaims that the river *Saraswati* is a goddess, who blesses her devotees with health, long life and poetic inspiration. The earthly river is only a partial manifestation of the heavenly deity. Six thousand years ago this river is supposed to have flowed through the region of *Rajasthan.* It was a huge river and the waves were so big that they could even break down mountains. It is said to have had its source in the celestial ocean and thus it was inexhaustible. But two thousand years ago it vanished and the region turned into a desert. It is believed that it became a subterranean river, which flowed underground and joined the two great rivers of India, *Ganga* and *Yamuna* in the holy place of *Prayaga.* This is the place where the three sacred rivers of the Indian sub-continent converge. Hence, this confluence is known as *Tirtharaja* or the king of all *tirthas.* It is said that anyone who stays on the banks of the *Saraswati* reciting the *Saraswati mantra*, will become a poet.

Anticipating her later nature as the goddess of learning, the hymns of the *Rig Veda* describe *Saraswati* as the one who inspires all songs and all gracious thought. In fact she is similar to the *Vedic* goddess of speech, *Vac.* The ability to turn the unintelligible sounds that come out of the mouth into forms that can be understood by others is a unique ability of the human being alone, and the Hindus have great respect for this. Hence, a goddess was created as the goddess of speech. Sound is the primordial stuff of creation. The *Vedas* declare that ritual speech is a most powerful tool for invoking the powers of nature and making them obey the will of man. It is the power of the goddess *Vac* that inspired the *rishis* and enabled them to hymn the divine. She is the mysterious presence that enables us to hear, see, grasp and express in words the nature of the world – both inner and outer. Thus, she is an essential part of our spiritual experiences. The *Vedas* describe her as a glowing being, benign and bounteous – who confers on everyone the riches of language. It is due to her grace that we can communicate with each other.

In the modern world we take language for granted but the ancient Indians venerated speech. When we come to think about it, we will realise that the ability to formulate complex concepts and communicate them through sound is a great accomplishment. The power to think is itself a great ability, but the power to communicate those thoughts to another, through speech, is a remarkable gift given to us by goddess *Saraswati.* The great grammarian *Panini* was considered a sage. He venerated the goddess and discovered the remarkable quality possessed by words to produce certain emotions in us. The words themselves are products of our thoughts but these words when articulated through the mouth, have the ability to transform other people's thinking patterns and produce still further thoughts. *Panini* was fascinated by words. His grammar is not a dull, routine and boring subject but the very source of inspiration and devotion. As the embodiment of speech, *Saraswati* is present whenever and wherever a word is spoken.

Since *Saraswati* is the goddess of speech, it follows that she is also the goddess of the intellect, which makes coherent speech possible. She is not only the power of knowledge but also the power of memory. She is behind this infinity of forms found in the universe and is responsible for the infinity of things created by the human mind. Thus, she is the mother of all sciences (*Sarvavidya Swarupini*) – she whose form is all sciences. Not only is she the mother of all sciences but also the mother of all arts. She inspires poets, musicians, writers and dancers. Whenever we see great culture or great art or extraordinary intelligence we can know that *Saraswati* has manifested herself. *Saraswati* has enabled the human race to become superior to other creatures, and has bestowed her grace so that mankind can stride across the world as demi-gods. Artistic creations and the power of knowledge, including philosophy, demonstrate the extraordinary ability of the human being to mould and refine the natural world into something noble and divine. Thus, *Saraswati* is the energy of cosmic creativity that is reflected in us.

Maha Saraswati is the Divine Mother's power of intelligence, perfection and order. *Maha Devi* lays down the large lines of the world order. *Maha Kaali* drives everything before her with her energy and impetus. *Maha Lakshmi* points out the beauty of their rhythms and harmony, and *Maha Saraswati* provides the intelligence, which details their organization and execution. She is the third of the goddesses who are worshipped during the nine-days (*Navaratri*) festival of worship of the Divine Mother. The first three days are devoted to *Maha Kaali*, who roots out our negative qualities, the next three days to *Maha Lakshmi* who plants in us all beauty and virtue, and the final three days to *Maha Saraswati* who finally gives us liberation.

Saraswati's symbols and character contrast dramatically with those of *Lakshmi*. *Saraswati* is clad in pure white and *Lakshmi* in red. *Saraswati's* only ornament is a pearl necklace or one of crystals, while *Lakshmi* bedecks herself with fabulous jewels. *Saraswati* holds books, pens and the lute in her hands while *Lakshmi* holds lotuses and the pitcher of plenty. *Saraswati* is associated with the wind – free and unbound – and thus she rides on a swan. *Lakshmi* is seated on a lotus and is associated with earth and water, bound and flowing. *Lakshmi's* name is coupled with many male divinities but *Saraswati* is associated with only *Brahma*, a god who is never worshipped. *Lakshmi's* colour is that of turmeric and gold while *Saraswati* is fair as the full moon.

Brahma is the creator in the trinity. As *Brahma Shakti* she is that power which enables human beings to create anything. Out of the nameless and formless, she makes this world of forms and names that we can experience.

She is the goddess of inspiration, eloquence and learning. All children have to worship her before they start their lessons. Many schools and colleges in India have statues of *Saraswati* to provide inspiration to the students. Initiation into all learning begins with an invocation to *Saraswati.* Before a child is sent to school, he has to go through a ritual called '*vidyarambham*' or the commencement of learning and for this the supreme deity to be worshipped is *Saraswati*, the giver of all knowledge.

As we have seen before *Saraswati* was originally the wife of Lord *Vishnu* but due to the curse of *Ganga* she was born on earth as a river. She was called *Bharati* since she came to the land known as *Bharata Varsha.* She is also known as *Vani* since she is the presiding deity of speech. Later she became *Brahma's* wife. However, she quickly over-shadowed her spouse. Hardly anyone in India worships *Brahma* but the whole country worships *Saraswati.* She is rarely shown seated next to him, even when they are seen together. Their relationship seems more intellectual than conjugal. She is his dynamic counterpart and holds the *Vedas* in her hands and thus she is said to be the creator of the three *Vedas.* Each *Veda* is connected with one of the elements. *Rig Veda* is connected to the earth, *Yajur Veda* to air and *Sama Veda* to the sky.

Brahma's creations are all mental. It is *Saraswati* who actually manifests these ideas, which are in the form of divine vibrations, into concrete forms. It is she who stirs the still lake of the undisturbed energy of the Absolute into the living stream of life. The first manifestation of the *Brahman* is *Sabda Brahman* or sound. This is called *spanda,* the mysterious vibration of sound that we hear as '*Aum*'. *Saraswati* is the living form of this sound, so she is known as *Nada Brahman.* In the *Rig Vedic* hymn known as the *Saraswati Rahasya Upanishad*, the goddess herself says:

"It was through me that the creator gained liberating knowledge,
I am Pure Being, consciousness, bliss, eternal freedom,
Unsullied, unlimited, unending.
My perfect consciousness shines in the world like a beautiful face in a soiled mirror.
Seeing that reflection I call myself you – the individual *jiva*,
Pretending to be finite."

Maha Saraswati is the Divine Mother's power for accomplishing all types of works and her spirit of perfection and order. There is none to beat her in the executive faculty. She is the drive behind the impetus of all nature. She demands exactitude and certainty. That is why science, crafts and techniques come under her province. Those who are blessed by her, have subtlety and patience, the certainty of the intuitive mind and the discerning eye of the perfect worker. Her will is scrupulous and indefatigable though it might be slow. She is conscious of every detail and insists on flawless performance. Nothing is too small or trivial for her attention. Both in the individual and in the universe, she moulds every part until it fits perfectly into the role meant for it. If one submits to her will, she will choose for us the right time and the right place and the right conditions to produce the perfect piece of work. She dislikes carelessness, negligence and indolence. Nothing short of perfection will satisfy her. She is ready to face an eternity of toil if necessary to bring perfection to her creation. If we are single pointed and determined to succeed, her hand will sustain our every effort. She is intolerant of falsehood and pretence. In the spiritual life, she is the one who drives us forward, provided we are sincere in our perseverance. She will never leave us until we have attained our goal.

Her form is beautiful. She is described as being as fair as the white lily, or the moon or the garlands formed by snow crystals. She is clad in spotless white garments. She is seated on a white lotus and carries the *veena* in one hand. She is worshipped by *Brahma, Vishnu* and *Shiva.* The white garments show that her form is that of pure *shuddha tattva* (purest element), the first emanation from the *Brahman.* Thus, she is entirely formed of *sattva guna*, which is the pure, spiritual thread of nature. Her *sattvic* nature dissociates her from the mud of existence, including the sap of fertility to which many of the other goddesses are closely related. Her motherhood is metaphorical. She gives birth to ideas and inspirations. She is said to have an ascetic nature and grants boons to those who perform *tapasya.* Therefore, she is not a goddess of the householder or the farmer but of the intellectual, of the ascetic – the student and the artist.

She is normally shown seated on a white lotus. This shows her transcendence. Although having its source in the mud, the lotus lifts its head and opens itself to the glorious sun, untouched by the muddy waters below. *Saraswati* inspires human beings to transcend their physical limitations and enter the realm of the arts and thus reach for the heavens.

Her vehicle, which is the swan, also points out her uplifting nature, far removed from the impurities of the natural world with its rhythms of growth and fertility. The word for swan is "hamsa" in Sanskrit. It can be cut into two words "ham-sa" or "so-ham". Every inhalation of ours has the sound "so" and every exhalation has the sound "ham". When you keep saying this rapidly it becomes "ham-sa". Therefore the swan which is Saraswati's vehicle denotes the breath of life. She is the one who gives us freedom from the thraldom of material life and takes us to the glories of a life beyond the senses. The swan is a symbol of spiritual transcendence in Hinduism. It is supposed to have the power to separate milk from water. So also great *yogis* have the power to separate the milk of immortal life from the water of material life. Such *yogis* are known as *paramahamsas*, or great swans. *Saraswati* is always gliding over this tangible universe of energy that we see, seated on her white swan, pointing out to us a different dimension of human existence above the physical world of the senses. Her realm is one of perfection, beauty, culture and grace.

Saraswati has four hands. One carries the *veena* or lute, which produces the vibration of life. The sound of the *veena* is the origin of the *Sama Veda.* One who has the ears of wisdom will be able to hear the whole world vibrating to the sound of her *veena.* If we put our ear to a conch we will hear that *Nada Brahman.* In fact the whole world of objects is nothing but the material manifestation of the sound of her lute. We know that the visible world is made up of forms and all forms have names and all names are only a combination of sounds. Thus, out of sounds come names or *nama* and from that is created form or *rupa.* Of all languages, Sanskrit is the one in which the sound of the word most closely approximates the form. The *rishis* made a study of the science of sounds, and found that all the *mantras* are sounds that carry within them the image of the form of the deity, which they are meant to invoke. Thus, everything we see or know is the vibration of *Saraswati's veena.* In another hand she carries the *Veda.* This suggests that she holds all knowledge in her hands, both material as well as transcendental. The *Vedas* signify the totality of all knowledge – both of things that can be known as well as that, which lie beyond thought.

In another hand she holds the spotless crystal *mala* denoting the necessity of putting *Vedic* knowledge into practice. The *japa mala* (rosary) indicates the necessity for continuous spiritual practice or *sadhana.* Thus, she stands for both the theory and practice of *yogic* knowledge. Every aspirant knows that continuous practice is essential for success in *sadhana.*

She is at once the origin and the conclusion of the evolutionary process of the *jiva* from ignorance to enlightenment. But it must be remembered that she not only gives us material knowledge but also supreme wisdom. The *jiva* in its entanglement with matter gets enmeshed in her role as *Maha Maya.* But at the end of its evolutionary cycle, when the *jiva* longs to trace its journey back to the source from which it came, it has to worship *Maha Saraswati*, for she is the giver of *Brahma jnana* or supreme knowledge. It is a circle in which the *jiva* is projected from knowledge, to ignorance and back to knowledge. *Maha Saraswati* is both the origin and conclusion of this process of evolution. The seeker of knowledge as well as the seeker of enlightenment has to look for her grace.

She is present in word form in every book. By reading the scriptures regularly we are worshipping her. By speaking the truth and by speaking sweetly we are worshipping her, for her *veena* has no discordant tones. During the nine days of the worship of the divine mother, in the month of October, the final day or the tenth day is called *Vijayadasami* – the day of victory when the aspirant finally cuts the knots of ignorance which have bound him to the mundane world, and gains victory over his ego and is united with the supreme. This day is dedicated to goddess *Saraswati.*

"Goddess of wisdom, who appears as syllables,
Words, sentences and understanding,
Goddess in whom all meaning inheres,
From beginingless time, grant me your grace.
Goddess who purifies and enriches the soul,
You who are the treasurer of intelligence,
Please accept these words, my humble offering!"

— "Saraswati Rahasya Upanishad"

Thus ends the twenty-second chapter of the *Sri Devi Lila* known as 'Saraswati', which describes the goddess *Saraswati.*

ॐ *Aim, hreem, kleem* ॐ

ॐ

Sri Radhayai Namaha!

CHAPTER TWENTY-THREE

RADHA

"O *Devi Radhika*! Your colour is like the white champaka flower.
Your face is like the autumnal full moon;
Your body shines with the spleandour of ten million moons,
Your eyes are as beautiful as the autumnal lotus;
Your lips are red as the *bimba* fruit;
Your loins are heavy and decked with a girdle;
Your gracious face is sweetly smiling;
Your breasts defy the frontal lobe of an elephant;
You are ever youthful;
Your body is adorned with ornaments;
You form the waves of the ocean of erotic love;
You are ever ready to show your grace to all devotees;
Your hair is braided with jasmine;
Your body is as tender as a creeper;
You are seated in the middle of the *raasa mandalam*;
One hand shows the mudra of fearlessness and the other of granting boons;
You are dearer to *Krishna* than his life.
O *Parameswari*! The *Vedas* reveal your true nature."

— *Sama Veda*

The advent of the Lord as *Krishna*, the *Purushottama* or the Supreme personality of God, is one that is well known to the world. But the esoteric significance of *Radha* – his soul companion – has not been fully understood.

Her life is inextricably connected with *Krishna* and she is hardly ever mentioned by herself. It is always *Radha-Krishna*. She was the daughter of a herdsman called *Vrishabhanu* and was born in the little village of *Barsana*, close to *Vraja* where *Krishna* spent his childhood. The *gopis* were milkmaids and some of them were the wives of the *gopalas* who were cowherds. The village they lived in was known as *Gokulam* or *Vraja*. *Krishna* was brought up as the son of *Nandagopa*, chief of the cowherds, even though his actual father was *Vasudeva*, a nobleman of the *Yadava* clan. Through fear of *Kamsa*, the king of their clan, his father transferred the baby *Krishna* to the village of *Vraja* and exchanged him for the baby girl who had just been born to their chief, *Nandagopa*.

His foster parents, *Yasoda* and *Nandagopa* fully believed him to be their son and he was brought up like any other *gopala* (cow-herd) boy. In the village of *Vraja*, and later in the woods and glades of the forest of *Vrindavana*, the boy *Krishna* performed many miracles that form the very core of his amazing life and are sung by bards to this very day. The cow-herd women doted on *Krishna* as a baby and as a child. But their interest changed to passionate longing for him when he grew older. Many of them were married women but none were able to resist his beauty and charm. Even though he was only twelve years old at that time, *Krishna's* appeal was irresistible. Everyone and everything was drawn to him – the cows, the herdsmen, the trees, and the boys. What wonder that the *gopis* felt as if they could not exist without him! There were hundreds of *gopis* and all of them felt that he alone was their Lord and Master. Nothing could deter the mad rush of their hearts towards him, not even the bonds of marriage.

The young *gopis* did forty-one days of adoration and worship of the Divine Mother, *Kartyayini*, and begged her to enable them to achieve their hearts' desire and get the son of *Nandagopa* – *Krishna* as their husband!

"Kartyayini, Mahamaye, Mahayogin, Yateeswari,
Nandagopa Sutam Devi, Pathim me kuruthe mama."

— *Bhagavad Purana*

In the month of *Chaitra*, they would bathe in the cold waters of the river *Kalindi* at four in the morning and worship the goddess with this *mantra*. Their idol was made out of the river sand. Finally, on the last day of their vow while they were bathing naked in the river, the Lord of their hearts arrived, looking like a veritable Cupid. He decided to teach them the most important lesson in the life of any true devotee. With a teasing glance in their direction, he took away the clothes they had left on the banks and perched himself on the branch of a tree. He hung the clothes on different branches and told them to come out of the water and get their clothes one by one. They begged and pleaded with him but he was adamant.

He asked them, "How did you get into the water"? "You must have left the clothes on the banks and jumped in naked. If you felt no shame being with each other, why should you feel shame with me? Don't you know that I am the *Paramatman* and you are part of me? There is nothing about you that I don't know".

At last they came out of the water one by one and received their clothes from his hands. He then blessed and promised them that he would satisfy their desires on the full moon nights of the autumn season.

This is one of the most misunderstood scenes in the life of Krishna. But it has a deep esoteric significance that has to be understood before we can proceed on the path of devotion. There are many bonds that separate the *jivatman* from the *Paramatman*. The main bond is the one of the body. Considering ourselves to be the body alone, we have wilfully cut ourselves off from our inner reality. As long as this sense of separation exists we can never attain union with the Supreme. The *gopis* have been eulogised as the greatest examples of pure *bhakti* or devotion to God, without any trace of selfishness. Even though this was the truth, they still had one bond left and that was the one to their body. This was the final attachment, which Krishna had to remove before he could grant them the fulfilment of their desires, which was union with him who was the embodiment of the Supreme Reality. This was the reason why he asked them to come naked and receive their clothes from him without shame and without the feeling of separateness.

The highest *yogis* in Hinduism are known as *avadhutas* or those who wear no clothes. These great souls have cast off their attachment to their bodies and as a symbol of this detachment they have discarded their clothes, since clothes symbolise one's attachment to the body. Before he could give them the ultimate experience, *Krishna* had to transform the *gopis* into *avadhutas*. This is the esoteric and deeply meaningful significance of this scene. We carry our impure minds before God and fail to understand his great mystery. We are incapable of having experienced true love even in our own lives since we are all hypocrites. So how can we ever understand the meaning of these two mysterious stories in the life of *Krishna.* We are never true to ourselves, so how can we be true to God?

The famous episode known as the *Rasa Lila* in which *Krishna* danced with the *gopis* took place in the forest of *Vrindavana* on the full moon night of the month of *Kartika* (October/November). The Lord took his stance under a tree in the forest at night just as the moon started to rise and played on his celestial flute. The notes were heard in far-off *Vraja* and brought thrills of delight to the hearts of the *gopis.* It is said that in the mad rush of their hearts towards him, who was the beloved of the whole of creation, the *gopis* forgot all their external bonds – their duties to their husbands, parents and even to their children. Leaving all their unfinished chores, hundreds of them ran to the forest, totally oblivious of everything except the call of their divine beloved. This was the enticing call of the *Paramatman,* the Supreme Soul, to the *jivatman,* the embodied soul encased in the gown of the body. How could they resist it? All the duties of a normal Hindu woman were totally forgotten.

The human being has only one basic duty, and that is to attain union with God. Until we realise this, we are bound to perform all the other duties imposed on us by the society and by our own nature and desires. But the moment this supreme duty becomes paramount in our minds, all other duties can be forgotten. Such a person has no more duties to perform, for she expects nothing from the world. Her entire dependence is on God alone and therefore she is exempt from all worldly duties. This was the state of the *gopis* of *Vrindavana* and that is why they are worshipped to this day as the greatest examples of devotion. Unfortunately, sensual minds fail to grasp the significance of these great episodes in the life of *Krishna* and make their own base interpretations of something that is most holy and exalted.

The full moon night in the month of *Kartika* was the day promised by *Krishna* to the *gopis* at the conclusion of their forty-one day vow. That day had arrived and they could not resist his call. In their eagerness to reach their beloved they had forgotten to put on their make-up or even to dress properly. No one noticed the state in which the others were, since their minds were concentrated totally on their beloved. The state of their mind was that of a meditating *yogi,* single-pointed and fixed on *Krishna.* He tenderly attended to the perfection of their toilette before leading them to the clearing in the woods, which was the perfect setting for the dance that is known as the *Rasa Lila.*

In this dance every *gopi* found herself to be partnered by a *Krishna*, so that there were hundreds of *Krishnas* and hundreds of *gopis.* There was yet another *Krishna* in the middle of the circle who was playing the flute and supplying the music for their dance. This is an allegory of the dance of life which the *Paramatman* plays with each *jivatman.* Each one feels that God is her very own, just as every *gopi* felt that *Krishna* belonged to her alone. At that time the ego reared its ugly head in the breasts of the *gopis* and they felt that they had conquered *Krishna* by their charm and beauty. At that moment it is said that the Lord disappeared from their midst and they were left bereft.

The only one who had no ego was *Radha* and that was the reason why she was *Krishna's* favourite. She lived in a world peopled by *Krishna* alone (*Krishnamayam jagat*). Some books say that she was married. But she cared not for any worldly ties. For a few short years, she lived in blissful companionship and love with her beloved. *Radha* is the supreme model of love for *Krishna. Radha's* love and therefore her fame are far above that of his wives. Why has this illicit love been extolled in the life of *Krishna,* is another pertinent question. This again has a deep esoteric significance. A wife gives up nothing to go to her husband. The marital ties are supported by the society and she has nothing to lose. In fact she gains the security of a husband and a fair name in society and may look forward to a protected life and an old age supported by her husband and the children to come. On the other hand, a woman who steals out in the middle of the night to meet her lover, is despised by society and has no rights over her lover. He might desert her at any moment. But she cares not for these material things. She is prepared to sacrifice everything for the sake of her love. She gives up her fair name and her chastity and demands nothing in return. She gives up everything that is precious to a woman without any thought of recompense. This is the height of selfless love! A wife's love can never compete with this. This is why the *Bhagavad Purana* extols the illicit love of the *gopis* as the highest of any form of love.

Only the soul which is prepared to give up everything for the sake of God will be accepted by him as his very own. Hence is *Radha* so dear to *Krishna.* The frenzy and ecstasy of their union is heightened by the constant threat of separation. At last the inevitable happens and *Krishna* leaves *Vraja*, never to return again. But his love for *Radha* never diminished and hers for him, for theirs was the union of the *jivatman* with the *Paramatman* and physical distance could never separate them. *Krishna's* love for *Radha* is depicted as being as deep as or even deeper than hers for him. The love that God bears for his devotee is far stronger than what the human heart can feel for God. Hence, all the great poems written in India about their amazing love affair, stress *Krishna's* love for *Radha* equally as hers for him.

The *Radha-Krishna* relationship typifies the pinnacle of all devotion and is a most graphic metaphor for the human-divine love affair. This relationship is what every devotee wants to achieve with her own *ishta devata* or favourite deity. The *Bhagavad Purana* does not mention *Radha's* name even though it does mention one *gopi* who was *Krishna's* favourite. However, there is a deep esoteric significance attached to the relationship between *Radha* and *Krishna.* It is a mystery that the ordinary human mind just cannot fathom. We rarely experience intense love in our lives. We are never true to ourselves and therefore never true to God. We are all mediocre devotees, with weak bodies and frail minds and raging emotions that cannot be controlled. The fire of supreme love cannot be contained within our weak frames.

The *Puranas* say, "Speech and mind turn back from that which they are not supposed to express or understand." Human beings have a certain mode of thinking which we are not prepared to change even for the purpose of attaining God. There is a fear in the human mind of losing the approbation of the society. There is also a fear of losing one's own individuality in the ocean of love that God offers. We are bound by the shackles of the society that divides us into men and women, rich and poor, good and bad, and Indian or American. Until we strip ourselves of these false values, like the *gopis* did, and stand naked before God, we will never be able to understand the mystery of love between *Radha* and *Krishna.* God is beyond all relationships. He demands nothing short of complete abnegation of the individual ego from the one who wants to be his beloved. All our prides and prejudices have to melt before God, the supra-relational Being. This melting of the human individuality is called *bhakti.* This is what *Krishna* demanded of the *gopis.* They were prepared for anything. There was nothing half-hearted or mediocre in their love for *Krishna. Radha's* love for him reached the consummation of any other form of love.

Later, poetical works and especially in the love poems of *Jayadeva* called *Gita Govinda,* the picture of *Radha* is clearly drawn. In the *Bhagavad Purana,* the play of *Krishna* with the *gopis* has a festive, joyful appearance like a carnival. In the *Gita Govinda,* the stress is on the sorrow felt by the woman (*Radha*) when separated from her lover. This is known as *viraha dukkha.* This is an emotion that is felt by all lovers of God when he fails to manifest himself even after years of constant prayer and supplication. This anguish of separation is something that has been experienced by every ardent devotee. These poems written by the twelfth century poet, *Jayadeva,* portray in full, the deep sense of despair and loneliness that the soul experiences when separated from the cosmic beloved. All *Jayadeva's* poems are written from the point of view of *Radha* and they take place in the secrecy and stillness of night in the woods, and they certainly do not have the approval of society. They explore the interior landscapes of a mind, obsessed by the love of God, in this case *Krishna.* But it can apply equally well to any devotee who has felt this sense of desolation and sorrow at the separation from God. The pathos in these poems will bring tears to the eyes of a loving reader.

Radha's illicit love for *Krishna* is also the central theme in the poetry of *Vidyapati* (1352-1448) and *Chandidasa,* also a fourteenth century poet. *Vidyapati* describes *Radha* as a woman of a noble family and *Krishna* as a common villager in order to show the extent of sacrifice that *Radha* was prepared to make in order to consummate her love.

She cares not for her status or her reputation. "If I go to him, I lose my home; if I stay I lose my love!" Is what she says. Needless to say, she always chose *Krishna* as any true devotee would. In recent times we find another such perfect example of true love that did not allow anything to stand in its path. *Mira,* the princess of *Mewar,* sacrificed her husband and her country and became a beggar in order to follow her beloved *Krishna.*

In the *Vaishnava* cult, which considers *Krishna* as the supreme incarnation of God, *Radha* plays a prominent role. In the sixteenth century, a great devotee of *Krishna* known as *Chaitanya,* was born in Bengal. In his own devotion to *Krishna*, he underwent the sufferings of *Radha.* She has continued to play a central role in the subsequent history of this movement.

In Hindu philosophy, the devotee is allowed to approach God in many ways. In the *shanta bhava* or the contemplative mood, God is considered as transcendent. In the *dasya bhava* or the role of the servant, God is the master. In the *vatsalya bhava* or the attitude of a parent, the Lord is thought of as a child. In the *sakhya bhava* or the role of a friend, the Lord is considered as a friend. Finally, the culmination of all devotional moods is said to be the *mathurya bhava* or the mood of ecstatic love in which the Lord is considered to be the lover as in the case of the *gopis.*

The superiority of illicit love is given great stress in all the schools of *Vaishnavism.* As has been mentioned before, married love has its basis on rights and obligations in which both partners have specific demands and duties. They may easily stop loving each other when either partner does not come up to these expectations. Even their physical love is characterised by selfish desire and is for the gratification of their sexual lust. It is known as *Kama.* There are no obstacles in the path of their love and thus it tends to become monotonous and boring.

The *Radha-Krishna* relationship, however, is based on *prema* or unselfish love. The impediments that *Radha* has to face only increase her love and longing. The long periods of separation help to enhance her feelings. There is no boredom. Her love is faced with risk and filled with insecurity. The painful periods of separation only augment the thrill of union. This is why this type of relationship has been extolled as the highest in the human-divine love affair. The devotee's affair with the cosmic beloved knows no waning or boredom. God is the perfect lover and the devotee has to be always on guard, always keeping her mind on him alone. God does not tolerate any adulterous behaviour on the part of the perfect devotee. She cannot have partial love for the world and partly for him. If she does, then like the *gopis* she will find that *Krishna* has deserted her. Then like *Radha*, she would have to weep and beg and pray incessantly till he deigns to reveal himself again. The Lord plays a game of hide and seek with the devotee. He is always free to come and go and the devotee often has to spend long periods in painful separation from him.

Radha is the paradigm of complete devotion. Her mind is totally obsessed with *Krishna*, and she cannot forget him even for a moment. Her total absorption in him is contrasted to the fleeting glimpses which meditating sages and ascetics attain of the Lord after arduous spiritual exercises. In many sects of *Vaishnavism*, especially in Bengal, *Radha* herself is worshipped. *Krishna* has many *shaktis* within himself; the most essential of these is the *hladini shakti* or the power of bliss. This power or *shakti* is the most sublime and refined essence of God. *Radha* is supposed to be the embodiment of this *shakti*. In this aspect, his sport with her is an expression of his dalliance with himself – the Supreme, revelling in his own bliss.

The *Devi Bhagavatam* identifies *Radha* with *Mula Prakriti* or the original cause of this universe. *Radha* is the presiding deity of *prana* and *Durga* of *buddhi*. These two *shaktis* guide the whole world. Liberation cannot be obtained without satisfying them. The six-syllabled *mantra* of *Radha* is '*Sri Radhayai svaaha*!' *Radha* is *Krishna's prana* and all *Krishna* worshippers should worship her first of all. She is the queen of *Vraja* and the chief participant in the *Rasa Lila*. The poem given at the beginning of this chapter is a hymn invoking her, which the devotee has to chant at the beginning of the *puja* done on the full moon night of the month of *Kartika*, when the *Rasa Lila* is supposed to have taken place. She is to be seated on a golden throne along with *Krishna* and worshipped as *Mula Prakriti*. Thus, we find that during the course of history, *Radha's* role changed from being the supreme devotee of *Krishna* to being considered as a goddess in her own right. This is to show us that God elevates his pure devotees to his own status.

"O friend, I cannot tell you,
Whether he was near or far, real or a dream
Like a vein of lightning,
As I chained the dark one,
I felt a river flooding in my heart,
Like a shining moon.
I devoured that liquid face,
I felt stars shooting around me."

— Vidyapati

Thus ends the twenty-third chapter of the *Sri Devi Lila* known as 'Radha', which describes the greatness of *Radha*, the goddess of love.

ॐ *Aim, hreem, kleem* ॐ

"Deep is my agony on this night of separation.
When will the streaks of golden dawn appear?
The moonlight is no comfort to me,
If I sleep I wake as if startled by a dream.
O Merciful One! Deprived of you I lie in anguish.
Bless me then with a vision of your face,
Lost am I save for love of you,
None can know the depth of my despair,
My moments of weariness.
Unless you stretch forth your helping hand O Lord!
How can I reach the further shore?"

— Mira Bhajan

ॐ

Vrindavanyai Namaha!

CHAPTER TWENTY-FOUR

TULASI

Namastulasi kalyani,
Namo Vishnu priye shubhe
Namo moksha prade Devi,
Namah sampad pradayini.

'Salutations to *Tulasi*, the auspicious,
Salutations to the propitious beloved of *Vishnu*,
Salutations to the goddess who gives liberation.
Salutations to the one who gives all prosperity."

— *Hymn to Tulasi*

Tulasi had been a *gopi* in *Goloka,* the celestial abode of *Krishna* where *Radha Rani* is the queen. Once she had incurred *Radha's* displeasure and been cursed by her to be born in the world as a human being. *Tulasi* had only one desire in her mind and that was to be united with Lord *Krishna* or *Narayana.*

She was born on earth as the daughter of King *Vrishadvaja* and the celestially beautiful *Madhavi.* The queen had become pregnant due to the blessings of a *deva.* She carried the baby for a hundred years and at last gave birth to a baby girl on a most auspicious day, the full moon day of the month of *Kartika*, at a time when all the planets were in favourable positions. The baby was an incarnation of *Lakshmi*, the consort of *Vishnu.* She was a most enchanting infant with all auspicious signs. She was named *Tulasi.* She remembered her past life perfectly and as soon as she reached the age of puberty she decided to go to the most ancient and spiritual spot in the *Himalayas*, known as *Badrikashrama*, to do *tapasya* in order to get Lord *Narayana* as her husband. Nothing and no one could deter her determination and she practiced austerities for many years, subsisting for a long time only on fruits, then on leaves, then air alone. At last *Brahma* manifested himself and told her to ask for a boon.

She informed *Brahma* that her only desire was to get Lord *Narayana* as her husband and she had done *tapasya* only with this aim. *Brahma* declared that getting *Narayana* as a husband was not such an easy thing and before she got her desire, she would have to go through a period of time as the wife of another person called *Shankachuda* who had been practicing penance for many years in order to get her as his wife. He gave her an outline of this person's previous life.

Shankachuda had been a *gopala* called *Sudama* who had been a close friend of *Krishna* in *Goloka*. *Radha* had cursed him that he would become a demon because he had become enamoured of *Tulasi*. *Brahma* told *Tulasi* that she would have to marry this *asura* since he was also a devotee of *Krishna* and had set his heart on marrying her. After many trials she would get the blessings of Lord *Vishnu* and be changed into a plant. This plant would be beloved by *Narayana*. No *puja* of his would be complete without the offering of *tulasi* leaves. She would be born in the forest of *Vrindavana* and would also be known as *Vrindavani*. All devotees of *Krishna* would have to offer *tulasi* leaves at his feet in order to please him. She would be as dear to *Krishna* as *Radha*. Thus, *Radha's* curse was truly a blessing to the whole world since the *tulasi* plant has high medicinal properties. *Tulasi* was very happy to hear this and continued to live in *Badrikashrama*, contemplating on the lotus feet of Lord *Narayana*.

In the meantime, the *gopala*, *Shankachuda*, who had been turned into an *asura* by *Radha's* curse, had been doing severe penance at the only holy spot dedicated to *Brahma*, known as *Pushkara*. *Brahma* appeared to him and told him to proceed to *Badrikashrama* where he would attain his heart's desire. When *Shankachuda* reached *Tulasi's* hermitage and saw her, his love for her in his previous birth overwhelmed him. He ran to her and knelt at her feet and begged her to marry him.

Tulasi told him that it was most unbecoming on his part to talk of marriage to a young girl without getting the permission of her parents. Then *Shankachuda* reminded her of their connection in a previous life which she already knew.

"I was a *gopala* named *Sudama*, a close friend of *Krishna* and I was born on earth due to *Radha's* curse. I fell in love with you in *Goloka* but could not associate with you for fear of *Radha*. But now I have been given the opportunity of marrying you, so will you consent to be my wife"?

Tulasi gladly agreed since it tallied with what *Brahma* had told her. Just then *Brahma* appeared on the scene and gave *Tulasi* in marriage to *Shankachuda*. Since it was a marriage by mutual consent there were no formalities. This is known as a *Gandharva* marriage and does not need any rites or the presence of priests. The couple continued to live in the hermitage in perfect harmony and love. At last when they tired of their solitude, *Shankachuda* took her back to his own kingdom. Soon he began to display his *asuric* tendencies and fought with the gods and dispersed them from heaven.

The despondent gods, headed by *Indra*, went with their eternal complaints to the Grandsire – *Brahma*. He professed his helplessness in this matter. They proceeded to *Kailasa*, the abode of *Shiva*. He told them that *Vishnu* was the best person to deal with this issue since *Shankachuda* had been his devotee in his previous birth.

Vishnu narrated to them the whole history of *Shankachuda's* previous birth. "O *Devas*! As you know, *Shankachuda* was my favourite attendant in *Goloka*. He is fully protected by the armour that I gave him when *Radha* cursed him. As long as he wears this, he is invincible so first of all I will have to go to him in the form of a Brahmin and beg him for his armour. *Brahma* has also given him the boon that he can be killed only if his wife commits adultery. Since his wife, *Tulasi* is dear to me and has done much austerity in order to procure me as her husband, I will personally approach her and tempt her. When she falls, as she is bound to do, *Shiva* will easily be able to kill him.

Shiva promised to help the gods and sent a messenger to *Shankachuda* asking him to return the heavens to the gods or come and fight with him. *Shankachuda* laughingly told the messenger to return to his master and ask him to get ready for battle. He then informed *Tulasi* of the impending encounter. She wept when she heard this and begged him not to go, for she had seen many ill omens.

Shankachuda said, "Be not afraid, O beauteous one! Everything happens due to the will of the *Maha Devi.* I have satisfied my desires with you and now it remains for you to fulfil your desire. You will certainly get *Narayana* as your husband so be not afraid. Everything which is meant to happen will happen with the turning of the wheel of time"!

In the morning, *Shankachuda* bathed and prayed to Lord *Krishna* and set out for battle with *Shiva.* It is said that the battle went on for many days without any fatigue on either part. It was then that *Vishnu* took the form of a Brahmin and came to the battlefield and begged *Shankachuda* for his armour. The *asura* who was noted for his great generosity immediately took it off and gave it to the Brahmin. *Vishnu* then took the form of *Shankachuda* and arrived at the palace. He went to *Tulasi* and took her in his arms. She thought that her husband had returned to her and complied with his wishes.

At this precise moment *Shiva* hurled the fatal trident at *Shankachuda.* When *Shankachuda* saw the spear coming, he immediately sat in *yogic* posture and fixed his mind on *Krishna.* The world-consuming trident now turned to ashes both the chariot and its occupant. To the amazement of all, they saw the *asura* take the form of a *gopala* and get into a celestial car, which had come for him. It is said that *Shankachuda's* bones were turned into conchs, which are considered most auspicious in *Narayana's puja. Lakshmi* resides in these shells and if the ceremonial bathing of a deity is done with water from a conch shell it is considered to be equivalent to bathing in all the holy rivers.

In the meantime, *Narayana* assumed his real form and gave *Tulasi* a vision of his beauteous countenance, blue in colour with lotus-petalled eyes.

When she saw this, *Tulasi* was grief-stricken and said, "O Master Magician! Why have you betrayed me? In order to help the gods you have cheated me and allowed your devotee to be killed. Your heart is like a stone so I curse you that you shall have to take the form of a stone"!

The Lord spoke gently to her, "O *Tulasi*! For many years you performed *tapasya* in the mountains to get me as your husband. Now that I have accepted you, why have you changed your mind? *Shankachuda* also performed great austerity to get you as his wife. Such rigorous penance cannot go unrewarded. Both of you have got your heart's desire. Divine ways are strange and inexplicable. Your husband who is a true *yogi* knew all about this. He has already gone back to *Goloka* and is residing in splendour and happiness with *Krishna.* You have a further role to play in the world. You will have to give up your earthly body, which will turn into a river known as *Gantaki.* Your hair will turn into a plant called *tulasi.* The leaves of this plant will be considered most sacred in all the three worlds and will be used in all *pujas* done to me. All holy rivers will reside at the foot of the *tulasi* plant and all places where you are cultivated will become pure and holy. I myself with every one of the other gods will remain at your feet and await the falling of a single leaf. I will get more pleasure from the offering of one *tulasi* leaf than I would get from the offering of countless gems and holy waters. *Puja* done in the month of *Kartika,* when you were born, will be even more effective. One who drinks *tulasi* water at the time of death will be freed from all sins. He, who wears a string of *tulasi* beads round his neck, will get the same benefit as one who has conducted a horse sacrifice".

"As for me, I will become the stones in the river *Gantaki* in compliance with your curse. These stones will be known as *Saligramas* and each will have a mark of *Vishnu* inside them. My devotees will adore these stones. They will bring auspiciousness to the household in which they are kept and worshipped. The best way to venerate them would be to pour *Ganga* water over them and offer *tulasi* leaves. The devotee who does this will get great prosperity and liberation at the end of his life."

Thus *Narayana* pacified *Tulasi* and told her, "O *Tulasi*! All my devotees will worship you. Everyone will keep you on his or her head. I myself will keep you on my breast, for you are a partial incarnation of *Lakshmi*". Thus saying, he took his leave of her. *Tulasi* gave up her life and became the river *Gantaki* as well as the sacred plant. In these forms she continues to bless all devotees of Lord *Krishna.* Lord *Vishnu* became the *saligrama* stones that are found only in the *Gantaki* River.

Devotees of *Krishna* or *Vishnu* perform *tulasi puja* on the full moon day of the month of *Kartika*, the day on which she was born on earth. One who worships her with devotion will attain the feet of *Narayana* and will attain liberation from the mundane world.

"A bliss lived in her heart too large for heaven,
Light too intense for thought and love too boundless

For earth's emotions in her skies of mind,
And spread through her deep and happy seas of soul,
All that is sacred in the worlds drew near,
To her divine passivity of mood."

— "Savitri" by Sri Aurobindo

Thus ends the twenty-fourth chapter of the *Sri Devi Lila* known as 'Tulasi', which describes the greatness of *Tulasi*, the goddess of the sacred plant.

ॐ *Aim, hreem, kleem* ॐ

Yad moole saaratheertane,
Yad madhye sarva devataam,
Yadagre sarva vedashcha,
Tulasim taam namaamyaham

"I bow to Tulasi Devi,
At whose feet reside all the sacred rivers,
In whose middle portion cling all the gods,
An in whose leaves are found all the Vedas."

ॐ

Vasundharayai Namaha!

CHAPTER TWENTY-FIVE

SITA

"Sita is all creation and the god of creation,
She is cause and effect, saints and demons, the elements, souls;
She is supreme virtue and supreme beauty,
The worlds are illumined by her form as the sun;
She adorns herself with lightning;
She is the evolving wheel of the cycle of time;
Merely by opening her eyes, she calls the worlds into being.
As her beautiful eyelids flutter closed,
The universe collapses.
She is the power of enjoyment, the tree of plenty,
The wish-fulfilling gem.
In two hands she bears fragrant lotuses,
Another hand signals the granting of boons,
While the fourth gestures, 'Don't be afraid';
She is the goddess *Lakshmi*, seated in yoga posture,
On her lion throne.
All the beauty you see around you, is hers alone,
Yes hers alone."

— *Brahma* in the *Sita Upanishad*

Rama was the seventh incarnation of *Vishnu* and is depicted as the example of the perfect man. He was the prince of the kingdom of *Kosala* and married *Sita,* the princess of the country of *Videha. Sita* was the model of wifely devotion and loyalty. Her love for *Rama*, unlike that of *Radha*, was based on strong marital ties. She is one of the most popular heroines in Hindu mythology, and is an example of the perfect wife to all young girls. *Rama* was the upholder of all *dharmas,* in all fields of life. He was the perfect son, perfect brother, perfect husband and perfect king. His life shows that a person holding a high political position should always put his loyalty to his subordinates before his personal interests.

Whenever *Vishnu* takes an *avatara,* his consort, *Lakshmi*, also takes on a bodily form. Thus, *Sita* was the incarnation of *Lakshmi* though she is also said to be the incarnation of *Vishnu's* other wife – *Bhudevi* or the earth deity.

The word '*sita*' means furrow and we find that there was a female deity called *Sita* who was known prior to the story of *Rama* and *Sita*, as given in the sage *Valmiki's Ramayana.* She was associated with agriculture and fertility. It is possible the *Valmiki* named the heroine of his book after this deity, for we find that *Sita's* origin was from the earth. In one of the *Vedic* hymns addressed to the Lord of the fields, the goddess, *Sita* is invoked.

"Auspicious *Sita*, come near,
We venerate and worship you,
That you might bless and prosper us,
And bring us abundant fruits."

In the *Kausika Sutra, Sita* is depicted as the wife of *Parjanya*, god of rain. She was the mother of gods, mortals and creatures and was invoked for growth and prosperity. In the *Paraskara Sutra, Sita* was the wife of *Indra,* god of rain and fertility. In the *yajnas* or *Vedic* fire ceremonies, she was offered cooked rice and barley in the sacrificial fire along with the other gods. In the *Vajasaneyi Samhita*, *Sita* was invoked by drawing four furrows on the sacrificial field. *Sita* is also one of the names of the goddess *Arya*, in the *Purana* known as the *Harivamsa.* Thus we notice that in the *Vedas* and other *Puranas*, goddess *Sita* has always had a close association with the earth and all its bounties.

"O goddess, you are the altar's centre in the sacrifice,
The priest's fee,
Sita to those who hold the plough,
And earth to all living beings!"

Sita's role is to make us aware of the necessity of a male power to awaken the fertility of the ploughed earth and, arouse and inseminate it.

The beautiful interaction between divine and human is brought out in all the ancient stories concerning *Sita.* The fertility of earth is the result of the interaction between sky and earth (god and man), between male and female, between the latent powers of the field and the inseminating effects of the plough, which opens the earth for the insertion of seeds into her fertile interior. The esoteric meaning of this is that human endeavour and noble actions are needed to ensure an unfailing supply of crops from the earth. If this good will is not there on our part, the earth deity will withdraw all her goods into herself. There are many *Puranic* stories showing this. In ancient texts, it was the king who played an active part in milking the cow of the earth and supplicating her to yield her produce.

However, *Sita* was not a very significant deity prior to the *Ramayana.* In the *Ramayana*, she was the daughter of the noble *Janaka,* king of *Videha.* He was involved in a royal ritual in which he had to plough the sacrificial field and he found a baby girl in one of the furrows. Hence she was named *Sita.* She was the personification of the earth's fertility, abundance and well-being. Thus *Sita* was no mere human being. Her birth was supernatural and her abilities and appearance are exalted throughout the text. She was called *ayonija*, not born from a womb. She was deeply associated with the primordial powers of the earth.

Even as a child, *Janaka* was astounded by her strength. She was able to lift a huge bow, which normally needed a hundred men to lift. *Janaka* vowed that he would give her in marriage only to one who could lift and string the bow. When she came of marriageable age, it was found that only *Rama*, the prince of *Ayodhya*, was capable of this stupendous feat. He broke the bow and married the celestially beautiful *Sita* who had already given her heart to him. Theirs was a love story beyond parallel. *Rama's* love for *Sita* and hers for him is the theme-song of many bards from that day to this.

Despite their great love for each other, *Sita's* story is one of sorrow from beginning to end. Thanks to the machinations of his step-mother, *Rama* was exiled to the forest for fourteen years on the very eve of his coronation. *Rama* being a noble soul, was unperturbed by this command of his father and was all set to go to the forest by himself. However, both his brother, *Lakshmana* and his wife, *Sita* insisted that they should be allowed to accompany him. When *Rama* pointed out the dangers of the forest to one as delicately nurtured as she, *Sita* replied that to a chaste woman, her husband was her God and apart from him, she might as well be dead.

"For a woman, it is not her father, her son, nor her mother, friends nor her own self but her husband who, in this world and the next, is ever her sole means of salvation. If thou dost enter the impenetrable forest today, O descendent of *Raghu*, I shall precede thee on foot. I shall happily live in the forest as I lived in the palace of my father, having no anxiety and reflecting only on my duties towards my Lord. Ever subject to thy will, docile, living like an ascetic, in those honey-scented woodlands, I shall be blissfully happy, for you will be near me, O illustrious Lord!"

When *Rama* pointed out to her the dangers and rigours of forest life, her reply was, "The hardships described by thee, will be transmuted into joys through my devotion to thee. Separated from thee I should immediately yield up my life. Which woman can live without her consort? Thou canst not doubt this truth where I am concerned. O *Rama!* I shall remain sinless by following piously in the footsteps of my husband, for thou art my God"!

For twelve years, *Rama* and *Sita* lived an idyllic life in the forest. In their thirteenth year of exile she was abducted by *Ravana*, the demon king of *Lanka*, and taken to his island kingdom. There she was severely tried by *Ravana* who wooed her diligently. He dared not touch her since he had been cursed that if he took a woman without her consent he would be struck dead.

With the aid of the monkey chief, *Sugriva*, and his able general, *Hanuman*, *Rama* found out the whereabouts of *Sita* and went to *Lanka*. He defeated *Ravana* and rescued his beloved wife. But her trials were far from being over. *Rama* accused her of infidelity and in order to prove her chastity, he asked her to undergo the ordeal of fire. Personally he had no doubts about her purity but in order to put an end to the doubts of people regarding the chastity of his queen, who had stayed for one full year in the court of the notorious *Ravana, Rama* put her to trial.

Sita was shocked at this accusation and commanded *Lakshmana* to make a pyre for her. After having been publicly denounced by her husband, it was better for her to die. When the fire was blazing, she circumambulated *Rama* and prepared to jump into the flames.

She addressed *Agni*, the god of fire thus, "If my heart has never ceased to be true to *Rama*, do thou O witness of all beings, grant me thy protection! As I am pure in conduct, though *Rama* looks on me as sullied, do thou, O witness of the worlds, grant me full protection!"

With these words she jumped into the blazing pyre but due to her innocence and faultless purity, *Agni* refused to harm her and brought her out unscathed. Even her flower garland remained unwithered in the flames.

All *puranic* stories have esoteric meanings. In this particular story, *Sita* is the individual soul, captured by the overpowering demonic forces of the material world. However she never forgets her divine beloved. God will always protect such a soul or *jivatman,* which remains faithful to the *Paramatman* throughout the temptations of her life and refuses to surrender to greed, lust and power. He will rescue her and carry her back to his own world. God loves every soul as passionately as *Rama* loved *Sita.*

Rama and *Sita* returned in triumph to *Ayodhya* where the citizens were waiting with great joy to welcome them back. The union of *Sita* and *Rama* represents the interplay between a powerful and virtuous king with a woman who symbolises the fecund forces of the earth. She was literally the child of the earth. The result of this auspicious relationship between kingly virility and earthly fertility was the kingdom of *Rama* known as *Ramarajya.* His reign was characterised by harmony, longevity of the people, order and abundant crops. Social, political and economic virtues dominated this society where the ruler was the epitome of *dharma* and his wife, the personification of womanly virtues.

Unfortunately for *Sita*, despite his passionate attachment to her, *Rama* placed his duty to his people and adherence to *dharma* before his duty as a husband. One was for the good of his country and people, whereas the other was for personal gratification. The welfare of his people was always kept above his own pleasure. In one of his incognito expeditions through the streets of *Ayodhya*, he heard his wife being maligned. He recalled the old saying, 'as the king so the citizens'. It was the duty of the ideal king to set a perfect example to his people. When the people heard that he had taken back as his wife, one who had lived in the court of another for a whole year, they were tempted to follow his example. Such behaviour would lead eventually to the degeneration of the moral consciousness of the society. As the upholder of *dharma*, he was forced to banish *Sita* to the forest even though he had just learnt of her pregnancy. This bitter decision to part from his beloved wife was made for the sake of his subjects. He commanded *Lakshmana* to take her to the forest and leave her there.

Sita knew nothing of his decision and went joyfully with *Lakshmana* to the forest. She had desired to be taken for a while to the hermitage of the sages where she had spent so many happy years with her husband. Just before he left her, *Lakshmana* gave her the unhappy news that she had been banished by the king, her husband. Even when she heard of this bitter decree, she did not blame *Rama*. She sent a message to *Rama* through *Lakshmana*, "O *Raghava*, you know that I am truly pure. You have renounced me for fear of dishonour, because your subjects have reproached and censured you. I am not distressed on my own account. It is for you to keep your fair name untarnished. The husband is a God to a wife. He is her entire family and her spiritual preceptor. Even at the price of her life, she must seek to please her Lord"!

Sita found protection in the hermitage of the sage, *Valmiki*, who is the author of the *Ramayana* and there she gave birth to twin sons. *Rama* lived a lonely life in the palace and refused to marry again even though both his priests and his subjects urged him to do so. He remained faithful to *Sita* in body and mind and refused to follow the trend of the age where kings were allowed to take numerous wives. At the end of many years, when his sons were twelve years old, *Valmiki* urged *Rama* to meet *Sita* once again and consider taking her back. *Rama* was eager to do so but once again he asked her to undergo a public ordeal that would convince his subjects once and for all about her innocence.

But *Sita* was fed up of life on this earth. She could bear no more and she begged the earth, her mother, to take her back to her bosom.

"If in thought, word or deed I have ever dwelt on my husband *Rama* alone, may the earth goddess, *Madhavi* receive me."

As she said these words, the ground shuddered and split open. A throne twined with all the creepers and plants of the earth rose up from the ground. On this was seated, the earth deity. *Sita* ran to her and was clasped to her bosom. The throne sank into the earth and the crack closed over it before the horrified eyes of the beholders. *Rama* ranted and raved and angrily demanded the earth to return his beloved to him but the ground remained silent and closed.

Rama lived for many years after this as a recluse, even though he continued with his duties as the perfect king and ruler. His life was lived in sorrow and he never took another wife, for *Sita's* image was enshrined in his heart forever. He made a golden effigy of *Sita* and used it in her place in all the religious rituals that demanded a wife's presence.

Sita's steadfast loyalty to her husband makes her the model of the ideal wife. Her life was inextricably bound with that of her husband. Throughout the *Ramayana*, her only thought was of *Rama's* welfare. Thus, *Sita* represents all the good qualities of a chaste woman and an ideal wife. Although other goddesses like *Parvati* and *Lakshmi* express many of these qualities, *Sita* is by far the most popular and beloved as the paradigm for wifely devotion, forbearance and chastity. The *Ramayana* is well known in every Hindu household and Hindu ideals have been modelled on the examples given in this book.

The Hindu tradition teaches a woman to emphasise those points in her character that would make her a model daughter, mother and wife. She is supposed to succumb to the demands of the society and not impose her own demands on it as the modern woman does. From childhood, women are taught to cultivate an attitude, which subordinates their welfare to the welfare of others, especially their husbands and children. This of course ensured an integrated society, since it produced a strong family unit that is the basic block of any social structure. The Hindu community is a mythologically instructed one, which provides numerous models and images that provide a pattern to which the individual may aspire. In the case of a Hindu woman the model is condensed to just one character and she is *Sita.*

"The wedding of the eternal Lord and spouse,
Took place again on earth in human forms;
In a new act of the drama of the world,
The united two began a greater age.
In the silence and murmur of that emerald world,

And the mutter of the priest-wind's sacred verse;
Amid the choral whisperings of the leaves;
Love's twain had joined together and grew one.
The natural miracle was wrought once more;
In the immutable ideal world,
One human moment was eternal made."

— "Savitri" by Sri Aurobindo

Thus ends the twenty-fifth chapter of the *Sri Devi Lila* known as 'Sita', which describes the greatness of *Sita*, the model of womanhood.

ॐ *Aim, hreem, kleem* ॐ

Samudravadane Devi
Parvatasthanamandale,
Vishnupatnim namastubhyam,
Paadasparsham kshamasva me.

"I bow to Devi, (the earth goddess) wife of Vishnu,
The oceans are your clothes,
And mountains your breasts,
Pray forgive me for placing my feet on you all the time."

ॐ

Savitryai Namaha!

CHAPTER TWENTY-SIX

SAVITRI

"A power dwelt in her soul too great for earth,
A bliss lived in her too large for heaven,
Light too intense for thought and love too boundless,
For earth's emotions lit her skies of mind
And spread though her deep and happy seas of soul,
All that is sacred in the world drew near,
To her divine passivity of mood,
A marvellous voice of silence breathed its thoughts,
All things in Time and Space she had taken for her.
In her they moved, in her they lived and were,
The whole wide world clung to her for delight."

— "Savitri" by Sri Aurobindo

In the *Vedas* the most famous goddess connected with the sun is *Ushas*, the goddess of dawn. Some of the most beautiful hymns of the *Rig Veda* are addressed to her. She is described as the daughter of the sky. Night is her sister. At times she is spoken of as the wife of *Surya. Ushas* is said to travel in a shining chariot, drawn by ruddy horses or cows. The *rishis* of the *Vedas* describe her in the most poetic terms. She is a beautiful girl dressed by her mother, a dancing girl covered with jewels and a gaily-attired wife appearing before her husband. Again she is like a fascinating damsel coming out of her bath. Smilingly she unfolds the irresistible power of her attraction and uncovers the cloth covering her bosom. Her quiet modesty is like a shy maiden, conscious of her beauty, ushered into society by her mother.

She dispels the darkness not only of the night but also the darkness of ignorance in the minds of human beings. She illumines everything, including the darkest recesses of the mind. She is the giver of both life and health. She causes the birds to fly from their nests and like the housewife she sends forth all creatures to attend to the needs of their day's routine.

She is eternally young since she is born everyday. Yet she is immeasurably old since she is immortal. She wears out the lives of successive generations, which disappear one after the other while she continues, undying. The souls of the departed are said to go through her and pierce the orb of the sun.

"Hail *Ushas*! Daughter of the sky,
Who borne upon thy shining car,
By ruddy steeds from realms afar,
And ever lightening draws nigh,
Thou sweetly smiling, goddess fair,
Disclosing all thy youthful grace,
Thy bosom bright, thy radiant face,
And lustre of thy golden hair."

Savitur refers to the sun god. The famous hymn to the sun god is known as the *Gayatri*. Actually *gayatri* is the name of the metre in which it is written. But the metre is conceived of as a goddess – *Gayatri*. In looks she is something like the *Vedic* goddess *Ushas*. The method and practice of the *Gayatri Mantra* is given in the *Savitri Upanishad*. Repetition of the *Gayatri Mantra* is compulsory for all Hindus. It is not meant only for the Brahmins even though the Brahmins were the custodians of this *mantra* for centuries. Even though it appears to be a hymn addressed to the sun, it is actually addressed to the Supreme Consciousness and is a prayer for enlightenment. It is universally applicable. It is nothing but a prayer for spiritual light addressed to the Almighty. It is addressed to '*Tat Savitur*' – 'that sun of Supreme Consciousness', which lights up everything, including the physical sun. The word *Savitur* is masculine and refers to the sun. The feminine counterpart is the goddess *Savitri*. This hymn has been regarded as the greatest of all *mantras*. If there is one *mantra*, which is common to all Hindus it is this:

"Aum Bhur Bhuvah Svaha,
Tat Savitur Varenyam,
Bhargo Devasya Dheemahi,
Dhiyo yo nah Prachodayat."

"Let us meditate on the Supreme and his glory,
Who has created this universe (earth, sky and heaven),
Who alone is fit to be worshipped,
Who is the remover of all ignorance,
May He enlighten us!"

At dawn we should turn our face towards the rising sun, which is the visible manifestation of the Supreme Reality and repeat this *mantra.* At mid-day we should think of the sun at its zenith and repeat the *mantra.* Again at sunset we should turn towards the setting sun and repeat it once more. It can be repeated as many times as one wishes. The *rishis* had a thorough knowledge of the subtle effects of sounds and they devised this *mantra*, which has great mystic power and which will enable the human being to expand his consciousness and allow us to reach the Supreme. Daily repetition of this mystical *mantra* with sincerity and devotion will help us attain our highest potential, both materially and spiritually.

The sun is the abode of the Supreme *Brahman.* It is the first visible manifestation of the Absolute. The *Rig Veda* glorifies the sun as '*Pratyaksha Devata*' or the visible divinity. Scientists are only aware of the physical properties of the sun but the sages discovered its spiritual aspect, which is directly linked with the evolution of life and the expansion of intelligence. The *rishis* realised that the sun has an active spiritual field. They found out that the energy of the sun was born out of the pulsating rhythm of the deep spiritual laws of the Supreme Spirit. They said that it was born out of '*rita*' or the cosmic law of harmony. The basis of the material sun is a great spiritual field, which they called *Surya Narayana.* The sun is not just a huge mass of atomic energy but a radiant mass of life-giving vitality to all creation. The spiritual values inherent in the sun express themselves in various degrees through different creatures and reach their highest expression in the human being. The sun inspires us to push forward and evolve to the unconditioned freedom of the Absolute. The *Gayatri*

Mantra throbs with this intense yearning on the part of the human race to evolve towards its highest potential.

Thus, *Savitur* is nothing but the Supreme itself. Hence the *Gayatri Mantra* is not just a hymn to the sun god but it is a paean of praise to the Supreme *Brahman.* The goddess *Savitri* is the presiding deity of the *Suryamandala* or the solar orb. She is said to be the mother of the *Vedas. Brahma*, in his role as custodian of the *Vedas*, was the first to worship her. The story of how she came to be born on earth is told in the *Puranas.* The great sage *Sri Aurobindo* has written a mystical poem about *Savitri*, which has a great depth of spiritual feeling and symbolism underlying it. In fact the poem is said to have been inspired by the *Lalitha Sahasranama.*

Once there was a king of the solar dynasty called *Asvapati.* He had a highly spiritual-minded queen called *Malati.* They had no children so their *guru, Vasishta*, advised her to worship the goddess, *Savitri.* She went to the holy lake of *Pushkara* and did *tapasya* for many years with no result. Dejected, she returned to the palace. Her husband told her not to worry and they should perform their austerities together. They did severe *tapasya* for a hundred years. At last a celestial voice announced, "Repeat the *Gayatri Mantra* for ten *lakhs* of times and your wish will be fulfilled."

At this time the great sage, *Parasara* appeared on the scene and told the king of the glory of the *Gayatri Mantra.*

He said, "O king! If you repeat the *Gayatri Mantra* just once, all that day's sins will vanish. One hundred repetitions will take away the sins of one year. One *lakh* destroys the sins of this birth and ten *lakhs* destroys the sins of other births. If a thousand *lakhs* is done, liberation is attained".

He then instructed the king on the type of *japa mala* or rosary to be used in counting.

"The *japa mala* should be made of the seeds of the white lotus or of crystal. It should be purified by dipping in milk or *Ganga* water and consecrated at the feet of one's favourite deity. If a person repeats ten *lakhs* of *mantras* on such a *mala*, he or she will receive the vision of the *Devi, Savitri.*"

The king performed the rites as commanded by the *rishi* on the fourteenth day of the black fortnight of the month of *Jyesta* (May/June) for fourteen years. He offered fourteen different types of fruits, flowers and incense to the goddess and distributed wealth to fourteen Brahmins. He used the following *mantra* to invoke her:

"I meditate on that *Savitri,* the Mother of the *Vedas,* who has the nature of *Aum,* and whose colour is that of burnished gold. Thou art effulgent like the rays of the noonday sun and adorned with many jewels and ornaments. Thou art the bestower of happiness and liberation, the consort of the Creator. May thou be gracious unto me."

Thus repeating this *mantra* and performing the prescribed rituals for fourteen years, King *Asvapati* and his queen got the vision of the goddess.

She said, "O king! I know your desire. Your wife wants a daughter and you want a son. You will both get what you want." Thus, having blessed them the goddess returned to the celestial regions.

Soon after, the king got a most beautiful daughter whom he named *Savitri* after the goddess.

When *Savitri* came of age, the king brought many proposals for her but she would have none of them. She had already seen the man she would marry in one of her excursions into the forest. He was called *Satyavan* and was the son of the blind king, *Dyumatsena.* The king had been deposed from his kingdom and had gone to the forest where he lived the life of a sage, accompanied by his faithful wife and son. King *Asvapati* was not happy with his daughter's choice even though he knew that King *Dyumatsena* was a noble man and he had heard that his son was the soul of truth and honour. At this time sage *Narada* came to his court and gave him another distressing bit of news. Looking at *Savitri's* palm, he told the king that her husband would die after just one year of marriage. The king was grief-stricken and exhorted his daughter to give up her scheme of marrying such a man. But she was adamant and prayed to her mother goddess, *Savitri,* to give her the courage to stick to her decision and also to give her a long life as the wife of *Satyavan.*

At last the king agreed and gave her in marriage to *Satyavan,* who took her back to his hermitage in the forest. For one full year *Savitri* prayed with all her heart to the goddess, *Savitri* to grant her the life of her husband. On the concluding day of her vow, which was supposed to be *Satyavan's* last day on earth, she insisted on accompanying him to the forest when he went to cut wood. As the day wore on, she noticed that *Satyavan* became more and more exhausted. At last he lay down with his head on her lap. Just at that time, *Yama,* the god of death, approached and took away *Satyavan's* life in a noose. With her perception sharpened by her austerities, *Savitri* was able to see all these happenings. She kept the lifeless body of her husband gently on the ground and followed *Yama.*

Yama saw her following him and asked her, "O *Savitri!* Why are you following me? No mortal can come with me to my abode. If you want to come with me you will have to shed your body. The time has come for the death of your husband and that is why I am taking him away, but your time has not yet come and you will not be able to follow me to the nether regions. It is only due to your great austerities that you are able to see me at all. The time of birth and death of each being is decreed by their *karma.* No one can go against their *karma".*

Savitri then asked him to explain the nature of *karma* and how it could be overcome.

Yama said, "*Karma* is produced by the actions of individuals and is of two kinds, good and bad. Those actions that do not go against the dictates of *dharma* are considered good and will result in beneficial *karma.* Actions done for the sake of God without expectation of reward increase devotion to God and lead to liberation. Now *Savitri,* return to your home and look after your aged parents. This is your *dharma* at the moment".

Savitri said, "A wife's *dharma* is to follow her husband wherever he goes. Where shall I go leaving my husband? Pray! instruct me, for you are the greatest of all teachers".

Yama said, "O *Savitri!* You are a portion of the goddess and hence you are precocious beyond your years and filled with knowledge. Ask three boons from me and I shall grant them".

Savitri immediately said, "Let me have a hundred sons by my husband *Satyavan.* Let my father-in-law get back his eyesight and his kingdom and let my father have many sons".

Yama agreed to this and swiftly *Savitri* said, "O gracious Lord! How will I get sons from *Satyavan* unless you give back his life"?

Yama was pleased by her presence of mind and perseverance and deep devotion to her husband and said, "My child, I am pleased with your devotion and intelligence. Worship *Devi Savitri* who is none other than *Mula Prakriti* and all happiness shall be yours. Take your husband and return to your home and live happily with him. Undertake the *Savitri* vow for fourteen years which is what your parents did and you will certainly attain liberation along with your husband".

Saying this, *Yama* blessed *Savitri* and told her to go back to the spot where she had placed the corpse of her husband.

When *Savitri* returned to the tree under which she had kept her husband's body, she found him getting up as if from deep sleep. He had no memory of what had happened and thought he had fallen asleep. She told him the whole saga and they rejoiced at his miraculous return from the land of the dead. They returned to the hermitage and repeated the wonderful tale. Soon after, *Dyumatsena* got back his eyesight and his kingdom and they went back to their land and worshipped the goddess as advised by *Yama. Savitri's* parents also got many sons as promised by *Yama.* All of them attained liberation from their mortal coils after many blessed years spent in conducting the affairs of the kingdom and worshipping the goddess *Savitri*, and by repeating the *Gayatri Mantra.*

"She pressed the living body of *Satyavan*;
On her body's wordless joy to be and breathe,
She bore the blissful burden of his head,
Between her breasts, warm labour of delight,
The waking gladness of her members felt,
The weight of heaven in his limbs, a touch
Summing the whole felicity of things,
And all her life was conscious of his life,
And all her being rejoiced enfolding his,
The immense remoteness of her trance had passed;
Human she was once more, earth's *Savitri*,
Yet felt in her illimitable change."

Thus ends the twenty-sixth chapter of the *Sri Devi Lila* known as 'Savitri', which narrates the story of Goddess *Savitri* and her descent to the earth.

ॐ *Aim, hreem, kleem* ॐ

ॐ

Kalaratryai Namaha!

CHAPTER TWENTY-SEVEN

SHIVADUTI

Ati saumythiraudrayai nathasthasyai namo Namaha!
Namo jagatpratishtayai Devyai krtyai namo Namaha!

"We prostrate before her who is at once most gentle and most terrible.
We salute her again and again.
Salutations to her who is the support of the world.
Salutations to the *Devi* who is of the form of volition."

— *Devi Mahatmyam*, Chapter V

The symbology of gods and goddesses in the Hindu pantheon covers an infinite array of forms, colours and depictions. Some are ravishing, some provocative, some kind and compassionate and others grotesque and barbaric. Some suggest spiritual powers and some material gains. In every case the structure is elaborately detailed and designed to evoke a corresponding response within the consciousness of the aspirant. The symbology is based on the eternal archetypal structure of the human beings' collective unconscious. These forms or *mandalas* are intended to draw out these archetypes from our unconscious as a magnet draws out iron filings. We have delineated a few of the benign forms of the *Maha Devi* and now we have to outline the characteristics of some of her fierce forms. She has two sides that portray the dual-faced visage of creation. To present the good and beautiful alone would be to give a lop-sided picture of life. Hinduism insists that both sides should be confronted and accepted before we will be able to gain a vision of her supreme form, which is beyond all duality. *Tantric* images often go beyond the boundaries of rationale. Some forms have sixteen hands and three eyes, some are naked and drinking blood, while still others are shown as carrying weapons of mass destruction.

Apart from their symbolic significance, these forms are the *tantric* way of asserting that life can never be fitted into one mould. This would simply denigrate the diversity of life. We have to experience life in all its multi-faceted aspects filled with contradictions before we can live it fully.

Many of these violent forms, which we shall discuss in this chapter, are mentioned at various times both in the *Devi Mahatmyam* and the *Devi Bhagavatam* as well as other *Puranas.* Apart from *Chandika* and *Kaali* one of the fierce goddesses referred to in the *Devi Mahatmyam* is *Shivaduti.* In the episode of the battle with the two *asura* brothers called *Shumbha* and *Nishumbha*, *Shiva* told *Chandika* to kill all the *asura* hoards that had been sent by them. At this there issued from the body of *Chandika*, an exceedingly fierce and horrific *Shakti* who came out howling like a hundred jackals. Turning to Lord *Shiva,* she ordered him to go as her emissary to the court of *Shumbha* and *Nishumbha.*

"Tell those two haughty *asuras* and all those assembled there that they have to give back to *Indra,* the three worlds which they stole from the gods. They will then be allowed to return to the nether world, which is their rightful domain. But if out of pride they refuse to obey my command, let them come for battle and allow my jackals to feed on their flesh!"

Since the *Devi* appointed *Shiva* himself as her ambassador, she came to be known as *Shivaduti.* She is another common figure on battlefields and other scenes of destruction.

Another group of goddesses mentioned in the *Devi Mahatmyam* are the *Sapta Matrikas.* They are normally said to be seven in number. They belong to the fearsome group of goddesses. When the *asuric* armies of *Shumbha* and *Nishumbha* approached *Chandika,* the male gods who were watching the whole episode with eager interest from the sidelines, created *Shaktis* or female counterparts of themselves to aid her. Seven such *Shaktis* were created and they resembled the male gods by whom they were produced. They had the same ornaments, vehicles and weapons as their masculine counterparts.

The first to arrive on the scene was *Brahmaani,* created by *Brahma.* She came in a chariot drawn by swans, carrying a rosary and a *kamandalu* or water pot. Next came *Maheswari,* created by *Shiva*, seated on a bull, wearing the crescent moon in her hair and snake bracelets on her arms and brandishing a trident. *Kaumari*, from *Kartikeya*, followed. She was seated on a peacock and carried a spear. *Vishnu's Shakti* called *Vaishnavi* was mounted on the eagle, *Garuda*, and carried the conch, discus, mace and bow in her hands. Her description is similar to that of *Vishnu* and in all the places that she appears, her use of the discus is specially emphasised. The *Shakti* of *Vishnu* in his *avatara* as the boar, *Varaha*, now came in the form of a boar and was known as *Varahi*. His *Shakti* created from the *avatara* of *Narasimha* or the man-lion was called *Nrisimhi* and came in the form of a lioness. One shake of her mane was enough to throw the stars into disarray. Finally there appeared on the scene, the *Shakti* of *Indra* called *Aindri* with thousand eyes, holding a thunderbolt in her hand and riding on the *Airavata*, the king of elephants. This group of *Shaktis* is collectively known as the *Sapta Matrikas*. All of them tried their best to kill *Raktabija* but he was invincible since he kept multiplying himself. At last *Chandika* called *Kaali* to expand her tongue and suck him dry.

After killing *Nishumbha* it is mentioned that the *Matrikas* vanquished the rest of the *asuras*. *Kaumari* pierced some with her spear. The sprinkling of sanctified water by *Brahmaani* repulsed others. Some were pierced by *Maheswari's* trident and some crushed to the earth by *Varahi's* snout. Others were cut to pieces by *Vaishnavi's* discus and many others by the thunderbolt discharged by *Aindri*. Along with *Kaali* and *Shivaduti*, the *Matrikas* devastated the demon hordes. After the battle, they danced and rioted, intoxicated with the blood of their victims.

Despite their names and appearances they are not really to be understood as the divine consorts of the male divinities but rather as the forms of the *Devi* herself. This is apparent from that portion of the *Devi Mahatmyam* when *Nishumbha* came face to face with her after she and the *Matrikas* had killed *Shumbha*.

He cried, "O wicked *Durga*, I am fighting alone and single-handed while you have so many at your command. That is why you were able to kill my heroic brother"!

In response to this, *Ambika* smiled and said, "There is none but me in all the fourteen worlds! I am alone. There is nothing other than me". So saying, she absorbed all the seven *Matrikas* and all the others who had been helping her, into herself.

In the *Vamana Purana* this fact is made even clearer since the *Matrikas* are seen to arise from different parts of the *Devi's* body and not from the male gods. In the *Matsya Purana*, *Shiva* commands the *Matrikas* to defeat the demon, *Andhaka*. After killing the demon, the bloodthirsty *Matrikas* proceeded to devour the gods, demons and people of the world. They refused to listen to *Shiva* and went on a rampage. *Shiva* then summoned *Narasimha*, Lord *Vishnu's avatara* as the man-lion and he created a host of benign goddesses who calmed down the terrible *Matrikas*.

The *Matrikas* never acted by themselves but only as a group, and they all shared the same characteristics. The *Puranic* accounts show them as the *Devi's* assistants who help her in combating demons but their wild, blood-thirsty characters are undiminished, whatever the role they play. Their characteristics are meant to portray those demonic traits in the human mind that refuse to be subjugated even with constant example and advice.

The *Bhagavad Purana* links them with other malevolent beings like *rakshasas, bhutas* (demons and ghouls), etc. The *gopis* made charms for the baby *Krishna* against the evil effects of these malicious beings. The *Purana* also gives instructions on how to overcome their evil effects.

The *Mahabharata* describes them as the mothers of *Skanda* in which role they seem to be connected in some way with the six *Krittikas* who nursed the infant, *Kartikeya*. They are known for the atrocities they wreak upon pregnant women and small children. There is a cult in many villages, which recognises their power and worships them in order to ward off their baneful effects. Sometimes the mothers appear as more than seven. Up to sixteen are mentioned.

Some *Jain* carvings of the medieval period portray a sculpture of the *Sapta-Matrikas* (seven mothers) with *Ganesha* as their guardian. The Buddhist goddess, *Hariti*, is also very akin to the *Matrikas*. Their forms are to be found in the great Buddhist university of *Nalanda*.

On the whole, they are given importance only because of the sinister role they play in the field of dangerous pregnancies, infant mortality, the joys of childhood and the mystery with which this joy and horror are intermingled. The issues they stand for are relevant to all life, hence they are found in some form or other in all the different sects of India. Research done by some modern scientists on consciousness suggests that there are some archetypal images, which trigger the unconscious to delve deep into the cosmic mind and come up with many strange facts, which the normal waking consciousness could never have known. We suppress them in the waking state but they come up in dreams and nightmares, especially in the case of children. The images found in Hindu scriptures have an ability to affect the subconscious in such a way that it gets into contact with the cosmic field of Super Consciousness with greater ease and helps to eradicate these primeval fears which all human beings have. The *Matrikas* are part of these archetypal images.

As we have seen earlier, the *Maha Devi* manifests herself in a great variety of forms. She is capable of producing goddesses from various parts of her body. Another group of goddesses, which are given prominence in *Devi* temples, are known as the *Mahavidyas* and are ten in number. They may be the *Shakta* version of the ten *avataras* of Lord *Vishnu* who appear from time to time when *dharma* declines. Some texts even claim that the *avataras* originally came from the *Mahavidyas. Kaali* is supposed to have become *Krishna* and *Chinnamasta, Narasimha.* This is only a theory. In actual fact, the *Mahavidyas* differ quite radically from the *avataras* of Lord *Vishnu.*

Their first appearance is connected with *Daksha's yaga.* As we have seen in the chapter on *Sati, Shiva* was not invited to this *yaga* and he refused to let *Sati* go. In her fury at his refusal, it is said that she multiplied herself into ten forms known as the *Mahavidyas.* They are *Kaali, Smashan Tara, Bhuvaneswari, Bagala, Dhumavati, Kamala, Matangi, Shodashi, Chinnamasta* and *Bhairavi.*

Kaali, as we have seen, has a fierce countenance, is naked, dwells in the cremation ground, holds a severed head in one hand and a bloody sword in the other. Her body is gaunt with ribs sticking out. She has thin, hanging breasts and a cavernous belly.

Smashan Tara is somewhat similar to *Kaali*, except in her size. She is the colour of collyrium, rests her left foot on a corpse and wears a tiger skin and a garland of severed heads. Her hair is braided in a single matted plait. She is fully pregnant, has full breasts and stands on a funeral pyre, wearing a girdle of arms.

Bhuvaneswari has a light complexion and a smiling face. She is said to nourish the three worlds and holds a piece of fruit in one hand. Her breasts are large and ooze with milk. She carries a goad and a noose.

Bagala has the head of a crane and is yellow in colour. She is seated on a throne of jewels. With one hand she appears to be beating an enemy with a club and with the other, pulling out someone's tongue.

Dhumavati is tall and pale with a stern, unsmiling face. She is toothless, her nose is large and crooked, her breasts long and pendulous and hair dishevelled. She is dressed in dirty clothes and looks like a widow. She holds a winnowing fan in one hand and her vehicle is the crow. She appears to be afflicted with hunger and thirst.

Kamala is a beautiful young woman with a golden complexion. Elephants pouring pitchers of water over her stand on either side. She is seated on a lotus and holds two lotuses in her hands. She looks like the Goddess *Lakshmi.* In fact, one of *Lakshmi's* names is *Kamala.*

Matangi is black in colour. She appears to be always intoxicated and reels about like an impassioned elephant. She has red, rolling eyes.

Shodashi is a young girl of sixteen. She is red in colour and is shown to be sitting astride the prone body of *Shiva* with whom she has obviously been having intercourse. They are lying on a bed, the legs of which are upheld by the gods, *Brahma, Vishnu, Rudra* and *Indra.* Sometimes she is identified with *Tripurasundari,* hence the reference to the bed upheld by the gods.

Bhairavi has a reddish hue and her eyes roll as if intoxicated. She wears a garland of severed heads. Two of her four hands hold a *japa mala* (rosary), and a book. One palm is held in the gesture of fearlessness (*abhaya mudra),* and the other in the symbol of conferring boons.

These are the *Mahavidyas,* which *Sati* brought out of herself. *Shiva* is supposed to have been frightened by these fearful forms that surrounded him. He gave *Sati* permission to go to her father's sacrifice if she withdrew them.

Even though a few of the *Mahavidyas* appear to have appealing forms, on the whole they are meant to be ferocious deities. With the exception of *Kaali,* they are not known to be warriors but are meant to project certain esoteric truths, which the *sadhaka* is supposed to find out for herself. Most of them play a part in *tantric* rituals. Their powers are meant to subdue the enemy by various methods. These powers include *maarana* or the ability to destroy the enemy, *ucchatana* – the ability to force a person to stop whatever he is doing, *kshobana* – which causes emotional disturbance, *mohana* – causing delusion and infatuation, *draavana* – causing people to run in terror, *jrimbhana* – which causes people to become lazy and keep yawning, and *stambhana* which causes paralysis. All these things are not just physical maladies but also mental and they can affect our spiritual life and spoil our *sadhana.* These *Mahavidyas* can be invoked to get rid of these emotional ailments and give us *moksha* or liberation.

Smashana Tara, as her name implies, is found only in cemeteries. '*Smashana*' is the Sanskrit word for the burning *ghat.* Her function is similar to *Kaali's.* Her devotees are the *aghoris* who worship her at midnight in cemeteries.

She is different from the Tibetan goddess, *Tara* who is a gentle soul and who is related to the *bodhisattva, Avalokitesvara.* As he is about to leave his body, he sheds a tear of compassion for those who are being left behind and this tear becomes *Tara,* who is thus the very essence of compassion. She is said to be a young girl of sixteen, playful and energetic with a sense of humour. In Tibetan lore, she is connected with their history and is their legendary queen and mother. Like *Durga,* she is supposed to come to the help of her devotees when they are in dire peril. Her compassion for suffering humanity is especially shown in her ability to snatch them from the jaws of death. Most of Tibetan Buddhism is fierce and heroic but *Tara* introduces a vein of tenderness and love.

Lama Lozang hymns her thus:

"O holy *Tara*! You know,
Everything that I have done,
My happiness and suffering, my good and evil,
Thus think lovingly of me, my only mother."

Chinnamasta is also one of the *Mahavidyas.* She carries in her left hand her own head, seemingly severed by herself with the sword held in her right hand. Her left hand carrying the head is raised upwards while the right is placed below. She is stark naked and her right leg is stretched out while the left is bent and crosses the right. Three streams of blood spout out of the stump of her neck. One falls into her own mouth and the other two into the mouths of the two *yoginis* who are on either side of her. She normally holds the head on a platter as if to make an offering of it. Beneath her feet lie *Kama,* the god of desire, and his wife *Rati* who are joined together in the act of love. They are stretched out on a lotus. The background for this gruesome representation is the cremation ground. The ghastly figure of *Chinnamasta* is a graphic portrayal of another great philosophic truth.

Creation and destruction are part of the cosmic process. The economy of the universe is kept in balance by a harmonious alternation of giving and taking life. The ever bountiful figure of *Annapurna* giving food, shows only one aspect of the process – that of giving. *Kaali* shows us the picture of the goddess severing the heads of others and demanding their blood as nourishment. The demons often sacrificed their own heads to the goddess. This represents the truth that the forces of the cosmos as depicted by the goddess require regular nourishment. Since we have received life from her, we are obliged to give it back to her. Life can only be maintained by ingesting the corpses of other beings, either animal or vegetable.

The *Chinnamasta* image actually conveys the same message but reverses the roles. She gives her own blood to herself and to her two devotees. Instead of taking the heads of her victims and drinking their blood, she takes her own head and drinks her own blood. She is nourished not by death but by the copulating couple beneath her. This is one of the most dramatic pictorial representations of the stark reality of life. It points out that life, sex and death are part of a closely inter-related system. None of them can exist alone. The whole scene, ghastly though it might appear to the casual viewer, becomes clear to the *sadhaka* who strives for a deeper meaning to reality.

This striking spectacle points out many truths, which we tend to cloak with a weak sentimentalism that masks our inherent inability to face the gory aspects of life. As far as nature, is concerned the sole necessity for sex is to propagate life, which in turn will decay and feed another life at another time and in another place. In other words life feeds on death, and is nourished by death. The copulating couple pump the goddess with their own life-giving energy which she in turn offers back to herself and to her children or devotees by the sacrifice of cutting off her own head! Life is portrayed by the copulating couple, death by the decapitated goddess, and the renewal of life by the *yoginis* drinking her blood.

The uninitiated may be shocked at the number of gruesome female goddesses depicted so realistically in Hindu mythology. To the initiate, however, the two types of goddesses only display the two sides of the coin of life as has been reiterated over and over again. *Lalitha* is worshipped on full moon days, for she represents consciousness at its most beautiful – full and resplendent like the moon. *Kaali* and all her counterparts are worshipped on new moon days when the sky is dark and nature herself appears in her most foreboding aspect. The allegory is to the human consciousness, which is still unawakened, cluttered with material desires and longs to be freed from this dark hold. *Kaali* extinguishes desire and *Lalitha* replaces the vacuum with liberating knowledge. *Kaali* typifies *sunyata* or void, while *Lalitha* is *purnata* or fullness. But what we should remember is that there is only one moon, whether waxing or waning, new or full. Thus, both *Kaali* and *Lalitha* are one and the same – pointing to the same truth from different viewpoints.

"The harmony of a rich culture's tones,
Refined the sense and magnified its reach,
To hear the unheard and glimpse the invisible,
And taught the soul to soar beyond things known,
Inspiring life to greaten and break its bounds,
Aspiring to the immortal's unseen world,
Leaving earth's safety, daring wings of mind,
Bore her above the trodden fields of thought,
Crossing the mystic seas of the beyond,
To live on eagle heights near the sun."

— "Savitri" by Sri Aurobindo

Thus ends the twenty-seventh chapter of the *Sri Devi Lila* known as 'Shivaduti', which describes the seven *Matrikas* and the ten *Mahavidyas*.

ॐ *Aim, hreem, kleem* ॐ

ॐ

Adi Shaktyai Namaha!

CHAPTER TWENTY-EIGHT

ADI SHAKTI

Indriyanam adhistatri bhutanam chakhileshu ya,
Bhuteshu sathatam thasyai vyaptidevyai Namo Namaha!

"She, who governs the senses of all creatures,
And who is present in the elements,
To the goddess of all pervasiveness, Hail! All Hail!"

As has been mentioned before, the *Shakta* cult is that which affirms the Ultimate Reality to be the duality of masculine and feminine – *Shiva* and *Shakti*, with greater accent on the feminine or *Shakti*. *Tantra* is the practical aspect of this cult and is an esoteric teaching handed down from *guru* to *shishya*. The Indian religious tradition is so rich that it has explored the heights and depths of the divine from all angles. With its typical fearlessness it has dared to describe the nature of the ultimate as consisting of all things, including the so-called bad and negative and ugly and wicked! Even though the *Shaktas* accept the presence of an all-pervading reality, it insists that this reality, which is termed *Shiva*, has a dual aspect – of consciousness and energy. *Shiva* is consciousness and *Shakti*, energy. *Shiva* is the static principle, which remains as pure unconditioned consciousness. It is only at the behest of *Shakti*, that *Shiva* is motivated to action. *Shiva* and *Shakti* are complementary to each other at every level. If he is *Shambhu*, she is *Shambhavi*, if he is *Maheswara*, she is *Maheswari*, if he is *Rudra*, she is *Raudri*.

The cult of the *Shaktas* is one that probes and analyses the nature of ultimate reality as feminine. *Shakti* is the kinetic power of the divine, so we find that even *Vaishnavites* (followers of *Vishnu*) and *Shaivites* (followers of *Shiva*) also worship *Shakti* or the goddess, as power. The expression

Shakti thus not only denotes the great goddess *Maha Devi*, but it also stands for the energizing power of any particular divinity. Unfortunately, *Shakti* worship has been misunderstood totally by most people including Indians themselves. *Shakti* worship is the worship of God's glory. *Devi* belongs to all sects, for she is the conscious power of the *deva* or of God. *Shakti* worship has its origin in the *Vedas* itself.

The *Upanishad* says, "*Parashakti*, the supreme power of God is the nature of God manifesting as knowledge, strength and activity. In fact we can say that everyone in the universe is a *Shakti* worshipper, for none can go without all these things. Physicists and scientists have proved that everything is pure imperishable energy. This energy is nothing but the divine *Shakti* that exists in every form of existence.

What are the vital aspects of the theory and practice of the *Shaktas*? *Shaktism* is dynamic Hinduism. It reconciles and amalgamates all aspects of Hindu philosophy. In the *Puranas, Devi* is known as the sister of *Vishnu* and the wife of *Shiva*, the mother of *Ganesha* and *Subramania*. Thus, she is the centre of all the great deities who are worshipped in India. The *Puranas* are considered to be one of the authorities on the *Shakti* cult. The *Brahma Vaivarta*, the *Skanda* and the *Kaalika* are the main *Puranas* that inculcate the worship of the Supreme as feminine. But the principal rites, rituals and incantations of this sect are found in a different source. The *bija mantras* that are used in *Shakta* rites are all derived from the *Tantras*.

The *Tantras* are therefore the main books on the worship of the goddess as *Shakti*. *Adi Shankaracharya* asserts that the books on *Tantra* are sixty-four in number. The authorship of these books is attributed to Lord *Shiva*. It is said that the sons of *Brahma* – *Sanaka, Sananda, Sanatana* and *Sanat Kumara* – begged Lord *Shiva* for a simpler method of *sadhana* than given in the *Vedas* and Lord *Shiva* taught them the secret doctrines of the *Tantras*.

Another and more popular theory is that *Shiva* taught these esoteric doctrines to *Parvati*. She asked him for an easy means of liberation for human beings who are born in this Iron Age of *Kali*, and he answered that *Tantra* was the easiest method of release. He disclosed this esoteric doctrine to *Parvati* and *Vishnu* confirmed them. The *Tantras* are therefore collectively known as the *Agamas* since they issued from the mouth of *Shiva*, were heard by the Mountain Goddess, and were sanctioned by *Vishnu.* (There are three syllables in the word a-ga-ma.)

In the *Shiva Tantra, Shiva* says, "The five scriptures (the four *Vedas* and the *Tantras*) issued from my five mouths. They correspond to the five directions – East, West, North, South and above. These five are known as the paths to final liberation. There are many scriptures but none are equal to the one 'above' (meaning the *Tantras*).

In the *Tantras* we find that *Brahman* is synonymous with *Shakti. Brahman* stands for the formless, Ultimate or *Turiya Brahman* that is ever united with *Mula Prakriti* or fundamental nature. *Shakti* is another name for *Mula Prakriti* united with *Turiya Brahman,* so they are not separate. *Brahman* cannot exist without *Shakti* nor can *Shakti* exist without *Brahman. Brahman* is static *Shakti* and *Shakti* is dynamic *Brahman.* This is the only difference. In *Tantric* books, *Shiva* stands for this *Turiya Brahman,* which is pure unconditioned consciousness.

The excellence of *Tantrism* lies in its emphasis on *sadhana* or spiritual practice. There can be no *siddhi* without *sadhana.* Complete knowledge of anything can only come by becoming that thing. To know *Brahman* (the Supreme), we must become *Brahman. Tantra* is popularly known as *mantra shastra* and *sadhana shastra,* for it is a practical science that makes use of *mantras.* This *sadhana* is not meant merely for transcendental benefits but also for material, for the *tantrics* consider the material world to be the foundation that upholds the spiritual structure. One has to start from the base to reach the summit. The *Vedic* '*Vac*' or creative word becomes the *adya spanda* or primal throb which finally develops into the seed sounds or *bijaksharas* used in *mantras.* From these sound vibrations they proceed to their Ultimate Cause or original throb that is the Supreme.

The *Tantras* give a set of rituals, *mantras* and *yogic sadhanas* that supplement the *Vedic sadhanas.* These are meant to give the fastest results if practiced properly. They are open to all castes and both sexes, unlike the *Vedic sadhanas,* which are meant only for the initiates, mainly *Brahmin* males. Thus, we find that especially in Bengal and South India, *Tantric* rituals have superseded the *Vedic* fire ceremonies. *Tantra* offers the means by which the undying reality within oneself can be uncovered through *yoga,* rituals, selfless service, art, and study and total dedication to the goddess in whatever form one conceives of her.

The meaning of the word '*tantra*' is found in the word itself. It is a combination of the two words, '*tanoti*' or 'expansion' and '*trayati*' or 'liberation'. It is the method of expanding the mind to its fullest capacity in order to attain liberation. Expansion of the mind allows us to experience a reality, which lies beyond the realm of the five senses. The knowledge derived through the senses is sadly restricted to the boundaries of space, time and causality. But if we know the technique of turning the mind inward, it will go beyond these boundaries and expand into the cosmic mind. When this happens, the apparent differences between matter and energy will disappear. Just as a river loses its limitations when it enters the ocean, so the individual mind becomes a receptor and transmitter of cosmic truth when it expands into the ocean of the infinite mind. There is an explosion of energy and the apparently small individual consciousness is freed from the thraldom of matter. It is only in this age that physics has accepted the fact that matter and energy are inter-convertible. Over two thousand years ago, *Tantra* went one step further and asserted that matter, energy and consciousness are all inter-convertible. Modern science is slowly and reluctantly coming to the same conclusion. Today, *Tantra* stands as the only spiritual tradition that has kept the sphere of practical application alive and uses it as a scientific treatment for the human mind and consciousness.

The ancient *rishis* dissected the human personality and made different sciences, which would raise each aspect of the personality to its highest potential, thus creating a holistic and complete human being. *Ayurveda* is a method of maintaining a perfect physical body while *Tantra* is a mental science, a meta-psychology, a method of exploring the mind and developing the range of one's perceptions. In fact it is the science of personality. *Tantra* declares that the path of liberation is open to every type of nature – sensual or spiritual, atheistic or theistic, weak or strong. It helps you to discover your own path. All human emotions like passion, fear, hatred, love, and anger are energy forces. If controlled, they can enable us to experience higher realities.

The universe possesses all possible qualities and attributes and each creature within the universe possesses a limited number of these qualities and attributes. The human psyche is actually a field of all possibilities even though we do not make use of it. The personality of an individual depends on his identification with a certain set of attributes. The Supreme according to *Shaktism* is *Adi Shakti* and possesses the ultimate personality, the supreme expression of the totality of manifested existence. Illness, according to *Tantra*, lies in having a limited, non-integrated personality. Health is derived both from internal balance as well as from harmony with the environment. On the physical level, our body's immunity lies in the number of white blood cells and anti-bodies that it has, similarly the strength of the mind lies in the degree of its personality integration. The aim of *Tantra* is to replace the limited human personality with an unlimited, permanent one. Anyone who continues to live with a limited personality can be considered to be diseased. Only those who choose to go beyond the three limiting factors of time, space and causality can be said to be in harmony with the cosmos and, therefore, truly healthy.

One of the areas of *Tantric* research was in finding out methods of prolonging one's life since that would give more time for integrating the personality and attaining harmony with creation.

A *Tantric* practitioner may fail to gain immortality in one lifetime but it is possible that he will get some extraordinary powers called *siddhis*. Wisely used, *siddhis* can accelerate one's spiritual evolution. But if they are commercialised, as they very often are by foolish *tantrics,* they will only bind one down more firmly to the wheel of cause and effect. Certain types of medicinal plants, metals and gems are all used in *Tantric* practices. They discovered the obscure secret of mercury, which has an infinite number of uses.

The *tantrics* also searched for the philosopher's stone, which would change base metal into gold, but esoterically speaking, the change they sought for, was the transmutation of the individual's limited personality to the gold of enlightenment, a state of unlimited consciousness. Though *Tantra* may seem too complex for the ordinary person, one cannot but fail to be filled with awe at the amazing thoroughness and attention to specific details that the ancient sages displayed in this science. Thankfully it cannot be exploited, for only one who can practice it in its every detail would be qualified to teach it and such practitioners are rare.

As has been mentioned before there is no *siddhi* or perfection without *sadhana* or spiritual practice. Essential to the procuring of any *siddhi* are the *sadhanas* that make use of *mantra, yantra* and *tantra.* A *mantra* is a particular vibration of the original throb of the cosmos and represents the sound body of one particular godhead in the structure of consciousness. *Mantras* are chanted during rituals in order to invoke the appropriate deities. All gods have their own *mantras,* which have the ability to conjure up the form of the deity when used repeatedly in the prescribed fashion. *Yantras* are a particular arrangement of the original light emanating from the Absolute. They represent the form pattern of a god. *Mantra* is the sound body of the deity and *yantra*, the form pattern. The nameless and the formless have thus been captured by the *rishis* into sounds and forms! *Yantras* are normally diagrams drawn on bark, crystal or copper plates. They can also be drawn on the ground with different coloured powders or sand. This is done before the commencement of a *yajna* or *puja.* All deities have their own *yantras.*

Tantra insists that no worship of the deity is complete without the worship of the deity's body in a material image, like an idol or a *yantra* or *chakra.* Inner worship leads one to the path of knowledge but for the full development of both the spiritual and material aspects of life, outer worship is necessary. It is more powerful and intensifies devotion and stabilises the inner realisation to the outer conditions. If this outer worship is done in an automatic and lifeless manner it will have no results but if it is done with knowledge, it can open up the body and mind of the aspirant to the heights of consciousness and delight. Any act, however mundane, if offered to the higher force within oneself, becomes a medium through which one can expand the awareness.

Tantra teaches that through the name and form of any deity it is possible to attain the nameless and formless *Brahman. Mantra,* the sound and *Yantra,* the form, are both to be used in the path mapped out by *Tantra.* Therefore, *Mantra, Yantra* and *Tantra* are all necessary for gaining *siddhi. Mantra* is the energy that moves the vehicle or *Yantra* according to the path as described by *Tantra.* The best *Yantra* is said to be the human body. The divine already resides within this body and if certain *tantric* rites are performed the individual will be able to reach her full divine potential. The highest self is said to be a priceless gem locked in a chest that is buried in mud. *Tantric* disciplines consist in cleaning away the mud of our petty desires and negativity and opening the treasure box in our brain to expose the gem of self-awareness within.

Tantric sadhanas are divided into three different types, to be used by diverse types of personalities. The *pashu* type is the *tamasic* individual whose life is akin to that of an animal in as much as he lives only for the sake of externalised enjoyments. Such an aspirant should perform external worship in its grossest form to control these urges. The *divya* or divine type has a *sattvic* temperament and tends to be introverted. Such a person need not bother with external rituals, even though he may continue to do it with devotion and knowledge. The *vira* or heroic type is *rajasic* in nature and likes activity. Such a person can perform both external and internal rituals. These people are capable of giving complete attention to every detail of the ritual. This is a most important point in all *tantric* rites. The true *divya* and *vira* types consider every act of daily life to be a ritual. Every breath is an offering to the *Adi Shakti.* Their whole life in an offering to the Supreme. Their goal is to awaken the inherent feminine *Shakti* or energy within, in order to attain union with the Supreme Consciousness known as *Shiva.* Every act of theirs is geared towards this consummation. Without awakening this energy, one can never attain the Supreme.

Tantra insists that there is no *mukti* (liberation) without *bhukti* (experience). Every experience that comes to the individual, whether good or bad, has to be accepted gratefully. This is because though *Tantra* affirms the existence of the transcendental *Brahman*, it also affirms the existence of the universe as a manifestation of the divine *Shakti.* So everything that takes place in the universe is also divine. The *tantric* does not mind regarding the world as *maya* so long as it is understood that this *maya* is nothing but the Divine Mother herself. *Tantric sadhana* is used for procuring material things as well, for they are the foundations on which the whole spiritual structure stands. The *sadhaka* depends totally on the magnanimity of the goddess to protect and provide.

There is a lot of difference in the *tantric* attitude to life and the attitude of some of the other schools of Indian philosophy. *Advaita* or monism stresses on unity. *Brahman* alone is real, so the world is unreal. If the world is unreal, then our view of the world also becomes clouded. The world is considered to be the source of pain and sorrow, for it is evanescent. *Adi Shankara* viewed the world from the transcendental point of view and thus concluded that it was unreal. *Tantra* on the other hand takes the standpoint of the *jiva*. To the *jiva*, the world is real and *Iswari*, the creator-goddess is also real. It is her *Shakti* that brings forth the creation out of herself, like the spider spinning a world of its web out of itself. The *tantrics* consider the goddess to be *Anandarupini* – pure blissful consciousness. From this they derive the idea that the universe is not only real but also joyful in character and meant for enjoyment. However, due to our desires for transitory things we are unable to enjoy this life as it is meant to be enjoyed.

Tantric rituals are sacrificial rites. Though herbs, minerals and sometimes even animals are used as offerings, they are only secondary to the true offering which is the sacrifice of one's limited self into the sacrificial fires of penance. Contrary to popular belief, *Shaktism* along with other schools of Hinduism affirms that a healthy physical and moral life is absolutely essential to the practice of *Tantra*. One, who has not refrained from evil acts and has no peace of mind and self-control, cannot attain God by any manner of means.

Tantrics are divided into two leading branches – the *Dakshinacharis* and the *Vamacharis* – the followers of the right-hand path and the followers of the left-hand path. *Dakshina Marga* is meant for those who seek steady progress with reduced danger of set-backs. The *Vama Marga* is described as fast, terrible and intense. On this path the chances of a fall are great unless the protection of a powerful *guru* is there. The rituals that involve sex and have made *Tantra* notorious, are part of this path. There is much misunderstanding about this even till this day. The *Vama Marga* is the most esoteric teaching of *Tantra* and, as has been said, should never be practiced without a competent *guru*, who has mastered the art and is capable of leading the aspirant step-by-step through this walk on the razor's edge, where the slightest fall could lead to death or insanity. It is also known as the *Kaula Marga*.

The *Dakshina Marga* or right-handed path devotes itself to the worship of the goddess in her most benign form while the left-handed path worships her in her most terrible and base forms. With the typical fearlessness of Hindu philosophy, *Shaktism* insists that worship of the goddess should reconcile all aspects of the deity – both good and so-called evil. Since she is *Adi Shakti*, she encompasses everything, so there is nothing that can be considered beyond the pale. This is one of the reasons why *tantric* practices have been a closely guarded secret. There is a great danger of them being misinterpreted and falling into wrong hands. One should never practice classical *Tantra* without a *guru* because there are no *tantric* texts that give accurate information about the rituals. All the texts either omit an essential step or give false information, so it is only through the *guru* that the esoteric information can be received. It is always handed down from teacher to disciple.

One of the first steps in *tantric* practice is what is known as *tattva shuddhi* or the cleansing of the elements that make up our material body. By continuous practice we can divinise these elements in our body so that they are no longer seen as gross matter but as forms of the divine *Shakti,* which is nothing but the Supreme Consciousness.

These elements are earth, water, air, fire and ether. To achieve harmony these elements must be purified. To experience Pure Consciousness we have to go beyond matter, which is made up of these five elements. The energy, which is locked in matter, is released and transformed by *tattva shuddhi.* The universe, including our own bodies has evolved out of *Shakti* or pure energy. Her cosmic counterpart is *Shiva* or Pure Consciousness. Although they have momentarily separated to give rise to the whole of creation, they are forever striving to unite in the human body in order to re-experience the cosmic unity from which they evolved. The whole object of *Tantra* is to attain this cosmic union.

Panchamakara is one of the many *tantric* rituals that aim at *bhuta-shuddhi* or *tattva shuddhi*, which is the purification of these five great elements. It is known as *panchamakara,* since the names of all the offerings start with the letter 'ma'. The offerings are *madya* (wine), *matsya* (fish), *mamsa* (flesh), *mithuna* (sex), and *mudra* (mystic gestures). These five have different meanings according to the type of aspirant who practices the ritual. The three types of aspirants have already been described. They are the *pashu* or *tamasic* type, the *vira* or *rajasic* type and the *divya* or *sattvic* type. The *tamasic* type alone is meant to follow the verbal meaning of the *panchamakaras,* or five offerings. The intensity of these five articles of worship, like the eating of fish, meat, wine, parched grain and having controlled sex is supposed to overthrow the dullness of the *tamasic* person and stimulate his brain. If the aspirant has been properly taught by a competent *guru,* this increased mental energy can help to hasten his spiritual evolution. A half-baked aspirant on the other hand will be overcome by this stimulation and descend into debauchery of the worst type.

Rajasic or *vira* types have active minds, which must be properly channelled. They need less stimulation and more control. So they use ginger instead of meat, radish instead of fish, boiled rice instead of parched grain, honey instead of wine, and flowers instead of sex in their *panchamakara* rituals.

The *divya* or *sattvic* types are naturally balanced and harmonious and do not require external aids to worship. To them meat is their own flesh that is eaten through fasting and silence and fish, is breath control through the practice of *pranayama.* Breath flows through the two nostrils like fish swimming in the river. Grain is the use of concentration techniques. Wine is the intoxication got from God, and sex is the union of one's limited ego with the Absolute. Esoterically speaking, *Madya* or wine is the nectar flowing from the *Sahasrara Chakra. Matsya* and *mudra* stand for the two *nadis* of the *Kundalini* – the *Ida* and *Pingala. Mithuna* is of course the joy of union of the *atman* with the *Paramatman* in the *Sahasrara Chakra* at the crown of the head.

Panchamakara is a fast, intense way of attaining *tattva shuddhi.* Each of these five offerings stands for one element. Meat stands for earth, fish for water, wine for fire, grain for air and sex for ether. By the correct use of this ritual, one can balance these elements in our body and thus achieve perfect harmony with the universe, which in turn gives perfect physical health that is so necessary for spiritual practice.

The doctrine of *Kundalini* and the *chakras* are also closely connected with the five great elements. When the elements have been thoroughly purified in an individual, the *Kundalini Shakti,* which is the individual equivalent of the cosmic *Adi Shakti,* has a free path upwards through the *chakras* and is able to meet and unite with *Shiva* in the *Sahasrara Chakra* in the brain. Each of the five lower *chakras* is the seat of the subtle form of one element. As each one is purified and harmonised, the *Kundalini* can free herself from their grasp. The *Lalitha Sahasranama* is an esoteric description of the rise of the *Kundalini Shakti.* Many methods like the *panchamakara* are advocated in order to enable this psychic force to rise. The chanting of the *Lalitha Sahasranama* with an understanding of its meaning is one of them.

The wonderful hymn of *Brahma* to the *Devi* in the *Brahmanda Purana* gives us a clue to the form of the goddess worshipped by the *Shaktas*. It is addressed to the goddess, *Adi Lakshmi* or *Kamakshi* who is said to be the mother of the *Trimurtis* (the Hindu trinity). She has the glorious form of light, and shines in the hearts of all. She is *Jaganmata* (Mother of the universe) as well as *Tripurasundari* (most beautiful in all the three worlds). She creates, preserves and destroys the universe but none can really know her. She is known only to herself. She is to be meditated upon by *Brahma*, *Vishnu* and *Shiva* as well as by *Indra* and the other deities. She is *Jnana Shakti* and it is at her command that the sun and moon light the earth and fire burns brightly. She is the immanent soul of all souls.

"There was no mind there with its need to know,
There was no heart there with its need to love,
All people perished in its namelessness,
There was no second; it had no partner or peer.
Only itself was real to itself."

— "Savitri" by Sri Aurobindo

Thus ends the twenty-eighth chapter of the *Sri Devi Lila* known as 'Adi Shakti', which describes *Tantra* – the cult of the *Shaktas*.

ॐ *Aim, hreem, kleem* ॐ

ॐ

Bhadrayai Namaha!

CHAPTER TWENTY-NINE

SMASHAN TARA

Srishti sthiti vinashanam, Shaktibhute sanathane,
Gunashraye gunamaye Narayani Namosthute!

"Salutations to Thee, O *Narayani*, the eternal,
Who is the power behind creation, maintenance and destruction.
Who consists of and abides in, the three qualities of primordial matter!"

Maya is the external garb of the universe. She is like a well-dressed, heavily made-up woman who appears beautiful and enticing. It is only when you remove her make-up that you discover her real form. The green colour and sour taste of a fruit is not its permanent state. Soon it will become yellow, ripe and sweet. So the green state is an impermanent one. So also is the case with *maya*. Her external garb is made up of the three *gunas* or qualities of primordial matter. It is only when you strip her of these adjuncts that you see her beauteous form as *Maha Devi*.

She is also known as *Shakti* since her projection of this universe is dynamic. *Shakti* is the energy that emanates spontaneously from the Supreme. Pure energy in any form is dangerous if not controlled. In *Tantric* philosophy it is *Shiva* who controls and conditions *Shakti*. He is the male aspect of the Supreme *Brahman*. He is depicted as having three eyes. *Maya* is his *Shakti* and contains the essence of duality, which is space, time and causation. As long as *Shiva* keeps his third eye closed, *maya* can have a full play. *Shiva's* two eyes, like ours, see only duality and when he keeps them open the world exists. However, with his third eye, the eye of transcendent wisdom, he can see only unity. So when he opens his third eye, the cosmos, which can exist only in duality along with its creatrix *Maha Maya*, will return to the plenum from which it was projected. So long as *Shiva's* third eye is open, nothing can exist. There is only *Pralaya* or the undifferentiated consciousness of Absolute Reality. When he closes his third eye, *Shiva* becomes subject to duality once again and *Maha Maya* appears in the forefront and the cosmos rises up.

The special sect of *Tantra* known as *Aghora*, belongs to the *Vama Marga,* which has been already discussed in the previous chapter. This is the left- handed path. In India the left hand is used for performing inauspicious actions like cleaning the lower orifices. *Shakti* controls the left side of our body. A man's wife is always seated on his left when they perform rituals together. In *Tantra*, the supreme deity is the Divine Mother. She is always standing on the left side of the devotee and helping him, so *Aghora* is indeed the left-handed path in more ways than one.

The word *aghora* means 'deeper than the deepest' or 'filled with light'. The aim of the *Aghora* and of *Tantra* is *laya,* which is a return to the state of undifferentiated consciousness. It gives many methods of achieving this *laya* or the union of the individual with the Supreme. In this, it is not at variance with the rest of Hindu religion, which also aims at the union of the *jivatman* with the *Paramatman.* The difference lies only in the methodology and words used to describe this union. In *Tantra*, this union is described through sexual metaphors. The personalised ego is considered to be feminine and the Absolute, male.

Due to the usage of sex in their rituals, there is a lot of misunderstanding about *Aghora.* But actually it is only under special circumstances that sexual rituals are employed to hasten spiritual progress. Even this has to be under the strict personal supervision of an enlightened *Tantric* practitioner or *guru.* Their practices include necromancy, use of intoxicants, sex and other forbidden and exceedingly dangerous types of rites. This has given *Aghora* a bad reputation. The truth is that *aghoris* try to overcome all mental differentiations between auspicious and inauspicious things, events and actions, and deliberately perform actions that might be considered inauspicious by most people. Everything is favourable to the *aghori* since everything comes from the Divine Mother. The sincere *aghori* depends totally on the power of the *Devi* to protect him. This protection is given only if the practitioner has developed absolute internal purity and takes up the practice only for the sake of spiritual progress and shuns every other type of power or *siddhi* that might come to him. Those who follow this way without the necessary purification of mind and body (*tattva shuddhi*) and without renouncing all sensory gratification, are bound to suffer tremendous repercussions, which might lead to madness or even death.

Commercialisation of the *siddhis* or special powers that might come to him as a result of these practices will also lead to his downfall. Hence you find that even in India there are very few true *aghoris*, for most people are incapable of making the incredible physical and mental sacrifices that the cult demands. It is truly a most dangerous path for the unwary – the razor's edge. Due to the difficulties on the course, most normal people are quite frightened to take up the path. So thankfully it cannot be commercialised like so many other paths in the Hindu religion.

Westerners, who were brought up in the conservative tradition of Christianity – and who were the first to come to India – condemned the *Aghora* as a sect who were steeped in sinful indulgence. They cannot be blamed for this, for their denunciation was based on ignorance. *Aghora* is far from being a type of indulgence. On the contrary, strict renunciation is the pre-requisite for initiation. Only when personal purity is perfect, is the aspirant allowed to perform rituals, which to the ignorant observer might appear hedonistic or sinful. *Aghora* is not a path of indulgence but a forcible transformation of the darkness of the individual consciousness to the luminescence of the Absolute. Renunciation is itself renounced when one reaches the Absolute state of perfection, for then nothing remains to be renounced. Before he reaches this luminescence the *aghori* is expected to plunge into the worst types of hell that the human mind can conceive of. Only then can he shake off the veil of ignorance and emerge into the sunlight of a supramental consciousness.

The *aghoris* are not content to sip the wine of the sweetness of life. They are determined to explore the very dregs of this cup of the wine of life. The *aghori* is like the lotus flower that revels in the mud in which it was born but when the time for blossoming comes, it shakes off the mud and raises its beautiful visage to the golden orb of the morning sun. Why dabble in such unsavoury things when Hinduism offers such sublime paths to the same goal, is a question often asked. The answer given by the *aghoris* is that it is the fastest path to liberation as well as to destruction!

The popular picture of an *aghori* is that of a wild-eyed ascetic with long matted hair, smeared with ashes from the burning *ghats*, skulking in cremation grounds, fighting with jackals over human carcasses! But the fact of the matter is that the true *aghori* may well look like an ordinary person. His practices are kept strictly private and his internal purity is unbelievable but such a one will not be interested in exposing himself to the curious gaze of the public. He practices in secret, in the dead of night in cremation grounds where none dare approach.

One of the immutable tenets of *Aghora* is that death is to be personified and deified. *Shiva* is known as *Mahakaala* or 'Death in the form of Time!' It is not physical death that the *aghoris* crave for but the destruction of all human limitations. Once he sets out to undertake the difficult rituals of the sect, the *aghori* is prepared either to succeed or die in the attempt. There is no middle course and no retreat. One who fears death should not embark on this path. It is meant only for those who have totally given up all fears, especially the fear of death.

Many of their rituals are conducted at midnight in burning *ghats* and cemeteries. These rites are done in a state of intoxication, seated next to a blazing funeral pyre, with flames shooting up into the blackness of the night. Most of their rites will always remain incomprehensible to the normal mind brought up with the prudish ideas of a conservative religious background. But lack of understanding should not make us condemn the practice.

Western philosophers experimented with the science of alchemy by which they sought to change the dross of base metals into gold. *Aghora* is similar to this but the base metal they seek to change is the animal-born mind of the human being. *Aghora* is one of the great discoveries of the Hindu religion which has dared to explore every facet of the human mind and find out methods of transmuting every aspect, even the basest, into the gold of enlightenment! It is one of the highest spiritual sciences that India has produced. *Aghora* is a mysterious practice and only those who are capable of laying aside their cultural clothing and plunging into the depths of their psyche will be able to discover the pearls within. It is not a path for the cowardly who want easy and safe methods of enlightenment. It is meant only for those who can leave the standard paths, which have few pitfalls and take to the path of the razor's edge, who dare to renounce their very lives if necessary, to find the jewel of enlightenment. Hinduism offers many safe paths to enlightenment in which the practitioner can lift himself up if he falls and restart his journey. But in *Aghora*, it is 'do or die'. If you fail, you fall into the deepest pits of hell and if you succeed you are the master of the universe! Nothing can harm you. You can roam about as you like, eating anything you like, drinking anything you like, for you are a walking corpse. Why should a corpse care about what it eats or drinks? Nothing can harm it. The cosmic *Shakti* is in possession of your body and you are like a *Yantra.* She plays through you and with you and allows you to enjoy the bliss. But of course this is the final stage and the *aghori* has to pass through many treacherous and highly dangerous disciplines before reaching such a stage.

It is the path of no return, a highly personal creed which puts at stake everything for the love of the Divine Mother and is prepared to relinquish every earthly pleasure for the sake of her love. The true *aghori* is not bound by the worldly bonds in which *maya* binds the ordinary mortal. He is intoxicated with the love of *Maha Maya.* His own identity is totally merged in hers so that he, as the personalised ego, no longer exists. *Mantra, Yantra* and *Tantra* are used to create the form of the deity in the aspirant's consciousness. After this the devotee and the goddess are expected to strictly keep to the type of relationship that suits him/her best – mother/son, lover/beloved, child/mother or just friends. This is known as *tanmayata.* One has to continue worshipping in this fashion until the relationship is fully stabilised. Eventually all traces of the devotee's original personality will be totally effaced and only the deity's personality will remain. This is known as *tadrupata* or attaining the same form.

The *aghoris* also practice the *panchamakara* ritual, which is basic to all *tantric* rites. A couple who wants to practice this in the correct way have to perfect the *Shiva Lata Mudra* in which all traces of animal desire are completely eliminated. The male identifies himself with *Shiva* and the female with *Shakti.* "Only one who has become *Shiva* will be able to worship *Shiva*!" is what they say. Thus, the couple should attain *tanmayata* with these deities before starting the ritual.

In the *Shiva Lata Mudra*, the man places his wife on his left thigh and cups her left breast with his left palm. The woman holds his penis with her right palm and clings to him like a creeper (*lata*). They do *japa* with the appropriate *mantras*. The man holds the *mala* or rosary in his right hand and she in her left. Soon they are so immersed in the repetition of the *mantra* that they both forget their individual personalities. She sees him as Lord *Shiva* and he worships her as the cosmic *Shakti*. They should be able to retain this attitude for at least three hours without any sexual excitement. There should be neither erection nor dilation! This can happen only when self-identification with the deities is complete. The concentration must be intense and the identification absolute. In fact, the couple will soon go into a state of *Bhava Samadhi* where they forget the mundane world and identify themselves wholly with *Shiva* and *Shakti*. Only couples, who have thus successfully practiced the *Shiva Lata Mudra* many times, are allowed to perform the *panchamakara* ritual in its purest form. Of course this is not always the case and many half-baked *yogis* perform the ritual and bring ruin on themselves and a bad reputation for the practice.

As we have seen in the previous chapter, the word *panchamakara* actually denotes the five types of offerings that are to be made in the ritual, all of which start with the Sanskrit letter 'ma'. These are *matsya, mamsa, mudra, madya* and *mithuna*, which stand for fish, meat, parched grain and certain hand postures, wine and the sexual act. To the couple that have become adept in the *Shiva Lata Mudra*, the partaking of these forbidden articles is no longer an act of indulgence but a sacrament. Since they have attained *tadrupata* with the deities, their physical bodies have attained total identification with these divine beings and they are the ones who are performing the rite and directly partaking of the offerings. Ordinary sex is for the gratification of the lust of the couple concerned, but in this *tantric* rite the partners have totally submerged their personalities with their chosen deities and offer themselves for the gratification of these gods alone. *Tantric* rituals are sacrificial rites like the *Vedic* fire sacrifices or *yajnas*. In this ritual the female is the fire into which the male offers his semen, just as ghee is offered into the *yajna kund*, or sacrificial pit in orthodox methods of fire worship.

Aghoris also use herbs and minerals like mercury and, sometimes, even animals as offerings. But it must be remembered that these are secondary to the true offering of one's limited self into the sacrificial fire of penance.

It is a very difficult path to pursue and the chances of a fall are legion. This is one of the reasons that *Aghora* has always been such a closely guarded secret.

The body of the *aghori* is always to be kept in a state of perfect health, since it is the *yantra* or vehicle that will enable him to reach his goal. His mind also should be fearless and free of worries. He has to be careful of what he eats and what he thinks while practicing these esoteric rites. The *bhuta agni* is the fire of austerity which enkindles the *jatara agni* or the fire of digestion. When the mind is weak and worried, the *bhuta agni* is weakened, which in turn weakens the *jatara agni.* This results in indigestion and disease. So the spiritual person should try to preserve his *bhuta agni* or spiritual digestion which will give him both mental and physical health. The best way to do this is to eat less. This is the reason why all religions insist on some type of fasting, which will improve health. As one's bodily hunger decreases, one feels an increased hunger for spiritual things. Sleep and sex dull both the *bhuta agni* and the *jatara agni.*

Alcohol is generally considered to strengthen the fire of digestion but it also has the effect of clouding the *bhuta agni.* The *aghoris* take alcohol and drugs only because they can keep their minds under control and use the drug with the appropriate dosage, needed to produce a heightened feeling of consciousness which will further their spiritual practices. If the drug overcomes them, as it does most people, it is of no use and will only end in downfall. Another reason why *aghoris* use intoxicants is because *Shiva* is supposed to take them and they think it will help them to identify themselves with the deity. It is only when they reach the height of their *sadhana* that they come to understand that *Shiva* is always in an intoxicated state of *atmic* bliss, and not in the temporary state of euphoria produced by drugs and alcohol. The *aghori* who wants to emulate *Shiva's* example has to gingerly tread this path of fathomless pitfalls and hang on to his *Shakti,* depending only on her to support him and stop him from falling!

Aghoris take all types of intoxicants like marijuana and hashish. But all these have to be taken in the proper way. The proper *mantra* has to be used before imbibing any of them. Then it becomes a rite and is no longer an indulgence. Again this is a very dangerous path since the mind has a thousand ways in which it can fool itself. Taking an intoxicant or drug without the appropriate *mantra* will ruin the *bhuta agni* and, consequently, the mind. This is because a lot of *karmas* are involved in taking intoxicants. Intoxicants can be useful in *sadhana* or they can severely damage one's psyche. It all depends on how one uses them.

Even with all these precautions, the body will deteriorate with the constant use of intoxicants, because the mind becomes partially free from the constraints of the body. So in all ordinary forms of *yoga* one will find that the taking of any type of intoxicant is strictly forbidden. Even in *Aghora* there is the constant pitfall that the practitioner may become addicted to the drug and unable to withdraw himself from it even after it has served its purpose.

The *Vedantins* declare, '*Brahma satyam, jagat mithya*' or '*Brahman* alone is real, the world is an illusion'. The *aghoris* claim that *jagat* or the world is equally real. The world is a direct expression of the *Maha Maya* who is an emanation from the *Brahman,* which is the Absolute Reality. So the world, which is a product of *Brahma Shakti*, has also to be real. They form parts of a harmonious whole. They are inter-dependent. The world may not be absolutely true but it has its own reality that is based on the truth of impermanence. It is as real as we are. Enlightenment does not mean that one enters into some white light. It is the natural state of one's mind and not something which has to come from outside. What enlightenment means is that one has lightened himself of the burden of *karmas* and debts that one has been carrying for many births. This lightening process is done through *sadhana* or religious practices and of course by the grace of one's *guru* and the Divine Mother. The *Vedic* religion is the religion of light – the light of all lights, the Supreme Light of Consciousness by which even the sun is lit.

Aghora on the other hand, is the religion of darkness – utter, absolute and abysmal darkness. Can anyone define light or truth? Similarly, can anyone define darkness? All we can say is that it is an absence of light. The deepest darkness is the darkness of a mind shrouded in ignorance. The light is the light of one's own consciousness. *Aghora* teaches one to embrace impurities, embrace darkness, for it is the veil of the *Maha Maya.* One has to catch her by the hair and drag her to oneself and force her to push one, through the darkness to the light within. All normal people are dreadfully frightened of *maya* because they are totally enmeshed in her web. *Maya* is the projection of the *Shakti* of *Shiva* into the outside world, and people fear her because they cannot control her. The *aghori*, however, identifies himself with *Shiva*, the Supreme within him and thus controls *maya*. From the mortality of earthly existence he propitiates the destroyer – *Mahakaala* (*Shiva*), and thus becomes immortal. Having controlled *Shakti*, he becomes luminent like *Shiva*.

The *Vedas* say, "Lead us from the unreal to the real, from darkness to light, and from death to immortality!" This is also the goal of *Aghora*. But the difference is that *Vedanta* tells us to proceed from the semi-darkness in which we exist and follow the path of self-enquiry, into the nature of the 'I' until we reach the light of the Absolute. *Aghora*, however, tells us to find out the nature of our darkness first and investigate both aspects of duality – the negative and the positive – until we go beyond into the state of non-duality.

Nothing is inauspicious to the *aghori*. His initiation has been in the burning *ghat* amidst the corpses, ghosts and spirits that roam around there. The foremost fear that he is taught to conquer is the fear of death. Attachment to the body has to be totally given up. If one clings to the body and fears death, one cannot perfect even the preliminary lesson in *Aghora*. To be an *aghori*, one has to go beyond all limitation and the greatest limitation is the limitation of the body. One has to embrace death while still being alive. He who has given up attachment to the body has nothing to lose and nothing to fear, for the greatest fear is the loss of the body through death. The mind has to be absolutely firm. Even if the most beautiful spirit comes to tempt one, he should remain firmly concentrated on *Shiva*. Ghosts and ghouls can throw hot coals in the cremation ground but he should be able to watch his skin burn with detachment and unconcern. It is only one who has controlled himself to this extreme extent, who can succeed in *Aghora*.

There are three things that bind us firmly to the body and these are food, sleep and sex. To welcome death while remaining in the body, one has to restrict all three. The more one indulges in these three things, the more one keeps craving for them. Gratifying them can eliminate other desires but these three will keep increasing in intensity the more one gives in to them. The more one eats, the more one wants to eat, the more one sleeps, the more one wants to sleep and the more one indulges in sex the more one craves for it. Unless one learns to curb these three, one can never make any true spiritual progress. Too much food makes one sleepy and sex exhausts you. *Aghoris* cannot afford to indulge in any type of relaxation. They have to be alert all the time. If one falls asleep in the cremation ground while practising some rite, one becomes psychically weak and any passing spirit will be able to enter the body and use it for its own purposes.

The '*Naths*' are an ancient tribe of famous *aghoris*. The great sage, *Goraknath* was their founder. Their prescription for spiritual advancement was to break up one's sleep and to cut down on food. Sleep is a form of death and overcomes the mind with a blanket of dullness that erases all that one has gained in meditation. So sleep should be reduced to the absolute minimum. They used a special plant for this purpose, which had to be ground and applied on the soles of the feet for thirty days, and this ensured that one could have control of both dreams and sleep.

To die while alive, means that a person has to eliminate all involuntary stimulation of the senses. One cannot salivate on seeing a tempting dinner. One cannot become aroused seeing a beautiful woman passing by, not even if she comes close enough to tempt the senses. One cannot even dwell on such things in memory and get a vicarious pleasure from them. When a person no longer reacts to this type of stimuli he is as good as dead. His body has dried up. The juicy thoughts which keep one bound to the body and are perpetually producing desires are no longer there. Only such a person is fit to imbibe the real juice of life – the nectar of immortality. Such a person may perform many things physically but they will not affect him, since he is totally unaffected by them mentally. He no longer reacts to physical stimuli. The *Bhagavad Purana* says that *Krishna* was a *nitya brahmachari* or a constant celibate even though he had many wives.

To die while still alive, means to extinguish duality altogether. The Absolute is One, not two, so all perception of duality has to be eliminated – pleasant and unpleasant, boring or exciting. A corpse does not care about any such distinctions. We are conditioned to think that corpses, skulls, menstrual blood and faeces are filthy and must be avoided at all cost. The very thought of using such things for rituals is nauseating to the common person. But the *aghori* makes use of all these things and is prepared to eat even human flesh from the cremation ground if it will help him gain his goal. *Aghoris* hang around cremation grounds and wait for the skull of a corpse to burst. They then swoop on the body and scoop the brain from within the skull before it is burnt and consume it. The brain is supposed to have some special properties that will help them in their *sadhana.* The goal of *sadhana* is to be able to accept everything in the world, both enticing and disgusting, with equanimity. *Tantra* actually is the non-rejection of all things and not the indulgence. Everything in the world is part of the *Maha Maya.* Duality is meant to delude the ego and assert her superiority.

The *Bhagavad Gita* declares that the enlightened soul is one who can see no difference between a clod, a stone and a diamond. All are different forms of matter and the diamond should not have more appeal due to its material value. Similarly, to the perfect *aghori,* a chocolate pudding, a clod and a lump of shit should have the same value! All are different forms of matter and should be treated as such! The only truly valuable thing on earth is the Supreme. Everything else is of equal value. It is the ignorant mind, which places different values on different things. The man of wisdom does not accept these differences even though he may be aware of them.

Have you ever paused to reflect on the number of murders, rapes, robberies, tortures and other heinous crimes that are being committed every moment in some part of the world or other? Who is responsible for this? No doubt it is each person's *karma* that brings such things within his orbit but even then why cannot an omnipotent God stop such atrocities? As has been discussed before, the Absolute *Brahman* does not concern itself with the running of the universe. Both the stage and the drama of the world are enacted by the *Parashakti,* the *Maha Maya* and she forces each one to take full responsibility for their actions. Ignorant fools, without a thought of the dreadful consequences of their appalling deeds, continue to commit one crime after another. But she knows it all and none can gainsay her! Can you imagine the amount of *karma* people accumulate? No wonder that the *jnanis* who are aware of the consequences of each *karma,* try to avoid actions altogether.

The *aghori* recognises the pitfalls of *karma* but forces himself to go beyond the fear and to see that it is all part of the whole. Everything is moving according to *Maha Maya's* divine plan. Every murder, every rape has its significance. One has to love everything, which takes place in the universe if one wants to go beyond duality and reach unity. When one sees One in All and All in One, one loses all fear. Fear exists only in duality. When a person sees only the *atman* in everything and himself as part and parcel of it, then who or what should he fear? Once a person gives up fear, the whole world is open to him because he has no demands. He has gone beyond anticipation and expectation. He anticipates nothing and expects nothing. He knows only to give because he always has so much and knows that nothing belongs only to him! He is the possessor of everything. The devotee sleeps like a baby in the lap of his Divine Mother, absolutely certain that everything will be provided for him. When death ceases to have a hold over him, then both time and causality cease to hold any fears.

Aghora is a path that is suitable only for a very special type of temperament. Everyone cannot practice it. Not only does the *aghori* strip off his clothes but he also strips his mind of every pre-conceived notion which society, culture and environment has clothed him in. He plunges himself into every possible type of so-called sin known to man, knowing that he has the power to draw himself out of it. He does this by complete surrender to the Divine Mother and is certain that she will draw him out after having purified him in the fire of his austerities. However, he is prepared to be tested at every moment, for that is part of her *lila.*

After having indulged in all types of intoxicants and narcotics, after having eaten all types of flesh including human and even offal and faeces without the slightest trace of disgust, the *aghori* comes to realise that the greatest narcotic, the greatest delicacy, the greatest bliss, is the name of God alone. He realises that the best drama is being enacted on the stage of his body and he himself is the main actor dancing the macabre dance of death with the destroyer himself, to the tune called by the divine *Shakti!* What joy can the world offer him? Clairvoyance, clairaudience, all the eight *siddhis* or extraordinary powers will be at his command. The Mother can deny him nothing but the strange thing is that now he wants nothing but her. He clings to her like a child and she in turn leads him to the Supreme from whom she has emanated. Such is the final state of the perfect *aghori* to whom the material world is but a toy that his divine Mother has given him to play with. He cares not for such trifles, for his body is aflame with desire for the cosmic beloved and he knows no other bliss but that of union with That! When one comes this close to the beloved there comes a time when he cannot continue to exist separately and his own personality is lost in that of the deity.

In his highest state the *aghori* becomes the greatest devotee. He is prepared to sacrifice everything in order to attain union with his deity. He is prepared to go to any lengths to attain the goal of his *sadhana.* No ordinary devotee can be as intense as an *aghori.* The *aghori* burns the candle of his life at both ends. It might not last through the night but while it does, it casts a lovely light!

"Life became a sure approach to God,
Existence a divine experiment;
The world a conception and a birth,
Of Spirit in Matter, into living forms.
Nature bore the Immortal in her womb,
That she might climb through him to eternal life."

— "Savitri" by Sri Aurobindo

Thus ends the twenty-ninth chapter of the *Sri Devi Lila* known as 'Smashan Tara', which describes *Aghora* – the left-hand path of *Tantra.*

ॐ *Aim, hreem, kleem* ॐ

ॐ

Chakrarajayai Namaha!

CHAPTER THIRTY

NARAYANI

"When the supreme Shakti, out of her own free will,
Takes on the form of the universe,
And gazes at her own throb,
Then the Sri Chakra comes into being."

— Yogini Hridayam

Yantra means an instrument, a machine or a storehouse of power. All forms of creation are nothing but energy, and a *Yantra,* due to its mathematical precision, is a powerhouse of inherent energy. It is drawn with lines, circles, squares and triangles. Within its concrete form it encloses the uncontrollable power of the deity. It limits the limitless within a figure of criss-cross lines that bind and channel the form of the deity. It creates a field of power that lives, breathes and moves with life, and within which the power of the divine can be invoked. These images exist within us but in order to perceive them we will have to develop a new way of looking at things, and sharpen our inherent faculty in which these images are stored. These images are pulled out of the vast Ocean of Consciousness that holds within it, all conceivable forms. As the awareness penetrates into deeper levels of consciousness, the inner experiences also change. They become more abstract. The forms we see in nature are only their gross representations, which are resting on their abstract subtle forms, and this is what the *Yantra* represents. The *Yantra* is the original form of everything in nature. Every image in nature can be represented by its linear dimension, which is the *Yantra.*

A *Yantra* is composed of a combination of the basic primordial shapes, like the *bindu* or point, a circle, a square and a triangle. The focal point of a *Yantra* is always the centre or *bindu.* It represents the point or nucleus, representing the seed from which creation has evolved and into which it will return – the process of creation and dissolution. It also represents the union of the two dual principles of the universe – *Shiva* and *Shakti*, consciousness and energy. The *bindu* represents the state of their union preceding creation. In the human body this focal point is found at the top back portion of the head. We will find that the *Brahmins* in India cover this spot with a tuft of hair.

Space cannot be circumscribed by anything less than three lines so the triangle is considered to be the first form to emerge out of creation. In its inverted form, it represents *Mula Prakriti* or the matrix of creation and the upward pointing triangle represents *Purusha* or *Shiva* or Pure Consciousness. In the *Sri Chakra* we will find this intersection of the upward triangle with the downward one many times, and this represents the downward thrust of energy which is met with an upward thrust of consciousness.

The circle represents the cycle of timelessness, which has no beginning and no end. It denotes eternity and implies the process of birth, life and death as an eternal cycle of events. The square is the substratum on which the *Yantra* rests and denotes the physical or terrestrial world that has to be transcended.

The *Yantra* is also known as a *Chakra* or wheel, representing constant movement. The *Chakra* signifies the constant and dynamic circulation of the power of the Infinite. The *Chakra*, like the *Yantra*, can lead us to the direct perception of the divine. The perfect lines of beauty, harmony and symmetry with which the Master Mathematician designs the universe, are caught in the *Chakra*. Just like the *Yantra*, it is drawn with lines, triangles, circles and squares. The lotus motif is frequently employed.

The *mandala* is always represented within a circle. The circle is a primal form and even our earth is in the form of a circle. Light waves move in a curve and thus bind space. The circular form is an essential part of the *mandala*. Any form that is pictorially created within the consciousness can form a *mandala*. *Tantric* iconography is filled with *mandalas* of the deities. These are often not the forms, which are visible to the gross vision, but the forms that are seen by the inner eye. An object can be visualised both from the outside and the inside but the difference is that when we visualise it from within, we catch a glimpse of what lies beyond the form.

The *mandalas* that we create will depend on our level of consciousness. The more evolved our mind, the more universal will be the *mandala* we create. Those who had transcended the material plane and become enraptured in some supracosmic ecstasy were the ones who created *tantric mandalas*.

Every civilization has its own *mandalas* and these give us a clue as to the level of consciousness of that society. These *mandalas* are created in the sub-conscious abyss of the mind, and hence they have a profound influence on the minds of those who look at it even though they may not be able to understand it. They can influence generations of people, long after they were made. That is why *tantric mandalas* have such a strong impact on us even today. All the ancient temple art of India were in the form of *mandalas*, since the artist was inspired by his inner vision and that is why they have withstood the test of time and exist as immortal and eternal ideas.

Even today *mandalas* are drawn in various colours in front of houses and for special rituals. The *mandala,* which is normally drawn before the commencement of any *tantric* ritual, is not a mere decorative image. It actually provides a potent and graphic focus for the operation of subtle forces – both internally and externally. Each deity has his or her own *mandala.* Concentration on the *mandala* awakens the deep-rooted *samskaras* within us and reveals unknown mysteries, in the form of dreams and visions. This is a psychologically subtle way of dispensing with a fearful enemy for which you have no outward defence. These *mandalas* are always aesthetic and are able to capture and direct our imagination, which is our link with our higher mind.

The *Vedas* speak of the supernal ether or *Akasa* as the abode of '*Vac*' or sound. *Tantra* calls this *Mahakaarana* or the cause of all causes. It is the storehouse of all sounds and is the permanent place of the light of all lights. From this mass of formless light, emerge the rays which fashion all forms during the course of evolution. *Deva* means 'the shining one' and the gods or *devas* are also emanations from this light. The formless radiance emits rays of definite forms and weaves them into the forms and features of the various gods. These lines of light that make the form-patterns of the gods are known as *Yantras* and *Chakras.* Contemplation on the Absolute can be done as a mass of ineffable light but if one wants to see the auspicious form of one's favourite deity, this light has to be codified into a definite pattern of rays and this codification results in the *Yantra* or the *Chakra*. *Tantra* says that by worshipping the *Chakra* or *Yantra* of a deity, one can immediately visualise the form and thus enable the god to manifest in front of our physical eyes. There is a wonderful passage in the *Isavasya Upanishad*, which says:

"The face of Truth is covered with a brilliant golden lid;
That do thou remove, O Fosterer of the law of Truth, for sight;
O Fosterer! O Sole Seer, O Ordainer! O illumining Sun!
O power of the Father of all creatures!
Marshal thy rays, draw together thy light;
The light, which is thy most blessed form, that in thee I behold.
The *Purusha* there and there,
He am I."

The above passage is a plea to the Ordainer asking him to mass the rays of his eternal light in a special formation so as to enable us to see the glorious form of the godhead.

The circle represents that principle which has no beginning and no end, perfectly symmetrical and equidistant from the centre. It stands for the radiations from the One Divine centre to the circumscribed field of action of the world. Triangles represent the triple worlds of creation – three lower and three higher. Each triangle enfolds the *yoni* or womb, which is the origin of everything and which stands for the Divine Mother. The *bindu* or dot in the centre normally denotes the Supreme. Both equilateral and isosceles triangles are made use of. A triangle with its apex turned up indicates the single-pointed aspiration of the *sadhaka* which raises her from the broad-based depths of her being to the heights of the divine. The triangle with its apex pointing downwards corresponds to the *Shakti* or grace of the Divine Mother that immediately responds to the efforts of the seeker. The figure formed by two triangles, intersecting each other, is known as the *satkona* or six-cornered figure and represents the rising aspiration of the *jivatman* which is being enfolded in the responding grace of the Mother. It is the ascent of the inner power, which is encouraged by the higher power, which descends to welcome it. When the Supreme *Shakti* out of her own volition takes on the form of the universe and turns her gaze on her own pulsation, the *Chakra* comes into being. The *Sri Chakra* is thus a master-plan for the manifestation of the universe drawn by the divine architect on the board of the Infinite!

The lotus is a flower that responds only to the call of light. It raises its head when the sun rises and closes its petals when it sets. The flower opens, petal by petal, and this signifies the gradual unfolding of the latent spirituality in us. That is why the lotus plays such a significant part in all *Chakras.* The centres of psychic consciousness in the human being are also known as *Chakras* and a lotus flower diagrammatically represents each of them.

The *Sri Chakra* is a *yantra,* which is known as the king of all *Chakras.* It is called *Chakraraja* in the *Lalitha Sahasranama* and constitutes the chariot of *Lalitha.* It is the most potent and famous of all *Yantras.* It is the eternal abode of *Tripurasundari,* the *Maha Devi,* and the supreme storehouse of all felicity. The *Lalitha Sahasranama* says:

"The *japa* of the king of *mantras,* the worship of the king of *Chakras* and the recital of the occult names are the fruits of no little *tapasya*!"

The *Sri Chakra* is the king of all *Chakras* for another reason also. It contains all other *Chakras* within it in the same way as the Divine Mother contains and sustains all other gods and goddesses. Therefore, it is said that by using the *Sri Chakra* one can worship any god or goddess. The vibrations that emanate from it are so positive that even a person who sits near it, is subtly influenced by it without their knowledge. Hence, it is set up in many centres of worship. *Adi Shankaracharya* is famous for having installed the *Sri Chakra* in all the temples that he visited or established all over India.

Modern mathematicians are astounded by the beauty and symmetry of this amazing figure, the secret of which they have not been able to fathom. The lines and angles are delicate and sharp. The curves and petals are round and smooth. Its intricate pattern defies all intellectual analysis.

The universe is a projection of the *Paramatman* in order to know Himself and to see Himself. The goal of life is a conscious and voluntary return of the *jivatman* back to the *Paramatman.* If the Divine Consciousness were only the inaction of unmanifest bliss, there would be no universe and no creation. The Supreme manifests Himself so that he might become conscious of Himself! The first manifestation is of light. This light contains within it the seed of an unformulated desire to manifest. *Tantra* calls this '*vimarsha*'. This *vimarsha* or seed-desire is the original *Shakti* or Mother Goddess. Whereas the colour of the light is pure white, the colour of the desire or *Shakti* is red since it pre-supposes the activity of *rajas*. This seed is the digit of desire. At this time the goddess is known as *Kameswari*. This desire creates a throb or *spanda*, which concentrates itself into a spot or *bindu*. It contains the seed of the entire creation. When it gets into the mood to create further it emanates as sound and is known as *Sabda Brahman*. This contains both *Shiva* and *Shakti*, so we get three points or *bindus*. These three form the primary triangle of the *Sri Chakra*. These three points stand for *iccha shakti*, *jnana shakti*, and *kriya shakti*. These are the powers of desire, knowledge and action without which the universe could not have been created. The three points also stand for the three *gunas* (*sattva*, *rajas* and *tamas*), which are the qualities of primordial matter. They also denote the three states of consciousness – waking, dreaming and deep sleep. The *bindu* or dot in the centre denotes the *Turiya* state of Pure Consciousness.

The *bindu* is the point of contact between the Creator and his creation. It is the drop that swells into the ocean of consciousness. It is the cipher by which everything else is deciphered. The *bindu* is the navel of the *Sri Chakra*, from which the whole of creation originates.

This *bindu* becomes the triangle and the triangle expands into the eight-edged figure, then to a ten-cornered figure and so on. Thus, the dot or *bindu* of the primary triangle transforms itself through a series of lines, triangles, circles and squares to the fully formed shape of the *Sri Chakra*. When the great goddess subjects herself to the division of the three *bindus*, she is known as *Tri-pura-sundari*. She is both the transcendent point in the middle of the primary triangle as well as the three points, which form the triangle. The figure of the *Sri Chakra* actually contains nine *Chakras*. The shape on the extreme outside is a square made of three lines, one inside the other. These lines are not joined, for they have four portals opening out to the four directions. This is the ground sketch representing the earth plane (*bhupura*). When we enter the portal we see three concentric circles, which are known as girdles. The space between the sides of the square and the girdles is a *Chakra* in itself, which is known as 'the enchanter of the triple worlds' (*trailokya mohana chakra*). Sixteen lotus petals are arranged next to the three girdles with tips pointing and touching the girdle and bases resting on another circle. This *Chakra* is known as 'the fulfiller of all desires' (*sarvasya paripuraka chakra*).

Inside this circle is yet another circle. The space enclosed by these two circles is smaller than the space formed by the sixteen lotus petals. Inside this space are arranged another eight lotus petals, with tips touching the centre of each of the sixteen petals. This *Chakra* is known as 'the agitator of all' (*Sarva sankshobhana chakra).*

Inside this final circle we come to the figure formed by the superimposition of five triangles with apex downwards, on four triangles with apex pointing upwards. This figure actually contains forty-three small triangles inside it. The outermost *Chakra* consists of fourteen triangles and is known as 'the giver of all auspiciousness' (*sarva soubhagyada chakra*). The next figure consists of ten triangles and is known as 'the accomplisher of all purposes' (*sarvartha sadhaka chakra).* Inside this is another ten-cornered figure known as 'the giver of protection' (*sarva rakshakara chakra).* Next comes an eight-cornered figure, which is 'the remover of all diseases' (*sarva rogahara chakra).* Inside this is the primary triangle with apex pointing down, which is 'the giver of all powers' (*sarva siddhiprada chakra).* In the heart of this is the dot or *bindu*, which is the seat of the *Tripurasundari* and is filled with unending bliss (*Sarva-anandamaya chakra).*

The *Sri Chakra* is thus formed out of the *bindu* and many intersecting triangles. The primary triangle, the eight-cornered figure, the two ten-edged figures and the fourteen-pointed figures are known as *Shakti Chakras.* The figures with eight and sixteen petals, and the three girdles and the three squares or *Bhupuras* are known as *Shiva Chakras.* Thus, the *Sri Chakra*, which is the body of *Shiva* and *Shakti*, is formed with four *Shiva Chakras* and the five *Shakti Chakras.*

We have seen how its original formation is out of nine *Chakras*, five pointing downwards and four upwards. The ones pointing downwards are known as *Shakti Konas* or triangles, and the four pointing upwards are known as *Shiva Konas.* The esoteric meaning here is that the dynamic *Shakti* is superimposed on the static *Shiva.* The amazing picture of *Kaali* dancing on the inert form of *Shiva* is a graphic representation of this.

The five *Shakti Konas* also stand for the five elements and the four *Shiva Konas* for *vidya*, *maya*, *Maheswara* and *Sadashiva.* These four principles, in combination with the five elements, produce the universes inherent in the *Sri Chakra.* Thus, every aspect of matter contains both *Shiva* and *Shakti,* in varying degrees of concentration. The *Sri Chakra* denotes both the microcosm and the macrocosm in the body of the two-in-one *Shiva/Shakti.* The following verse describes this union.

"His body is the dense sky, which she embraces secretly. Their breath of love spreads a hidden beauty all around. Their dance in space causes a series of universes and glittering stars as though they were the beads of perspiration caused by their intense bliss of union."

— Sri Kapali Sastriar

We have already mentioned that the *bindu* is the *kamakaḷa* or the digit of desire of the Supreme. It is the essence of love and bliss. So each *Chakra* is a gradual development of that initial drop of love and bliss. Hence, every aspect of life is meant to be filled with love and bliss.

The figure of the *Sri Chakra* also provides an esoteric path of return for the *jivatman,* from the external world of matter to the point of unending bliss – the *bindu.* The outermost *Chakra* as we have seen is known as 'the enchanter of the three worlds' and the *jivatman* who has come under the spell of the goddess in this *Chakra* can remain for many lifetimes, enjoying her play of beauty and becoming. After indulging in this for an incredible amount of time, the individual hankers to possess and own all this. She fulfils this desire in the next *Chakra* known as 'the fulfiller of desires'. But the more the *jiva* possesses the more he desires, so the mind is filled with agitation. And thus he passes to the next *Chakra* called 'the agitator'.

After staying in this *Chakra* for many births of such agitations and unfulfilled desires, the *jiva* decides to penetrate further into the labyrinth of his own consciousness and discover the source of bliss. This is the *Chakra* of 'auspiciousness'. From now on, progress becomes easier for the *jiva,* for divine grace is felt to be flowing towards him. All protection is provided in the next *Chakra* and the disease and disharmony felt by the aspirant is removed. This in turn leads to all perfection and the attainment of powers or *siddhis.* From here it is but a step to reach the *bindu* or drop of bliss from which the whole journey started. Thus, the *Chakra* is a two-way map showing the descent of the Divine into inert matter and the ascent of the *jivatman* back to the point of bliss from which it started its journey. The lesson the individual has to learn is that a perfect surrender to the Mother, will have the effect of incurring divine grace.

The *Sri Chakra* can also be pictured in the human body. The *bindu* is contacted at the top of the spinal column in the *Sahasrara Chakra* on the crown of the head. The *trikona* or triangle is at the base of the spine in the *Muladhara Chakra.* The *Kundalini,* which is the coiled energy of the Divine Mother in the *Muladhara Chakra*, travels upwards until it attains union with *Shiva* in the *bindu.* The whole of creation is the outcome of the union of the *bindu* with the *trikona* – of *Shiva* and *Shakti.* All aspects of creation contain both these principles – the static and the dynamic. When the dynamic aspect is in the forefront, it is called *Shakti* and when the static aspect is projected, it is known as *Shiva.*

Various formulas are given in ancient texts as to how the *Sri Chakra* should be drawn. In the *Kaula* tradition of the left-handed path of *Tantra*, the circle is drawn first and then the bases of the nine triangles. In the *Samaya* method, the primary triangle is drawn first and the *bindu* placed inside and then the sides are extended to form the rest of the figure. Both the paths follow the same method for drawing the outer petals, the three girdles and the outer square. One important point to remember is that the petals should touch each other and no space should be left between each. Since the *Sri Chakra* is used with the intention of getting the most auspicious things of life and finally liberation itself, the colour to be used in drawing it should be red. Saffron mixed with cow's milk is recommended for drawing it for a *puja.* It can also be made on copper, silver or gold plates and installed permanently in a house or the *puja* room with the appropriate *mantras.* Then it acts as an armour of protection.

When the *Sri Chakra* is made in an upright form, it is known as the *Meru.* Here the nine *Chakras* are on different elevations and not on the same plane. This elevated figure is a representation of Mount *Meru,* which is considered to be the axis of the earth.

Many methods of worshipping the *Sri Chakra* are given, but one of the easiest is by reciting the thousand-and-one names of the *Devi* in the *Lalita Sahasranama.* She is greatly pleased if *puja* is done with *vilva* or *tulasi* leaves or lotus flowers. Worship of the *Sri Chakra*, especially on full moon nights, is highly recommended. If one worships the *Devi* on full moon nights by using the *Sri Chakra* and reciting the *Lalita Sahasranama*, one attains the form of the goddess. This is the outer method of worship of the *Sri Chakra.*

When inner worship is done, the *Sri Chakra* is identified with the subtle centres or *Chakras* in the body. One can mediate on it either on the *Manipura Chakra* situated in the navel or in the *Anahata* or heart *Chakra.* After deep meditation, the *sadhaka* starts to hear the *nada* or sound that emerges from the cave of the heart. This turns into the radiance from which creation originally started. Very soon the small individual personality is shattered in this blast of light and dissolves into it. His sense of identity with the body, mind and intellect is completely dissolved and he becomes filled with bliss and light alone.

"While there one can be wider than the world,
While there one is one's own infinity."

....

"The deathless Two-in-One,
A single being in two bodies clasped,
A diarchy of two united souls,
Seated absorbed on deep creative mood;
Their trance of bliss sustained the mobile world."

— "Savitri" by Sri Aurobindo

Thus ends the thirtieth chapter of the *Sri Devi Lila* known as 'Narayani', which describes the *Yantra* known as the *Sri Chakra.*

ॐ *Aim, hreem, kleem* ॐ

ॐ

Kundalinyai Namaha!

CHAPTER THIRTY-ONE

DEVI KUNDALINI

Manastwam, vyoma twam, marudasi, marutsarathirasi,
Twamapastwam, bhumistvayi, parinatayam, nahi param,
Twmeva svatmaanam, parinamayitum vishvapurusha,
Chidanandakaaram, haramahishi-bhavena bibrushe.

"O Devi *Kundalini*! You are mind, space, air, fire, water and earth.
Nothing exists beyond you.
You have transformed your form of blissful consciousness,
And taken on the shape of the universe."

The *Upanishad* seer says, "Even if man acquires the capacity to roll up the sky like a piece of leather, there would not be an end to sorrow unless he realises the Effulgent One within".

The Supreme Consciousness residing in the *Sahasrara Chakra* at the top of the head is the Effulgent One within. *Kundalini Shakti* is the cosmic energy of the Divine Mother, which lies coiled up in the *Muladhara Chakra*, at the base of the spinal column. The word '*kundala*' means coiled. Her form is like that of a coiled serpent; hence she is known as Mother *Kundalini.* She is the mystic fire of primordial energy. She is a fiery occult power, the force, which underlies all organic and inorganic matter. She is *Parashakti,* the subtlest and most potent form of energy. This is not a physical energy like electricity but a spiritual potential. This cosmic power is found in all human bodies and lies dormant in the *Muladhara Chakra* in the centre of the body, at the root of the spinal column. As a cosmic reality it has no form but in the human body, *yogis* have discerned that it has a coiled-up shape, which can be made to rise upwards by the use of certain techniques. Even though all human beings possess this *Shakti,* very few even know that they have it. Naturally they have no idea how to make use of it. The method of awakening this dormant energy in us is called *Kundalini Yoga* and is actually a part of *tantric* discipline even though other types of *yoga* also recognise it. *Kundalini Yoga* is also known as *Laya Yoga* and is the culminating meditative experience. Various rites and practices to awaken this force have been suggested by all the paths of *yoga,* which are taught in Hindu philosophy.

When Consciousness manifests as energy or *Shakti,* it possesses the twin aspects of potential and kinetic energy. The *Kundalini Shakti* represents a polarisation of these two energies. The human body is the potential pole of the energy of the Supreme. The latent energy of the *Devi* is stored in the *Muladhara Chakra.* It becomes dynamic only when it is stirred to action through different types of *yoga.* Then it moves upwards from the *Muladhara* in order to unite with the quiescent Supreme Consciousness in the *Sahasrara.* These two are like the poles of a magnet. Even though the Supreme Consciousness permeates the entire human organism, it is given a specific location in the human body. It is seated in the *Sahasrara Chakra* located at the crown of the head.

Kundalini Shakti is primordial, cosmic power and cannot be trifled with. Attempts to rouse it without proper knowledge of the technique can cause great damage both mentally and physically. All *tantric sadhana* aims at awakening this *Shakti* and making her unite with her Lord, *Sadashiva.*

The same amount of thought which western scientists gave to probing the secrets of external nature were given by the sages of India to discovering the secrets of our internal nature. The detection of this energy, called the *Kundalini Shakti,* is one of their most amazing discoveries. Using the tool of their minds they priced open the secrets of the universe and discovered that these secrets lay within themselves. They underwent years of rigorous research on their minds and practiced intense self-denial and austerities before they discovered many amazing facts about the *Kundalini Shakti.* The details of the path are so minutely described by them that we have to conclude that it was the true description of their personal experience. It was only after verifying these truths many times that they passed on the information to their disciples who, in turn, confirmed it and thus made it into a purely scientific truth which could be verified in the minds and bodies of every human being, provided they had the courage to set out on a voyage of this unchartered territory. Spiritual research needs more than physical courage. It needs the ability to control our animalistic tendencies of sex, gluttony, smoking, drinking, over sleeping and jealousy, cheating others, thinking ill of others and doing harm to others. One needs to follow a strict code of ethical conduct for many years before venturing to practice these techniques.

Scientists have only a physical view of energy and they think it to be a blind phenomenon without any mental characteristics. According to them, all manifestation of energy takes place by accident. The seers, however, realised that physical energy is actually derived from Pure Consciousness or *Chit Shakti.* The life force is known as *Prana Shakti* and is derived from *Chit Shakti.* All forms of physical energy and the very evolution of life are influenced by this *prana.* It is only very recently that modern physicists have become aware of this energy. Max Planck talks about a force of the spirit that sets the atomic particles in oscillation and concentrates them into minute solar systems.

Science is the result of the mind's perception of the phenomenal world. It gives us only one aspect of reality. It can never understand that other levels of reality exist outside of their perception. It can never appreciate this truth since it is not able to fit it into its neat little scheme of the world as perceived by the five senses. Today, when the twenty-first century human being is faced with the horrifying Frankenstein of his own making, who is threatening to totally wipe out all his precious discoveries with the dropping of just one nuclear bomb, he is forced to pay heed to the words of wisdom uttered by India's sages more than five millenniums ago! Though our scientific discoveries have advanced in leaps and bounds, our spiritual evolution seems to have become stagnant. We have learnt to split everything, including the atom, but have not found out the method of uniting humanity into one civilized whole.

Modern thought, which is influenced by western science, divides life into spiritual and secular. This is an unnatural division, which gives a fragmented vision of life. This is the main cause of our mental suffering and inability to find peace within. We are totally unaware of the vast spiritual power, which lies dormant in us. It is only by tapping this source that the human being can evolve to his/her highest potential. Different fields of enquiry cannot be kept in water-tight compartments. At some point all of them have to merge, for life is a holistic phenomenon. The ancient seers of India were well aware of this and they evolved an all-comprehensive vision of the ultimate unity of all life in the universe.

The macro-cosmos is inherent in the micro-cosmos. The human being is a microcosm in which all the components of the macrocosm are found in minute perfection. Whatever exists outside exists in us. All the *tattvas* or elements, which make up the macrocosm, exist in us. The macrocosm is said to contain fourteen *lokas* or worlds, seven below the earth and seven above. These are also found in the body of man. *Lokas* refer to those astral regions in which the fruits of one's actions or *karmas* can be experienced. The seven upper worlds are *Bhuh*, *Bhuvah, Svah, Tapa, Jana, Maha* and *Satya.* These have their corresponding locations within the seven *Chakras* or centres of spiritual energy, which are found in the spinal column and brain.

The *Chakras* are centres of the spiritual energy of *Parashakti*, situated in the astral body along the physical spinal column. They are lotus-shaped whorls of spiritual energy. The first six *Chakras* are located along the spinal column and the seventh in the brain. It must be remembered that these are centres of spiritual energy and cannot be perceived by the physical eye. They lie along the spiritual *nadi* or path known as the *Sushumna Nadi,* which is situated in the physical body within the spinal column. Starting from the base of the spine upwards, these *Chakras* are known as *Muladhara, Swadhishtana, Manipura*, *Anahata, Vishudha, Ajna* and *Sahasrara.* Each *Chakra* has its *bija* (seed sound), its *tattva* (element), *guna* (quality), *Deva* and *Devi* (presiding deities) and its *nadis,* which are formed like the petals of a lotus. These petals or *nadis* resonate to the vibrations of the different sounds of the Sanskrit alphabet. Each letter denotes one *mantra* of the *Devi Kundalini.* The supreme power of the Divine Mother, known as the *Kundalini Shakti*, lies coiled up in the *Muladhara.* She has to be awakened by continuous *sadhana* or spiritual practices. Once she has risen, she has to be forced up through the other five *Chakras* and made to unite with *Sadashiva* or the Supreme Consciousness, which lies in the *Sahasrara Chakra* at the crown of the head.

Each element or *tattva* within the *Chakra* has its own geometric form representing a specific power as well as its own colour, function, presiding deity and *bija mantra* or mystic vibration. The *yogic* vision has described these *Chakras* in the form of lotus flowers with varying numbers of petals. The *Muladhara* has four petals, *Swadhishtana* has six, the *Manipura* has ten, the *Anahata* has twelve, the *Vishudha* has sixteen, and the *Ajna* has two. There are fifty petals in all, corresponding to the fifty letters of the Sanskrit alphabet, which are euphonically contained within the petals. These fifty multiplied by twenty, becomes thousand. The *Sahasrara Chakra* has thousand petals, indicating infinity. The vibrations produced by each petal correspond to one letter of the Sanskrit alphabet. Each has a colour of its own. Every sound is a *mantra* of *Devi Kundalini.* These sounds exist in the petals in a latent form. They start manifesting and vibrating only during intense meditation.

The descent of consciousness into the forms of matter can be followed in the *Chakras* of the human body. In the *Sahasrara Chakra,* the Supreme Consciousness is united with *Mula Prakriti*, which is the nature of the goddess manifesting as knowledge, strength and activity. *Mula Prakriti* is the unmanifest potential of Nature and is the energy of the Divine Mother. As we saw in the chapter on '*Lalitha*', she is capable of sustaining two forms – manifest and unmanifest – simultaneously. She is *Satchidananda Swarupini* or the form of bliss as well as *Bhavani* or the form of becoming. From her come the higher manifestation of intelligence known as *sattva buddhi*, *ahamkara* or ego, *manas* or mind and the subtle locations of the senses or *indriyas.* These are situated between the *Ajna* and *Sahasrara Chakras.* From this emanate the *tanmatras* or the subtle essences of the senses, which evolve into the five gross elements. These are *akasa* (etheric space), *vayu* (air), *agni* (fire), *apas* (water) and *prithvi* (earth).

All evolution proceeds from the subtle to the gross. Therefore, what we call solid matter actually emanates from the ethereal realm. Even though the mind and the five elements pervade the entire body, there are certain centres where they are predominant. The *Ajna Chakra* is the centre of the mind and the five lower *Chakras* are the centres of the five *tattvas* or elements. The human being is a microcosm in which the all-pervading Spirit evolves into the form of mind and matter through the *bhutas* or *tattvas.* Hence, the *tantrics* insist that the first step on this path should be *nadi shuddhi* and *bhuta shuddhi* or *tattva shuddhi.* They maintain that the final spiritual experience can only be gained after this purification. Evolution has been from subtle to gross and the path to perfection lies in re-tracing the way by which we have evolved – that is from the gross elements to the subtle *tanmatras* which in turn fold back into the *Parashakti*, which is nothing but the *Para Brahman*.

As has been mentioned before, during the period of the evolution of the cosmos, the universe unfolds and expands from the seed sound '*hreem*'. This vibrating mass of energy continues to differentiate and expand in different wavelengths. This energy evolves into the gross plane by the fifth differentiation and creates the fifty articulate sounds or *varnas*. '*Varna*' means colour and each sound has its corresponding hue. The universe of forms is created from the combinations and permutations of these fifty primeval sounds. Predictable forms can be produced from sound. Experiments have found that notes produced on certain instruments can be traced on a bed of sand to form certain geometric patterns. In order to produce a particular form, a specific note at a particular pitch must be generated. Underlying all the forms of the physical world are the oscillating wave-lengths of the fifty primeval sounds in varying combinations. Sound is potential form and form is manifest sound. The alphabets of the Sanskrit language are directly derived from these primordial sounds.

The *Chakras* are also the centres of *Prana Shakti* within us. *Prana* is the vital force. It is a psychic energy. All life energy that is manifested in the world is through *prana*. Without it not even a leaf can move. Heat, light, electricity, magnetism are all manifestations of *prana*. Breath is the external expression of *prana*. By doing the *yogic* exercise called *pranayama* or control of breath, one can influence the subtle *pranic* force. Mind cannot operate without *prana*. So control of breath implies control of *prana*, which in turn leads to control of the mind. Within the human being, this *prana* assumes five different functions known as the *Pancha Pranas*. These control respiration, digestion, dreaming, evacuation and blood circulation. These functions are located in the different *Chakras*. When we control the breath and direct it by the force of our will to different parts of the body, we can cure diseases and revitalise ourselves. This has been recognised in modern times and many people practice what is known as *pranic* healing. If we can control the *prana* within us, we can slowly learn the method of controlling the universal *prana*. This is how certain *yogis* perform miracles.

The physical body has certain plexuses, which correspond with the location of the *Chakras*. The *Muladhara* corresponds to the sacrococcygeal plexus, the *Swadhishtana* to the sacral plexus, the *Manipura* to the solar plexus, the *Anahata* to the cardiac plexus, the *Visuddha* to the laryngeal plexus and the *Ajna* with the two lobes of the cerebellum. Above this lies the mind or *manas* in the middle cerebrum and finally the *Sahasrara*, corresponding to the upper cerebrum, the function of which is still to be discovered by science.

These six *Chakras* are thus vital centres of psychic energy, which affect various essential physical functions within the body. They influence and govern the gross body outside the spinal column, which is co-extensive with that section of the spinal column in which they are situated. The *Muladhara* is the physical centre, controlling elimination. It is the subconscious centre. The *Swadhishtana* governs generative organs and is the sex centre and controls the movements of greed and lust. The *Manipura* governs the digestive organs. It is the centre of the higher vital life forces and passions. The *Anahata* is the seat of the cardiac and respiratory forces and controls the emotional centre. The *Visuddha* is the broadcasting system and is connected with the external mind. The *Ajna Chakra* is the control room of motor activity, the centre of the will, inner mind, occult vision and dynamic thought. The *Sahasrara* is the master switchboard. It is the centre of higher consciousness. It is the intuitive mind that can connect with the astral planes and the cosmic mind.

The body may be divided into two main portions. The head and trunk form the main part and the legs, the other. The centre of the body lies between these two, at the base of the spine. The spinal cord runs through the whole body and supports it. It can be termed as the axis of the body. The legs and feet are the grossest part of the body, since they show less signs of consciousness. The head and trunk with the spinal column, which contains white and grey matter, are more highly developed. The body and legs below the centre contain the seven lower or nether worlds or *lokas,* which are upheld by their respective *Shaktis* or sustaining powers. From the spinal column upwards, to the cerebral centres, consciousness manifests freely. The seven upper worlds or *lokas* are situated here.

The *nadis* are tubes of astral matter, which carry psychic currents. They have no connection with nerves and arteries or veins. Even though physical correlates are given to specify the whereabouts of these *nadis* and *Chakras*, it must be understood that they are not actually situated in the physical body but in the astral body. They are made of subtle forces that are not visible to gross perception. The word '*nad*' means motion in Sanskrit. It is through these *nadis* that the *pranic* current or life-force moves and flows. They are not perceptible to the gross senses. Only their action can be felt. They disappear with the disintegration of the organism at death. Post mortem examination will not be able to reveal their whereabouts, just as it will not reveal the location of the mind!

The body is filled with innumerable *nadis*. They have a vital role in *Kundalini Yoga*. Out of these countless *nadis* the three which play a most important part in our body are called *Sushumna, Ida* and *Pingala*. Out of these, the *Sushumna* is the chief. It extends from the *Muladhara Chakra* at the bottom of the spine to the *Brahmarandra* at the crown of the head. This *nadi* passes through the hollow cylindrical cavity of the vertebral column. Inside the *Sushumna* is another *nadi* called the *Vajra Nadi* that is radiant like the sun and filled with *rajas*. Inside this is another called the *Chitra*, which is pale like the moon and is *sattvic*. Within this lies the slender tube of the *Brahmanadi*. When the *Kundalini Shakti* is awakened, its passage upwards lies through this. The *nadi* called the *Ida* is on the left side and the *Pingala* on the right side of the spine. All the *nadis* spring from a place called the *Kanda*, which is shaped like an egg and is placed just above the *Muladhara Chakra*. This is another great psychic centre.

On the physiological plane, we find that there are two cords known as the sympathetic and para-sympathetic cords that lie on either side of the spine. As we have seen before, the *Ida* and *Pingala nadis* also lie on either side of the spinal cord even though they do not correspond with these sympathetic nerves. *Ida* starts from the right testicle and *Pingala* from the left. They meet the *Sushumna Nadi* for the first time at the *Muladhara Chakra* and make a knot there. This is known as the *Brahma Granthi* or the knot of *Brahma*. The three meet again at the *Anahata* or heart *chakra* and this knot is called the *Vishnu Granthi*. They meet for the third and last time at the *Ajna Chakra* and make a knot, which is known as *Rudra Granthi*. The current of the *Ida Nadi* goes out through the left nostril and *Pingala* through the right. *Ida* is known as the *Chandra Nadi* or the *nadi* of the moon and has a cooling effect on the body. *Pingala* is known as *Surya Nadi* or the *nadi* of the sun and represents heat. *Ida* is that which nourishes the system and *Pingala* is that which digests food. When the *nadis* are clogged with impurities, one cannot meditate and the body becomes unhealthy. One has to practice *pranayama* in order to purify them. The *Chakras* are said to look like lotus flowers. Actually their petals are made of the number of *nadis* that surround it. The *nadis* determine the number of petals.

Muladhara means root centre. Four important *nadis* emanate from the *Muladhara Chakra* and give it the characteristic four-petalled lotus shape. All *nadis* resonate to the sound of the letters of the Sanskrit alphabet. The letters corresponding to these four *nadis* or petals are *vam, sham, shham* and *sam.* These petals are crimson coloured. This *Chakra* is located at the base of the spinal column. It lies between the reproductory organ and the anus. It is just below the *Kanda,* which is the egg-shaped junction from where all *nadis* arise. This *Chakra* is what supports the rest of the body. The *tattva* or element of this *Chakra* is *prithvi* or earth, and is found in the centre of the lotus in a square *mandala* that is yellow in colour. It resonates to the *mantra,* '*lam*' which is the *bija mantra* or seed sound of the earth element. This *Chakra* corresponds with *Bhu Loka* or the planet earth. The *Swayambhuva Linga* of *Shiva* is also to be seen in this *Chakra. Devi Kundalini* lies, face downwards, at the mouth of the *Sushumna Nadi* with her face on the head of this *linga.* She is curled up into three-and-a-half coils like a snake. The three coils represent the three *gunas* of *Prakriti* – *sattva, rajas* and *tamas.* The half represents the *vikritis* or modifications of *Prakriti. Ganesha* is the presiding god of this *Chakra* and *Dakini,* the goddess. The animal connected with this is the elephant. The *Brahma Granthi* or the knot of *Brahma* is in this *Chakra*, since this is the place where the *Ida* and *Pingala Nadis* meet the *Sushumna* for the first time. The seven nether worlds lie below this *Chakra.* The *yogi* who concentrates on this *Chakra* gets full knowledge of the *Kundalini Shakti* and the method of awakening it. Levitation or control over the gravity of the earth is one of the *siddhis* that can be attained by concentrating on this *Chakra.*

The *Swadhishtana Chakra* is located within the *Sushumna Nadi* at the root of the reproductory organ. *Swadhishtana* means 'one's own place'. It corresponds to *Bhuvar Loka.* This *Chakra* controls the lower abdomen, kidneys, uterus and reproductory organs in the gross body. Six *nadis* emanate from this, which give it the appearance of a six-petalled lotus. The colour of the petals is vermilion. The vibrations of these *nadis* correspond to the letters *bam, bham, mam, yam, ram and lam.* The *tattva* associated with this is *apas* or water, which is found in a space, shaped like the crescent moon, which is pure white in colour. The seed sound of this *Chakra* is '*vam*', which is the *bija mantra* of *Varuna,* the god of waters. The presiding deity is *Brahma* and the goddess or *Shakti* is *Rakini.* The animal connected with this is the crocodile. He who concentrates on this *Chakra* will lose all fear of water and will even be able to walk on water.

The third *Chakra* is known as *Manipura* and is located in the region of the navel. *Manipura* means 'full of rays'. This has control over the liver, stomach and spleen and corresponds to the physical location of the solar plexus. It is a most important centre. Ten *nadis* emanate from this that makes it appear like a ten-petalled lotus. The petals are dark purple in colour. The vibrations produced by these *nadis* correspond with the Sanskrit letters *dam, dham, nnam, tam, tham, ddam, ddham, nam, pam,* and *pham.* The element, *Agni* is located in a deep red triangle with its apex pointing downwards in the centre of the *Chakra* with the *bija mantra,* '*ram*'. This is the seed sound of *Agni* or the god of fire. This *Chakra* corresponds with *Swar Loka* or the heavenly region. The presiding deity is *Vishnu* and the goddess or *Shakti* is *Lakini* or *Lakshmi.* The animal connected with this is the ram. The *yogi* who concentrates on this *Chakra* will have no fear of fire and will remain unscathed even if thrown into a blazing conflagration.

Next comes the *Anahata Chakra,* situated in the region of the heart corresponding to the cardiac plexus. *Anahata* means 'soundless sound'. Twelve *nadis* emanate from this that are deep maroon in colour. The sounds produced by each *nadi* correspond to the following Sanskrit letters – *kam, kham, gam, gham, gnyam, cham, chham, jam, jham, jnyam, tam, ttam.* In the centre is a hexagonal shape that has a dark smoky aura. Here resides the *vayu tattva* or the element of air. It has the *bija mantra* of *vayu* – '*yam*'. It corresponds to the *Mahar Loka.* The *Bana Linga* is located here. The presiding deity is *Isha (Rudra)* and the *Shakti* is *Kakini.* The animal connected to this is the antelope. The *nada* or sound of *Sabda Brahman* is heard from this *Chakra.* In fact the *yogi* in deep meditation can hear many astral sounds emanating from this *Chakra.* This is the second place where the *Ida* and *Pingala nadis* meet the *Sushumna* and form a knot, and this knot is known as *Vishnu Granthi* or the knot of *Vishnu.* This *Chakra* is full of *sattva* and one who meditates on this will find his heart overflowing with love for the whole of creation. He will also have control over the element of air and will be able to fly.

The *Visuddha Chakra* is placed at the base of the throat and corresponds to the laryngeal plexus in the physical body. *Visuddha* means purity. The sixteen *yoga nadis* that emanate from this are smoky purple in colour and give it the shape of a sixteen-petalled lotus. The sounds produced by them are *am, aam, im, eem, um, oom, rim, reem, lum, loom, em, aem, om, aoum, um, ah.* The *tattva* is *akasa* or ether. This *tattva* resides in the centre of the *Chakra* in a circle that is pure blue in colour. The seed sound of this element is '*ham*'. *Jana Loka* is located here. The presiding deity is *Sadashiva* and the goddess is *Shakini.* One who concentrates on this *Chakra* will get knowledge of past, present and future.

The *Ajna Chakra* is situated in the space between the two eyebrows, known as the cavernous plexus in the physical body. *Ajna* means the command or order of a holy person. It corresponds to *Tapo Loka.* The seed *mantra* here is found in a pure white circle that is the seat of the mind. It has two *nadis* or petals on either side that are also pure white in colour and vibrate to the sound of the letters *ham* and *ksham.* The element here is *avyakta*, the primordial cloud of undifferentiated energy and matter from which the five elements emanate. The presiding deity is *Paramashiva* in the form of a swan. The *Shakti* is *Hakini.* The *Ida* and *Pingala Nadis* meet the *Sushumna* for the final time at this junction and this knot is known as *Rudra Granthi* or the knot of *Rudra.* The *Lalitha Sahasranama* says that the goddess *Lalitha* herself is the one who cuts all the three knots (*Rudra Granthi, Vishnu Granthi* and *Brahma Granthi – vibhedini*). It is only after cutting these three knots that one can have access to *Sadashiva,* who resides in the *Sahasrara Chakra.* One who concentrates on this will be able to destroy all the *karmas* of previous lives. He becomes liberated – a *jivan mukta.* She or he can acquire all the major *siddhis* or supernormal powers. *Yogis* consciously fix their *prana* here at the time of death.

Above these six lotuses, we have the seventh, which is known as the *Sahasrara.* This means thousand-petalled. All the others are intimately connected with this. Situated at the crown of the head, it corresponds to the pineal gland in the physical body. One thousand *nadis* are found in the *Chakra,* which makes it look like a thousand-petalled lotus. The fifty letters of the Sanskrit alphabet are repeated twenty times in these petals. This is the location of *Satya Loka.* It is the abode of Lord *Shiva* in his aspect as the *Para Brahman* or Supreme Consciousness. When the *Kundalini Shakti* is united with *Sadashiva* in this *Chakra*, the *yogi* enjoys supreme bliss and goes into another state of consciousness called *samadhi.*

The *Brahmarandra* is an orifice at the crown of the head. The literal meaning is the hole of *Brahman.* The physical counterpart is the fontanel, which is very soft in a baby but hardens with age. The *jivatman* or the embodied soul enters the body through this opening at the time of birth. When a *yogi* departs from his physical body, he bursts open the *Brahmarandra* and departs the way he came. The *prana* escapes through this opening and thus he attains immortality. The *prana* of ordinary individuals goes out through one of the other orifices of the body.

Thus, Mother *Kundalini* is Pure Consciousness itself. She is *Prana Shakti* as well as *Parashakti* – the life force and the Supreme force. It is by this *Shakti* that the world of matter exists. It is the subtlest form of energy. Creation, preservation and dissolution are all found in her. She maintains both the individual body as well as the cosmos through this subtle *prana.* She is the dynamic working power of the universe.

The equilibrium of the universe is maintained by a polarity of positive and negative, static and dynamic. In *Kundalini Yoga*, it is said that the static ground force, or *Shiva*, resides in the seventh *Chakra* known as the *Sahasrara.* The dynamic feminine power or *Shakti* lies in the *Muladhara*, at the base of the spine. It is the manifestation of cosmic power in the body and is in a dormant, potential state. In *Kundalini Yoga,* this divine power that lies asleep in every human being is aroused and pulled upward through the six *Chakras* till it reaches the *Sahasrara Chakra*, which is the seat of *Sadashiva*, the Supreme Consciousness. This is the height of the meditative experience.

The static *Shakti* of the *Kundalini* can be vitalised by *pranayama* and other *yogic* processes and made dynamic. When it is completely vibrant, the *Shakti* rises and passes through the various *Chakras* and finally unites with *Shiva* in the *Sahasrara*, and the two poles become one. The *yogi* attains the state of consciousness known as *samadhi.* In this state, even though the body continues to exist, the person appears inert since his individual consciousness is no longer fixed on his body and the objective world, but has been united with the Supreme Consciousness. *Yogis* have been known to stay in this state of suspended animation for many years. The question may be asked as to how such a body manages to sustain itself. There is a continuous dripping of nectar from the *Brahmarandra* when this union takes place, that sustains the whole organism for an incalculable period of time. When *Devi Kundalini* sleeps, the human being is awake to the world and clamouring and fretting for materialistic objects. When she is awake, the individual no longer hankers for the world of the senses and is awake only to the Supreme Reality. He is asleep to the world of duality and enters into the state of unity. The so-called happiness of the world turns into an ecstasy beyond words. The *Bhagavad Gita* says, "That which is night to the *yogi* is day to the ordinary man and what is day to him is night to the *yogi*".

In worldly-minded people given to purely physical pleasures and sexual enjoyments, this *Kundalini* power is never awakened. It lies dormant throughout their lives. The power has to be stimulated through some form of spiritual practice and not through the acquisition of wealth or any other form of material control. When an aspirant seriously practices all the disciplines as given in the *Shastras,* under the guidance of a qualified *guru*, the layers of ignorance veiling the *Kundalini* begin to be cleared and are finally torn asunder, and the energy is pushed upwards through the *Chakras.*

Even when it is awakened, it does not proceed directly to the *Sahasrara* unless one is an exceptionally pure *yogi.* It must be moved forcibly from one *Chakra* to another. A great deal of concentration and patience is needed in order to aquire this. It may also drop back and have to be forced up again with great effort. Even if it goes up to the *Ajna Chakra*, it is difficult to keep it there. Only great *yogis* have been able to keep it there for any length of time. When it goes up to the *Sahasrara,* union takes place but again it need not remain long in that state. It can slip back. It is only after long and continuous practice that the adept experiences permanent union and final liberation. The speed with which it is aroused depends entirely on the aspirant's longing for liberation, purification of the *nadis,* dispassion and stage of evolution. In course of time, the Divine Mother herself awakens the power and gives the *sadhaka* the knowledge as and when he or she is ready for it. Until the *sadhaka* is able to absorb it fully, nothing of importance will be revealed to him.

There are many methods of locating the *Chakras.* They can be located both from the front and the back. When we do it from the back, our concentration has to move along the spinal cord from *Chakra* to *Chakra.* If one approaches from the front, the concentration has to move from the base of the spine to the navel, the heart, the throat, etc. The consciousness has to be kept alert always so that it is receptive to the inner vibrations that denote an energy centre. The *Chakras* may also be focussed upon by chanting '*Aum*'. At the *Muladhara, Aum* has to be chanted at the lowest pitch. As we move up, the pitch has to be raised by one degree for every *Chakra.* The *Aum* sound gradually becomes imperceptible. Another method uses the Indian musical scale to locate the centres. There is a strange relationship between the seven notes of the scale and the seven major *Chakras.* '*Sa*' corresponds to the *Muladhara*, '*re*' to the *Swadhishtana*, '*ga*' to the *Manipura,* '*ma*' to the *Anahata,* '*pa*' to the *Visuddha*, '*da*' to the *Ajna* and '*ni*' to the *Sahasrara.*

The petals of the lotuses in these *Chakras* are initially closed and drooping but as the *Devi Kundalini* pierces their centres, the blossoms lift their heads and bloom in all their glory, emanating a divine light and fragrance, and reveal their esoteric secrets. The more the *Kundalini* advances the more the *yogi* also advances on the spiritual path. When it reaches the *Ajna Chakra*, the *yogi* gets a vision of his personal god and when it reaches the *Sahasrara*, he loses his individuality in the ocean of *sat, chit* and *ananda. Shiva* and *Shakti* become united and the *yogi* becomes a fully illumined sage or *jivan mukta.* Even the ignorant individual knows that he wants happiness. To get this he uses whatever means that come to his command. Unfortunately, he does not realise that the happiness of the world is a pale reflection of that bliss which lies within him and which he can taste, if he only knew the method of finding it. *Kundalini Yoga* is one such method.

As in all other *tantric* practices, the technique of awakening the *Kundalini* can be learnt only after attaining ethical perfection. Otherwise it will lead to spiritual and physical downfall. Before starting this *yoga*, one has to follow a strict discipline. Practitioners have to cultivate the following qualities – non-violence, celibacy, perseverance, patience, acceptance, sparse eating habits, humility, honesty, and selfless service to others.

This mysterious power directly affects the mind and if an undisciplined aspirant practices it, he or she can even become insane. First of all, one has to be detached from the lure of worldly pleasures. She has to be free from desire, anger, greed and jealousy. She has to have *deha shuddhi* (a pure body), *nadi shuddhi* (purified *nadis*), *mana shuddhi* (pure mind) and *buddhi shuddhi* (purified intellect). *Pranayama* has to be practised to cleanse the *nadis*. The mind becomes steady with the practice of *pranayama*, so it is absolutely necessary to do it before meditation.

The necessity of a spiritual guide on this path cannot be over-emphasised. As in all *tantric* practises, the pitfalls are many and one has to be guided by a proper *guru*. The *Kundalini* can be roused by different methods advocated in different *yogas*. The *Hatha yogis* use *pranayama*, *asanas* and *mudras*. *Bhakti Yoga* advocates devotion and perfect surrender to one's personal deity. *Raja Yoga* stresses on concentration, meditation and control of the mind. *Jnana Yoga* supports the exercise of the analytical will, and *Tantra* advocates *tattva shuddhi* and the use of *Mantras* and *Yantras* in rituals. The type of *sadhana* that one uses will depend on the nature of the person. It is the *guru* who should give the proper advice on this point. Any one of these paths may be used with great success by a selected few. But for most people, a combination of methods might be more effective. When the *Kundalini* travels from one *Chakra* to another, layer after layer of the mind becomes open and the *yogi* acquires psychic powers known as *siddhis*. Many misguided people take to the practice only for the sake of attaining these powers. They use these powers to gain name, fame and wealth and this eventually leads to their downfall. This power is meant to be used for the benefit of the world and for furthering spiritual evolution and not for selfish ends.

The *Yoga-Kundalini Upanishad* is the eighty-sixth among the one-hundred-and-eight important *Upanishads*. It is a most important work on *Kundalini Yoga*. It prescribes methods by which the *prana* can be controlled and the *Kundalini* aroused and taken to its consummation in the *Sahasrara*. *Pranayama* and other *yogic* processes are described in detail, by which the state of *samadhi* can be attained. However, it is a path filled with pitfalls and it is essential to have a proper guide or *guru*. All *yoga* has but one purpose and that is the attainment of unity with the Supreme Consciousness. Every type of *yoga* is an attempt at the self-transformation of the base metal of individual consciousness into the pure gold of Supreme Consciousness. Many of the ordinary paths of *yoga* can be followed safely by even an ignorant practioner, but *Kundalini Yoga* is an occult science. It can lead one to the heights in the shortest possible time but it can also precipitate us to the lowest depths of darkness of the mind.

As mentioned before, when the *Kundalini* sleeps, the human being is awake to the joys of the world. When it awakes, the human being also awakes to the light within him. Some of the signs of the awakened *Kundalini* are that the body becomes light as air. We begin to possess an inexhaustible fund of energy and become divinely intoxicated. During meditation we will behold divine visions, tastes, smells and sounds. But these are only the side-effects. If one gets deflected from the true purpose of the *yoga* and runs after these tantalising things that the *Devi Kundalini* dangles before the unwary, one will never attain his true goal. This is the time to be assiduous in the practice and never let up until the final goal of unity with the Supreme Consciousness is achieved. In this state the *yogi* experiences cosmic love, peace, fearlessness and harmony. When the *Kundalini* unites with *Sadashiva*, nectar starts to flow from the *Brahmarandra* to the *Muladhara*, flooding both the astral and physical bodies, satisfying the presiding gods and goddesses of the various *Chakras*, and thus filling the person with *Paramananda* or supreme bliss.

What we have to understand from the study of the various *Puranas* is that there is a deep philosophy underlying all the traditional Hindu methods of worship and the various *Puranic* allegories. The path of spiritual *sadhana* is shrouded in a mystery that is not apparent even to the *sadhaka*. We may imagine that we are the ones who have started this *yoga* and who have been successful in it, but the fact is that even the heroism and strength that we put into it, is the force of the Divine Mother working within us. A child may shake off its mother's restraining hand and run forward, secure in the knowledge that she is right there behind him. Similar is the case with us. Whatever intelligence, we may possess, whatever extraordinary gifts and powers we might have, are but a pale reflection of her mighty powers. She walks beside us and steers our course from within. Everything that is worthwhile in our existence we owe to her alone. Her watchful vigilance never falters even for a second. Those who have full faith in her can walk blind-folded on the path of life, for they can be sure that she is guiding their footsteps throughout the way.

If we allow the cosmic mother to fill us with her love and beauty, our problems will vanish. As the child feels secure when holding the hand of the mother, so the devotee of the mother has no cares for he knows that his beloved mother is always beside him. Every human being, regardless of their sex, should try to develop motherly qualities. Then only will we be able to love the whole universe and all the people in it. We must not limit our love to our children alone but learn to look on everyone as our child. This is the only way in which humankind can attain peace. Most of us would have experienced the glory of the unqualified love that a human mother can give. This is only a ray of the flooding sunshine of love that the Divine Mother can give us. The wine that *Chandika* quaffs before the battle with *Mahishasura* is a divine nectar that she will give to all her devotees. May all taste of this divine beverage and attain the perfection that every human being is capable of.

The *Devi Chandika* promises, "I will be present wherever my glories are sung and wherever I am worshipped with true devotion. My power destroys ill health and bestows prosperity. It protects and restores peace. By the mere remembrance of my name, one crosses over all troubles and sorrows. My devotees will always be protected from all types of fears".

"I am the queen of the universe, the giver of all wealth and fruits of works.
I am intelligence and omniscience.
Although I am One, through my powers I appear as manifold.
I cause war for protection; I kill the enemy and bring peace on earth.
I stretch out heaven and earth.
I have produced the Father.
As the wind blows by itself, so I produce all phenomena by my own will.
I am independent and responsible to none.

I am beyond the sky, beyond this earth.
My glory is the phenomenal universe;
Such am I by my own powers."

— *Rig Veda* X Hymn 125

Thus ends the thirty-first chapter of the *Sri Devi Lila* known as 'Devi Kundalini', which describes Goddess *Kundalini* and the practice of *Kundalini Yoga.*

ॐ *Aim, hreem, kleem* ॐ

Aparaada sahasraani,
Kriyanterhanisham maya,
Dasyomiti maam matva
Kshamaswa Parameshwari.

"O Parameshwari! Please consider me as thy slave,
And forgive me for the thousands of mistakes that I have committed."

— Kshama Prartana (Prayer for forgiveness),
Devi Mahatmyam

ॐ

Shivapriyayai Namaha!

CHAPTER THIRTY-TWO

SHIVANI

Poems on the Divine Mother

by Vanamali

Ya Devi sarvabhuteshu, thushti rupena samsthita,
Namasthasyai, Namasthasyai, Namasthasyai Namo Namaha!

"O Goddess, who resides in all creatures in the form of contentment, Hail to Thee! Hail to Thee! All Hail to Thee!"

Down the corridors of Time I fled,
With you in hot pursuit.
Along the sands of Space I ran,
With your breath upon my back.
The whys and wherefores of Causality,
Held me in endless thrall.
Catch me as I fall
O Mother!
Catch me as I fall!

ॐ ॐ ॐ ॐ ॐ ॐ ॐ ॐ ॐ

Let me be a bird and build a nest in your heart,
Let me be a flower to be trampled by your feet.
Let me be the dewdrop glistening in your locks.
Let me be the moonbeam caught in your eyes.
Let me! O let me! O Mother mine!
Let me be thine!
Let me be thine!

ॐ ॐ ॐ ॐ ॐ ॐ ॐ ॐ ॐ

Why play hide and seek with me?
I care not for the game.
Between the rocks of infinity?
You have eluded me.
Tossing me like a ball,
Between the rows of insanity.
Beguile me not with your beauty,
Disgust me not with your crudity,
I care not for this game.
Lift thy veil and let me glimpse,
Thy sweet face of eternity

ॐ ॐ ॐ ॐ ॐ ॐ ॐ ॐ ॐ

Far have I wandered,
Past heaven and hell.
Crossing the threshold of infinite time,
Arriving on planet earth at last.
But where are you?
Why have you deserted me?
In this barren waste of beguiling charms?
Charm me not O charming one,
I care not for your sweets,
Reveal thyself, reveal thyself!
I want nothing else.

ॐ ॐ ॐ ॐ ॐ ॐ ॐ ॐ ॐ

Caught am I in the strands of your hair,
Bewildered by thy ugliness,
Terrified by thy harshness,
Why the slap when all I asked was for a touch,
Wherefore the storm and the wreckage?
Wherefore the war and the carnage?
What lesson do you teach, O terrifier?
Is there no reprieve?
Call you this a game?
More terrifying than reality,

Release me, O Mother,
Release me from this game.

ॐ ॐ ॐ ॐ ॐ ॐ ॐ ॐ ॐ

O *Maya*, *Maha Maya*,
Thou hast me in thrall,
Bound am I by thy beauty!
Caught by thy charm.
Thou hast me in thrall,
My sweet delight,
Enchantress of the three worlds,
Catch me if I fall.

ॐ ॐ ॐ ॐ ॐ ॐ ॐ ॐ ॐ

Vishnu Maya! *Maha Maya*! *Maha*! *Maha*! *Maha Shakti*!
Greater than the greatest,
Beguiler of the gods,
Do you now seek to beguile me?
I am already caught in your golden net,
Flapping like a helpless fish,
Show your strength and cut the strands,
Release me from these strangling bonds.

ॐ ॐ ॐ ॐ ॐ ॐ ॐ ॐ ॐ

Why have you deserted me, O Mother!
Will a mother abandon her baby in the woods?
Will a mother kill her foolish child?
If not, then why have you forsaken me?
I stumble in a jungle called life,
I drown in a lake called tears.
Alone and helpless, an orphan am I,
Desolate on the sands of time,
Clinging to the creeper called death.
Which in turn is upheld by thee!

ॐ ॐ ॐ ॐ ॐ ॐ ॐ ॐ ॐ

Take me to the moon, the fair moon of thy face,
Take me to the sun, less brilliant than thy form,
Waft me to the stars, which swing from your hair,
O *Sundari*! *Tripurasundari*!
Reveal thyself!
Give the gift of divine sight,
Disclose to me, thy exquisite face!

ॐ ॐ ॐ ॐ ॐ ॐ ॐ ॐ ॐ

Why call me'
If you didn't want me?
Why woo me,
If you didn't love me?
But having wooed and having won,
Why thrust me to the darkness,
Groping like a blinded worm,
For something it knows not what,
Crying for one speck of light,
For one star, for one ray,
In the blinding darkness of a lonely night!

ॐ ॐ ॐ ॐ ॐ ॐ ॐ ॐ ॐ

Have I not longed for you thru' many lives?
Have I not cried for you thru' countless births?
Where have I failed?
What have I left undone?
That you should ignore me like this?
O Mother! Cut asunder the knots of my ignorance,
Enfold me in your soothing arms.
Let me inhale thy sweet perfume,
Let me nestle in your soft bosom.

ॐ ॐ ॐ ॐ ॐ ॐ ॐ ॐ ॐ

Bereft am I – desolate,
Cast on the lonely beach of life,
Prey to every passing wave,

Lashed by the relentless tide.
Will you not grasp my outstretched hand,
Rescue me from this friendless land.

ॐ ॐ ॐ ॐ ॐ ॐ ॐ ॐ ॐ

Sing to me of eternity, O Mother!
Sing to me of glory!
Tell me those gentle tales,
Of devotees you have helped.
Let me hear the music of the spheres,
Of astral worlds where live those fortunate ones,
Who are beloved to thee,
That I may hear and perchance,
Learn to beguile thee!

ॐ ॐ ॐ ॐ ॐ ॐ ॐ ॐ ॐ

Forgive this foolish one, O Mother!
Countless are my mistakes,
Courage have I none, yet,
Dared have I to disclose the sweetness of thy tales,
Thy grace alone guided me, controlled me.
Can you forgive yourself?
For this poor scribe was but an instrument,
A note in the lute of fair *Saraswati*!

ॐ ॐ ॐ ॐ ॐ ॐ ॐ ॐ ॐ

Give me thousand tongues to describe the glory,
Give me a million eyes to drink in thy beauty.
O thou indescribable!
I have attempted the impossible
Lakshmi - Enchantress
Intoxicated am I by the beauty,
Enchanted by the glory,
Blinded by the compassion of thy loving glance.
Overwhelmed by the depth of thy infinite grace,
Bemused by the moods, thy forms of play,

O Lakshmi – Enchantress!
What can I offer thee,
Who has given me, my all,
This alone I have to call my own,
An this I give to thee with untold love.
My prostrations,
O Mother,
From now till infinity.

ॐ ॐ ॐ ॐ ॐ ॐ ॐ ॐ ॐ

Above the highest mountain,
Below the deepest sea,
Beyond the depths of my unchartered mind
Lies the hidden treasure
I have no instruments but my poor mind
To search for Thee
Where should I go
But beyond the mind
In that leap to the unknown
I lose my precious self
So dear to me, so close to me
My solitary companion
Alone am I but not anchorless
From behind I am caught in a tight embrace
"I was waiting for this", came the voice
Waiting for you to lose yourself
So that I could catch you
And become one
Nay! How could we become one
We were never two but always one
I knew it but you never did
Where did you wander, where stray
Never did you take a step by yourself
I was ever striding beside you
Waiting, waiting for you to call
For you to find that you were never alone

My precious self, my very own
Where can you go without my support?
Where hide, that I cannot find?

ॐ ॐ ॐ ॐ ॐ ॐ ॐ ॐ ॐ

O Kaali with the flaming sword,
Behead these millions
They are but puppets made for destruction
Construct another crore
And destroy them again as a game!
What is this but a man making factory
But why give us feelings?
Why give us love?
Why not hate and lust alone?
Why this endless clamour of the senses for gratification
When they can never be satisfied
Why the endless craving for love
When it doesn't exist.
Not even in you, for you are above everything
Alone, serene, unaffected
By the storms and typhoons of life
Above love and hate
Beyond pain and sorrow
The uninvolved participant in the game of life

ॐ ॐ ॐ ॐ ॐ ॐ ॐ ॐ ॐ

I place these poems at the lotus feet of the Divine Mother along with this book, which you alone have instigated. May your blessings fall on all those who read it as well as on this poor scribe. May we be released from this forest of *samsara* (illusory world), and attain your supreme state.

Thus ends the thirty-second and final chapter of the *Sri Devi Lila* known as "Shivani". It is a garland of wild flowers which *Vanamali* has gathered to offer at the lotus feet of *Devi*.

ॐ *Aim, hreem, kleem* ॐ

GLOSSARY OF SANSKRIT TERMS

abhaya mudra	sign of fearlessness
adharma	non-righteousness
Adi Shankaracharya	the founder of *advaita*
advaita	philosophy of non-dualism
advaitin	one who practices this philosophy
adya spanda	the primeval throb of creation
Agastya	a great sage
Aghora	extreme sect of *tantric* philosophy
aghori	follower of this sect
agni	fire
ahamkara	ego
Airavata	name of *Indra's* elephant
Ajna Chakra	psychic spot between the eyebrows
ajnana	ignorance
ajna-shaktis	forces of *Lalitha*
akasa	etheric space; first of the elements
akasa ganga	*Ganga* flowing in the heavans
akshaya patra	the pot of never ending food
Alakananda	tributary of the *Ganga*
amrita	nectar of immortality
Amsuman	*Bhagiratha's* grandfather
Anahata Chakra	psychic centre near the heart
ananda	bliss
ananga	bodiless; name of *Kama*
ananta	endless; serpent on which Vishnu sleeps
antah-karana	inner tool; consists of mind, intellect, ego and *chitta*

ap; apas	water; fourth element
apana vayu	pranic current controlling the lower portion of the body
apsara	celestial dancer
Arjuna	one to whom the advise of the *Bhagavad Gita* was given; the aspiring human being
Arundhati	wife of sage *Vasishta*
Aryan	belonging to the *Aryan* race
Asamanjas	great-grandfather of *Bhagiratha*
ashrama	refuge; sanctuary
ashta-shaktis	eight forces of *Lalitha*
Ashwatthama	son of *Drona*
Asikni	wife of *Daksha*
astra	missile
asura	demon
asuric	pertaining to the *asuras*
Asvapati	father of *Savitri*
aswamedha yaga	horse sacrifice
aswin	seventh month of the lunar calendar (october/november)
atman	soul or inner spirit
aum	primeval sound
avadhuta	one who wanders naked and owns nothing
avatara	incarnation of god
avidya	ignorance; nescience
avidya maya	veiling power of the goddess
avyakta	unmanifest
Ayodhya	capital city of Lord *Rama*
ayonija	not born from a womb; *Sita*
ayurveda	science of medicine
Badrikashrama	pilgrim spot in the *Himalayas*
Badrinath	modern name for the same
Bana	18th century poet; author of *Chandikashtakam*
bana linga	name of linga in the *Anahata Chakra*

Barsana	name of *Radha's* village
Bhagavan	one who has all the six lordly characteristics
Bhagiratha	prince of the solar race who brought *Ganga* to the earth
bhakta	devotee of god
bhakti	devotion
bhakti yoga	*yoga* of devotion
bhand	an explective
Bharata Varsha	ancient name of India
bhava samadhi	state of super consciousness
Bhavabhuti	18th century poet who wrote a poem on *Chamunda*
buddhi shuddhi	cleansing of intellect
bhuh; bhur	the earthly plane; material world
bhukti	enjoyment
bhupura	squares round the three *Chakras*
bhuta	primary element
bhuta agni	fire of spirituality
bhuta shuddhi	purification of the elements
bhuvah	one of the astral worlds; world of becomings and desire which is the pivot for action; constitutes the mid-world of man
bija	seed
bija mantra	seed sound
bijaksharas	*mantras* of the seed sounds of the deities
bindu	spot, dot; mystic dot from which creation emanates
bindusaras	lake of drops
Bodhisattva	realised soul who incarnates to help others; Buddhist term
Brahma granthi	knot of *Brahma*; found in the *Muladhara Chakra*
Brahma jnana	knowledge of the Supreme
brahma nadi	psychic tube through which the *Kundalini* rises
brahmarandra	orifice at the top of the skull

brahmin	member of the priest caste
Brighu	famous sage; expounder of *Brighu Samhita*
buddhi	intellect
Chaitanya	effulgence; great 16th century saint of Bengal
chaitra	a lunar month; march/april
Chakra	wheel; psychic whorl of energy
Chakraraja	king of *Chakras; Sri Chakra*
Chandidasa	poet of the 14th century
chandikashtaka	eight verses on *Devi Chandika*
chandra nadi	psychic enfolding through which *Kundalini* passes
chaturyuga	period of time comprising four *yugas*
chid	consciousness
chidagnikunda	eternal pyre in which all creatures are consumed
chintamani griha	room in which *Lalitha* resides; made of the fabled jewel *chintamani*
chit shakti	the force of pure consciousness
chitra nadi	the hollow psychic tube inside the *brahma nadi*
Chitrakarma	sculptor who created *Bhandasura*
Chitrakuta	hill on which *Hanuman* resided
chitta	super consciousness
daitya	demon
Daksha	father of *Sati*
dakshina marga	right hand path of *Tantra*
dakshinacharis	followers of this path
Dakshineswara	famous *Kaali* temple in Bengal
danava	demon
dasya bhava	attitude of a servant
deha shuddhi	purification of the body
Deva	shining one; god
Devi	goddess

Devi suktam	Rig Vedic hymn to the goddess
Dhanya	sister of *Mena*
dharma	law of righteousness
Dipawali	festival of lights
Diwali	same as Dipawali
divya	celestial; filled with light
draavana	ability to make people to run in terror
dukkha	sorrow
Durga puja	nine day festival of *Devi Durga*
Durvasa	sage known for his anger
Dussera	last day of the nine-day festival of *Durga*
dvaita	duality
Dwapara yuga	third epoch
Dwaraka	Lord *Krishna's* capital
Dyumatsena	*Savitri's* father-in-law
ganapatyas	sect who worship *Ganesha*
ganas	*Shiva's* entourage
gandharvas	celestial singers
Ganga	river goddess
Ganga sagar	mouth of the *Ganga*
Gangashtakam	eight verses to *Ganga*
Gangotri	source of the *Ganga*
Gantaki	river in Nepal
Garuda	eagle vehicle of Lord *Vishnu*
gayatri mantra	famous *mantra* to the sun god
geyachakra	chariot of *Lalitha*
ghat	safe place to bathe in the river
ghee	clarified butter
Gokarna	famous temple town in South India; dedicated to *Shiva*
Gokulam	village where *Krishna* grew up
Goloka	celestial world of *Krishna*
gopala	cow-herd boy
gopi	milk maid
Goraknath	famous *tantric* sage

guna	string; one of the three strands of nature; *sattva, rajas, tamas*
gunatita	one who has risen above the *gunas*
gupta shaktis	secret force of *Lalitha's* army
guru	spiritual preceptor
Haridwar	pilgrim centre on the *Ganga* in North India
hatha yogi	one who practices *hatha yoga*
Himavan	king of the *Himalayas*
hladini	power of bliss
hreem	esoteric *mantra* of the goddess
ham	seed *mantra* of the element of *akasa* or etheric space
iccha shakti	desire to create
ida	important *nadi* that lies on the left side of the *Sushumna*
indriyas	sense organs
ishta devata	favourite deity
jagat	world
Jahnu	name of a *rishi*
jana (loka)	one of the *lokas* or celestial planes of existence; world of creative delight
Janaka	king of *Videha*; father of *Sita*
japa	repetition of the *mantra*
japa mala	rosary used for *japa*
jatara agni	fire of digestion
Jayadeva	composer of the *Gita Govinda*
jiva	the spark of life; individual soul
jivan mukta	liberated soul
jivatman	embodied soul
jnana	spiritual knowledge
jnana shakti	knowledge of the process of creation
jnana yoga	*yoga* of knowledge

jnanendriyas	five organs of knowledge – ear, skin, eye, tongue and nose
jnani	man of wisdom
jrimbhana	ability to cause people to become lazy and keep yawning
jyesta	lunar month; mid of May to mid of June
Kailasa	abode of lord *Shiva* in the *Himalayas*
kaala	time
Kalavati	daughter of the manes
Kali yuga	the fourth epoch in which we are living
Kalidasa	great poet; devotee of *Kaali*
Kalindi	river in *Vrindavan*
kalpa	an epoch or age of *Brahma* – the creator
kalpataru	wish fulfilling tree
Kama	god of love; desire
Kamadhenu	wish fulfilling cow
kamakala	a digit of desire
Kamakelitarangita	name of *Lalitha*; one who overflows with love and desire
Kamakhya	famous temple in Assam; *siddha peeth*
kamandalu	water pot carried by *sanyasins*
Kamarupa	ancient name of *Kamakya*
Kanakadara Stotram	poem by Adi Shankara on *Lakshmi*
Kanchipuram	pilgrim city in Tamil Nadu
kanda	source of all *nadis*
kanta	beautiful
Kapila	a famous sage
kara	hand
karma	action; duty
karma yoga	the *yoga* of action
karmendriyas	five organs of action – tongue, hands, legs, genitals, anus
karmic	pertaining to the law of *karma*
Kartika	lunar month; mid of october to mid of november

kaula marga	a path of *Tantra*
Kauravas	100 princes of the *Kuru* dynasty; dark forces of the universe
kaustubham	ruby on the chest of Lord *Vishnu*
kirichakra	one of the chariots of *Lalitha*
kona	corner
kosha	sheath
kri	denotes *rajas*
Krishna Dwaipayana	name of *Vyasa*, author of the *Puranas*
krishnamayam jagat	world filled with *Krishna* alone
krita yuga	the first epoch; also called *Satya yuga*
kriti	creation
Krittikas	the constellation known as pleiades
kriya shakti	ability to create
krodha	anger
kshatriya	the warrior caste
kshobana	ability to create emotional disturbance
kundala	coil
kundalini	psychic coiled spiritual power at the bottom of the spine
kundalini yoga	study of the *kundalini* power
Kunti	mother of the *Pandavas*
Kurukshetra	battlefield of the *Kurus*; the field of human consciousness
lakh	hundred thousand
lam	*bija mantra* of the earth element
Lanka	the island where *Ravana* ruled
laasya	dance with slow movements which *Parvati* does
lata	creeper
laya	dissolving
laya yoga	*yoga* of dissolving in the supreme
lila	cosmic play
linga	sign; phallic symbol of *Shiva*
linga sarira	astral body

lobha	gain; greed
loka	astral world
lolakshikamarupini	one with tremulous eyes; *Lalitha*
maarana	ability to provoke death
Madhavi	name of *Lakshmi*; earth goddess
Madhu; madhu	a demon; honey
madya	liquor
maha	great; glorious
maha pralaya	dissolution which takes place in the night of *Brahma*
maha puranas	great *Puranas*, eighteen in number
maha tattva	great element; refers to *Shiva*
mahakaarana	the great cause; *Shiva*
mahakameswarastra	missile of Lord *Shiva* used by *Lalitha* to kill *Bhandasura*
mahamoha	the great illusion
mahapadmatavi	place where *Lalitha* kept her chariots
mahar (loka)	one of the astral worlds; world of vastness and pure thought and will
Mahratta	name of a person who lives in the state of Maharashtra
makara	crocodile
mala	garland; necklace
malati	jasmine flower
mamsa	meat
mana shuddhi	purification of the mind
manas	mind
Manasarovar	lake in the *Himalayas*; lake of the mind
mandala	mystic design
Mandara	mystic mountain
Mani Dwipa	mystic island in which the *Maha Devi* resides
Manikkavachakar	famous devotee of Lord *Shiva*
manipura chakra	the stomach *chakra*
manoja	aspect of love; one of the joints of *Mantrini's* chariot

Mantra	mystic sound
Mantra shastra	the knowledge of *mantras*; *Tantra*
Manu	the first of the law-givers
manvantara	an age of one Manu; 4,320,000 human years
Markandeya	ancient *rishi* who continues to live for a whole *manvantara*
mathurya bhava	the feeling of intense love
matsya	fish
maya	illusion; power of the *Maha Devi*
maya shakti	power to create illusion
medhas	discriminative intellect
Medhas	name of a sage
Mena	mother of *Parvati*
Meru	celestial mountain; axis of the world
Mewar	princely state of North India
Mira	great devotee of *Krishna*
mithuna	coitus
mithya	unreal
mohana	ability to attract and delude
moksha	final liberation from mortality
mudra	mystic sign
mukti	liberation
muladhara chakra	the first *chakra* found at the base of the spine
Mysore	princely state of South India
nad	motion; movement
nada	sound of creation
nada brahman	*Aum*; pure consciousness manifesting as sound
nadi	astral tube of energy
nadi shuddhi	purification of these tubes
naimittika pralaya	*maha pralaya*; the night of *Brahma*
Nalanda	ancient Buddhist university
nama	name
Nandagopa	foster father of Lord *Krishna*

Nandi	bull vehicle of Lord *Shiva*
Narada	celestial singing sage
naraka chaturdasi	14th day of the lunar month on which the demon *Naraka* was killed by Lord *Krishna*
Narayana parvata	mountain at the back of the temple of *Badrinath*
narayanastra	missile of *Narayana*
naths	sect belonging to the *aghoris*
navadhanyas	nine types of grains
navaratri	nine-day worship of the divine mother
nirakara	without form
nirguna	without the three qualities of nature – *sattva rajas* and *tamas*
nitya	eternal
nitya pralaya	dissolution of individual awareness during sleep
paasupata	arrow of *Shiva*
padmasana	lotus posture for sitting
panchamakaras	the five offerings in *Tantra* starting with '*m*'
Pandavas	sons of *Pandu*; virtues expressed by the evolved person
Panini	famous Sanskrit grammarian and saint
paramahamsa	the great swan; title given to highly evolved saints
paramanu	speck or smallest particle of matter
paramanukala	speck of time
Paramatman	the supreme self; *Brahman*
Parasara	father of *Veda Vyasa*
paraskara sutra	*vedic* hymn
pasha	rope (of ignorance which binds the soul)
pashu	animal
patala Ganga	name of *Ganga* in the nether world
peepul	fiscus tree

peetha	seat; spots where parts of *Sati's* body fell
pingala	the *nadi* on the right side of *Sushumna*
pra	exalted; superior
Prajapati	patriarch
Prakriti	executive will of the *Purusha*
prakritika pralaya	complete dissolution when all the universes revert to their original cause
pralaya	dissolution; flood; period of repose
prana	the life breath; the cause of human life
prana shakti	the life force
prana vayu	the five forces or winds which control all the involuntary actions
pranava	the *mantra* '*aum*'
pranayama	science of breath control
prasada	grace; left-overs of offerings to god
prayaga	confluence of rivers
preeti	highest form of selfless love
prema	love between lovers
prithvi	earth
puja	ritualistic worship of god
punya tirtha	holy river
puranas	hindu scriptures; 18 in number
puranic	pertaining to the *Puranas*
purnata	fullness
Purusha	supreme soul; witness of the play of *Prakriti*
Pushkara	holy city dedicated to *Brahma*
raja yoga	*yoga* for the stillness of the mind in order to unite with the supreme; method is given in the *Patanjali yoga sutras*
rajas	one of the three gunas of *Prakriti*; passion, energy, desire
rajasic	energetic; passionate; active
rakshasa	a giant of darkness and evil; violently egoistic with uncontrollable passions
ram	seed *mantra* for the element of *agni*

Ramakrishna	great Bengali saint of the 20th century
Ramarajya	the reign of *Sri Rama*, noted for its all round social perfection
ramya	pleasing; beautiful
rani	queen
rasa lila	the dance of *Krishna* with the gopis in the forest of *Vrindavan*
rasi	moon sign
Rati	wife of *Kama* – god of love
rishi	truth seer; seer-sage; composers of the *Vedic* hymns were *rishis*
rita	truth in action; working of *sat* or reality in the cosmos
Rudra Granthi	knot of *Rudra* situated in the *Ajna Chakra* between the brows
rupa	form
Sabda Brahman	emanation of consciousness as sound
sadhaka	one who practices spiritual disciplines
sadhana shastra	name of *Tantric* philosophy since it insists on some form of practice
Sagara	ancient king of the *Surya* dynasty; ocean
saguna	having form and all qualities of nature
Sahasrara Chakra	psychic centre at the top of the skull
sakhya bhava	approach to god as a friend
saligrama	stone found in the *Gantiki River* in Nepal which has the image of *Vishnu*
samadhi	super conscious state
samana vayu	one of the five winds which takes care of involuntary actions; controls digestion
samaya	conservative path of *Tantra*
samsara	the world of cyclical movement; world of transmigration
samvit	intelligence
Sanaka	one of the four boy-saints

Sananda	they are the eternal powers of the divine, ever youthful, who lead
Sanat Kumaras	people to the truth
Sanatana	fourth of the boy-saints
sanatana dharma	eternal law of righteousness; name of Hinduism
sankalpa	intention; determination
Sarabha	fabled animal; half-bird, half-dragon
sarga	primary creation
sari	six metres long cloth draped round the body by Indian women
sarira	body
sarva rakshakara chakra	giver of all protection
sarva sankshobana chakra	agitator of all
sarva siddhiprada chakra	giver of all powers
sarvaanandamaya chakra	giver of unending bliss
sarvarogahara chakra	remover of all diseases
sarvartha sadhaka chakra	accomplisher of all purposes
sarvasaubhagyada chakra	giver of all auspiciousness
sarvasya paripuraka chakra	fulfiller of all desires, these are the names of the *chakras* surrounding the *Sri Chakra*
sat	being; reality; existence
satkona	two intersecting triangles which form six corners
sattva	one of the *gunas* of *Prakriti*; balance, harmony and equilibrium
sattvic	pertaining to *sattva*
satya	truth
satyaloka	the astral world of *Brahma*; world of highest truth
Satyavan	name of prince who married *Savitri*
Saundaryalahari	poem in praise of the Divine Mother's beauty by Adi Shankaracharya
Savarni; savarnika	epoch of *Manu* in which the story of the *Devi Mahatmyam* took place

shaiva	sect who consider *Shiva* to be the supreme reality
Shaivites	followers of this sect
Shaktas	sect who consider the goddess as the supreme reality
Shakti	power; energy of the goddess
shakti peetha	place where part of *Sati's* body had fallen, filled with divine energy
Shaktism	philosophy of the *Shaktas*
Shankachuda	demon who married *Tulasi*
shanta bhava	peaceful approach to god
shanta murti	peaceful aspect of the godhead
shastra	scripture
Shatagni	blazing weapon of *Agni*
shava	corpse
Shiva lata mudra	one of the sexual practices in *Tantra*
Shivaji	great king of Maharashtra
shuddha tattva	purest element
Shuka	son of *Vyasa*
shunya	void; zero
shunyaka	*Bhandasura's* city of voidness
siddhi	supernatural power
Sita	wife of *Rama*; form of the earth deity
sloka	verse
smashana	burning ghat
smriti	collective name for the *Puranas*
Sonitapura	another name for *Bhandasura's* capital
Souryas	worshippers of *Surya*, the sun god
spanda	initial throb of creation; vibration
sraddha	faith
Sri	auspiciousness, prosperity; *Lakshmi*
Sri Chakra	supreme *Yantra* of the goddess
Sri Suktam	*Rig Vedic* hymn to *Lakshmi*
Srimad	excellent; venerated
srimati Jahnavi	the excellent *Ganga*
Srinagar	name of *Lalitha's* city

sringararasapurna	filled with the intoxication of beauty
Sripura	sanctum sanctorum of *Lalitha*
sruti	collective name for the *Vedas*
stambhana	ability to induce paralysis
sthuti	praise
stotram	hymn
Sudama	friend of *Krishna* in *Gokula*
Sudarshana Chakra	*Vishnu's* weapon; the wheel of time
Sugriva	monkey-king who helped *Rama*
Sumeru	name of a mountain
sunyata	voidness
Suratha	name of a king in the *Devi Mahatmyam*
surya nadi	astral tube called *pingala*
suryamandala	the aura of the sun
suta	one who recites the scriptures
svah	heaven; world of purity
swadha	wife of the manes
Swadhistana Chakra	name of psychic centre placed at the root of the reproductory organ
swar	heavenly region; world of light; pure psychic state
swarga sopana sharani	name of *Ganga*; ladder to heaven
swayambhuva linga	name of *linga* in *Muladhara Chakra*
tadrupata	attaining the same form (as the deity)
tamas	one of the three gunas of *Prakriti*; darkness, ignorance, inertia
tamasic	having the qualities of *tamas*
tanmatras	subtle elements, corresponding to the five elements or *tattvas*
tanmayata	melting of the devotee's personality into that of the deity
tanoti	expansion
Tantra	system of worshipping the divine as *Shakti* or divine energy
tantric	pertaining to *Tantra*

tapa	one of the astral worlds above the earth; world of infinite will
tapasvin	male who practices austerities
tapasvini	female who practices austerities
tapasya	spiritual force; austerities for gaining spiritual and material powers
tarpana	offering of water to the manes and to the sun god
tattva	essence of anything; the five elements
tattva shuddhi	purification of the elements in our body
tandava	dance of *Shiva*
tirtha	holy waters
tirtharaja	king of holy confluences; refers to *Triveni* in Allahabad where *Ganga, Yamuna* and *Saraswati* converge
ti	stands for *tamas* in *pra-krit-ti*
trailokya mohana chakra	enchanter of the triple worlds; *chakra* surrounding the *Sri Chakra*
trayati	liberation
treta yuga	the second age or cycle of evolution; only three-fourths of truth is to be found in this *yuga*
trikona	triangle
trimurtis	trinity of *Brahma, Vishnu* and *Shiva*
Trisati	hymn on the goddess *Lalitha*
tulasi, Tulasi	the holy basil; name of a goddess
turiya	fourth state of consciousness which underlies all the other three states; *samadhi* state
ucchatana	ability to force a person to stop
udana vayu	vital breath which directs the currents upward; aids spiritual development
uttama purusha	the supreme person
vac	power of sound or speech
Vaikunta	transcendental abode of *Vishnu*

Vaishanava	pertaining to *Vishnu*
Vaishnavism	philosophy of those who consider *Vishnu* to be the supreme reality
Vaishnavites	those who follow this philosophy
Vaisya	merchant cast
Vaitarini	*Ganga's* name in the nether regions; gift of a cow at the time of death
Vaivasvata	name of the *Manu* in that *manvantara*
vajra nadi	*nadi* inside the *Sushumna*
Valmiki	author of the *Ramayana*
vam	seed sound of the element of water
vama marga	left hand path of *Tantra*
vamacharis	those who follow this path
vamakesi	one with beautiful hair; name of *Lalitha*
vamanayana	one with beautiful eyes; name of *Lalitha*
vamsa	lineage
vanamala	garland of wild flowers; *Vishnu* and his *avataras* always wear this
Varanasi	famous temple town of North India; specifically for *Shiva*
varna	colour; caste
vasana	inherited or acquired tendencies of the mind
Vasishta	a famous sage; guru of *Rama*
vatsalya bhava	love of the parent for a child; one of the modes of approach to god
vayu	wind
Veda Vyasa	sage *Vyasa* who compiled the *Vedas*
Vedanta	collective name for the *Upanishads*
vedic	pertaining to the *Vedas*
veena	indian lute
Videha	capital city of *Sita's* father, *Janaka*
vidya	knowledge
vidya maya	illusion through knowledge
Vidyapati	16th century poet, devotee of *Krishna*

vidyarambham	ceremony to denote the begining of studies for a child
Vijayadasami	day of victory; last day of the nine-day worship of the Divine Mother
vikritis	modifications
vikshepa	the wavering quality of the mind
vilva	tree whose leaves are used in the worship of *Shiva*
vimarsha	seed desire; quality of *Maha Devi*
Vindhya	mountains of Central India
Vindhyachala	famous temple town dedicated to the goddess
vira	heroic
viraha dukkha	poignant sorrow of seperation
Virini	one of the wives of *Daksha*
visarga	secondary creation
Vishnu Granthi	knot of *Vishnu*; found in the *Sushumna nadi* in the *Manipura Chakra*
Vishnupadi	name of *Ganga*; coming from the feet of *Vishnu*
Vishuddha Chakra	name of a psychic spot in the throat
viswarupa	cosmic form of the lord
Vraja	village where *Krishna* grew up
Vrindavan	forest where *Krishna* played with the *gopis* and *gopalas*
Vrishabhanu	name of *Radha's* father
Vrishadvaja	name of *Tulasi's* father
vyana vayu	life breath which governs circulation
Vyasa	a famous sage; compiler of the *Vedas*; author of the *Puranas*
Yadava	name of *Krishna's* clan
yajna kund	the pit where the fire sacrifice is conducted
yajna; yaga	fire sacrifice
yajnashala	hall where the fire sacrifice is held
yaksha	celestial being; controllers of wealth

yam	seed sound for the element of wind
Yamuna	name of the river on whose banks *Krishna* sported with the *gopis*
Yantra	mystical mathematical figure
Yasoda	foster mother of *Krishna*
yoga	any path which leads to union with god; divine union
yoga nidra	spiritual sleep
yogi	man who practices *yoga*, saint
yogini	lady who practices *yoga*
yoni	vulva
Yudhistira	*Arjuna's* eldest brother
yuga	an age; an epoch

ॐ *Aim, hreem, kleem* ॐ

SCRIPTURES

Agama Shastras	scriptures for the formal worship of *Vishnu*, *Shiva* and *Shakti*
Agni Purana	scripture which extols *Agni*, the god of fire
Bhagavad Gita	holy song; advice of Lord *Krishna* given to *Arjuna* on the battlefield
Bhagavad Purana	*Purana* which extols *Krishna* as the supreme incarnation of *Vishnu*
Brahma Vaivarta Purana	one of the *Maha Puranas*
Brahmanda Purana	*Purana* in which the *Lalitha Sahasranama* comes
Brighu Samhita	scripture designated to the sage *Brighu* which gives the astrological details of all the future generations
Chandi	popular name of the *Devi Mahatmyam*
Devi Bhagavatam	*Maha Purana*, which describes all stories of *Shakti*; most famous *Shakta* literature
Devi Gita	advice given by the *Devi* to the mountain, *Himalaya* in the *Devi Bhagavatam*
Devi Mahatmyam	scripture which glorifies *Durga* and her killing of the various demons; most powerful of the *Shakta* literatures
Devi Purana	same as *Devi Bhagavatam*
Durga Saptashati	another name for *Devi Mahatmyamam*
Harivamsa	*Purana* glorifying *Vishnu*
Isavasya Upanishad	most famous of the *Upanishads*
Kumara Sambhava	poem by *Kalidasa* on the advent of *Kartikeya*, son of *Shiva*
Kurma Purana	a *Maha Purana*

Lalita Sahasranama	thousand-and-one names of the Mother Goddess as *Lalitha*
Lalithopakhyana	portion of the *Brahmanda Purana* which deals with the story of *Lalitha*
Mahabharata	the epic story of the *Kuru* Dynasty by *Vyasa*
Mahanirvana Tantra	one of the *tantric* scriptures
Maha Puranas	eighteen in number, attributed to sage *Vyasa*
Markandeya Purana	*Purana* in which the *Devi Mahatmyam* or *Chandi* is mentioned
Matsya Purana	one of the eighteen *Puranas*
Narada Purana	one of the eighteen *Puranas*
Pancharatra	*agama* dealing with the worship of *Vishnu* and his incarnations
Ramayana	epic poem on the life of the avatara, Rama by sage *Valmiki*
Rig Veda	the oldest of the four *Vedas*
Sama Veda	*Rig Veda* chanted musically
Savitri Upanishad	in which the practice of the *Gayatri mantra* is given
Skanda Purana	*Purana* which deals with the exploits of *Skanda* or *Kartikeya*
Tripura Rahasya	poem which extols *Lalitha*
Upanishads	end portion of all the *Vedas*, dealing with highly spiritual and philosophical matters
Upa Puranas	subsidiary *Puranas*; 18 in number
Vajasaneyi Samhita	part of the *Rig Veda*
Vamana Purana	*Purana* eulogising the *avatara* of *Vishnu* as the dwarf man
Vayu Purana	*Purana* pertaining to the wind god
Vedas	most ancient books known to humanity; four in number – *Rig*, *Sama*, *Yajur*, *Atharva*
Vishnu Purana	*Maha Purana* extolling *Vishnu*
Yajur Veda	one of the four *Vedas*
Yoga Kundalini Upanishad	deals with the nature and practice of *Kundalini Yoga*

ॐ *Aim, hreem, kleem* ॐ

NAMES OF GODS

Adi Shesha	serpent on which Lord *Narayana* reclines
Agni	god of fire
Ananta	another name for *Adi Shesha*; denotes endless time
Ardhanareeshwara	single form of *Shiva* and *Shakti*; half-male and half-female
Aruna	charioteer of the sun god
Aswins	the two divine physicians
Avalokiteswara	embodiment of compassion; incarnation of *Buddha*
Bhava	*Shiva*; being
Brahma	creator in the Hindu trinity
Brahman	the transcendental Absolute; beyond thought and description
Brihaspati	preceptor of the gods
Chandra	moon god
Dakshinamurti	*Shiva* as the universal teacher
Dik	god of space
Ganapathi	leader of the *ganas*; *Ganesha*
Ganesha	son of *Parvati*; elephant god venerated by all sects of Hinduism
Hanuman	monkey god; son of the wind god; chief helper of *Rama* in the *Ramayana*
Hara	*Shiva*; one who removes sins
Hari	*Vishnu*; one who removes sins
Hayagriva	horse-faced demon to kill whom *Vishnu* took a horse-faced incarnation
Indra	king of the demi-gods
Iswara	divine as Lord and ruler of the universe;

	personal god in all systems
Janardana	name of *Krishna*; giver of all that people ask for
Kalki	the tenth *avatara* of *Vishnu*, still to come
Kama	god of love and desire
Kameswara	*Shiva*
Kartikeya	general of the gods; son of *Shiva*
Krishna	supreme incarnation of *Vishnu*
Kshetrajna	god as the inner witness
Kubera	god of wealth
Kumara	name of *Kartikeya*
Lakshmana	brother of *Rama*
Madhusudana	*Vishnu*; slayer of the demon, *Madhu*
Maha Vishnu	the harmoniser and maintainer in the trinity
Maha Yogi	*Vishnu*; *Krishna*; Lord of *Yoga*
Mahadeva	the great god; *Shiva*
Mahakaala	*Shiva*; god of destruction
Maheswara	*Shiva*; the great Lord
Manmatha	another name of *Kama* – the god of love
Mayan	architect of the gods
Narasimha	the half-man, half-lion incarnation of *Vishnu*
Narayana	Lord *Vishnu* who lies on the serpent, *Sesha* on the cosmic waters
Nataraja	*Shiva* as the cosmic dancer
Para Brahman	Supreme Consciousness without form or attributes
Parjanya	another name for *Indra*; giver of rain
Pradyumna	son of *Krishna*
Pratyaksha Devata	sun god whom we can see before us
Purushottama	the supreme person; *Krishna*
Raghava	Lord *Rama*; born in the line of *Raghu*
Rama	seventh incarnation of *Vishnu*; hero of the epic, *Ramayana*
Rudra	the fierce form of *Shiva*
Sabda Brahman	the *mantra* '*Aum*'; the Absolute as sound
Sadashiva	the enternal entity of *Shiva* corresponding

	to *Brahman*
Shambhu	*Shiva*
Shanmukha	*Kartikeya*; six-faced one
Sharavanabhava	*Kartikeya*; born among the reeds
Shiva	the destroyer in the Hindu trinity
Shukra	preceptor of the demons
Skanda	*Kartikeya*; the war god
Soma	moon god
Subramania	another name of *Kartikeya*
Sundaramurti	name of *Shiva* as the most handsome one
Surya	sun god
Surya Narayana	spiritual aura of the sun god
Turiya Brahman	the Absolute which is ever united with *Mula Prakriti* or the creative force
Uttama Purusha	the supreme person; *Krishna*
Vaasudeva	*Krishna*; one who is immanent in all creation
Vamana	fifth incarnation of *Vishnu*; the dwarf man
Varaha	third incarnation of *Vishnu* as the boar
Varuna	god of waters; god of the sea
Vayu	god of wind
Vinayaka	another name of *Ganesha*
Virabhadra	incarnation of *Shiva*
Vishnu	the harmoniser in the Hindu trinity
Vishvakarma	architect of the gods
Yama	god of death

ॐ *Aim, hreem, kleem* ॐ

NAMES OF DEMONS (*ASURAS*)

Andhaka	blind son of the demon, *Hiranyaksha*
Balahakas	seven brothers in *Bhanda's* army
Bhanda; Bhandasura	asura born out of the ashes of *Kama*
Chanda	general of *Shumbha's* army
Dhumralochana	general of *Mahishasura's* army
Durgama	*asura* killed by *Durga*
Durmada	general in *Bhanda's* army
Hayagriva	horse-faced demon who stole the *Vedas*
Hiranyakashipu	famed king of the demons; father of *Prahlada*, famous devotee of *Vishnu*
Hiranyaksha	elder brother of *Hiranyakashipu*; *Vishnu* took the incarnation of the boar in order to kill him
Kaitabha	one of the two demons born out of *Vishnu's* ears whom he killed with the help of the goddess
Kamsa	evil uncle of *Krishna*
Karambha	demon who practiced austerities in order to beget sons
Kuranda	*Bhanda's* best general
Madhu	one of the two demons born out of *Vishnu's* ears
Mahabali	great demon who was slain by *Vishnu* in his incarnation as *Vamana*
Mahisha; Mahishasura	buffalo demon killed by *Durga*
Munda	one of the generals of *Shumbha's* army

Naraka	a demon who incarcerated many princesses in his dungeon; *Krishna* killed him and released the princesses
Nishumbha	one of the two *asuric* brothers killed by *Durga* in the *Devi Mahatmyam*
Raktabija	friend and ally of *Shumbha*; every drop of his blood which fell on the ground turned into a clone of himself
Rambha	*asura* who became *Raktabija* in another life
Ravana	king of *Lanka*; he abducted *Sita*, wife of *Rama*
Shumbha	one of the two *asuric* brothers killed by *Durga* in the *Devi Mahatmyam*
Sugriva	*Shumbha's* minister; king of monkeys
Taraka	fierce demon to kill whom *Kartikeya*, son of *Shiva*, was born
Visunga	general of *Bhanda's* army

ॐ *Aim, hreem, kleem* ॐ

NAMES OF GODDESSES

Adi	first; description of *Shakti*
Adi Shakti	first emanation of the goddess
Aditi	mother of the gods
Adya	primordial
Aindri	female counterpart of *Indra*
Ambika Amba	female counterpart of *Shiva*; source of his power
Anandarupini	one whose form is bliss
Annapurna	giver of food
Aparajita	the invincible
Aparna	name of *Parvati*; one who subsists on leaves
Arya	another form of *Adya*; *Sita's* name in previous birth
Ashta Lakshmis	the eight *Lakshmis*; givers of all types of felicities to human beings
Ashtadevis	goddesses who were guardians of the eight directions
Atiguptarahasya	secret police of *Lalitha's* army
Bagala	one of the *Mahavidyas*; has the head of a crane
Bala	*Lalitha's* daughter
Bhagavati	one who has all the six qualities or bhagas; omnipotence; ability; excellence; beauty; omniscience; non-attachment; feminine of *Bhagavan*
Bhagirathi	name of *Ganga*, since she was brought to the earth by *Bhagiratha*

Bhagya Lakshmi	one of the *Ashta Lakshmis*; giver of fortune
Bhairavi	feminine of *Bhairava*; one who brandishes a bloody sword
Bharata Mata	Mother India
Bharati	name of *Saraswati*
Bhavani	*Parvati*; becoming; feminine of *Bhava* or Being
Bhu Devi	the earth goddess
Bhuvaneswari	ruler of the earth
Brahma Shakti	the power of *Brahma*
Brahmaani	feminine counterpart of *Brahma*
Chamunda	one of the names of *Kaali*; slayer of the two demons – *Chanda* and *Munda*
Chandi	short for *Chandika*; epithet of *Durga*
Chandika	*Durga*
Chinnamasta	one of the *Mahavidyas* who holds her own decapitated head in her hand
Cybele	goddess of ancient Phrygia
Dakini	presiding goddess of the *Muladhara Chakra*
Dakshayini	*Sati*; daughter of *Daksha*
Dandanatha; Dandanayika	general of *Lalitha's* army
Demeter	goddess of ancient Greece
Devi	goddess; filled with light
Devi Kundalini	the goddess of the *Kundalini Shakti*
Dhana Lakshmi	one of the *Ashta Lakshmis*; giver of wealth
Dhanya Lakshmi	one of the *Ashta Lakshmis*; giver of grain
Dhumavati	one of the *Mahavidyas*
Durga	virgin, warrior goddess; born out of the various powers of the male gods
Gaja Lakshmi	one of the *Ashta Lakshmis*; one who is seated on an elephant
Ganga	the holy river
Gauri	name of *Parvati*; the golden coloured one
Gayatri	goddess of the *Vedic* hymn to the sun; a poetic metre
Hakini	presiding goddess of the *Ajna Chakra*

Hariti	Buddhist goddess
Indrani	wife of *Indra*
Ishtar	goddess of ancient Assyria
Isis	goddess of ancient Egypt
Iswari	the goddess as ruler of the universe; feminine of *Iswara*
Jaganmata	mother of the world
Jahnavi	name of *Ganga*; daughter of the sage *Jahnu*
Jwalamalini	one of *Lalitha's Shaktis*; one who makes a garland of fire
Kakini	presiding goddess of the *Anahata Chakra*
Kalaratri	name of *Durga*; the great night of destruction
Kaali; Kaalika	goddess in the form of all devouring time
Kamakshi	name of *Lalitha*; one with love-filled eyes
Kamala	*Lakshmi*; one of the *Mahavidyas*
Kameswari	name of *Lalitha*; giver of desires
Kartyayini	virgin goddess to whom the *gopis* prayed
Kaumari	feminine counterpart of *Kartikeya*
Kaushiki	form of *Parvati*, which came out of her bodily sheath or *kosha*
Kumari	daughter of *Lalitha*
Kundalini Shakti	the force of the *Kundalini*
Lakshmi	goddess of auspiciousness and wealth
Lalitha; Lalithambika	most benign form of the *Maha Devi*; born to destroy the demon, *Bhanda*
Maheswari	feminine counterpart of *Maheswara* or *Shiva*
Madhavi	the earth goddess
Maha Devi	the Divine Mother; all other goddesses are her *Shaktis* or powers
Maha Kaali	the great *Kaali*
Maha Lakshmi	the great *Lakshmi* who is independent, not attached to *Narayana*
Maha Maya	the great delusion
Maha Medha	the Supreme intellect
Maha Nidra	the great sleep
Maha Prakriti	the great *Prakriti* or root cause of creation

Maha Saraswati	*Saraswati* as an independent principle
Mahavidyas	ten ferocious aspects of the goddess
Mahamoha	the great deluder
Maharatri	the great night of delusion
Mahasuri	the great demoness; appellation of the goddess who contains both good and bad
Mahishasuramardini	name of *Durga* when she slew the demon, *Mahisha*
Mantranayika; Mantrini	general of *Lalitha's* army; power of the repetition of the *mantra*
Matangi	one of the ten *Mahavidyas*
Maya Shakti	the delusory aspect of the *Maha Devi*
Medini	name of the earth goddess
Moharatri	the great night of delusion
Mohini	incarnation of *Vishnu* as a female of great beauty in order to dupe the demons who had stolen the nectar
Mula Prakriti	the transcendental feminine force which lies submerged in the *Brahman*
Narayani	one of the names of *Durga*
Navadurgas	the nine aspects of *Durga*
Nrisimhi	the feminine counterpart of *Narasimha* – the man-lion incarnation of *Vishnu*
Padma	*Lakshmi*; lotus
Padmavati	*Lakshmi*; born from the lotus
Parabrahma Swarupini	the goddess who is no different from the *Parabrahman* or transcendental Absolute
Parameshwari	the supreme feminine power
Parashakti	the supreme feminine force
Parvati	wife of *Shiva*; daughter of *Himavan*
Prakriti; Devi Prakriti	the original force which emanates from the transcendental *Mula Prakriti* and produces this universe of forms
Radha	beloved of *Krishna*; *Prakriti* incarnate
Rajarajeshwari	queen of queens
Rakini	presiding goddess of the *Swadishtana Chakra*

Rati	wife of *Kama* or *Manmatha*, the god of love
Raudri	feminine counterpart of *Rudra* or *Shiva* as destroyer
Rukmani	princess of *Vidharba*; wife of *Krishna*
Sampatkari	general in *Lalitha's* army
Sandhya	goddess of dawn and twilight
Santana Lakshmi	one of the *Ashta Lakshmis*; giver of progeny
Sapta Matrikas	the seven fierce forms of the *Maha Devi*
Saraswati	goddess of arts and sciences; wife of *Brahma*
Sarvavidya Swarupini	*Saraswati*; the embodiment of all wisdom
Satakshi	name of the *Maha Devi*; one with a hundred eyes
Satchidananda Swarupini	the inherent form of the *Brahman*; existence, consciousness and bliss
Sati	wife of *Shiva*; daughter of *Daksha*
Savitri	goddess of the sun; wife of *Satyavan*; famed for the power of her chastity
Shakambari	name of *Maha Devi*; one who carries a sheaf of corn
Shakini	presiding goddess of the *Vishudha Chakra*
Shakti	force; energy; power of the *Maha Devi*
Shankari	feminine counterpart of *Shankara* or *Shiva*
Shiva Shakti	the female energy of *Shiva*
Shivadhuti	fierce incarnation of *Durga*; one who sent *Shiva* as an ambassador to a demon
Shivani	beloved of *Shiva*
Shodasi	one of the *Mahavidyas*; young girl of sixteen
Sita	wife of *Rama*; princess of *Videha*
Smashan Tara	one of the *Mahavidyas*; found in burning ghats
Tamasi	delusion; one of the names of the *Maha Devi*
Tantrini	one of the chief attendants of *Lalitha*
Tara	Tibetan goddess; gentle in nature
Tirasankarani	one of the *Shaktis* of *Lalitha* who caused the opposing army to become blind
Tripurasundari	most beautiful in all the three worlds

Tulasi	wife of the demon *Shankachuda*; the holy basil
Uma	name of *Parvati*; lit. meaning 'don't go'
Ushas	Vedic goddess of the dawn
Varahi	female energy of the boar incarnation of *Vishnu*, called Varaha
Vac	*Saraswati*; the personification of the spoken word
Vagadeeswarees	warrior goddesses of *Lalitha's* army
Vaishnavi	feminine energy of *Vishnu*
Vani	*Saraswati*
Vara Lakshmi	one of the *Ashta Lakshmis*; giver of boons
Vidya Lakshmi	one of the *Ashta Lakshmis*; giver of knowledge
Vindhya Vasini	goddess who resides in *Vindhyachala*
Virya Lakshmi	one of the *Ashta Lakshmis*; one who gives courage
Vishalakshi	name of the *Maha Devi*; one with large eyes
Vishnu Shakti	the feminine energy of *Vishnu*
Vrindavini	another name of *Tulasi*
Yantrini	one of the chief attendents of *Lalitha*
Yashaswini	a *Shakti* created by *Lalitha*
Yoga Nidra	goddess in the form of sleep

ॐ *Aim, hreem, kleem* ॐ

MANTRAS

(AS THEY APPEAR IN THE CHAPTERS)

ॐ *Ganeshaya Namaha!*	Salutations to Lord *Ganesha*
ॐ *Brahmanyai Namaha!*	Salutations to the Brahman
ॐ *Aim Hreem Kleem*	The three forms of the *Maha Devi Saraswati*, *Lakshmi* and *Kaali*
ॐ *Adbhutacharitrayai Namaha!*	Salutations to the one with amazing stories
ॐ *Ambayai Namaha!*	Salutations to Mother *Amba*
ॐ *Sri Matre Namaha!*	Salutations to the Divine Mother
ॐ *Devyyai Namaha!*	Salutations to the goddess
ॐ *Aim, Hreem, Kleem, Chamundayai-Vicchai Namaha!*	The most auspicious nine-syllabled *mantra* of the *Maha Devi*
ॐ *Paramatmikayai Namaha!*	Salutations to the one who is the form of the *Paramatma*
ॐ *Prakrityai Namaha!*	Salutations to *Prakriti*
ॐ *Ambikayai Namaha!*	Salutations to *Ambika*
ॐ *Sarvabhuteshwaryai Namaha!*	Salutations to the goddess of all creatures
ॐ *Rajnyai Namaha!*	Salutations to the queen
ॐ *Maheswaryai Namaha!*	Salutations to the great goddess
ॐ *Bhavanyai Namaha!*	Salutations to *Bhavani*; the form of becoming
ॐ *Ishwaryai Namaha!*	Salutations to the goddess
ॐ *Mahashaktyai Namaha!*	Salutations to the great power
ॐ *Kamakshyai Namaha!*	Salutations to the goddess with eyes filled with love
ॐ *Durgayai Namaha!*	Salutations to *Durga*; remover of evil

ॐ *Chandikayai Namaha!*	Salutations to *Chandika*; the fierce one
ॐ *Raudrayai Namaha!*	Salutations to the wife of *Rudra* – the terrible one
ॐ *Chamundayai Namaha!*	Salutations to the slayer of *Chanda* and *Munda*; *Kaali*
ॐ *Sathyyai Namaha!*	Salutations to *Sati*; the personification of Truth
ॐ *Shivaayai Namaha!*	Salutations to the auspicious one
ॐ *Yoginyai Namaha!*	Salutations to the female yogi
ॐ *Mahamayyai Namaha!*	Salutations to the great deluder
ॐ *Bhuvaneswaryai Namaha!*	Salutations to the goddess of the universe
ॐ *Gangayai Namaha!*	Salutations to *Ganga*
ॐ *Mahakalyai Namaha!*	Salutations to the great *Kaali*
ॐ *Lakshmyai Namaha!*	Salutations to *Lakshmi*; goddess of auspiciousness
ॐ *Saraswatyai Namaha!*	Salutations to *Saraswati*; goddess of learning
ॐ *Radhayai Namaha!*	Salutations to *Radha*; beloved of *Krishna*
ॐ *Radhayai Svaha!*	The *mantra* of *Radha*
ॐ *Vrindavanyai Namaha!*	Salutations to the goddess *Tulasi*, also known as *Vrindavani*
ॐ *Vasundharayai Namaha!*	Salutations to *Vasundhara* – the earth goddess
ॐ *Savitryai Namaha!;*	Salutations to *Savitri*
Tat Savitur Varenyam	I bow to that sun god, *Savitur*; part of the *Gayatri* hymn
ॐ *Kalaratryai Namaha!*	Salutations to the great night of delusion; *Brahma's* hymn to *Adi Shakti*
ॐ *Adi Shaktyai Namaha!*	Salutations to the the primeval force; power of the universal Mother Goddess

ॐ *Bhadrayai Namaha!*	Salutations to the giver of auspiciousness
ॐ *Chakrarajayai Namaha!*	Salutations to the king of *Chakras*; reference to the *Sri Chakra*
ॐ *Kundalinyai Namaha!*	Salutations to the goddess of the *Kundalini*
ॐ *Shivapriyayai Namaha!*	Salutations to the beloved of *Shiva*

"Mantra heenum, kriya heenum
Bhakti heenum Sureshwari,
Yad poojitam maya Devi,
Paripoornam tadastu me."

"O Devi! I beg of you to make perfect,
This puja of mine, which is,
Devoid of chants (mantras), actions (kriyas), or devotion (bhakti)."

ॐ *Aim, hreem, kleem Chamundayai Vicchai Namaha* ॐ

BIBLIOGRAPHY

1. *The Srimad Devi Bhagavatam*
2. *Devi Mahatmyam; Durga Saptashati; Chandi*
3. *Hindu Mythology* by WJ Wilkins
4. *Kundalini Yoga* by Swami Shivananda
5. *Sri Chakra* by S Shankaranarayanan
6. *Savitri* by Sri Aurobindo
7. *Aghora* by Svoboda
8. *The Living Goddess* by Linda Johnson
9. *The Lalitha Cult* by Dikshitar
10. *Devi Mahatmyam – Chrystallization of the Goddess Tradition* By Thomas B Coburn

ॐ *Aim, hreem, kleem* ॐ